MASSES AND MAN

MASSES AND MAN

NATIONALIST AND FASCIST PERCEPTIONS OF REALITY

GEORGE L. MOSSE

WAYNE STATE UNIVERSITY PRESS

Detroit, 1987

Library of Congress Cataloging-in-Publication Data

Mosse, George L. (George Lachmann), 1918–
    Masses and man.

    Reprint. Originally published: 1st ed. New York :
H. Fertig, 1980.
    Includes index.
    1. Nationalism—Europe.   2. Europe—Politics and
government—1789-1900.   3. Europe—Politics and
government—20th century.   4. Fascism—Europe.
5. Jews—Germany—History—20th century.   I. Title.
D363.M65 1987   320.5'4'094   87-6131
ISBN 0-8143-1895-9

Design by Albert Burkhardt
Printed in the United States of America

The following page constitutes an extension
of the copyright notice.

For permission to reprint copyright material, the author is indebted to the following:

2. *Literature and Society in Germany*, reprinted from *Literature and Western Civilization*, Vol. V, *The Modern World*, II, *Realities*, edited by Professor David Daiches and Anthony Thorlby, © 1972 Aldus Books, London, pp. 267–299.

3. *What Germans Really Read*, first published as "Was die Deutschen wirklich lasen. Marlitt, May, Ganghofer," *Popularität und Trivialität*, ed. Reinhold Grimm and Jost Hermand, Athenäeum Verlag, Frankfurt-am-Main, 1974, pp. 101–121.

4. *Death, Time, and History*, first published as "Tod, Zeit und Geschichte. die völkische Utopie der Überwindung," *Deutsches utopisches Denken im 20. Jahrhundert*, ed. Reinhold Grimm am Jost Hermand, Verlag W. Kohlhammer, Stuttgart, 1974, pp. 50–70.

5. *The Poet and the Exercise of Political Power: Gabriele D'Annunzio*, reprinted from *Yearbook of Comparative and General Literature*, No. 22, 1973, pp. 32–42.

6. *Caesarism, Circuses, and Monuments*, reprinted from the *Journal of Contemporary History*, Vol. VI, No. 2, 1971, pp. 167–184.

7. *The French Right and the Working Classes:* Les Jaunes, reprinted from the *Journal of Contemporary History*, Vol. 7, No. 3–4, 1972, pp. 185–208.

8. *The Heritage of Socialist Humanism*, reprinted from "The Legacy of the German Refugee Intellectuals," *Salmagundi* (Skidmore College, Saratoga Springs, N.Y.), ed. Robert Boyers, No. 10–11 (Fall 1969–Winter 1970), pp. 123–140.

9. *Toward a General Theory of Fascism*, reprinted from *International Fascism, New Thoughts and New Approaches*, ed. George L. Mosse, Sage Publications, London and Beverly Hills, 1979, pp. 1–45.

10. *The Mystical Origins of National Socialism*, reprinted from *The Journal of the History of Ideas*, Vol. XXII, No. 1, January–March 1961, pp. 81–96.

11. *Nazi Polemical Theater: The* Kampfbühne, first published as "Die NS Kampfbühne, in *Geschichte im Gegenwartsdrama*, ed. Reinhold Grimm and Jost Hermand, Verlag W. Kohlhammer, Stuttgart, 1976, pp. 24–39.

12. *Fascism and the Avant Garde*, first published as "Faschismus und Avant-Garde" in *Faschismus und Avant-Garde*, ed. Reinhold Grimm and Jost Hermand, Athenäeum Verlag, Frankfurt-am-Main, 1980.

13. *The Secularization of Jewish Theology*, first given in 1976 as an address at the centennial symposium of Hebrew Union College, Jerusalem.

14. *The Jews and the German War Experience, 1914–1918*, reprinted from *The Leo Baeck Memorial Lecture*, No. 21, Leo Baeck Institute, New York, 1977, by permission.

15. *German Socialists and the Jewish Question in the Weimar Republic*, reprinted from *Year Book XVI* of the Leo Baeck Institute, London, edited by Robert Weltsch and Arnold Paucker, 1971, pp. 123–155.

In memory of

MERRILL JENSEN

Acknowledgments

While writing these essays over the years I have accumulated numerous and pleasant debts. Many of the problems raised here have been discussed with Renzo De Felice, Stanley Payne, Walter Laqueur, Anson Rabinbach, and Paul Breines. The late Jane Degras, Janet Brindsmaid, Ann Adelman, Steven Lampert, and Steven Uran helped to improve the quality of these essays. Howard Fertig suggested the making of this book, and his advice and counsel were indispensable throughout the manuscript. Many of the ideas and analyses in this book were formulated and refined while teaching graduate and undergraduate students in Madison and Jerusalem. The following libraries were important for my research: the Bayrische Staatsbibliothek, Munich; the Wiener Library and the British Library, London; the Bibliothèque Nationale in Paris; and the Hebrew University Library as well as the Library of the University of Wisconsin. The dedication of this book to the late Merrill Jensen expresses my personal gratitude to a friend who made me a colleague many years ago, when encouragement mattered most.

G.L.M.
Madison, April 1980

Contents

PART III

MASSES AND MAN

ONE

Introduction: Nationalism and Human Perceptions

D ESPITE THEIR apparent diversity, these essays have a common method and theme. They deal with the mobilization of private discontent into collectivities that promised to transcend the anxieties of the modern age. Nationalism was the most important such collectivity, promising a happy and healthy world protected against the rush of time. These essays analyze the various ways in which men and women have used nationalism in order to keep control over their lives. From the end of the last century onwards, these lives were lived in an ever more complex and impersonal society where all seemed in motion. This was a nervous age, as contemporaries saw it, threatening to wipe out the traditional distinctions between the normal and the abnormal, the permitted and the forbidden—a time when human discourse threatened to break through all that was held sacred and private in life. Nationalism promised to restore order and the respect for immutable values, and to maintain clear distinctions between the accepted and the unacceptable—guidelines upon which men and women could model their life to escape confusion.

For most of the men and women who fill these pages, the slogan "Masses against man" summed up their fears of modernity and the struggle to retain their individuality within an ordered universe, at a time when many who had placed their hopes in chang-

1

ing the social and political order were rapidly disillusioned. Ernst Toller drafted his play *Masse Mensch* in 1919, when postwar Germany's revolution seemed to have run its course and a new orthodoxy threatened to replace the old. Ideals of freedom had been transformed into the wish for domination. "Doctrine above all," proclaims Toller's man without a name who champions the masses; "I love those to whom the future belongs." "Man above all," counters his heroine; "you sacrifice present men to future doctrine."[1] In retrospect this exchange seems commonplace, after we have seen the hopes of the postwar revolution collapse into the arms of Stalinism or into a social democracy now occupying the liberal space in politics. But at the time Toller wrote, the failure of revolution to bring about the instant liberation of man was an awesome discovery. The revolutionary hopes of Toller lived on in the socialist humanists discussed in this book, while nationalist ideas gained influence among orthodox socialists, as we hope to demonstrate. For example, it has lately been shown that the same Jewish stereotype which provided the staple of nationalist thought surfaced in popular German socialist literature.[2] Nationalism triumphed in the age with which we are concerned: the individual would fulfill himself within a historical tradition that gave him roots and tribal shelter. To a large extent, nationalism determined the nature of all other collectivities ready to absorb private discontent before and between the wars.

The setting of these essays is a Europe in the grip of intense industrialization and urbanization. Modern nationalism and the Industrial Revolution grew up together in a dialectical relationship, formally opposed to each other while at the same time agreeing to collaborate. The nation appropriated the past, preindustrial myths and symbols in order to veil the actual speed of time, the increasing polarization of the social structure. It pointed backward to a usable past and forward to an arcadia of unspoilt nature and recaptured innocence. The native landscape with its flowers, woods, and mountains stood outside the rush of time and the nervousness of the age. The quest for nature was linked to the quest for history—the appropriation of a classical, medieval, or Renaissance past—which took place not only in nationalist ideology but also in the private lives and tastes of the bourgeoisie. Nationalism could lay a claim to totality, a lifestyle that provided a past for those afraid of the present. Municipal and national buildings imitated classical temples, Gothic cathedrals, or Renaissance palaces; private villas were increasingly built in the Renaissance style; and sometimes, at least in Germany, prosperous bourgeois families of the fin de siècle had themselves portrayed in Renaissance costumes. These huge canvasses are not remembered today, but then they were part of the wave of historical paintings attempting to recapture, as accurately as possible, the principal events of the national past. Christian traditions were joined to nature and history, the "sacred" being integrated into the nation, as the rituals which accompanied Gabriele D'Annunzio's exercise of power clearly show. From ritualized mass meetings, to the emotional absorption of the native landscape, to the imitation of historical styles, to a bizarre nationalist mysticism—nationalism wove a garment for itself it is the aim of this book to dissect and examine.

Nationalism did not seek to destroy the process of industrialization; on the contrary, it deliberately furthered it in order to increase the country's might and prosperity. But industrialization was kept subordinate to an anti-industrial ideology, treated as technological advance rather than as leading to a new perception of the world. The scientific discoveries of the age were carefully separated from the larger considerations of nationalist ideology, politics, or social life. As our discussion of fascism hopes to show, the frightening process of industrial and scientific change was embedded in pastoral, historical, or sacred traditions, perceived as a means to an end that would transcend industrial society; indeed, ever since the beginning of the nineteenth century there had been those who sustained both the industrial ideal and its moral rejection. By the end of the century, this simultaneous approval and rejection was brought into harmony through the national ideal. To be sure, many men and women had no such fears, basing their liberalism squarely upon industrial and scientific advance. But we are here concerned with nationalists rather than with bourgeois liberals, with the strength of this particular collectivity rather than with the optimistic and positivist outlook of some of the bourgeoisie of the nineteenth century.

However, even a robust positivism made an attempt to veil that progress which was publicly praised. For example, Theodor Fontane's *Jenny Treibel*, set around the year 1874, provides us with one of the best portraits of bourgeois life at the fin de siècle. The industrialist Treibel and his family occupy a villa which, though close to the factory, is shielded from it by a large garden, and it is into this garden that one's eyes are drawn. Nature becomes an integral part of the house.[3] The heavy, comfortable furniture documents a well-being based upon prosperity. The Treibels lived within well-defined social rules and Jenny presided with great calm over their elaborate social functions. Yet Jenny Treibel felt a certain dissatisfaction with this lifestyle; she tried to reach out for "higher things" like art and literature in order to inject some romantic interests into her life. Eventually, order and discipline won out over emotions that might escape control. The Treibels were not untypical for a large section of the German upper bourgeoisie in their lifestyle and also in their longing for higher things. In the long run, nationalism could take care of the emotions, the longing for the romantic within an ordered life, and so reinforce the anti-industrial industrialism symbolized by the garden placed between the villa and factory.

The Treibels provide a German example of the functions nationalism could perform. Although a majority of these essays are set in Germany, countries like Italy and France are not neglected, and provide the comparative dimension necessary to understand the people and movements discussed in this book. Everywhere nationalism had many faces, appropriating the hopes of men and women, making alliances with conservatives, liberals, and radicals alike. For conservatives, it promised to maintain or restore the traditional hierarchies; for liberals, it promised a framework of order and moderation within which steady progress was thought possible; and for radicals, a means of democratization and an attack upon the supposedly materialistic and complacent values of the bourgeoisie. While nationalism encouraged foreign expansion, it also appropriated what it could of the various ideologies and political and social movements within each nation. It proved flexible here, willing to make contradictory alliances. Beneath its basic function as a collectivity disguising even while assimilating modernity, each nation contained different nationalisms: conservative, liberal, or radical. These essays concern the radical, democratic nationalism that wanted to transform man and society. This was the kind of nationalism the Jacobins exemplified in revolutionary France, attempting to substitute themselves for the traditional liberal and conservative hierarchies. Toward the end of the nineteenth century, such nationalism was used as a weapon against a supposedly corrupt Establishment unable to integrate the people with the nation.

The radical Right became a revolutionary force in the last decades of the nineteenth century, one that attacked finance capitalism and the ruling élites but did not want to nationalize the means of production. Private property was to be maintained and a hierarchical society advocated, based not on social or inherited status but upon service to the nation. Nevertheless, it was this revolution rather than that stemming from Marxism which was to have startling successes in the Europe between the wars. Its shock troops were to a large extent bourgeois youth, an élite of high school and university students in revolt against the positivism, materialism, and entire lifestyle of their elders. They agreed with Nietzsche's assertion that ordered society puts the passions to sleep. Some, like the young Expressionists, went to extremes; they wanted to ride with the speed of time and confessed themselves potential murderers whenever they saw a comfortable bourgeois.[4] Others, like the dramatist Franz Wedekind in Germany, created boys and girls eager to throw over sexual taboos, hungry to discover the sensuality of their own bodies. Against the sure calmness with which the Treibels sat enthroned, they wanted to experience all life had to offer, not to die without having lived, in Oscar Wilde's famous phrase.

To be sure, much of this revolt of the fin de siècle had its origins in the boredom that often accompanies prosperity. Youth looked for excitement; for new meaning in life; for the "great events" their fathers feared; for demonstrations, adventure, and war. Nationalism became the means through which many of them fulfilled their dreams, providing a dynamic faith that promised community and self-fulfillment, offered the excitement due to a true believer, and saw life as a permanent festival. There were other young people, more disciplined though hardly less emotional, who through the youth movements found a true faith—not in the saber-rattling nationalism of their elders but in the internalization of the national landscape, historical traditions, and customs. Yet the shock troops of this revolution were not youth alone; their elders joined too, though in lesser numbers, and at times members of the working classes were attracted to the revolt. Various aspects of this revolution are discussed as part of our analysis of a radical nationalism, including the working-class movement "*Les Jaunes.*"

This was an antibourgeois bourgeois revolution, a play within a play, but serious for all that. Class war was rejected as a revolutionary strategy, and instead, these revolutionaries proclaimed a war between generations—a conflict that would provide the vocabulary of this revolution from the end of the nineteenth century through the Third Reich. For all its political and social purposes, the bourgeois antibourgeois revolution tended to concentrate at first upon changing manners and morals, as well as on the creation of a literary and artistic avant garde. But it soon attempted to reach out to the people, as many of the following essays illustrate. It inspired the "generation of 1914," which flocked to the colors; it was strengthened by wartime camaraderie; and after the war, it declared open season upon parliaments, liberals, and socialists.

This bourgeois antibourgeois revolution was part of the search for the Third Force that would transform society, rejecting both orthodox socialism and the Establishment. Those advocating this Third Force were for the most part men and women obsessed with the importance of absolute values, opposed to the so-called hypocrisy of political tactics and compromise. Advocates of the Third Force included left-wing intellectuals such as the socialist humanists discussed below, but for the most part they were nationalists, who believed that the values contained in the national community were crucial to the self-actualization of man. The worship of youth as against old age, the idealization of "manliness," gave dynamic to this ideology, leading eventually to the search for a new fascist man. These essays continue and extend that probing of the Third Force begun in my *Germans and Jews*[5] in the hopes of contributing to the understanding of a movement that occupied so many minds of the Right and Left between two world wars. It saw orthodox socialism and existing bourgeois society as fragmenting man, and instead attempted to integrate the masses with the nation through shared perceptions of reality.

The political liturgy practiced so successfully by D'Annunzio at Fiume was one way to accomplish such integration; another was through Caesarism, circuses, and monuments, as used by the national socialists in France. Several essays in the first part of the book discuss the penetration of this nationalism into specific groups like the workers or the heterogeneous masses looking for faith and stability. But the greatest number of essays attempt to probe popular conceptions of reality and their relation to nationalism through literature. People do not necessarily believe what they read, but popular literature read in the hundreds of thousands can tell us something about the hopes and longings of the men and women this nationalism attempted to capture. To a certain extent, popular literature filters human perceptions, and at the very least it coincides with a good many of them. Popular literature seems a valid means of analyzing the integration of men and nations—a process expressed in another form through the political liturgy of nationalism discussed in my *Nationalization of the Masses*[6] and in several of the essays that follow.

While radical nationalism found it easy to infiltrate important social and political groups, it proved much more difficult to penetrate popular literature, at least in Germany. Although much of this literature was rooted in specific local traditions, in the native landscape and soil, this did not necessarily lead to a nationalist point of view. For example, Berthold Auerbach, who in his *Village Stories* (1843) created the German peasant novel, believed that he was writing about the particular within the universal. Auerbach, perhaps one of the most popular literary figures of nineteenth-century Germany, held that there was no contradiction between commitment to individuality and religious tolerance on the one hand and the struggle for German unity on the other. Popular literature—so he wrote at mid-century—must exemplify all of these, never losing from view that literary characters, however rooted in their locality and nation, must exemplify a common humanity.[7] This attitude was not to last, at least as far as the peasant novel was concerned; here nationalism penetrated successfully, sweeping Auerbach and his village stories into oblivion. By the time Hermann Löns wrote his *Der Wehrwolf* (1910), the single most popular modern peasant novel, the peasant himself exemplified Germanic virtues embattled against those of other peoples and nations. Yet the tradition in which Auerbach had written continued to dominate most of German popular literature; nationalist and volkish novels never won a clear victory over a more tolerant and humane approach to letters, despite the fact that much of German literature did become involved in the quest for German identity.

Germany was to have no deep tradition of revolutionary literature, as the essay on "Literature and Society in Germany" shows. But those writers who called for a specific German faith or exalted the past never dominated popular reading habits. They did reflect the turning away from the Enlightenment: even the liberalism of writers like Marlitt and Ludwig Ganghofer was embedded in a Germanic romanticism, and concerns for national identity were close to the surface. Still, as that essay demonstrates, the virtues advocated as exclusively German were not always aggressive or filled with chauvinism. Yet, if we look at both the tradition described in "Literature and Society," and that analyzed in "What Germans Really Read," it is clear that most best sellers retained a universalism that may have made the particular more meaningful, especially the sentimentality which fills such novels. Surely it is better to rejoice in a pure heart which, while rooted in Germanic nature, is shared with all humanity. But such sentimental universalism never led to a political concern with equality and freedom for all peoples. The writers discussed in "Literature and Society" engaged the settled bourgeoisie, while the discussion of other popular writers points to a lower social group, though by no means exclusively: literary tastes are not firmly anchored in the social structure. Nearly all of the plays and novels dealt with in "Literature and Society" reflected the ideals and tastes of the solid bourgeoisie, while those described in "What Germans Really Read" spread this image downward into the population. This was not the literature of the bourgeois antibourgeois revolution, which is only referred to whenever expressionism or plays like Franz Wedekind's *Spring's Awakening* are mentioned. Yet fascism managed to tame this revolution into the acceptance of the bourgeois literature rather than that which had accompanied the revolt of youth. The essay on the Nazi theater shows clearly how literary tastes could be manipulated when linked with the continuing longing for action.

What the Germans read in large numbers from the fin de siècle through the Third Reich were local tales, fairy tales or adventure stories whose moral pointed to a sharing of humanity, compassion, and freedom as part of the quest for national identity. It remains to be seen if this held true for other nations, though England certainly shared in these tastes. Such utopias were for the most part opposed to the exclusiveness of modern nationalism; they stressed individuality rather than collectivities. Yet reading them did not stop men and women from joining fascism or the radical Right; as we shall see, even Hitler shared in this popular taste. Popular literature was largely regarded as a fairy tale that would come true only after nationalism had cleared the way.

This literature pointed to a distant future; the good society was inherent in the present, to be actualized only when the time was ripe. Yet such ideas remained so strong that nationalism could proclaim itself tolerant and accuse its enemies of intolerance. The absurd claim was directed against the Jews in particular, but also against all of those who stood in the way. Most European ideologies laid claim to the core of the liberal tradition, Marxism as well as nationalism, and in so doing transformed liberal ideas into empty rhetoric, a stick with which to beat all enemies. The individual fulfilled himself in the collectivity, which alone really mattered; the virtues of tolerance and compassion were not abolished but annexed and monopolized by the nation. Nationalism was a scavenger ideology, which absorbed all that had become rooted in popular perceptions, integrating it with its ideals of history, nature, and the sacred in life.

The nationalism of the radical Right led into the fascist movements after World War I. Here, the bourgeois antibourgeois revolution was no play within a play, no mere breeding ground for a cultural avant garde. The nationalist utopia in which so many of the fin de siècle youth had found refuge, and to which some of the avant garde turned between the wars, produced a powerful mass movement. To be sure, other forces also went into the making of fascism, but the connection between those men and movements discussed in the first section of the book and those in the second is obvious and real. The essays in the first part of the book attempt through literature or social movements to probe human perceptions before the coming of fascism, and in the second part, to see these perceptions shape a reality that affected all Europeans. The third section analyzes several aspects of the relationship between Jews and Germans in the face of the dynamic assertion of nationalism. While "The Secularization of Jewish Theology" attempts to show how current German and bourgeois values came to displace traditional theology, the experience of World War I might well be called the climax of Jewish assimilation in Germany. Judaism received an increasingly Protestant structure: reverence toward God was said to be furthered by hymns rather than prayer, and the Protestant chorale was adopted because it was originally based on the Psalms and the Bible, "expressing our religious feelings to perfection."[8] At the same time patriotism became a part of Jewish life, together with emphasis upon so-called middle-class virtues. Jews were emancipated into the German Wars of Liberation (in which Jews fought for German unity), while the bourgeoisie was finally rising to a position of power and influence in Germany.

Still more important, Jewish assimilation is analyzed in this book through the adoption of Christian and German symbols: the cross as a military decoration, and World War I as a Christian metaphor centering upon the cult of the fallen soldier with its rhythm of death and resurrection. This appropriation of symbols was no conscious act of submission to an ever more aggressive and predatory nationalism, but a natural consequence of the process of assimilation. The overwhelming number of Jewish soldiers in World War I never experienced any overt conflict between their Jewishness and the acceptance of Christian myths and symbols described in the essay on the German Jews and the war experience. Indeed, this essay has elicited a great deal of anger from those who survived the war experience. Is the historian justified in making judgments in retrospect which so radically differ from those made by many who wore the uniform years ago? Sometimes the vision of those present is limited. For example, while it would not have occurred to any Jewish soldier of World War I to object to the Iron Cross because of its Christian symbolism earlier, during the Wars of Liberation such decorations were thought insulting to Jewish sensibilities. Moreover, those who experience an event usually see and remember only what went on around them, and even this is filtered through their memory. The historian, while taking their witness into account, must attempt to see the full picture, to place individual experience in the context of the past and the future. Historical distance enables him to climb up onto the hill in order to see where the path came from and in which direction it leads, to get a clearer view than those who follow its tortuous course through the valley below.

The essays on Jewish assimilation continue the emphasis upon human perceptions filtered through myths and symbols that are at the core of our historical analysis. Here the historian becomes an investigator of myth. Not only nationalism but all modern ideologies attempt to express themselves through symbols which men and women can grasp, which they can see and touch. The twentieth century, the age of mass politics and mass culture, has become visually oriented rather than tied to the printed word. This visual orientation had always existed among a largely illiterate population, but now with the refinement of photography, the film, and political ritual, it became a major political force. Myths, symbols, and stereotypes largely determined political thought between the two wars, as the essays illustrate. We can no longer ignore the acceptance by Jews of Christian symbol and myth as irrelevant, just as we cannot ignore myth and symbol as a crucial part of modern mass politics. The Jewish stereotype has been frequently investigated and its importance in determining attitudes toward the Jew generally recognized. But the importance of myth and symbol was not confined to anti-Semitism or racism, though the strength of anti-Jewish imagery is documented in this book by its effect upon the Social Democrats, who attempted to reject all prejudice. During the first part of the twentieth century, men and women increasingly perceived the world in which they lived through myth, symbol, and stereotype.

This was the way in which many ideas were supplied, in the attempt to cope with an age of industrialization and urbanization, an alienation from nature and from man's own individuality. Men and women longed for a new wholeness in their lives; they reached out for totality. People were no longer content to divide their lives into separate compartments, some dealing with politics, some with work, and some again with leisure. Such undoubtedly was the reality, but in times of rapid change a hunger for totality came to the fore—the yearning for a fully furnished house. Both Hegel and Marx had understood this longing when they condemned the division of labor as exemplifying the dehumanizing consequences of industrialization. Nationalism also wanted to make life whole again by abolishing the division of labor. But here once more it finished by keeping what it had condemned, not abolishing the division of labor but integrating it into the national mystique in an attempt to transcend the problem. Radical nationalism advocated a hierarchy of function, a division of labor; but beyond this it proposed a hierarchy of status, in theory fluid and open to all, depending on their service to the nation. Throughout these essays we find men and women wanting to make their life whole again and using the national collectivity to achieve this purpose.

The longing for totality was accompanied by a strong urge to appropriate immutabilities: the landscape, national traditions, history, and even the sky. All of these were thought to stand outside the rush of time, helping men to keep control, introducing something of the sacred into individual lives. World War I heightened such perceptions, making it possible to transcend harsh reality by appropriating the immutable forces of nature, climbing mountains, flying in the skies.[9] Nationalism represented itself as an immutable and sacred force, using history and nature to demonstrate the greatness of the nation. The longing for totality and for immutability helped integrate man with the masses.

What room remained then for individuality? Nationalism helped to define the norm, supported conformity in manners and morals, and promised to protect traditions. The nation reinforced the nuclear family as the policeman of youth, though the family might rival the nation as the center of individual allegiance. As the social, political, and economic crises deepened between the wars, the family became an ally of the nation rather than a threat, though something of the rivalry remained within National Socialism. The nation reinforced the calm and order which the bourgeoisie desired.

This can be illustrated by the attempt to control that revolt against manners and morals which had inspired some youth ever since the fin de siècle. The nation came to the aid of those concepts of sickness and health which by mid-nineteenth century had come to define sexual normalcy. Thus a French medical dictionary tells us that a nation's greatness depends upon its capacity for moral outrage when confronted with sexual excesses or "perversities."[10] The emergence of population as an economic and political problem did not merely broaden the discourse about sexuality, as Michael Foucault has noted;[11] it encouraged the nation to act as a guardian of sexual normalcy and moderation. It had a large stake in the rise and decline of populations, and in the people's health, which was more often than not linked to their fitness to serve in the army.

The nation helped to restrict individuality through the primacy of collectivism, and also by its support of strict manners and morals, by linking control over sexual excesses and abnormalities to the very effectiveness of the national collectivity. The nervousness of the age was symbolized by the so-called abnormal, the nonconformist, the avant garde in literature and art. At times there was room for the avant garde, but never for nonconformist manners and morals. The degree of artistic and literary individualism permitted depended upon the respective roots of radical nationalism. Italian fascism, with its Futurist and syndicalist tradition, permitted greater scope for the art and literature of modernity than Nazi Germany, with its single-minded emphasis upon the national past. But as the essay on "Fascism and the Avant Garde" seeks to show, individuality was tolerated only so long as it did not menace the basic conformity and consensus which nationalism desired.

The avant garde, like the Jews, were outsiders (small wonder that they had an affinity one for the other). Both stood outside historical tradition and thus menaced the historical foundations of nationalism. The Jews could not share in the national past, however much they tried, and the avant garde by and large thought history irrelevant to their present concerns. The outsider was tolerated as long as he was entertaining, but this tolerance ended if as a group he made alliances with other more powerful forces in society. The homosexual count of Charlus and the Jew Swann were readily accepted in the satiated society of the noble Guermantes in Paris because they were entertaining without posing a threat to its existence. What Proust observed at the turn of the century in *Remembrance of Things Past* would hold true with equal measure for the first Jew in an Oxford common room or the black at a liberal cocktail party. How much the normal could tolerate the abnormal is one more question which might be asked of these essays. Did mass triumph over man here as well?

Nationalism and the bourgeois lifestyle with which it was allied showed a great talent for cooptation—the ability to absorb new impulses and turn them to their advantage. Many of the young people who fought the war between the generations at the fin de siècle were tamed into the collectivity of nationalism, while part of the avant garde was coopted into the mainstream of life. This process will be amply illustrated in the essays which follow. There were those who attempted to stem the tide. The socialist humanists attacked the concept of mass man on behalf of individual freedom and rationality. They are included here as the counterpoint to that nationalism which fills the rest of the book: their ancestors can be found in those young democratic writers who tried to make their mark on German letters during the crucial period in German history between 1848 and 1914 discussed in "Literature and Society in Germany." They lost out then, just as the socialist humanists lost out in between the wars. It was the collectivity which triumphed, the morals and manners of the nineteenth century which were destined to last because of the process of cooptation and assimilation, but also because normalcy promised to curb the speed of time, to disguise the frightening advances of industrial society. The past, the present, and the future were no longer shrouded in mystery, but could be read by members of the national community.

These essays, then, are concerned with the national myths, symbols, and stereotypes that made it possible for many men and women to confront the burdens of life: they are the filters through which reality is perceived. Having described the main thrust of this book and the problems with which it is concerned, the time has come to say something about the method used to probe radical nationalism, though the method can hardly be divorced from the content and the questions it raises.

In any analysis of the past, what counts is the objective reality and human perceptions of it. Historians have traditionally tended to concentrate on only one part of the dialectic between perception and reality: they have mined the social, political, and economic realities in which men and women lived, and on occasion have elevated the outward circumstances of men's lives into historical laws. Within such laws, men and women were said to have little freedom of choice because historical necessity usurps individuality. Such economic, social, or political determinism is indeed comfortable to live with; it introduces immutable forces into the historical process itself, making it easier for the historian to cope with a changing reality or to face an indigestible past. But however much they may be limited by objective reality, men and women do have choices to make. Indeed, that reality tends to be shaped by the perceptions men and women have of it, by the myths and symbols through which they grasp the existing world. Myths and symbols serve to internalize reality and to infuse it with the fears, wishes, and hopes of man. Men and women act upon reality as they perceive it, and thus they help to shape it as well.

The dialectical relationship between historical reality and human perception allows no crude determinism. Some men and women perceive themselves to be helpless in the present and project their individuality upon the future, but even so this despair and hope will shape their particular version of reality. These essays deal with the perceptions of men and women, one half of the ongoing dialectic between the human and objective forces of history. That is why our sources are so often literary, and why the visual is so important, as we saw earlier. The building of myths and symbols—how men and women mediate between their own identity and the given realities of life—is more often than not based upon what literature supplied and what they could see and touch. It is no coincidence that nationalism, as the mediating force between perception and reality, represented itself as largely a literary and aesthetic movement.

This book, then, is a study in the history of human perceptions, in the mediating forces between the individual and his world. That such forces drove men and women to seek shelter in collectivities demonstrates the increasingly impersonal and abstract reality in which they lived. But the development was not inevitable and had many levels of meaning, some of which we hope to clarify. Analyzing the myths and symbols through which men and women perceive their world can give us an insight into the personal and political choices by which they tend to cope with reality and thus help to shape the future.

The chief problem facing any historian is to capture the irrational by an exercise of the rational mind. This becomes easier when the irrational is made concrete through rational acts within the terms of its own ideological framework: rites like those practiced at Fiume provide a good illustration. The various expressions of radical nationalism which fill this book may seem irrational and even bizarre, but they are a logical consequence of the presuppositions and the functions of modern nationalism. An earlier generation of scholars working in the Weimar Republic, living in the shadow of National Socialism, believed that the irrational could be tamed into a framework of rational thought by an exercise of the rational mind. They examined the myths of the past in order to ensure a rational approach to the construction of present society. Men like Aby Warburg and Ernst Cassirer believed that a scholarly, historical, and philosophical investigation of myths and symbols would lead to the integration of what was nonrational in the rational critique of culture. We can no longer share the optimism of such men, based as it was upon the idea, as Cassirer formulated it, of humanity's progressive enlightenment until man realizes the rational basis of his existence.[12] But as a historical method and approach rather than politics, their investigations gave us new insight into historical reality based upon human perceptions.

If this is one scholarly tradition from the past that is relevant to the approach to history of this book, the renaissance of Marxism in the Weimar Republic focused attention upon the mediations between individuals and objective reality which we have tried to explain. The young Georg Lukacs, Max Horkheimer, and Theodor Adorno sought to analyze human cognition in order to destroy the determinism of Marxist orthodoxy. What counted were not simply the modes of production, but how the historical reality which they created was mediated, how it affected man's consciousness. Self-understanding was crucial; it meant grasping life as a whole. Only if men and women had gained an understanding of the interrelationship between literature, art, politics, and aesthetics could they join the class struggle in order to transform society. However, in actuality, this approach to revolution meant the primacy of culture: cultural criticism as a revolutionary force. These men also based their theory upon a belief in the rational mind, which would grasp the totality of life through true rather than false mediation, true rather than false consciousness. Here once more it is the approach to history, with its analysis of the perceptions of men, which is important for our purposes. These socialists soon despaired of the political relevance of their own convictions.[13]

These approaches to history, reinforced by parallel sources such as John Huizinga's emphasis upon symbols as necessary personalizations and concretizations of abstract ideas, remain valid, though the fears of dictatorship that inspired them seem to have passed in the West. After World War II, liberalism revived once more—when it had long been pronounced dead—and individual freedom fought back against mass man. The hunger for totality seems to have lessened in the years after the war, perhaps because it had proved so disastrous in creating false collectivities. Yet eventually a renewed opposition to the Establishment once again desired a fully furnished house. The model of the new Left was not the radical Right but the Marxist renaissance of the Weimar Republic. For all this, bits and pieces of radical nationalism are still lying about, ready once more to absorb private discontents. Man, so it seems, can easily be enticed into the masses; and nationalism, which had played the Pied Piper in the past, remains one of the most enduring temptations.

The brand of radical and democratic nationalism with which we are concerned has proved more dangerous to individual freedom than either conservative or liberal nationalism. Those other nationalisms lacked the revolutionary dynamic and all-inclusive claims of the nationalism which built upon the bourgeois antibourgeois revolution of the fin de siècle, strengthened by the war experience and the turmoil which followed. Yet for all that, even this radical and democratic nationalism could at certain moments itself provide an alternative to the chauvinism that has filled these pages. Its emphasis upon the inner processes of men and nations could turn such nationalism away from the necessities of domination. For example, Martin Buber and Robert Weltsch as Zionist leaders exhorted their followers to concentrate upon the inner development of the Jewish nation, upon its cultural heritage. By living a national life based upon such principles, Jews would attain a harmonious relationship with the whole world. Here, nationalism supported human dignity instead of a blind submission to the collectivity; for such men, the nation was a step toward a union of all mankind.[14] There was no need to abolish all differences between men, but instead to integrate these with the concerns of all mankind. The ideals of these Zionists were not so different from the belief of the liberal Berthold Auerbach, quoted above, that the particular must be a part of the universal, that one could work for German unity without abandoning humanity.

That this nationalism did not prevail does not make it any less relevant. As nationalism refuses to go away, as every minority con-

tinues to search for its national identity, the task of giving nationalism a human face becomes all the more pressing. Nothing in this
book is meant to deny the necessity of nationality; not only has it
been dangerous in the past to be a people without a nation, but the
national community rightly conceived can be a source of strength
and pride, humanizing rather than brutalizing its members. Such
must remain our hope: one day the history of this humanistic
nationalism will be written, for its history must be recaptured
in order to show the unrealized possibilities for good inherent in
nationalism. This book is a warning, instead, a cautionary tale
which, by analyzing a nationalism hostile to human freedom, one
that substitutes masses for men, seeks to encourage the never-ending search for a humane definition of nationality. To be sure, this
seems a utopia expressed by only a few pioneers in the past, for it
was easier simply to denounce all nationalism. But if nationalism
with a human face is not realized, we might once more abandon
the world to oppression and war.

We have set it as our task (and not only in this book) to analyze
nationalism at its most extreme in order to produce a confrontation
between men and masses.[15] It is the task of the historian to destroy
old myths in order to encourage new confrontations with reality.
History, after all, is a continuous process, which contains possibilities for both good and evil. That the history with which we are
concerned saw the victory of evil over the good does not mean that
mankind is unable to surface from the sea of pain which radical nationalism has caused. To plumb the depth of evil might strengthen
the forces for good, fill men's consciousness with the need to transform chauvinistic into a humanistic nationalism. If such a hope did
not exist, there would be no sense in the unpleasant task of chron-
icling the illusions of domination that follow, even if this book also
contains men and women devoted to human creativity and liberty
—those who refused to idolize false gods.

PART I

TWO

Literature and Society
in Germany

D URING THE NINETEENTH CENTURY, Germany became
estranged from many of the traditions of the Enlightenment and the French Revolution that had found a home in
other Western nations. The basic fact about German history since
the eighteenth century has been the failure of the Enlightenment
to take root.[1] Instead Germany looked inward, to its own supposed traditions of the past, obsessed with the problem of national
unification. But this is not the whole of the German story. Toward
the end of the century, Germany was emerging as one of the most
important industrial nations: growing and self-confident. Moreover, the German working classes had been organized into the
strongest socialist party in Europe. Historians have long sought to
analyze the complicated factors that formed German attitudes in
the second half of the nineteenth century and that were to cast
their shadow into our own time. The thought and attitudes current
in Germany seemed to reject the liberalism that emerged in other
industrial nations, and to stultify the rise of a bourgeoisie wedded
to ideals of freedom and equality.[2]

Literature can be of the utmost significance in determining pecu-
liarly German attitudes in an age of rapid industrialization and rising self-confidence. The relationship between literature and life is
necessarily a complex one, but for Germany the kind of literature

that was admired was deeply involved in the German quest for identity. The revolution of 1848 stands at the beginning of our analysis. That revolution seemed at first to have given liberalism a place in German life, and the radical uprisings that accompanied the revolution could have given Germany a vital revolutionary tradition of its own. Writers responded to both these impulses, especially those of "Young Germany," and those associated with the ideas of Karl Marx. Perhaps a literary tradition both liberal and revolutionary could have helped to form German attitudes, the more so when a strong socialist party came into being after Germany was unified. But this was not to occur, and the literature that triumphed was that which was concerned with national identity as well as the ideals of German bourgeois society. The major part of this essay will be concerned with such literature, which was to form the attitudes of those who lived in German-speaking lands. But in order to see why nationalist and bourgeois literature triumphed, it is crucial to examine the failure of the impetus that sprang from the revolution of 1848: why Germany, in the second half of the nineteenth century, was barren of a tradition of letters that might have called for liberty and equality against the inherited inequalities of life.

Before and during the revolution of 1848, a group of writers known as "Young Germany" vociferously opposed the social reality of Germany, wanting to bring about greater freedom within the society that they knew. These men were liberals whose call to freedom and revolt, in the tradition of the Enlightenment, had a certain abstract quality: they were more interested in moral than in social questions. Moreover, in the face of a growing hostility from authority they retreated into an attitude of resignation, not untainted by cynicism.[3] When such literature was revived toward the end of the century, in the form of expressionism or naturalism, it had a similar cynical and abstract quality: the revolutionary action it invoked had nothing to do with barricades but was concerned with literary sensitivity, which at best could lead to changes in manners and morals. To be sure, there are exceptions to the lack of a revolutionary literary tradition. Germany was, after all, the country of Marx and Engels, and they did arouse the enthusiasm of some writers and poets. The only creative artist with whom both revolutionary leaders were satisfied was Georg Weerth (1822–

1856), one of the writers to attempt a realistic portrait of the working man. Yet his works are, for the most part, satires on the existing order, and do not fuse literature with revolutionary dialectic. Engels praised him above Goethe for his capacity to express a natural sensuousness.[4] Two other, more important writers also enjoyed the friendship and support of Marx and Engels, although never wholly or consistently. Georg Herwegh and Ferdinand Freiligrath were revolutionary poets, but both, characteristically, were aroused by the radical impetus of the revolution of 1848 rather than by any specifically Marxist experience.

Georg Herwegh (1817–1875) provides perhaps the most important example of a writer and poet who continued his commitment to revolution through 1848 and on to his death in 1875. Herwegh clung to the concept of freedom, and saw that this must encompass the workers as well as the middle classes. Freedom for him was more concrete than it had been for the "Young Germans," and it included a sharp and bitter critique of capitalism. Significantly, the editor of his works, writing in the 1890s, failed to understand how this commitment could outlast the fact of German unity and lead to a bitter criticism of the new Reich. This commitment to freedom and democracy (Herwegh, like Marx, had supported the democratic uprising in Baden in 1848) was permissible in 1848, but was regarded as subversive once the Reich had come into being[5]— an indication of the changing atmosphere in Germany to which most writers succumbed.

Herwegh carried on, exclaiming in a poem that unity was an empty shell, and so was the law, if the oppression of men continued. Capitalism and the complacency of the liberals were to blame, and he composed poems on this theme after 1870, just as he had written some of the most famous poems on the need for revolution before and during 1848. His friend Ferdinand Lassalle (1825–1864), with some justice, described Herwegh as *"un nouveau Mirabeau,"*[6] but a Mirabeau who worked in lonely eminence without penetrating the Establishment or gathering a revolutionary following. Lassalle's own themes centered upon national heroes such as Franz von Sickingen, whose drive for freedom Lassalle endowed with a decidedly romantic appeal. Herwegh was not interested in past German examples but in the overthrow of the existing order.

Ferdinand Freiligrath (1810–1876) wrote some of the most stirring poems of 1848; eventually he joined the editorial staff of Karl Marx's *Neue Rheinische Zeitung* and the League of Communists as well. His poems, which had praised humanity in general and were not devoid of melodramatic effects (e.g., *Ça Ira!* in 1846), later became imbued with a vision of proletarian misery and the longing for a true equality. A poem such as *"Die Toten an die Lebenden"* (The Martyred Dead Speak to the Living, 1848) is replete with revolutionary fervor, a call for an uprising that would fly the red flag over the barricades. Freiligrath followed Marx into exile in 1851, but in London he underwent a change that was to last until his return to Germany and his death. He drifted away from the circle of Marx and Engels, asserting a love of freedom and equality that, like that of the earlier "Young Germans," was based on a moral impetus rather than on sustained social analysis. Love for humanity in general, and for the republican form of government in particular, took the place of the call for revolution against the existing order. Finally, Freiligrath found that he could no longer deny the progress made by Germany under Prussian leadership. The national mystique threatened to displace the cry for change and even the exaltation of humanity.[7]

The "Young Germans" and these revolutionary poets had believed that literature should play a vital role in the formation of a new society. However, their emotionalism and moral impetus had left the solid ground of social reality far behind. Even Herwegh refused to submit to the discipline of a social movement and, in spite of his sympathy for it, never joined the League of Communists. Marx and Engels failed to create a literary movement that might accompany their quest for social justice. Yet, later in the century, the Naturalist movement seemed to give a second chance to the creation of a revolutionary literary tradition in Germany. By that time the socialists had united, and the strong Social Democratic Party might have taken advantage of this literary genre to construct a socialist literature where earlier efforts had failed. For the Naturalists were better able to penetrate reality than the enthusiastic heralders of revolution of an earlier day.

Gerhart Hauptmann (1862–1946) made his name by portraying realistically the misery of the Silesian weavers and the reaction of the ordinary people to their plight. *Die Weber* (*The Weavers*, 1892) stressed the importance of the environment in which they lived and worked. But this very stress upon the environment demonstrated the difficulty of fusing such naturalism with a revolutionary tradition. The movement tended to become an environmentalism that alerted society to the fate that awaited many of its members. It could be used to inspire action in order to change that society, but naturalism tended to ignore the idealism that might point to a better future and that was vital to a socialist and revolutionary impetus. Man became a cipher, dehumanized by his industrial environment, and showed little potential for improving his station in life. Eventually many Naturalists themselves sought an ideal, and most of them found it not in socialism, but within a romantic sentimentality fortified by the national mystique.[8] Gerhart Hauptmann himself trod this path, showing once more the force of a German literary tradition that could stifle all attempts to use literature as an instrument of fundamental social and political change.

Socialist critics rightly chided Hauptmann for failing to show how the weavers could escape their lot. And although Social Democrats acclaimed him as the principal representative of modern art, their chief critic, Franz Mehring, added at once that "modern art is not great art."[9] Socialists could find no rapport with the modern art of their time and thus had no model upon which to build a contemporary socialist literature. Their way out was to stress the German classics: Goethe, Schiller, and even Mörike. Such a turning back into history was not likely to forge a link between socialists and the creative artists of the times, a link that Marx had thought important for the founding of a revolutionary tradition. Éduard Bernstein summed up the socialist dilemma: in the struggle toward the socialist goal, discipline and organization must prevail, and in this respect the artist was an outsider. Once the socialist society had come into being, there would be a great artistic flourishing.[10]

The creation of socialist literature was in the "future."[11] But what literature were the people to read and hear in the meantime? An effort was made to found a theater that would rouse the masses against the injustices of the times. The Freie Bühne (Free Theater), 1889, concentrated upon naturalist themes, presenting plays by Hauptmann, Ibsen, and Strindberg. Its successor, the Freie Volksbühne (Free People's Theater), 1890, was eventually taken over by the trade union movement, but it continued to produce plays that the bourgeoisie also enjoyed. To be sure, the workers had their own plays, which were performed by amateurs, but these plays were didactic, and the plots tended to be swamped by the educational message. The doctrine of surplus value had to be explained at some length from the stage, and sentiment was handicapped by the moral that true love was possible only between Socialist Party members.[12] Apart from such plays, attempts at a radical theater merely transmitted the predominant bourgeois culture to the working classes.

Even when self-conscious proletarians such as Max Kretzer wrote novels and poetry, their work seldom rose above the level of descriptions of the *triste milieu*; or, as in the case of Karl Henkel, it merely echoed Nietzsche's call to arms against the bourgeoisie. Minna Kautsky (1837–1912), mother of the socialist theoretician Karl Kautsky, wrote novels that advocated the ideals of social democracy and glorified the fighting spirit of proletarians who refused to be robbed of their humanity. Although she succeeded in picturing the awakening of class consciousness and the corruption of the upper classes, her friend Engels was right when he criticized her sentimentality and her simplistic notions of the social struggle.[13] A working-class, even a socialist, literature did exist during the Reich, but it was sporadic at best, and only a very few writers attempted to link their creative talents to the goals of the workers' movement.

To summarize, then, we can say that by the end of the nineteenth century, all attempts to create a German literature founded on revolutionary principles, and on the rhetoric of equality and freedom for all peoples, had been swept aside by the growth of a national mystique and by the ideals of bourgeois society. Characteristic of the preoccupation with nationalism was the search for a new religion that would cement German unity—a theme that evoked a more powerful response in the minds of Germans than ideas of radical change in the social structure. As we come to the mainstream of German literature during the second half of the century, we must proceed by examples, ignoring many important writers and their works. But we shall see the emergence of a pattern that, together with the failure of a revolutionary tradition of freedom and equality, can help to explain many of the attitudes that have formed the German politics of our time.

Wilhelm Jordan (1819–1904) is forgotten today, but in the 1860s he traveled up and down Germany reading his version of the *Nibelungen* saga to large, enthusiastic audiences. Jordan was one of several writers who wanted to create a Germanic religion to supersede the "sterile Semitism" of traditional Christianity. Like his more famous contemporary Paul de Lagarde, Jordan used the tradition of German idealism and a reviving national consciousness in order to create a faith based upon a return to ancient German sources of inspiration. His initial enthusiasm for the revolution of 1848 was forgotten in the effort to prove, through a recreation of Germanic sagas, that the Volk were endowed with a spiritual revelation, a creative instinct more vital than that of other peoples.

The practical result of the Germanic faith was to be a "reverential duty and unceasing work," as Jordan put it,[14] an attitude toward the world that contrasts markedly with that of Herwegh, but that most of his fellow writers shared, even though it was not usually expressed in German epic verse. However, Jordan was no racist. His argument concerned religion and the nation: everyone born in Germany could participate. Like many others of his generation, Jordan was influenced by the Greek heritage, and in a rather confused way he connected this with the Germanic tradition. When writing about the Greeks, however, he repeats his main thesis: the Semitic religion had penetrated into Greece and prevented the Greeks from transforming the Homeric ideal into reality. Jordan's ideas and goals may sound strange, but he had a wide audience in a literary genre that attained some popularity.

Wilhelm Jordan demonstrates the euphoria of national unity in which writers and artists joined so whole-heartedly after 1871. Their revolution was that which Bismarck had brought about, and the stress upon unity meant that all dissension must cease. Social problems and the maladjustment of a nation forging ahead to world power could be overcome through the creation of a spiritual unity among all inhabitants. To be sure, poverty existed and so did the toiling masses, but such problems would vanish if the ruling classes treated them with sympathy and if the lower classes responded with good will. Men like Jordan and most national liberals were at one in this view of society, and much contemporary German literature echoed this "idealistic" emphasis.

One example of this is the growing number of writers who

reached back into the German past in order to prophesy the national future. The historical novel was not confined to Germany, of course; at this time it achieved immense popularity throughout all western Europe. But after 1848 the craving for national unity came to predominate within the German variant of this literary genre. Victor von Scheffel's *Ekkehard* (1855) maintained its popularity for the rest of the century. The preface to this work states explicitly that the historical novel should assume the role that had been taken by the epic poem during the youth of the Volk: the artistic interpreter (not to say mythmaker) of national history. The novel centers on the monk Ekkehard and his life in monastery and castle almost 1,000 years ago. This was a time of "naïve, yet vital" conditions of life, and strong beliefs that not even our "rationalistic fury" can deny.[15] Ekkehard demonstrates a virile courage against the enemies of the Reich (the Huns), a Reich that was unfortunately fragmented after the death of Charlemagne. Here nothing is small and petty; everything has a transcendent greatness. The native landscape of the Bodensee (Lake Constance) area forms a vital part of the plot. Scheffel built the national mystique into a skillfully constructed novel, and his view of true Germanism stresses the virility and immediacy of all personal relationships. Here, as we shall see, he is close to the themes of the peasant novel and the adventure stories of Karl May.

The Königsberg historian Felix Dahn (1834–1912) followed in these footsteps. His *Der Kampf um Rom* (*The Fight for Rome*, 1867) rivaled *Ekkehard* in popularity, and Bismarck himself confessed that this was the only book he had read twice.[16] Dahn had intended to write a didactic novel, although the struggle of the Goths against Byzantium for the control of Italy was also a good adventure story. The hero of Dahn's book is a people: the Goths, ancestors of the Germans, and endowed with the primeval virtues that give them strength and confidence in their mission. They are defeated not so much by Italian and Byzantine cunning as by the influence of the southern environment. Italian luxury, rationality, and love for intrigue sap Gothic strength and will.

Dahn paints the Germanic ideal in strong colors: honesty, loyalty, and an absence of guilt characterizes the whole nation. These qualities of character were also praised by Jordan in his version of the *Nibelungenlied*. Side by side with these virtues stood the love of freedom and representative institutions. Dahn, like many historians before and after him, resurrected the Germanic tribal organization (*Comitatus*) as the true origin of democracy and contrasted this with Byzantine despotism. The tribal assembly, with its free debate, was an integral part of the national ethos, and the German longing for national unity was closely linked to this political ideal. Typically, Dahn belonged to the progressive wing of the National Liberal Party, and only after a personal conversation with his hero Bismarck, in the 1870s, did he move further to the political right.

Throughout the novel the Goths represent virtue and strength; the body mirrors the soul. The concept of beauty that informs such fiction (and not fiction alone) borrows from a Greek ideal and from Germanic mythology intermixed with romantic preconceptions. The blond and blue-eyed Goths echo a Germanic myth that is based upon those Germans whom Tacitus described so favorably. The emphasis on the right proportions of body and face, the athletic and sinewy build, all go back to the Greek examples. A particular ideal of beauty is found throughout Dahn's pages, and this ideal became an integral part of the German self-image. If we add to this ideal the virtues of the Goths, we have put together the "Aryan type" that was to play an increasingly important part in German literature from 1848 onward,[17] and was to reflect ever more sinister attitudes in the twentieth century.

The noble woman is part of this image, and here Dahn adopted the motif of Sir Walter Scott's *Ivanhoe*. The beautiful Jewess Miriam is in love with the future king of the Goths, Totila. This love serves to ennoble Miriam (and her father), but it has no effect on her brother, who in the end betrays the Goths to their adversaries. Moreover, this Jewish youth mirrors in his outward appearance the evil that resides within his soul; he is small, puny, and in all ways unattractive. Dahn uses this Jewish stereotype, which had already emerged into popular consciousness and which became the foil to the Germanic ideal of beauty. Yet Dahn was not consciously a racist; Miriam and her father show that Jewishness can be redeemed through a true assimilation to the Germanic ideal.[18]

Dahn's other works never approached the popularity of this novel. He wrote stories and poetry about the Germanic gods that preached patriotism and involvement with the past of the people. Not surprisingly, he abandoned Christianity in favor of a pantheism that stressed the unique religious experiences of every Volk. Dahn, like Jordan and many others, was preoccupied with the creation of a Germanic religion that would cement the new nation. But this cement, instead of leading to a Byzantine despotism, was to include an ideal of free political discussion. There was nothing in this Germanic image that threatened German bourgeois society and its ideals. The virtues we have outlined were aspired to by the German middle classes, and the ideal of beauty could easily be accepted as part of these virtues. The ideal of strength and of the "honest fight" (such as the Goths waged against Byzantium) was integrated with Social Darwinism, nationalism, and the idea of progress, reflecting the restraints that German bourgeois liberalism imposed upon itself.

Germany's newly found self-confidence resulted in a strong emphasis on the inevitability of progress. Viewed in national terms, this progress meant the retention of the status quo in a society that seemed already designed to make such progress possible. This status quo was not defined solely in terms of national unity, but also through an emphasis on the individual standing outside the sphere of direct political involvement and yet within a society that allowed him to unfold his own unique potential. The works of many German writers said, in effect: "Here in the nation that we have at long last created is a society that is rooted in tradition and yet allows you to develop your own creativity and worth. There is no need to concern yourself with politics or the social structure; instead you must look inward to develop your individuality within this world." A character in a novel by Paul Heyse put it succinctly: "the possible, the useful, the purposeful, and the necessary are and remain relative goals; it must be the task of the statesman to educate the public to a respect for law so that as many free individuals as possible may live harmoniously together." [19]

Whereas Felix Dahn's novel symbolically depicted the growth and direction of German nationalism, Gustav Freytag's *Soll und Haben* (*Debit and Credit*, 1855) symbolized the ideal of German bourgeois existence. This novel attained an even greater popularity than *Der Kampf um Rom*. The hero is not the Germanic people but a Germanic merchant house, its "heroic" qualities residing in the fact that it is old and established, devoted to "honest work" within the limits of the small town in which it operates. At one level an aristocrat, Rothsattel, provides the contrast; he is a spendthrift and prone to luxury, but his fortune is saved by the merchant house of Schröter, and he departs to settle on his eastern estates. Gustav Freytag (1816–1895) did not want to abolish the nobility; on the contrary, he believed that every class had its place in the nation. It is a mistake for the count of Rothsattel to dabble in finance, which is the business of the "honest bourgeoisie." His role is to recapture his strength and sense of mission by colonizing among the slaves. The real contrast in this novel, however, is between the house of Schröter and the Jewish house of Ehrenthal: the contrast between Christian honesty and stability and Jewish nervousness and false dealing. This contrast includes those who belong to both houses, and the stereotypes are the same as those Dahn was to draw later. The whole way of life of the two households is involved: Schröter's establishment is old, solid, clean, and comfortable; Ehrenthal's is dirty, small, and cramped. At the Schröters', all is *Gemütlichkeit*; at the Ehrenthals', hatred and rootlessness predominate. The quality of family life is central to this contrast, for at the Ehrenthals' there are quarrels and opposition between parents and children, whereas the Schröters lead a happy and settled existence. Given the importance of the family as the basis of the bourgeois ideal (a topic to which we shall return), this contrast is of the utmost importance. Wilhelm Jordan wrote that all ideals culminate in Germanism, but singled out for praise the "sacredness" of the family group.[20]

The ending of Freytag's novel mirrors once more the ideal he has set forth. The nervous, unsettled, Jewish youth, Veitel Itzig, drowns in a dirty river, but the Christian apprentice marries the Schröters' daughter and enters fully into the settled life of the ancient, honorable merchant house. Everyone gets his just deserts and the didactic nature of the novel is fully revealed.

Like Dahn, Freytag was no racist. He advocated the complete assimilation of Jews, and the thrust of his portrayal is directed against Jews as members of a foreign culture and civilization. He lived in Breslau, close to the masses of East European Jewry (as Dahn lived in Königsberg in the same frontier region), and his view of these Jews dominates the stereotype. This contrast between Jew and German was to fascinate many later writers, though none in the nineteenth century was as popular as Freytag or Dahn.[21] Yet the roots of the racist anti-Semitism of the twentieth century were laid in this popular literature, even if Germany did not stand alone in emphasizing the contrast. East European Jewry *did* form a separate culture and civilization in Europe, and as this was highly visible (partly because of the emigration of Jews into the West), it also provided the most exposed target against which to measure national differences.

Freytag wrote other works that emphasized the historical connection between past and present. He liked to trace back each of his subjects to its historical roots in order to discover an organic principle relevant to national concerns. The middle classes became such a concern in Germany, which was very slow to shed its feudal structure—and, indeed, never did so entirely during the nineteenth century. Typically, the middle classes were regarded as a restless and disruptive element within a nation that prized organic development, especially after the revolution of 1848. Freytag's "settled" merchant house, firmly rooted in its locality, provided the ideal of bourgeois existence. The hero of *Soll und Haben* mentions that the Poles do not possess such a settled middle class, whereupon his friend replies: "This means that they are devoid of culture."[22] The limited horizons of this bourgeois ideal involved a very restricted definition of culture, and a dread of change.

Friedrich Wilhelm von Hackländer's novel *Handel und Wandel* (*Trade and Change*, 1850) was one of the few earlier novels that, like *Soll und Haben*, centered on a bourgeois milieu. Here also speculation and risk-taking are derided in favor of "honest work." Life, even commercial endeavor, should be bound to one locality—the truth of this maxim being established when the hero is driven insane by the twin evils of foreign travel and reckless commercial speculation. Freytag himself ceased all correspondence with foreigners toward the end of his life.[23]

Such works reflect the reality of social values in Germany during the period of industrialization. Here the old patriarchal value structure existed side by side with the industrial process. In Germany, as Ralf Dahrendorf has remarked, the process of rapid industrialization produced social effects quite different from those in England and France. For one thing, Germany maintained a class structure that dated back to the preindustrial age;[24] the liberalism that exerted so strong a hold on the French and English bourgeoisie had little following in Germany—though Freytag thought of himself as a liberal, and Dahn came from a liberal background. The shift away from a revolutionary tradition in German letters, which we have observed, is connected not only with a concern for national unity but also with the value system and structure of the German bourgeoisie.

The emphasis on rootedness, on the small provincial town rather than on the big city, pervaded the country and its literature at the very time when cities were growing and the working classes increasing in power and restlessness. Novels, even those of great popularity, fought a rearguard action against this development. *Die Chronik der Sperlingsgasse* (*The Chronicle of Sparrows Alley*, 1857) by Wilhelm Raabe (1831–1916), centers upon the loneliness of the individual within the metropolis. The book is drenched with the pessimism of "evil times." The central character clings to life within the small street in which he lives, a microcosm of the urban scene behind which the great world looms as in a dream. Strobel, the diarist of the *Sperlingsgasse*, is an introspective individualist, and typifies the "characters" that many German writers offered their readers during this period. Friedrich Theodor Vischer (1807–1887) continued this tradition with *Auch Einer* (*Also a Person*, 1879), which presents an individualist who flouts the community of men and goes his own unorthodox way.

But such individualism is always circumscribed. Vischer's lonely hero praises the nation and affirms his love for his Volk. Raabe's Strobel clings not only to his alley but also to a belief in a mystical creative power (a belief evidently derived from the writings of Schopenhauer). The necessary parallel of the particular and the universal preoccupied such men. Berthold Auerbach (1812–1882), the founder of the German peasant novel, summarized this feeling in 1846: the more freely the individual is able to develop his potential, the greater the feeling of community that is released within his soul.[25] Such idealism was held to resolve the conflict between individuality and an organic view of life, between the ideal of freedom and the desirability of rootedness and order. These ideas were put into a framework of historical development, a nostalgia for the life of the past that had furthered this combination of freedom and ordered existence.

The harmony that comes with a settled existence also provides the theme for many of the novels of Theodor Fontane (1819–1898).

Prussia dominates his works—not the militaristic Prussia, which he abhorred, but Prussia as the "middling state of affairs" that typifies the values that lie at the root of Fontane's outlook on the world. Moderation is at the center of these values: "Brandenburg was the one country that never produced any saints, but where, on the other hand, no heretics were ever burned either."[26] Man must make peace with his fate and his society, for ultimate happiness will always elude him. The tragedy of *Effi Briest* (1895) lies in her unwillingness to come to terms with her fate and in a lack of personal stability that leads her into adultery. For Fontane, moderation means not only adjustment to reality but also common sense as opposed to blind adherence to principles. The actions of Effi Briest's jealous husband are inspired by abstract principles, so that, when he kills her lover in a duel, he is incapable of the satisfaction of feeling true human passion toward his enemy.[27]

Moderation allied to sobriety, incorruptibility, honesty, and dedication to duty are the virtues that distinguish the citizens of Brandenburg-Prussia. To be sure, these are bourgeois virtues, but Fontane, like other writers discussed in these pages, believed that those who possessed them formed a true nobility regardless of class; and, unlike other writers (such as Paul Heyse), Fontane did not confuse the good life with opulence: modesty and simplicity are integral to the virtues he praised so highly.

The protagonist of *Frau Jenny Treibel* (1893) lacks both these virtues. Through her marriage she has risen from low birth into the upper ranks of bourgeois society. As the wife of a prosperous merchant, her newly found class consciousness corrupts her judgment. Jenny Treibel's chief characteristic is possessiveness: she not only clings to her station in life but also tries to rule everyone around her. In face of her attempted manipulation of his daughter's life, a kindly academic is forced to exclaim: "If I were not a professor, I would become a Social Democrat." Fontane, in this novel, contrasts the classical ideal ("become what you truly are yourself") with the false ideals of Jenny Treibel.[28] There is nothing wrong with rising out of your social class, provided that this enlarges your horizon rather than constricting it. Fontane is not attacking the virtues the bourgeoisie exalted, but castigating the selfish possessiveness that governs Jenny Treibel's outlook upon her new world. His ideal embraces those qualities that all writers in the mainstream of German letters had also praised, but he goes beyond them in emphasizing that adjustment to society also means gaining distance from the hurly-burly that society represents.

Fontane's heroes are pessimists who manage to overcome this pessimism and to gain harmony in their personal lives. Prussian virtues are central to this harmony, but a firm connection with Prussian history helps toward their attainment. Dubslav, the principal character of *Der Stechlin* (1898), or the evangelical sisters in *Wanderungen durch die Mark Brandenburg* (*Ramblings Through the Mark Brandenburg*, 1862–1882), have their roots in the Prussian past. Although Fontane denied the usefulness of a hereditary nobility, his stress upon the Prussian past inevitably makes most of his heroes a part (or at least a reflection) of the Junker class and its values. His definition of the Prussian heritage is bound up with the landscape within which it was formed, and works such as the *Wanderungen* attempt to combine Prussian history and the Prussian landscape into one indissoluble whole. This idea was not new. Many of the historical novels that we have discussed attempted this kind of fusion. The German ideal of rootedness, of the foundations for a settled society, included a wished-for harmony between those families that had long shared the fate of the nation, and the landscape that had helped to shape their destinies.

In the historical novel, as in the peasant novel, this concept of harmony tended to narrow the range of vision and promote an intolerant nationalism. In Fontane's work, however, the author's sense of history gives "distance" to his characters, enabling them to rise above society and to come to terms with their fate. In *Stechlin*, Dubslav typifies Fontane's harmonious man: not only does he possess the Prussian virtues but he is opposed to narrow definitions of class and culture, and inveighs against a one-sided pride of nationality. Dubslav is tolerant because he is at one with his fate as well as with the history and landscape of his native soil. Fontane reached back into the past not in order to prophesy the national future, but to use the past to encourage virtues far removed from the exuberant nationalism or bourgeois acquisitiveness of his time.

Nothing in Fontane conflicts with the ideals of the bourgeois world of which he himself was skeptical; no call to revolt is sounded in his pages. He shared Raabe's pessimism about his own times;

in his case, too, this pessimism led to a concentration on the individual rather than on society. His characters seem to withdraw from the world, because "quiet is better than noise."[29] But the emphasis is always on the effort to overcome this pessimism in one's own personal life and to emerge settled, harmonious, and with that larger view of man and his struggle that characterized the Prussian imagination. However large this view, it was still circumscribed by its connection with Prussian history and the Prussian landscape, and by an emphasis upon virtues that give Fontane's works their singularly old-fashioned character.

The limited horizons of German letters led to a change in the attainable ideal that many writers presented to their readers. German unity had for long provided such an ideal, but after it was attained in 1870, writers increasingly began to praise the good and the beautiful as a goal of life that stood outside any concern with society or politics. The status quo would include a utopia that everyone could share. The work of Paul Heyse (1830–1914), the most celebrated and admired novelist of the Wilhelmine era, illustrates these ideals.

Heyse had supported the revolution of 1848 in his youth, and had even cheered the democratic uprising in Baden. After the failure of revolution, however, he shed his revolutionary fervor and began to recommend the quiet and orderly development of society.[30] He was called to Munich by King Ludwig II of Bavaria, and became, for a time, a member of the court's "round table," where literary matters were discussed and papers presented. Heyse's patron at Munich was the poet Emmanuel Geibel (1815–1884), who had also repudiated his initial enthusiasm for the ideals of 1848 in order to become the "herald of German nationality." Geibel's poem "The Death of Tiberius," for example, presents symbolically the transfer of the empire from Romans to Germans. Tiberius, dying, drops his scepter out of the window, and it is caught by a German legionnaire who has seen Christ die on the cross. Geibel was much admired as the high priest of poetry, a reputation he himself did much to encourage. Heyse became something of a high priest as well, though his work was never as portentous and heavy-handed as Geibel's.

Heyse (and indeed the whole Munich group) has been accused of avoiding the darker aspects of life in favor of an emphasis upon beauty and form.[31] There is some truth in this criticism, but it ignores the fact that the quest for beauty was only part of a world view that Heyse projects in his novels.[32] In his most famous novel, *Kinder der Welt* (*Children of This World*, 1873), he emphasizes the need to come to terms with the reality of life; he advises the new generation not to withdraw either into a rejection of the world for the sake of religion, or into martydom for the sake of a cause, and asserts that individual worth will improve the quality of life on earth. What is needed is the good will of all men. A master craftsman who wants to reform the world and suffers many disappointments is advised to remain within the limited circle of his profession and his small town: if he tills his own soil and works honestly at his craft, he will create a better society than those who theorize about social conditions and politics.[33] Heyse typically praises the "golden mediocrity" of some, provided it is not hedged about with pretentiousness.[34]

Individualism stands in the foregound of the novel: man must trust in his own worth, and neither the state nor religion should practice intolerance. These liberal maxims are combined with the contention that the individual can best unfold his personality within his own milieu, and develop an appreciation of the beauty contained in the world through pride in himself. This beauty is defined in Wilhelminian terms; Heyse's novels abound in descriptions of paintings and furniture that are judged through the conventional taste of the time. As for the working classes, the hero of *Kinder der Welt* founds a working-class cultural club and praises a capitalist who lets his workers buy shares in his firm. It is interesting to note that during the revolution of 1848 such workers' "cultural" clubs (*Arbeiterbildungsvereine*) had the political purpose of spreading democratic ideas. Heyse's club has no such purpose; it unites workers and the bourgeois leadership, who attend lectures on natural science that demonstrate the falseness of organized religion. The lower classes (Heyse wrote in one of his short stories) must be encouraged to attain bourgeois consciousness.[35]

Although Heyse was strongly opposed to the idea of nationalism in terms of an all-powerful state, his liberalism was essentially negative in quality; he praised individualism—but only the kind of individualism that renounced any political participation: above all the harmony of the existing social order must be preserved. The revolutionary in *Kinder der Welt* gives way to a hero who believes in a settled life that will culminate not in social or political change, but in the appreciation of the good that life has to offer. It is not surprising that Heyse was so highly regarded in his day. His novels echoed the German bourgeois ideal, and it must have been comforting to read such works in a Europe that was neither quiet nor settled in its political and social order.

Paul Heyse had a host of followers, and his ideas appeared in many other novels of the time. Georg Hermann's very popular *Jettchen Gebert* (1906) is of special interest in this connection. Georg Hermann (the pen-name of Georg H. Borchardt, 1871–1943) set his novel in a Jewish milieu, and so it throws light on contemporary ideas about the assimilation of German Jews into bourgeois society. The Jewish element is merely superimposed on an idealization of the bourgeois way of life that Heyse and others had prized; it consists mostly in the names of characters and in certain religious holidays that are observed with bourgeois opulence. To be sure, the heroine Jettchen suffers an unhappy love affair and finally commits suicide—her lover being deemed "unsuitable" because he is both a Gentile and a penurious intellectual. But here, as elsewhere, Hermann is making a general plea for tolerance and damning the worship of wealth. The life led by the Geberts is in other respects praised, because it is a settled life where (as one character puts it) not much attention is paid either to a quest for the so-called higher things of life or to the changeable, drunken, and fleeting aspects of existence. Life within its own prescribed limits is the ideal for Hermann, as it was for Heyse: "life," so Hermann writes in a preface to his novel, "is a game and we must not take it too seriously." "Everything comes as it well must" is Hermann's fatalistic view of the world—a view that contrasts with Heyse's optimism. For both writers, however, a settled bourgeois life provides the best way of coping with the joys and disappointments of human existence.

Georg Hermann's own fate was tragic: the writer who so lovingly described the bourgeois milieu of Berlin perished at Auschwitz. Stefan Zweig was correct when he wrote to Georg Hermann, after the Nazis came to power, that "it will one day be noticed as a peculiar sign [of the times] that it was precisely the Jews who painted the most lasting portrait of Germany at the turn of the century and after the war."[36] Nevertheless the German bourgeoisie had expelled the Jewish bourgeoisie from their midst, accepting the Jewish stereotype that Dahn and Freytag (among others) had drawn in such stark colors. Hermann had praised the limited horizons entailed in the way of life of his characters; but they had become too limited to contain those whom he thought to be such prime examples of this way of life.

Paul Heyse linked his idealization of the bourgeoisie to excellent literary form, intimately connected with the past traditions of poetry and society. The Naturalists advocated an unlimited idealism that could lead only to anarchy.[37] Felix Dahn criticized the Naturalists in a similar manner. They acted wildly, as if nature were ugly and mean, whereas in reality "beautiful truths" and "beautiful human nature" exist on earth.[38] Heyse himself linked literary form to a life of work and duty culminating in the vision of a world of beauty and light. When such beauty is attached to an idealization of existing society, literary form becomes part of tradition and the status quo.

The primacy of personal relationships over any larger concerns is implied or expressed in all works written by the most admired Wilhelmine writers. But these personal relationships were not anarchic; they were given literary form through their connections with the settled and traditional order, which was expressed in these works by family relationships. Heyse's *Kinder der Welt* is filled with sentimental attachments of husband to wife, or with the love that exists between brothers. Jettchen Gebert suffered, at least in part, because she was in danger of destroying the fabric of her family. The family symbolized the very essence of the bourgeois way of life, and this symbol reached its greatest prominence in the work of some novelists at the very moment when the family structure came under attack by Naturalist and Expressionist writers. A whole world separates the solid families of writers such as Heyse from the cruel and despairing parents in Frank Wedekind's *Frühlings Erwachen* (*Spring's Awakening*, 1891), in which the family is the victim of strife between generations. The significant point here, of course, is that writers such as Heyse (who clung to tradition) and writers such as Wedekind (who explored the "pathology" of traditional bourgeois values) both started from the assumption that the family structure is the true microcosm of society at large.

The works we have discussed were widely read by middle-class readers, and they demonstrate the general direction of German literature in the second half of the nineteenth century. Yet the world views held by these writers infiltrated the population at large from works that attained mass circulation through cheap editions or lending libraries. However slight the literary merits of such fictions, we should not underestimate the extent to which they may confirm and sharpen—even if they do not create—ideas about the value systems in society.

At first glance the highly successful books of Marlitt (the penname of Eugenie John, 1825–1887) are sentimental love stories. But if we look closer we discover the same value system that the other, more critically appreciated writers had advocated. Marlitt's ideal was an "even-tempered, harmonious family life." Here children must obey their parents and man must assume authority over woman, for woman is destined "to found a happy family and not to fill her head with facts and figures."[39] Society depends on a social hierarchy, though not one founded on inherited privilege; sentimentality and refinement are the criteria of true social status. Marlitt's definition of sentimentality includes compassion toward the poor, a paternalism that will alleviate their present misery.

Within her novels men and women rise in the social scale only by accepting bourgeois manners and morals, including the ideal of "honest work." (In fact, many of her characters move upward in the social scale through marriage rather than through their own endeavors.) It has been observed, with justice, that German literature lacks its Horatio Algers, and this serves to remind us of the realities of the German class structure, and especially of the dominance of preindustrial attitudes within the industrial nation. Small wonder that Marlitt inveighs against the social climber, the pusher, and those who threaten the organic fabric of life: no unfettered individual effort is allowed in her world. Perhaps Marlitt's ideal can best be summed up in her own words: "There is something very beautiful about [this] ancient bourgeois order . . . everything stands or lies in its accustomed place . . . one is immediately at home."[40]

"To be at home" was another definition of the limited horizons necessary for a good and beautiful life. Within the limits of such rootedness, however, Marlitt emphasized her optimism about man's potential and individual worth. The worst crime society can commit is the degrading of man to the level of a machine, making him serve others and deny his own will. Marlitt enthusiastically supported Bismarck's fight against the Catholic Church, which she believed to be oppressive, and instead she advocated a pantheism brimming with Christian sentimentality. Individual freedom plays a part in her novels, as it did in Dahn's *Der Kampf um Rom*, but it is circumscribed by the narrow bourgeois ideal that she advocated. Marlitt was no strident nationalist; although she was loyal to Bismarck's state, her characters do not stress their Germanism. Indeed Marlitt, like the other writers to be discussed in the next essay, advocated tolerance toward Jews and respect for all peoples and nations. However, the environment in which they live, their roots in the locality, accentuate the provincialism that fills these novels, and that at the same time restricted the vision of such popular writers.

Marlitt was the favorite author of the *Gartenlaube* (*Gazebo*), a journal that, at its height, had the unparalleled circulation of half a million copies. This journal attempted to perpetuate the tradition of 1848, praising Voltaire and Rousseau as champions of freedom, and eulogizing Kant for attempting to exalt reason as the basis of society and economics.[41] However, the further the revolution of 1848 receded into the distance, the greater the stress it laid not only upon Voltaire and Rousseau but also upon the need for order and social hierarchy. Bourgeois manners and morals provided the foundations for a better and settled life, and nothing must be allowed to challenge this tradition.[42]

The vision of life that we have discussed was not solely confined to novels in a bourgeois setting. The peasant novel had a long tradition in Germany, and Berthold Auerbach, who had popularized this type of work, was still alive in the decades following the revolution of 1848. His novels of village life idealized the simple peasant and the upright village priest. Ludwig Ganghofer (1855–1920) proved to be the most successful practitioner of this genre within the unified Reich. He was on the best-seller list of 1900, side by side with Tolstoy; even in 1957 he was still greatly admired, many Germans putting him in the company of such men as Gustav Freytag, Thomas Mann, and Ernest Hemingway.[43]

The peasant was used to symbolize a strength and virility not yet sapped by the all-pervasive modernity. Ganghofer's peasants are "examples of men within whom the primeval forces, the healthy instincts, and the force of life have not changed into the unhealthy, restricted, and average."[44] Moreover, Ganghofer's characters were drawn with sufficient realism for his readers to regard them as a reflection of life itself. His peasants tend to be superstitious, even mean and quarrelsome; but this, after all, is life: men should be recognized for what they are, and the reader should learn how to build a better future out of such a recognition. Ganghofer was an optimist; for him the genius of human existence, with all its secret recesses, will lead men to the light, if only they can break out of the fetters of culture (by which he meant urbanism and modernity). Life is hard, but it has potential if it will be guided by the inspiration of nature. Interestingly enough, in his youth Ganghofer had admired the cynical and worldly Heinrich Heine. However, by the 1880s he had repudiated his former hero, and he called this repudiation "a step toward health." That step had begun with his discovery of the mountains, the "sacred landscape" that symbolized for him the unspoiled force of nature.[45] At the same time Ganghofer turned from cynicism to optimism: men will find the force to break the fetters of artificial culture.

He constructed an elaborate utopia in which every person would have his own land, and where euthanasia would be the lot of the congenitally sick. Such concepts are uneasily combined with traditional liberal virtues. Laws, not men, must rule in this state. There must be freedom of religion and for the creative artist. Above all, every man must know the joys of home and hearth, which so many peasants actually possess: the family would be safeguarded, and bachelors would pay most of the expenses of the state.[46] We are back with the praise of bourgeois virtues, of a German bourgeois utopia, that Marlitt had typified at another level.

The German peasant novel never expanded into a true glorification of the primitive, after the manner of Gauguin and many French writers.[47] Instead, the tradition of the German peasant novel stressed an approach to nature that deprived it of that wild primitivism that threatened all forms of civilized life. Marlitt was also fascinated by nature, but her nature becomes a friendly landscape where the contours of the mountains are "soft and glowing."[48] Ganghofer's nature is more wild and rugged, yet in the last resort it also is tamed through the peasant's feeling of belonging, of identification with the land.

Human nature is tamed through providing a home for man: we are back with Marlitt's ideal of a society where everything lies in its accustomed place. Unlike the characters in Marlitt and the previous writers discussed, however, Ganghofer's peasants are involved with the struggle for life, where the qualities of shrewdness and cleverness can bring success. Such an emphasis upon struggle comes close to a glorification of force. Ganghofer was too sentimental to take this step, but Hermann Löns (1866–1914), his successor in popular esteem in this genre, combines the glorification of primitivism with an equal emphasis on the naked force necessary to protect this way of life from the corruption of modernity.

Stories of adventure in foreign lands could also be used didactically, and this combination brought enormous success to Karl May (1842–1912). May overshadowed even Marlitt and Ganghofer in popularity; indeed, he may well be called the most popular German writer of modern times. Adolf Hitler once said that Karl May had opened his eyes to the world,[49] and he certainly opened the eyes of generations of readers during the first half of the twentieth century. Between 1892 and 1913, over one and a half million copies of his collected works were published, and by 1938, this total had risen to nearly seven and a half million.[50] May's novels centered on the Orient or the American West. Both Kara Ben Nemsi in the Orient and the trapper Old Shatterhand march through dangers in strange lands, and emerge victorious over the evil that confronts them. Both master life—a life filled with persecution, mysterious secrets, and labyrinthine intrigues. These are the anxieties of modern urban existence transposed to the deserts of the Orient or the North American plains. Perhaps it is the fairy tale element in May's works, coupled with the lure of adventure, that accounts for his great popularity. He himself stressed the didactic nature of his works, but, like many of the writings discussed in this essay, they could be read without embracing the author's world view.[51] Yet, even if we grant the complexity of the relationship between an author's world view and his readership, the close integration of world view and plot must have had an impact on the attitudes of those who read and enjoyed such works.

Kara Ben Nemsi and Old Shatterhand typify the morality that

inevitably wins its battles, for as May himself tells us: "along the paths which Winnetou and Old Shatterhand rode, no mean actions were tolerated."[52] Evil is always punished. The hero combines kindness, and even sentimentality, with strong and decisive action, in order that virtue shall triumph everywhere. May glorifies the virtues that other novelists had also praised; but he surrounds them with a fighting spirit directed against those who would destroy them. The confrontation between good and evil is direct and simple. For Karl May, king, fatherland, and law are necessary institutions that give roots to man. Such roots help man to rise above the purely material plane to the highest ideal on earth: that of becoming a noble soul (*Edelmensch*). May's utopia offers "a symphony of liberating thought"—the strong and noble souls whose wills are directed toward uprooting lawlessness and the evil instincts of man.[53]

May thus connects heroism with both Germanism and Christianity. "You Germans," says one of his characters, "are a peculiar people, sentimental and yet when necessary you stand and fight."[54] The school reformer and volkish thinker Ludwig Gurlitt described one of May's American Indian heroines thus: "she is modest and strict with herself . . . yet tender and of a deep soulfulness, filled with true femininity like Kriemhilde: an Indian woman with a German heart."[55] Karl May believed that Germany was the true repository of the virtues he praised, and that no German could do much wrong either on the North American plains or in the deserts of the Orient. But he never lapses into a strident nationalism: for him the American Indians are nobler souls than the whites who try to destroy them. His Germans in foreign lands fit themselves into the customs of other peoples; they tend to be Germans and men of the world at the same time. May's heroes also emphasize their Christianity, and as missionaries among primitive peoples they teach love and good manners not only by personal example but also through the use of force.

The hero dominates each of the novels, and becomes the personification of authority, a man who through his true nobility exemplifies the triumph of courage, love, and compassion in the wide confines of nature, following out God's plan for the world. The pantheism that surrounds and, in a sense, guides May's heroes toward the light, also suffuses the ideal society that Marlitt sets before us. For both, this is an inner piety that disdains any outward effect. Such inner piety supported the "pure heart" that would make a new and better life possible on earth. God's spirit and the inspiration of a "pure heart" will lead men out of the jungles of the city toward a genuine society where bourgeois virtues will reign. Neither for Marlitt's hierarchical society nor for May's hero is political freedom an essential part of this utopian longing. Force plays its part, but it is dedicated to defeating evil—in the guise of all that is morally deficient, and lacking in compassion, sense of family, or the will to protect noble souls.

The tendency to view the world in moral terms predominated among such writers. The specific moral pattern that accompanied the rise of bourgeois society provided the foundations and the cement for the ideal commonwealth of men. Sobriety, hard work, and an emphasis on action play a large role in these novels, but virtue is also defined as including good manners, the "respectability" that contemporaries associated so closely with middle-class virtue. Morality and good manners were an integral part of the concern for society: the conventions society had produced also served to define it.

Those writers who rebelled against these literary norms took the view that conventional respectability merely served to distort the realities of life, and that the acceptance of bourgeois virtues deflected the individual from his search for personal integrity. The Expressionists revolted against the bourgeois image of society, but their revolution, in large part, centered upon the individual in his relationship to the conventions that surround him. Max Brod's *Schloss Nornepygge* (*Nornepygge Castle*, 1908), which came early in the Expressionist revolt, lamented the ability of the hero to "pierce through" the fool's paradise in which most people lived, for such insight transformed him into an outsider, naked and defenseless. Mozart's *Don Giovanni* provides the theme of the book, and Don Giovanni himself appears in order to demonstrate how such heroes can lead mankind toward liberation. Nevertheless the book's hero (or rather anti-hero) remains in his indifferent isolation. The rejection of the "home" that so many writers had helped to build for their readers left Expressionists with a feeling of isolation. As a result, many Expressionist writers longed to be fully and irresponsibly alive, and this marked a personal vitalism that saw man as a self-contained unity. "Am I not alive—am I not life?" cries a character in one of Georg Kaiser's earliest plays.[56]

The influence of Nietzsche, himself in revolt against the predominant patterns of social life, is unmistakable in such vitalism. This was a revolution, but not on the pattern of 1848, for society and politics were rejected in favor of individual perception and ecstasy. Nietzsche's phrase, "society puts the passions asleep,"[57] characterizes the attitude of many Expressionists toward the realities and miseries of life. The bourgeois writers had turned the vision of a better life toward "beauty and goodness" attainable within the framework of existing social reality. The Expressionist writers rejected this reality, drifting off into a vitalism that encompassed, at one and the same time, a Nietzschean ecstasy and a pessimism about life itself. The "new" Expressionist man believed in acting out the demands of his own chaotic soul. Sincerity to oneself did not mean settling into a home where everything had its appointed place; it meant hurling oneself against the conventions of society. In Wedekind's *Frühlings Erwachen*, the schoolboys face repression and punishment because they embrace what is only natural—sex—and society punishes men for such acts.

With the approach and the beginning of World War I, however, many Expressionists were moved to adopt more overtly political positions. The central character of Georg Kaiser's *Die Bürger von Calais* (*The Burghers of Calais*, 1914) challenges traditional patriotism; he commits suicide in order to persuade his fellow citizens to give hostages to the English and accept defeat, rather than condemn the city and all its inhabitants to death. The preservation of man, not his destruction, must be the goal of politics. Action must be guided by reason in the cause of the love of mankind.

However, the love of man and the pacifism that inspired Expressionist writing during and after the war were based more upon emotion than upon social analysis: the attempts of Expressionists to improve society "floated, as it were, in a sea that swept towards a shore of infinite promise."[58] It is not surprising that so many Expressionists ended up in the arms of nationalism and bourgeois society. Max Brod became a Zionist; Hans Johst, a prominent early Expressionist, went on to make his name as a Nazi writer. Gottfried Benn's poetry, before and after World War I, was filled with visions of disease, decadence, and death; he also wrote Dionysian hymns to the human ego. But by 1933 he was praising the logic of history as the absolute value to which man had to relate himself, and making speeches exalting the "new man" of the Third Reich.[59] Expressionism had proved to be an ineffectual and disappointing revolution. The new literary forms of the movement and its considerable artistic freedom provided no compensation for those who had wanted no less than to change the minds of men. German bourgeois society had survived in such strength that it eventually absorbed the very men who had attempted to storm its ramparts. A Nietzschean revolt led by creative artists was clearly not an effective way to accomplish a revolutionary task. Their frame of reference proved both too vague and too limited: the conventions they hated were merely symptoms, not the cause, of the sickness that they discerned in the society of their time.

The German bourgeoisie, however, discerned no such sickness before World War I. It rejoiced in a status quo that combined a supposed dedication to individualism with an emphasis on traditional manners and morals, and the national mystique. The mainstream of German letters followed this path. Liberal attitudes were undermined by the longing for a settled and ordered existence that would not threaten the Establishment. Nevertheless, as the new century opened, one powerful voice protested against the course that liberalism had taken in Germany.

Heinrich Mann attempted to link German liberalism with the tradition of the French Enlightenment. Mann had passed through nationalism and expressionism in his early youth, and now he exalted the rationalism of the French tradition, castigating the romantic and irrational attitudes prevalent in German society. His novel *Schlaraffenland* (*Land of Cockaigne*, 1900), exposed the hypocrisy of the German *haute bourgeoisie*: millionaires applaud plays showing the misery of the working classes, but then go about their business as usual; life is regarded as a game where appearances are more important than reality, and where corruption has eaten into the very fabric of society. The exclamation of the book's chief character—"feeling is all that matters"—goes to the heart of Mann's condemnation of Wilhelmine Germany, because feeling is opposed to those rational attitudes that alone can produce a democratic society where freedom and justice reign.

For Mann, the ruling classes use their power in order to corrupt man's rational faculties: his ability to grasp what is true, good, and right. The anti-hero of his novel *Der Untertan* (*The Man of Straw*, 1918) worships "the power that rules over us and whose feet we kiss."[60] This power is exercised in the name of an ordered and settled existence, and it ruins those whom it cannot manipulate. Within the novel this power triumphs, even if not for ever; the kindly socialist who is deprived of his office and livelihood continues to praise the "spirit of humanity" that will eventually triumph; for power that cannot spread goodness and kindness throughout the world is not destined to last.[61]

Mann saw the outbreak of World War I as the natural consequence of the use of power for irrational and tyrannical purposes. His famous essay *Zola* (1915) was one more attempt to recall Germany to the sanity of the French rational tradition—a true liberalism that would defeat the irrationalism that had led the nation into militarism and oppression. Mann fully shared the optimism characteristic of the French Enlightenment: the people have the ability to construct a democratic society; it is the misuse of power by a "dried-up" Establishment that stands in the way of the inevitable perfection of humanity.[62] With singular courage Mann looked forward to the defeat of Germany, for only such a catastrophe would open the way for the abolition of militarism and capitalism in favor of the "ideal republic of the future."[63]

The defeat of Germany and the revolution of 1918 failed to establish the ideal republic, however, and Heinrich Mann now called for a "dictatorship of reason," exhorting the hapless president of the Republic to exercise absolute power until the people could be freed from the yoke of "darkness and madness" that Wilhelmine rule had thrust upon them. Once again he reaffirmed his faith in the "rational spirit": it alone could bring democracy.[64] The economic problems that Germany faced were secondary, mechanical difficulties that could be tackled successfully provided the right spirit was present. This belief in the primacy of the spirit links Mann to that German idealism he hated so much, and to the abstract longing for freedom of the "Young Germans"; it is small wonder that he never joined any of the existing socialist parties. His novels are filled with the spirit of rationalism and humanism, but they are devoid of any Marxist social analysis and have no direct place in the movement to create a socialist literature.

In spite of this, Heinrich Mann did attempt to change the course of German letters. He was not interested in the Expressionists' chaotic search for freedom or in Nietzschean cries of revolt. As he wrote in 1917, "Why should the beautiful preference of the mature eighteenth century for goodness and the recognition of human equality not be recaptured?"[65] His books were widely read: *Schlaraffenland* had sold 100,000 copies by 1929, and *Der Untertan* sold 150,000 copies shortly after its appearance in 1918.[66] Nevertheless, it was too late to reestablish the influence of French rationalism over the German mind; that opportunity had been missed with the failure of the revolution of 1848. Instead, the mainstream of German letters continued to reflect the rejection of this particular liberal and revolutionary tradition.

Thomas Mann's reply to his brother's essay on Zola was rooted in a deeper and more abiding stream of German thought. *Betrachtungen eines Unpolitischen (Reflections of an Unpolitical Man*, 1918) summarizes many attitudes that we have already discussed. Whereas Heinrich Mann had seen in the self-satisfied German bourgeoisie an obstacle to the realization of the ideal republic, Thomas Mann praises bourgeois existence as *the* truly German lifestyle, summarizing this way of life as *Ordnung, Folge, Ruhe* (order, progression, quiet).[67] Thomas Mann stresses order and ordered progress, concepts that his brother had condemned as serving to disguise the misuse of power. The bourgeois virtues that Thomas Mann exalts in other works also inform his idealization of this style of life: hard work, devotion to duty, and good manners.[68] So it is not surprising that he also praises the patriarchal relationship between employer and laborer.[69] He recalls Theodor Fontane in his attitude to the quiet and ordered life; but his emphasis on patriotism and on the metaphysical depth of the German soul further restricts his vision.

Heinrich Mann had also praised the bourgeois virtues of duty, punctuality, and moderation,[70] but he equated bourgeois democracy with French democracy, whereas his brother believed that middle-class life was the logical outgrowth of German idealism. Thomas Mann's pessimism about the political potential of the people led him to an acceptance that, in the political realm, might makes right. His brother, in contrast, asked: ". . . what is power if it is not justice?" Thomas Mann combines praise of the bourgeois way of life with cynicism about the possibilities inherent in human government. The ideal republic of his brother's dreams was nothing more than a fantasy, which was irrelevant to the reality of German life.

In the *Betrachtungen*, the outward forms of government are dismissed as unworthy of serious consideration; this follows from the distinction he makes between culture and civilization. The "rich inner life of the soul," which determines individual development, is what makes for true culture, whereas civilization is a matter of mere outward forms, a superficial preoccupation with the here and now. Thomas Mann castigates the "love for demonstration and manifestos" as a shallow rationalism that merely encourages a generalized love for humanity.[71] The *Betrachtungen* is filled with confessions of faith in humanism, but this humanism turns out to be a hidden substance residing within the soul of the Volk. All that is truly "genuine" must be inner-directed; it expresses itself outwardly solely through the lifestyle of the bourgeoisie. For Thomas Mann, a cultured bourgeois is a "romantic individualist,"[72] but in reality he himself romanticizes the whole bourgeois way of life, with its settled tradition and its rootedness where, in Marlitt's phrase, "one is immediately at home."

For all that, the unpolitical man turns political in time of war. Then the bourgeois is "at his place" in the national struggle and no questions are asked. War is the cement of national culture, the antidote to the cancer of civilization that threatens to dissolve society. Thomas Mann was deeply influenced by Nietzsche, although he does not echo Nietzsche's cry of revolt against the bourgeoisie. Instead, he emphasized the philosopher's opposition to democracy, his "anti-radicalism," as he calls it. But it is to Nietzsche that we can trace his exaltation of primitivism—his belief that in war such primitivism is an outburst of the Volk soul with which the German artist must keep in touch.[73]

The *Betrachtungen* was written under the influence of a war experience that engulfed many Germans in a wave of Nietzschean ecstasy, but it is free of the harsh polemics against Germany's enemies that had become fashionable among so many of his fellow writers. The tone, with some exceptions, is moderate; the arguments are advanced with an air of judicious restraint. To be sure, there is little in the book to foreshadow Mann's conversion to democracy only three years later (although, even after this conversion, he remained withdrawn from the world, preferring a quiet life among his own immediate circle).[74] Yet it is the *Betrachtungen*, rather than the works of his brother, that is in the mainstream of the German literary tradition, for it summarizes many attitudes that dominated Wilhelmine society.

The works of overtly volkish and nationalist writers never attained the popularity of the books considered in these pages.[75] Although the former were hostile to the bourgeoisie, they rejected a true change in the social structure in favor of a "change of attitudes." Their writings were in the process of becoming racist, whereas overtly racist views were absent from the popular works that have concerned us here.

German literature reflected a quest for identity within a new nation undergoing rapid industrialization. The foundations were laid for the future in the rejection of Western liberalism and in the failure to combine creative art and literature with revolutionary theory. During World War I, Thomas Mann's attacks upon enlightenment and rationalism were in the tradition of this nineteenth-century rejection. By the time Mann repudiated his own views, during the years of the Weimar Republic, it was already too late, and a national socialist revolution that none of these writers would have desired was about to engulf bourgeois and socialist alike.

We must now extend this analysis of German literature and society by focusing upon Marlitt, Ganghofer, and May, the most popular writers of the fin de siècle. For such works, read in the millions, will serve to sharpen and refine our ideas about the value systems of German society. They shared the limited horizons of German letters, as we have seen, but they also put forward ideas about man, morality, and society that need further elaboration if we are to understand how bourgeois society wanted to see itself. Their vision penetrated downward into the lower orders through the popularity of those novels, which in straightforward fashion reflected the popular taste.

THREE

What Germans Really Read

G ERMAN POPULAR LITERATURE can give us an insight into German attitudes, hopes, and longings. Its relationship to social and political reality was complex, yet our analysis of the German popular novel at the end of the nineteenth century does lead to some conclusions about the connection of this literature with the fateful course of German history during our own age.

Jost Hermand has written about the great variety of styles at the fin de siècle, which runs from naturalism and impressionism to the quest for the Holy Grail.[1] While such variety no doubt existed, the overwhelming content of the popular literature of this age is characterized by those limited horizons which, as we saw earlier, gave German literature as a whole its peculiar cast during most of the nineteenth century. German literature was deeply involved in and reflected that quest for identity which accompanied the political movements for national unification, providing a sharp reaction to modernity. Whereas England and France produced literature read throughout the West, Germany no longer did so; its cultural horizons were too constricted and the self-conscious quest for identity was far too intense.

Popular literature is a part of this quest: here we have little variety of style or indeed content. The very sameness of this literature gives it its significance, for it reflected, in a more or less constant fashion, the aspirations in the moral and political world of most of the population. There can be little doubt that it cut across classes and that we cannot simply identify it with the servant maid in her attic or the hardpressed *petit bourgeoisie*. The current runs too deep, the editions into too many millions, for us to take a restricted view of the audience. The very sameness of style and content meant that these novels struck a sympathetic chord and had managed to establish significant contact between the authors and their masses of readers.

Such contact was successfully established and maintained because the men and women who wrote for mass circulation never lost sight of their readers. It was a conscious attitude on the parts of E. Marlitt (the pen-name of Eugenie John, 1825–1887), Ludwig Ganghofer (1855–1920), and Karl May (1842–1912), who alone between them saturated the popular market. Their books are inconceivable without their readers. The even tenor of these works can tell us relatively more about immediate feelings and aspirations than either the literature of revolt against bourgeois society, which consciously pointed to a tenuous future, or the volkish literature, which had a far more restricted market.

The settings of their novels differed: Marlitt focused on the small town, Ganghofer on peasants and huntsmen in the high mountains, and May on the plains of North America or the deserts of the Orient. Marlitt constricted her horizons, while the two others dwelt upon the infinite "contrasts with the prison which civilized men calls his home."[2] Karl May had a special aversion to any confinement, for he had actually spent time in jail during his youth. Ganghofer's attitude is similar: within the wise confines of nature, we find all that is primeval, healthy, and full of strength.[3] Marlitt differs: she praises the old bourgeois order: "everything stands . . . in its accustomed place . . . one is immediately at home."[4] Her small towns and the houses within them are indeed homely, not to be compared with the prairies or wild mountain lands.

But this contrast turns out to be imagined rather than real, and through this insight we can penetrate a major reason for the novels' appeal. We confront a seemingly contradictory longing for wide-open spaces and equally strongly for rootedness, for being at home, which informed the mind of millions during the Second Reich. Adventure and restfulness, infinity and a settled order—

these deep and contradictory yearnings were harmonized through popular literature. Marlitt, May, and Ganghofer took up a tradition that limited the romantic and localized the cosmic spirit: not within the Volk, but within the bourgeois order.

This is an important and significant point. At mid-nineteenth century, the romantic impetus and the impetus of modernity were both tamed through rootedness in the Volk. Later, in the twentieth century, it would be said that "with the victory of National Socialism the limitations upon the dynamic spirit of man, which at first frightened us, are transformed into a feeling of restfulness."[5] Popular literature at the fin de siècle shared this view-point only in part: restfulness was combined with activism, and neither of these was rooted in the volkish fate.

How did Karl May's heroes conquer the prairie? Certainly not through fire and sword. Although the stable social and political conditions of Germany are absent in the American desert, May's Old Shatterhand throughout the series of novels beginning with *Winnetou* (1893) attempts to exemplify law and order. For, as he tells us constantly, "in the prairies bad palefaces hide from the laws of the good palefaces."[6] When he has conquered the bad men, he does not kill them but brings them before judge and jury. He is apt to preach sermons about the evil of hate and revenge. Punishment must follow sin; that is part of human and divine justice,[7] but cruelty must be avoided and so must the unnecessary spilling of blood. Old Shatterhand got his name from the way in which he knocked out his enemies without killing them.

Karl May does not foreshadow Nazi brutality, indeed, his whole work is a plea for compassion combined with law and order. Even the prairie has its rough and ready laws; thus no thief is allowed to be punished except by his victims.[8] Yet May also writes about the cruel law which says that the weak must give way to the strong, assumed to be an integral part of God's creation. This law is exemplified by the struggles that take place on the prairie and by May's resignation to the sad fate of the Indians he loves. Social Darwinism fuses with law and order in his novels, as the two did in the Second Reich. But here the good inevitably triumphs—and does so through adventures that were fascinating to read. The "cruel law" of survival gave May's work its dynamic, his morality *tamed* this into a view of life which his audience shared in full measure. Social Darwinism was not a threat to the triumph of good in the world (God had guaranteed this also), but instead provided defeat for the bad, and thrilling adventures with predictable outcomes for the onlookers.

Ganghofer conquered his rugged terrain in a similar fashion, yet without the overt emphasis on law, order, and justice. He was not writing about the North American plains but about the German landscape, and made use of the traditional unity between man and Germanic nature. To know this nature is to read a mystical book through which one attains clarity and rest, loses the folly of speculation, and becomes in turn a specimen of healthy nature.[9] Indeed, such a bond would rid men of all evil instincts. But even so, this oneness of man and nature entails struggle and adventure (once again essential to hold the reader's interest), while it is tamed into respectability through the triumph of the good and the beautiful. "Hardness" in the struggle for life is never an evil for either May or Ganghofer; instead, "tenacious force" is considered an essential element of the heroic. Such heroism, however, must not be confused with brutality. The hero exemplifies the moral order, law and justice: he does not stand above or outside these principles. The fight is either among equals according to rules of chivalry, or for the protection of justice from oppression, stealth, and arrogance.

The hero fulfills the ideal of mankind within a landscape replete with danger and mystery. By fulfilling this ideal, he tames it and brings about an acceptable combination of struggle and order. Marlitt's heroes, too, though in their quite different setting, appeal to traditional morality. Women should not be exposed to the problems and temptations of business life, but instead are predestined to found a happy family.[10] Their struggles are usually (but not always) inward ones, not exemplified by nature. Sentiment, emotionality, and tenderness characterize Marlitt's ideal people; unlike Karl May's heroes, they could never have been martyred by Indians without shedding tears. Yet here also, adventure is combined with what Marlitt calls "balance"; that is, the existing order tempered by fairness and tolerance. Such a balance formed a "beautiful soul," to cite one of Marlitt's favorite phrases. Schiller had already used the term "beautiful soul" in connection with a "tranquility springing from the balance which is created, not by a stagnation of power, but by the unity of nature and reason (. . . *ruhe aus gleichgewicht, nicht aus dem Stillstand der Kräfte—einheit von vernunft und natur)."* [11] Marlitt's "beautiful soul" contains a balance that is less dependent upon reason than upon nature and sentiment; still, the ideal of tranquility and of activism remains intact.

Clearly, in all of these novels the status quo included a utopia that everyone could share. Such a utopia exemplified not only moral virtues but, above all, an ideal of beauty, which served to summarize and define it. Ganghofer continually focused upon and illustrated such beauty. Thus the heroine in the novel *Gotteslehn* (1899) is a girl who went blind in the month of May and for whom it therefore always remains spring. Small wonder that he ended the preface to one novel: "1906, at Munich, as the sun shone on a winter's day." [12] The sun symbolism is strong here, obvious yet traditional. The concept of beauty in the popular novel was linked to the most widespread aesthetic tradition of the nineteenth century. Beauty resides in the beholder because, as Friedrich Theodor Vischer, the famous aesthetician, said, in a bourgeois world of chaos and disorder it had retreated into the human soul. When it breaks through into reality our alienation is ended, for beauty reflects a healthy and happy world. For Vischer, the projection of beauty upon the outward world meant the need for myth and symbol; this would make men feel at home in a reality other than that of daily life in an industrial society. [13] Vischer's aesthetic clarifies the function of beauty in the popular novel, and beyond this, that of German national festivals and ceremonies.

Beauty provides something exceptional in its penetration of reality. An examination of the role of festivals in the novels of the fin de siècle has shown that such festivals were consistently depicted as the high points of life because they interrupted the banal and daily routine, providing a symbolic contact between this drab world and the exceptional, healthy and happy world where alienation is ended. [14] The loving decoration of the room in which a festival is to take place is a manifestation of deep longings. The popular novel made daily life into one continuous festival, an orgy of the beautiful. This beauty is romantic; sunsets and early morning dew abound. But, as in Vischer, beauty also includes the principle of order. Once again we confront the taming process, for chaos must be rejected.

Marlitt's beauty is the "old accustomed order," where everything is in its place, and her descriptions of interiors are particularly revealing in their equation of beauty and *gemütlichkeit*. Ganghofer's mountains are now and then surrounded by dark shadows, but it is the beholder who disperses them from his own mind; they can have no power over a childlike soul.[15] Here, in conformity with the predominant aesthetic culture, the beholder imposes order upon wild nature. And for Karl May, too, nature embodies the principle of order as typified by the punishment of sin. In his long descriptions of the prairies, they are wild only when the villains meet a deserved death within them; otherwise, the desert landscape is mysterious, but the hero always imposes his principles of order and beauty upon it. Thus, in the midst of prairie, Old Shatterhand recalls the words of the poet Uhland, and when he is about to die of thirst in a hostile desert, he thinks about the ordered family life in his German home and is saved. Metaphors taken from the *settled* life of the old country are frequently used. Hobble-Frank confronting hostile Indians remarks: "I am as calm as the milestone at the side of the road."[16] This provides an obvious contrast to the prairie he roamed where the only milestones were Indian tracks that laymen could not read. The ordered world of Wilhelminian Germany served to tame the disordered world of the American plains, which indeed proved receptive to such analogy in the midst of its own peculiar beauty.

The healthy world symbolized by beauty is eternal. Hegel had already written that the accidental must not mar the principle of beauty. Because the word "beauty" exemplifies a healthy world, happiness is an integral part of it, and in this context death loses its sting. Ganghofer's blind girl is thrown into an abyss by her lover, who then himself commits suicide rather than have the "eternal May" confronted by the evils of reality. But this is a sweet *Götterdämmerung*, and not the sacrifice of a *Wiltfeber*, the Germanic hero killed by lightning. The importance of understanding and conceptualizing this idea of beauty cannot be stressed too much. It entered the popular vocabulary of Germany. The exclamation "How beautiful!" was a commonplace in these novels, and the basic concept clung to did not vary much throughout the nineteenth and twentieth centuries. Eventually, this would become a pattern in mass politics and its rituals; the drama and the adventure contained within them a principle of order and beauty. It was not merely in Germany that such aesthetic apply to politics; for as we shall see in a succeeding essay, it also informed Gabriele d'Annunzio's exercise of political power.

This was a secular religion, which had grown up hand in hand with German nationalism during the nineteenth century. National myths and symbols were, from their beginning, closely connected to a concept of beauty, but also to Christianity: thus Ernst Moritz Arndt believed that national festivals should begin with a quiet prayer; patriotic festivals also borrowed the liturgical rhythm of Protestantism.[17] Moreover, pietism and its concept that "the fatherland is within you" obtained a major place in the growth of German national self-consciousness and self-representation. This has a direct bearing upon the popular novels of Wilhelminian Germany. For here, too, the symbols of a healthy and beautiful world were connected to a pietistic faith which, in many ways, provided the foundations of the ideal personality they advocated.

Marlitt's ideals of beauty and goodness are also bound to the "rich life of the soul." A pietistic soul sees its faith personified in all of God's creation. This is the freedom with which she is concerned, and it is opposed by fundamentalists, by Catholics, and indeed by all who would restrict such pietism. Moreover, before God's creation, all men are equal. Marlitt condemns arrogance and lack of compassion. As beauty always penetrates reality, so man is basically good but merely perverted by organized religion; in spite of all sorts of humiliations, one of her Cinderellas exclaims: "I love mankind and have a high opinion of it."[18] As pietism was inner-directed, so too was Marlitt's ideal of freedom and compassion. Yet Marlitt thunders against imposed poverty or slavery. Human dignity, based upon the proper functioning of "pure heart," comes first. Here both May and Ganghofer agree. Old Shatterhand has himself composed a pietistic Ave Maria; he talks continually about the oneness of God and His creation, celebrating Sunday even in the prairie through an act of divine contemplation. Winnetou died a Christian, indeed, had been a true Christian long before he was killed. His soul was reflected in consistently noble actions. Winnetou, Old Shatterhand, and Marlitt's heroes provided a commentary and illustration of the statement made by one of the founders of German pietism, Philipp Jacob Spener (1680): "it is a mark of true rebirth, that a man reborn does good out of his inner nature, from his heart, and this though he may feel that his flesh has no such desire. . . ."[19]

The way men dress, their outward appearance, matters little; rather, their deeds tell the story. May draws this lesson from the ragged and outlandish sight that "westerners" present to the outsider, which would have been derided by the civilized world. "Clothes do not make the man." The proverb is used by these novels to demonstrate that a true heart leads to noble deeds, and that this is how God wants it to be. The exception to this credo is also significant: Dress is irrelevant, but a man's face is not. Old Shatterhand constantly recognizes a noble soul through a person's facial expression. Biological ideas about the intertwining of looks and soul are always present. The novels reflect one deep current in German thought, that the outward structure of man does indeed mirror his soul. But at this point there is no racism involved, though such popular notions would make it easier to include when the time came.

The pietistic objection to organized religion led to a true tolerance, such as May felt toward Indians, and Marlitt as well as Ganghofer toward the Jews. In Marlitt's *Heideprinzesschen* (1872), the central character is a baptized Jewish girl who is driven to insanity by Christian intolerance. A servant girl hates Jews, but only the Jews who crucified Christ, for how can one hate "innocent people who were brought into the world and educated in the old faith?" Men must overcome their "dark heart," and practice toleration in their newly found innocence until "I had no wish, no unfulfilled longing, my heart was filled solely by tenderness."[20] This is the true Christian attitude, and it corresponds to May's treatment of Indians and Negroes. Ganghofer's Joseph is a doctor who attempts to cure the blind girl. He has been humiliated and castigated as a Jew, and the evil monks accuse him of sorcery.[21] But when he puts on his philacteries, he sees and feels the splendor of nature. Not only is anti-Semitism nonexistent in these novels, but toleration is emphasized within a pietistic Christianity.

The limits of this toleration are, once more, illuminating. It stops short of the obliteration of class and national differences. Karl May's introduction to *Winnetou* reads like a charter for oppressed Indians; nevertheless, Old Shatterhand refuses to marry an Indian girl: "this cannot be done by a European."[22] He does not explain this, merely taking it for granted. Tolerance, of course, did not extend to revolution, a direct consequence of unbelief. Klekih-petra, a German who educates the Apaches in virtue, atones for having been a revolutionary. His eyes were opened through an encounter with a poor family who sheltered him after defeat. Klekih-petra discovers that through his speeches he has misled the husband, now languishing in jail. "They had been poor but content," and the revolutionary robbed them of their happiness.[23] The lesson learned by the "white father" is obvious: contentment, that healthy and happy world as revealed through beauty, depends upon order—and order depends upon God the creator of the universe. Ganghofer is even more blatant. When a hunter grumbles about his employer's injustice, he is told that he should not accuse his master, for if one sees the world through healthy spectacles, it must be clear that everything is justly distributed.[24] Marlitt believes that class differences do matter. When an ostensibly poor girl marries into a good family, it turns out later that she is of noble birth. Yet, class differences never mean differences in virtue; indeed, the nobility is always depicted as less admirable than the laboring poor.

As virtue alone counts, class differences which must be kept intact for the sake of order are not of great importance. Personal relationships are what matter. Virtue cannot and must not destroy the existing social order, but the individual can raise himself inwardly above it and receive love in return. Such love, Ganghofer tells us, is a firm bridge which, if you trust it, will carry you across all the vagaries of life.[25] The need for such love is also common to Marlitt's heroes. While the concern with love infuses the novels with some sexual content, in reality this love stands free of such encumbrance; it is the gift of God and is obtainable between men and women. This emphasis upon personal relationships suffused with love is illustrated through the stress placed upon happiness within the family structure, which typifies the highest bliss man can attain.

Count Tasse, in one of Ganghofer's novels, sacrifices his fortune and pride to keep the family intact, until finally the "angel of happiness" walks quietly through the room.[26] One of Marlitt's characters is a villain because, through his religious bigotry, he robs his daughter of the "pure happiness of family life."[27] Old Shatterhand often thinks back to such times of well-being. And in Marlitt's novels, the family has a traditional structure: the man must lead and children must beg forgiveness from parents.[28] But in spite of such authoritarianism, in the last analysis personal relationships must be based upon the dignity of each individual.

The belief in man's dignity is aptly reflected in the work ethic, which all of these novels praise and exalt. Marlitt's heroines work relentlessly and with pleasure, but never as slaves. Work is an expression of personality, part of the knowledge that (as Karl May puts it) we must accept responsibility for all our actions.[29] Indeed, work is lifted out of the class structure to become a manifestation of the noble deeds Christian men perform of their own free will. Virtuous Apaches and palefaces agree that only what one has earned by the sweat of one's brow possesses merit.[30] May, in his exaltation of work, even praises the city of San Francisco, where no one wastes time and everything works smoothly as a result. Moreover, men of all origins live peacefully together: the English, the Chinese, even the "dirty Polish Jew."[31] (Like beauty, work reconciles men to the world they live in and leads to inner and outward harmony.)

Both work and beauty exclude the "demon passion,"[32] for that clouds a clear view of the world. This absence of passion has nothing to do with rationality, but refers to a tradition that is once more a part of the nineteenth-century vision of beauty. Vischer defined the functional concept of beauty, but J. J. Winckelmann and the classical revival in eighteenth-century Prussia provided its lasting content. Winckelmann likened beauty to the unity of an ocean, which appears smooth and still at a distance though it is constantly in motion.[33] Passions were not excluded, but were subsumed under the archetypal classical form. The classical revival, and Winckelmann in particular, synthesized the classical and the romantic traditions by attempting to subsume romantic passions under the classical form. National symbols had produced this synthesis long before these popular novels were written. Indeed, the mausoleum erected to Karl May after his death repeats the pseudo-classical style so popular in national monuments: the town of Radebeul received a smaller *Walhalla* (the Bavarian monument to German unity), this time in Saxony rather than on the banks of the Danube. Winckelmann did for romanticism what Kant tried to accomplish with reason—he contained it within boundaries which, in Winckelmann's phrasing, transformed turbulence into "noble simplicity and quiet greatness" (*edle einfalt und stille grösse*).[34] These words could be applied to all the heroes and heroines of popular literature.

Reality was infused by the healthy world that beauty and love represented. Passion was dissolved into harmony of form; restlessness became anchored in rootedness. A rootedness, however, that lay not in the nation itself, but in a morality which in turn sprang from deep pietism. The class structure remained intact, but was at the same time transcended by the priority given to human dignity and to personal rather than mass relationships. We cannot describe these social attitudes as merely patriarchal, for they were also rooted in the proud individualism of Winnetou or Old Shatterhand. Popular literature presented an unchanging liberalism, not only in its concept of work but also in its plea for toleration and human dignity; a world filled with beauty and harmony could not tolerate racism, bigotry, or class-bound virtue.

What, then, of the nation? Reverence for the past was seen as part of the universal harmony, though this past was not necessarily a national one, as it emphasized the traditional bonds among men rather than those that formed them into a specific tribe. "Reverence," a word used constantly, meant rather opposition to the dissolving acid of modernity. Yet Germanism did enter this vision: Ganghofer's landscape and Marlitt's virtues were often defined in terms of "the noble German family life."[35] But the best complete picture of the ideal German has been transmitted to us by Karl May. If we gather together his scattered references to the German character, a significant picture emerges.

Old Shatterhand is German, and so are the other heroes: Sam Hawkes, Klekih-petra, and the rest. Germans, even in the wilderness, recognize each other through their intuition. They long for the time when this instinctive recognition will become true national unity. But Germans are also recognizable through outward signs: the "good-natured laugh which spreads across the face" typifies true German origin. They are "peculiar individuals" (*Sonderbare Käutze*) because although they look like uncouth bears, they show compassion even for their worst enemies.[36] Germans are chivalrous, fight only when attacked, and spill human blood, if at all, only in self-defense. Moreover, the German is modest; he never asks for more than is his due. Germans abhor slavery, mass murder, and the Ku Klux Klan; but they are also hard. The only tears they cry are tears of joy.[37] Indeed, their emotions are always disciplined: they love to sing, but pious songs—and in choirs. Their vision of the faraway fatherland includes eventual retirement in a small town or rural setting.[38] Culture, moreover, is a part of German character, and Old Shatterhand is no less of a man, as some of his enemies mistakenly believe, because he plans to write books.[39] Small wonder that May praised *Gelehrsamkeit* (learning). In his youth he wanted to become a teacher, and in 1902 bought a doctorate from a nonexistent Chicago University. Culture, however, was not to be confused with book learning, for May reflected the bourgeois ideal of *Bildung*: centered upon inner growth and self-development.[40] Cultured yet hard, compassionate yet just, emotional yet disciplined, the German faced the world. He was lovable and could give love; he was abroad but treasured the values of home, family, hard work, culture, and pietism, which accompanied him wherever he went.

But this German was no chauvinist, even though Old Shatterhand decorated the tomb of an Apache with the German oak.[41] For these virtues sprang from God and were common to all men, if they only willed it. In fact, the Indians possessed them in high measure, more so than most Germans; there were good and bad white men as well as good and bad Indians. May's novels show a correspondence between the life of the German pietistic settlers in the prairies and of those who lived in the compound of the Apaches. Both were free men; for example, Indians refused to take money as a sign of gratitude because that would degrade them to the status of slaves.[42] Virtue reigned in both settlements, even if the Indians retained some customs that good white men like Klekih-petra and Old Shatterhand wanted to undercut. If such heroes were imperialists, they also rejected the use of power. Through their own example, they spread the virtues God grants all men as a gift.

Such abstention from violence is facilitated by the myth that surrounds the hero. The "power of his personality" and his "legendary fame" enable Old Shatterhand, at times, to get his way without the use of force. Moreover, the hero has "magic" qualities, at least in the perception of his opponents. Old Shatterhand's famous rifle provides a good example: its very sight serves to paralyze some of his opponents, though in reality it is simply a new invention by an ingenious gunsmith. Karl May was well aware of the power of myth; his writings exemplify that "longing for myth" which so many contemporaries detected within the fragmented society of the Second Reich.[43] The essence of such a myth must be the good and the virtuous, symbols of a happier life. Certainly, Old Shatterhand and Winnetou symbolize such a myth. As Winnetou puts it: "My arm is raised against evil men and protects him who has a good conscience."[44] The emphasis on conscience, once more, connects virtue to the world of Lutheran pietism.

The hero does, at times, resort to violence, but May's basic distaste for such acts comes out again when "cleverness" is prized as a substitute for the shedding of blood. The heroes of *Der Schatz im Silbersee* (*The Treasure in Silbersee*) outwit their opponents: "a small deception which is not a lie, because it led to the saving of lives without doing harm to the red man."[45] Virtue can be bent only this far on behalf of the dignity of man. But for the heroes, as well as for all other good men, their basic individualism and its pietistic heritage (which May stressed) prevented any descent into chauvinistic nationalism. Standards of judgment were provided by a moral universe, which the best Germans presented to others.

Ganghofer's view of Germanism was similar. He continually stressed the humanistic values, though like May he also pleaded for German unity. Perhaps he placed somewhat more emphasis on the Volk, for Ganghofer's settings were, after all, German. The only specifically Germanic quality he ever mentioned was cleanliness,[46] but this implied order as well. And Marlitt too shared May's views. The old-fashioned virtues of course remained, but none of this abandoned the solid ground of toleration and recognition of the dignity of others.

Historians have tended to focus on that German literature which reflected national self-confidence combined with an exaltation of war.[47] But such writing, widespread though some of it was, could not compete in popularity with the popular literature that failed to translate national self-confidence into national chauvinism. Yet there is something profoundly German about this literature and the readers it reflected, which can best be characterized as "provincial." Indeed, none of these writers traveled widely or with much curiosity. They were served solely by their fantasies. These were steeped in the ambiance of the times, in the aesthetics and the virtues that had become commonplace in Germany. Even apart from the edge against modernity, provincialism was a feature of the German mind created specifically by a German tradition of romanticism, classicism, and the quest for national identity. As mentioned earlier, the rise of national self-consciousness coincided with the aesthetic synthesis of classicism and romanticism. While this ideal world remained a literary utopia even after 1871, the image became universalized. Germandom itself furnished only one factor in the equation, and not necessarily the dominant one.

Although Adolf Hitler once remarked that Karl May had opened his eyes to the world,[48] these popular novels were not the direct forerunners of National Socialism. The statement must be understood literally. For Hitler's manichaean universe was fundamentally opposed to virtue as these novels defined it. Yet National Socialism found it easy to enter into an alliance with the world which popular literature advocated; indeed, the overall popularity of Nazi letters was partly based upon the annexation of this tradition. It is typical that Hitler praised not only May's rich fantasies but in particular the decency and the ability to master life shown in his novels. May's virtues were precisely those which Hitler wanted to defend against all enemies; both men were formed by the morality and culture typical of Wilhelminian Germany. Hitler saw no contradiction between discussing Winnetou with his nephew as an example of the mastery of life and his racial world view.[49] The Indian had come to represent German virtues just as even earlier an admirer had characterized Winnetou's sister as "an Indian woman with a German heart."[50] The morality, the dream, had become detached from its actual setting.

Whatever Hitler's private view, the official Nazi state was pledged to transform the dreams of Marlitt, Ganghofer, and May into existing reality. Surely if Nazi art and literature continued the praise of beauty, and at times even of toleration, it ruled through a dictatorship that these authors would have rejected as contrary to human dignity. Instead, the real weaknesses of this world of popular literature were revealed in 1933.

It had been only a dream, never corresponding to reality. The opposition to modernity precluded a consideration of concrete dilemmas, so that slums, economic crises, and urbanism hardly entered the picture. The form a government took was unimportant outside of the notion that it must unite rather than divide; Marlitt condemned the hate sown by political parties.[51] She praised Bismarck, not for his politics (which hardly concerned her) but for his religious policy. He fought the Catholic Church and that was service enough. The dream these novelists presented transcended reality. This was inevitable, for permanence and immutability were necessary for a healthy world.

Marlitt, more than Ganghofer or May, was aware of certain social problems. Strikes and the laboring poor do exist in her writing, though strikes, of course, were condemned even if the cause was justified (in one case decent housing) because they could only lead to violence, behavior directly antagonistic to the exercise of virtue.[52] The individual stood in the center, practicing by example, like Old Shatterhand or Ganghofer's heroes. They were optimists by nature, for they fulfilled God's plan for the world. Such heroes were characterized by activism: "the will of a single man who is strong," wrote Ganghofer, "has done more good on earth than all the feeble love [which priests preach]."[53] But strength was paired with opposition to brutality and injustice. These heroes were far from Nietzsche's ideal, nor were they the Hitlers of the future. They stand, once more, in the pietistic tradition of the eighteenth century, rather than in the dictatorial tradition of the twentieth.

This in itself is important. For the dream stood still as the world advanced. The pressures became greater, the frustrations endless. The Nazis, well aware of the continuing popularity of this literature, retained its themes but attempted to infuse them with volkish substance. Josefine Berend-Totenohl's *Der Femhof* (1934) was one of the most popular novels on the party's approved list.[54] *Der Femhof* continued the tradition of peasant novel unchanged except for two instances: one villain is described as belonging to a foreign gypsy race, and the novel has a tragic ending. Nazi literary critics believed that the tragic hero was particularly suited to the soul of the German Volk. This linkage of tragic and heroic typified the depth of soul which all Germans were supposed to possess.[55] Moreover, it provided a restless dynamic important for a new political movement, directly opposed to the self-satisfaction and happiness which writers like Ganghofer evoked.

Yet the combination of traditional themes and volkish substance, however shallowly executed, was rare in the Third Reich. Because he seemed to advocate close relations between Germans and "lesser races," Karl May earned the disapproval of many party organizations, and editions of his works were kept at a minimum.[56] But May could not be held down. Even if certain party organizations wished to minimize his influence, others disagreed. For example, in the propaganda film about the élite Nazi educational institutions, the so-called *Nationalpolitischen Erziehungsanstalten* (1939), we see one boy reading Karl May, while others play with a ship's model or with a fortress crowned by a tank.[57] Hitler himself never abandoned his admiration for Winnetou and Old Shatterhand. In spite of the paper shortage during the war, his personal headquarters ordered 300,000 copies of *Winnetou* for distribution among the troops.[58] The dream itself was more important than the fact that not only Germans but Indians, too, exemplified it.

Writers like May, Marlitt, and Ganghofer continued to be sold in numbers that left their volkish rivals far behind.[59] Even under the Third Reich volkish fiction never managed to keep pace with this popular literature, just as in earlier years volkish books had vegetated on the fringes of popular reading matter.

Germans were steeped in what we may call liberal literature. This was certainly not a fault, but it was fatal that these writings had no guidance to lend to the present because their relationship to reality was so tenuous. Ganghofer's Irimbert, having been walled up by evil monks for several years, exclaims: ". . . I live! For my heart is filled with joy and dreams."[60] The worker, the petit bourgeois, the businessman could not rise to embody the character of an Irimbert in the face of an urban and industrial world that seemed to close in upon them. As a result, they continued to read these novels as a utopia, while turning elsewhere for political and social fulfillment.

German reality and German popular literature had seemed for some people to coincide during the Wilhelminian Reich. Certainly the principles of aesthetics and morality these novels embodied were widespread, and so was the feeling that the Second Reich embodied a social order which would encourage them. But after World War I this correspondence was no longer the case, and such literature became a fairy tale—albeit one that continued to cry out for fulfillment. During the Third Reich this fulfillment was sought in directions that clashed with the ideal of these novels. They became a utopia that must be reached by a different path, though constantly kept in mind. Old Shatterhand must triumph. But he could do so only after Adolf Hitler had cleared the way.

The utopia of popular literature was reinforced by a volkish utopia, which attempted to integrate the nation with the triad of death, time, and history, forces that shaped life itself. Those writers concerned with this volkish utopia descended into dark and mystical spaces rather than exemplifying a happy, healthy German and bourgeois family life. It is with the defeat of Germany and the economic, social, and political collapse after World War I that this utopia came into its own. The more secure and complacent times in which the writers of the fin de siècle lived gave way to the Weimar Republic.

FOUR

Death, Time, and History: Volkish Utopia and Its Transcendence

> And he that overcometh and keepeth my work
> unto the end, to him will I give power over
> nations: and he shall rule with a rod of iron . . .
> and I will give him the morning star.
> —Revelation 2:26–28

D URING MANY centuries of European life the longing for
utopia created an apocalyptic view of history, in which the
present was superseded by visions of the future. The need
for a more clearly outlined program of the last things was met by
the book known as the *Revelation of St. John the Divine*, but the
apocalyptical books of the Jewish tradition were also highly prized,
by Jews and Christians alike. These various books of the Apocalypse were composed around a dialectic that might well be described as the "dialectic of utopia," in which man has to live
through earthquakes, witness the stars falling from Heaven, and
see Jerusalem destroyed, and where war, famine, and death must
strike mankind. Yet at the same time that man passes through the
valley of darkness he is led ever closer to God, until at the seventh
trumpet call the rule of God commences, and a new Jerusalem de-
scends from Heaven to replace the old. God now sits in judgment
over all who are evil, and especially over the enemies of the Volk.
Paradise returns from behind the mountains of the north where it
has taken refuge.

Within such a dialectic, the ideal of "overcoming" assumed cosmic proportions. All the scourges that preceded the rule of God
had to be overcome, and in this way the passage of time was abolished. The apocalyptic image of history allowed history to over-

come itself; death, too, lost its sting, as merely one episode in the rush of time to obliterate itself. The seventeenth-century mystic Jakob Böhme expressed it well: ". . . how everything is make-believe by which man passes his time in restlessness";[1] for the reality lies behind this restless surface, which is but a reflection of the striving for God and toward the last things. German idealism went hand in hand with a mystique that attempted to penetrate the eternal substance of man and nature: Existence without end, where there is no death or life, as the novelist Hermann Stehr once put it.[2] "In overcoming is joy," to quote a phrase of Böhme.[3] Such struggle alone could reveal the new Jerusalem, and only through intense suffering could it be achieved.

Jakob Böhme was one of the crucial transmitters of apocalyptical thought in Germany. It was no accident that in 1901 Martin Buber wrote his doctoral thesis on Böhme, through whom he could demonstrate the continuing relevance of this tradition. Buber in his work stressed the creativity of struggle, while pointing out that beneath this struggle all matter, including man, moves relentlessly toward a more perfect unity of the whole universe. Man contains within himself both the need to struggle and the image of a divine unity.[4]

Buber represents one good example of the perpetuation of the mystical longing for utopia in the twentieth century. But many others were inspired by Buber's stories of the Hassidim, which are closely related to the mysticism of Jakob Böhme. The young Georg Lukacs dreamed that he himself might be descended from the Baal Shem.[5] At the beginning of this century, a whole generation of youth was fascinated by a mystical utopian revival. The apocalyptic tradition was alive and well in early twentieth-century Germany, despite the fact that instead of providing a revolutionary dynamic, as it had done at times in earlier centuries, it would come to be annexed by the German Right and even by National Socialism. To be sure, after World War I, Ernst Bloch attempted in his *Thomas Münzer* (1921) to claim the apocalyptic tradition once more for revolutionary ends; but he soon lost it to counterrevolutionary forces.

The apocalyptical tradition, with its emphasis on the abolition of time and the overcoming of death, was especially popular after World War I. Death had claimed millions, and that horrible memory was assiduously kept alive through hundreds of books and monuments. But death now also involved the fatherland: did defeat mean national death? How could one assert that those fallen in the war had redeemed the fatherland rather than died in vain? These questions were intertwined with the ever-present fear of modernity, of unrest and chaos, which was the mark of the rapid passage of time. Clearly, the ideal of a utopia always present as an "essence" beneath the surface, but one that would emerge through suffering and defeat, was most relevant after the war, as was the thought that such true reality lay beneath the passage of time and moved inevitably toward a divine unity. The attraction of the apocalyptical tradition was and always had been its "inwardness"; this was a fact which neither Ernst Bloch's *Thomas Münzer* nor the Marxist revolution could rupture.[6]

The tradition was reflected in several kinds of literature after 1918: it is seen directly in the *Paracelsus* legend, for which Erwin Guido Kolbenheyer's trilogy set the tone and is also present in much of the literature glorifying the war experience. Moreover, the publishing of sagas and fairy tales (usually for the first time) had a direct relationship to this particular utopian tradition. Finally, the literary dreams of a coming Third Reich belong here as well. All of these genres were well suited to describe the dilemmas of the Weimar Republic, but they were also taken over by National Socialism. The utopia with which we are concerned became the National Socialist utopia: the dialectic of the necessity of suffering, struggle, and overcoming, the concept of death as make-believe, part of a transparent, negative reality against the steady movement toward paradise—all these connect the Nazi experience with a deep European tradition.

Kolbenheyer's *Paracelsus*, published in 1925, can introduce us to the utopia utilized by the National Socialists which is our particular concern. His work broke with earlier images of Paracelsus as the magician and the hypnotist who in one novel even deciphered the language of the Egyptian Sphinx.[7] Kolbenheyer's *Paracelsus* is quite a different figure, engaged in trying to overcome suffering, misery, and despair. He fights the elemental in order to shed all earthly loyalties on behalf of a freedom that will enable him to penetrate to the "essence" of the universe and experience the divine unity of all matter. Paracelsus's "joy of overcoming" is linked to an appreciation of nature as a direct reflection of divine unity (similar to Jakob Böhme, once more). This alchemist Paracelsus believed that matter always strives to transcend itself, and so also must man, who is part of matter: "Whoever searches for nature finds marvelous miracles."[8] Paracelsus is redeemed at the end because he has persevered despite suffering, illness, and despair in his search for the "essence." That essence is now redefined by Kolbenheyer. It still means the divine unity of God and nature, but is exemplified by the idea of the Volk. Kolbenheyer stresses a Germanic continuity that will surface as part of the divine utopia.

But to enable the "essence" to become reality, there must be as little contact as possible with the contaminated modern world. Paracelsus withdraws into a solitude unconcerned with the passage of time; living in the countryside or the small town, "the ear is deafened by the rhythm of the world."[9] The city becomes a symbol for hostility to nature: foreign grain is brought to its mills, foreign flax clothes the people. Where God, nature, and Germanism are rejected, the essence that paves the road to utopia is lost.

Kolbenheyer robs the apocalyptical tradition of its revolutionary element by emphasizing the internalized continuity of time and nature. The *Book of Revelation* speaks of the "new Jerusalem," and this fact led Ernst Bloch, at about the same time as Kolbenheyer, to envisage the apocalyptical tradition as a revolutionary force. Paracelsus, like Thomas Münzer, longed for a "new May"; in Bloch's *Münzer*, this belief leads to revolution, "the dawn of the apocalypse roars toward this world of faith, and it measures its absolute truth by that apocalypse, the metapolitical, yea, metareligious principle of all revolution: the beginning of freedom for the children of God."[10] Kolbenheyer's Paracelsus also attained freedom from chains, though not in order to revolutionize the world but rather to restore the paradise of an eternal Germanic past. The apocalypse becomes a reactionary utopia, and so will it remain; for Kolbenheyer rather than Bloch was to be typical of the German road to utopia.

Kolbenheyer's *Paracelsus* was a tract for the times. The defeated and humiliated nation had to keep its substance intact by refusing to compromise with the world until the time was ripe. For Kolbenheyer himself, the time was ripe on January 30, 1933, when he actively supported the Nazi cause; for in that movement he saw a surfacing of the volkish essence, the "only possible form of the national and volkish movement,"[11] which Paracelsus had preserved in evil times. The Nazis enthusiastically adopted his *Paracelsus* trilogy, though Kolbenheyer himself gradually withdrew from his political involvement, partly through hurt pride and disappointment in the political pragmatism of Nazi organization.

Nonetheless, Paracelsus lived on in the form which Kolbenheyer had given him. For example, in 1943, a Paracelsus drama was supposed to be substituted for *Everyman* at the Salzburg Festival. Richard Billinger wrote a drama that projected Kolbenheyer's hero into the war situation. This time, the question posed centered upon the overcoming of death: "all that is alive must pay its due to death."[12] Nature now had the specific function of building a golden wall that death could not climb; however great the distress on earth, all matter, including the substance of man, moves relentlessly toward paradise. For Billinger, Paracelsus himself fails: he dies prematurely because he has compromised with earthly pleasure and given in to society. Here too the volkish prophet is obliged to keep himself pure. Billinger's *Paracelsus* is no longer Kolbenheyer's hero, but the themes are still the same, now squarely concentrated on the overcoming of death.

The emphasis upon death did not have to await World War II; it preoccupied writers who wanted to explain away the defeat of World War I, and to banish the thought that the fallen had died in vain. This attitude is startlingly exemplified by a book issued in 1927 illustrating the more than seven hundred "shrines of honor" (*Ehrenhaine*) that had been built during the Republic for the war dead. The dead, this work tells us, are not really dead at all; they climb out of their graves and visit us at night in our dreams. The glorious dead are resurrected within ourselves, helping to construct man's unchanging spirit (that is, his essence), and therefore to bring about a "German miracle" (*Deutsches Wunder*). What is that miracle? It is the belief that Germany is not defeated and that the time has come to reconstruct the Reich and to save its lost honor.[13]

The fallen become part of the "eternal German" (as Kolbenheyer's *Paracelsus* was called),[14] those who preserve their basic nature from all contamination with the passage of time, and whose Germanic souls grow steadily in spite of death and defeat. To give another example of this theme: Franz Schauwecker's *Aufbruch der Nation* (*The Rise of the Nation*, 1930) asserted that those who sacrificed themselves for the nation passed on the essence of Germanism to a postwar generation. It made no difference whether the war ended in victory or defeat, for the fallen would still transmit the Germanism, raising it to a new height, far above prewar indifference.

The concepts of destiny and fate play a large role in apocalyptic novels about the war. Although a part of the apocalyptic tradition of striving and overcoming, such concepts were also part of many other traditions such as Protestantism and the Enlightenment. Yet in this apocalyptical tradition, the final end is attainable on earth in all its divine unity; "the kingdom of God begins on earth and not in heaven," as Kolbenheyer's *Paracelsus* put it.[15] Paracelsus and the fallen in the war are all part of that destiny, which through death and suffering leads to a glorious end, for they helped to transmit the essence of Germanism through the ages uncontaminated by the passage of time. The Volk is the vessel of God.

These themes were used and repeated by National Socialists. The slogan chanted by the Hitler Youth on Heroes Memorial Day put it in a nutshell: "The best of our people did not die in order that the living might be dead, but instead that the dead become alive."[16] Nazi literature is filled with images of death, just as the celebration of the martyred dead, whether for fatherland or party, became one of the most successful festivals of the Nazi year. Heinrich Anacker, during the Nazi struggle for power, wrote in his poem "Golgotha" that no one could renounce that torture which Christ himself had suffered, everyone would be nailed to the cross; Everyman faces his Golgotha. But the implied moral of the poem is that resurrection through National Socialism follows the cross and thus death has lost its sting. To be human, according to Anacker, means to stoop before fate and yet still see the stars.[17] Gerhard Schumann, perhaps the most celebrated Nazi poet, wrote that "death loves us because we love life."[18] Death respected the Nazis because he sensed that they hated and defied him. Death can be defeated if we are ready to challenge him, Schumann said. At the same time, with every death the flag waves mightier.

Finally, Alfred Rosenberg put it succinctly: death and life are not contraries, but linked to one another. Through the benevolence of God's fate, these contraries are dissolved within eternity. But this eternity can exist on earth as soon as the whole Volk understands the laws of life and fate which govern it. Death creates new life and, we might add, thus continually renews the Volk's march toward finality.[19]

Death is constantly dissolved into a higher synthesis; it is part of sacrifice for the Volk, the true vessel of God. The concept of the Third Reich repeats such dialectic: "we must have the strength to live by antitheses,"[20] Moeller van den Bruck tells us, but these antitheses are themselves eventually dissolved through the struggle of the Volk toward the ideal Reich. The internalization of what Bloch called the "dawn of the apocalypse" is evident: Paracelsus and the fallen heroes and martyrs transcend the flow of time or history and are part of a continuity that stands beyond reality. Thus isolated from the rhythm of daily life, Germanism could easily follow its movement toward God and the Reich.

Hand in hand with this thought went an emphasis upon élitism, for it was felt that the masses were incapable of appreciating such continuities, living as they did merely on the surface of things. Kolbenheyer believed that he was a lonely conservator of the volkish substance, and many other writers thought likewise. This belief was part of a long tradition that had suffused much of the nineteenth century. Clearly, here was an opening for esoteric ideas and fantasies which the more respectable volkish writers rejected. Yet because of the necessity of loneliness and isolation from the evil present, volkish thought could fuse with theosophical elements to posit a small circle of "cognoscenti," or a single prophet who preserved the German essence against all odds.

The novel *Osning* (1914) by Ernst Wachler provides a good example of the trend: deep in a cave in a Germanic wood lives a sage who alone has preserved the "secrets" of the Volk. This sage forms a circle of cognoscenti who will transmit his secret when he dies. The initiates have been purified through their despair and suffering: "endless is the struggle but the victory is certain."[21] Again, the writer and painter Fidus formed such a circle of secret German wisdom, together with his disciple Gertrud Prellwitz. For Prellwitz, new life will grow from death, whether that of the individual or the nation, for life is eternal like the Easter fire. For writers like Fidus and Prellwitz, the Germanic worship of light and sun fuse with the Christian idea of redemption. Wotan and Christ both labored to save the Germanic Volk.[22]

These writers were part of the upsurge of prophets and prophecies at the close of World War I. A whole battalion of such men and women preached their gospel throughout Germany or settled for a time on Monte Veritá, near Ascona. Some thought they were Christ; others sought redemption through vegetarianism or nudity or desired to ward off dangerous odors by donning woolen underwear.[23] Obviously, these were transitory phenomena, and so were the novels of Wachler and Prellwitz. But they demonstrated how easy it was for an inner-directed utopia to slide off into esoteric ideas and practices. In fact, a sectarian streak dwelled in almost every volkish writer, which is perhaps why the Nazis found it so difficult to deal with them.

But if volkish literature could veer toward such bizarre utopias, it could also annex a quite different and much more important genre: the fairy tale. Such tales could give body to the eternal substance of the Volk—something that had been left rather vague by men like Kolbenheyer. Now the fairy tale was said to concretize the roots and essence of the Volk. Scholars in the past had held that fairy tales were, indeed, national myths; but in the twentieth century, typically enough, there was some attempt to connect them to the tradition of popular utopian prophetic and apocalyptical literature. It was widely believed that the crux of a fairy tale could be grasped through its vision of another world.[24] Hans Friedrich Blunck, an indefatigable reteller of sagas and fairy tales in the interwar years, believed that the heroes of old were close to modern Germans and could help them to focus their sights upon the future of the Volk.[25] For Blunck, fairy tales released "immeasurable secret powers," they crystallized extrasensory perceptions.[26] One Nazi writer explained that because it is supposedly "naïve," a fairy tale can bring to light the substance of the Volk buried beneath the garbage of modernity.[27] In short, the fairy tale was a reflection of the life of the Volk soul. As such, it must be "pure" in its rejection of modern complexities and foreshadow a utopian goal as well. The Nazis were fond of reiterating the idea that those fairy tales that concentrated upon the daemonic and its victory were foreign imports into the Germanic world.

As an illustration of the Nazi interpretation of a fairy tale, we can look at *Snow White and the Seven Dwarfs*. This tale becomes a story of redemption as Snow White's awakening is said to symbolize the liberation of the racial soul. The Seven Dwarfs whose homecoming makes this awakening possible are, in fact, messengers from the volkish subconscious, which, like Wachler's sage, lives hidden away in a wood.[28] Actually, such a Nazi interpretation is not so far removed from what the Brothers Grimm had in mind: we stand at the climax of a tradition rather than at its beginning.

Fairy tales had always held a place in the school curriculum, but in Nazi Germany they were thought to be all-important vehicles toward instilling an understanding of Germanism from an early age. The fairy tale, so the Nazi Party held, can show us the constant component of the Volk, its idealism and will to survive. The ancient fairy tale was the eternally valid model for all literature. Such tales, moreover, cannot be modern inventions relying on reason and artificiality (*Kunstmärchen*).[29] Hitler himself seems to have had a taste for them. We possess one story of how he read fairy tales during the war to an admiring circle of women while his entourage was kept waiting outside.[30] No doubt that fairy tale served as a literary substitute for the modern psychology which the Nazis rejected. But long before they assumed power, in 1924, Arnold Zweig had already praised the fairy tale as presenting a convincing truth, while the psychological novel was symptomatic of a lack of soul.[31]

No real distinction was made between fairy tales and sagas; writers like Blunck treated them interchangeably, except that sagas were set within some definite segment of history. But even so, the saga also pointed to a future beyond its immediate setting. Both fairy tales and sagas, we are told, preserved the dream of the Reich throughout the long night, so that everyone could bathe in the light of the distant goal.[32] For Blunck also, the Nazis seemed to bring that goal within reach, and though he was no racist he joined the movement as a fellow traveler. The Nazis not only annexed the literary genres we have discussed but also seemed to typify a "new dawn" to most of their practitioners. However, it was logical that a movement which proclaimed itself a "revolution of the spirit" should continue a utopian tradition that looked inward rather than to outward effects.

Fairy tales did not have to be connected to nationalism. They could, like Ernst Wiechert's tales, serve to console Germans unhappy under the Nazis and further to console those suffering during World War II. His marvelously sensitive fairy tales were meant to fulfill both these functions; the utopian element was present as good triumphed over evil. For Wiechert, fairy tales opened doors into the final judgment of God, symbolized by the splendor of golden halls and gardens that radiated their light out into the icy night. Ultimately, life on earth and life beyond earth reached hands and reconciled all differences—an outcome not unlike the final unity which Kolbenheyer's *Paracelsus* managed to attain.[33]

I have left what must be the most popular of all modern fairy tales to the last: Agnes Günther's *Die Heilige und Ihr Narr* (*The Saint and Her Fool*), which sold nearly a million copies between 1913, its date of publication, and 1945. (It is available in paperback again today.)[34] That this story is indeed a fairy tale there can be little doubt: the heroine's silver dress and golden slippers document it, as well as, once again, the German wood, which is always vital in framing the action. The heroine, "Little Soul" (*Seelchen*), is, as one early commentator put it, "surrounded by a light which penetrates the darkness all around her, amid prophecies which point to the future . . . to perfection."[35] The heroine is a champion of "overcoming": she transcends temptations, despair, and evil (symbolized by her stepmother), in order to face a death that leads to true freedom. But in Agnes Günther's novel, the dawn of the apocalypse is embedded in pietistic thought: "Little Soul" obeys God in all things without asking wherefore. Passivity before one's destiny leads to the final reward. These elements we have seen in the other works discussed, and it is quite possible that pietistic ideals informed most of them. For pietism was an integral part not only of German Protestantism but of German nationalism as well. Moreover, pietism in the nineteenth century had also been influenced by the thought of Jakob Böhme, that inspirer of apocalyptical utopias.[36] Pietism too believed in eternal, hidden substances, at times equated with the fatherland "which is inside you."[37] "Little Soul" is part of an eternal substance here, for in her second sight she identifies with the life and suffering of an ancestor many centuries earlier. "Gisela" (the name of her double), wrongly accused of being a witch, had to pass through great distress and suffer a cruel death. But she symbolizes the promise of last things: "her hair was as a golden river woven from the gold of heaven's door."[38]

The inwardness of the heroine, the chivalry of her husband, the wood, and the castle are all specifically Germanic, for Günther has written a German fairy tale. The idea that this kind of utopia is promised to the Germans, that here alone death and time will end, is implicit or explicit in all these works. This is what Hermann Stehr meant when he wrote in 1914 that the Germans were the only people whose blood demanded that religious ideals be translated into political action.[39] A leading Nazi literary journal then defined the religious as symbolizing the return of man to those ideas that derived from the past and were present behind outward appearances.[40]

Given this Nazi definition, we can see that all the literature we have discussed was highly political inasmuch as it deepened a Germanic utopia congenial to the political Right—a mixture of traditionalism, spiritual continuity, and uplift. But this utopia was also directed toward affirming the necessity of struggle and suffering while at the same time explaining them away, asking for death and sacrifice even while transcending them; and, finally, emphasizing the eternal quality of the Volk and of nature thus ending the rush of time. All this could be used to oppose a dialectic of eternity, comfort, and restfulness against the Marxist dialectic of reason, criticism, and struggle.

The novelist Hermann Stehr brought out the implications of such an approach to utopia, to the good and beautiful life. His two-volume novel, *Der Heiligenhof* (1918), states the "inwardness" of such a world view clearly: "The conditions of the soul must produce the political system and not vice versa . . . otherwise man acts as if he wants to build a house for someone not yet born. . . ."[41] Blindness is the road to holiness for Helena, the heroine of the novel. Her soul is not confined, but sees all the world as in a flood of light. Proper sight unduly emphasizes the outside world. For example, only through our eyes do we know death. When Helena regains her sight, all the evils of the world begin to press in upon her. But in the end these evils can be overcome through love, which leads man to a greater unity with himself and the world.

This work contains almost every cliché advocated by volkish thought. Women are virginal; the almost holy Helena is put into a faint when one lecherous man touches her fully clothed bosom. She has been defiled. Manliness is prized, as are the clean and orderly farm and the good peasant life. The landscape is made to come alive, and nature forms one unity with the earthy characters of the novel. Yet contemporaries were struck by the work. Arnold Zweig had the highest praise for it, pronouncing it a wonderful fairy tale. *Der Heiligenhof* seemed to exemplify a poet who was free of the bonds of time, not unlike the quality that had been so admired in the famous Paul Ernst.[42]

At the time he wrote the *Heiligenhof*, Stehr proclaimed his intimate friendship with Walter Rathenau, who through financial contributions had made Stehr's career as a writer possible. Moreover, Stehr professed himself a passionate adherent of the Weimar Republic.[43] But he repudiated his past when the Nazis came to power, and even falsified his own work to cut all ties. For example, in 1934, Stehr asserted that in *Wendelin Heinelt* (1906) he had shown how a worker was led from class struggle to brotherly love. In reality that tale contains nothing about class struggle, but is a fairy tale which concludes with a forecast of heaven on earth where no one fears death any more.[44]

This change of heart would not be worth mentioning on the part of a writer who is today forgotten if it did not bring out the political implications inherent in such mysticism. Stehr's *Heiligenhof* was praised as the greatest work of modern German mysticism.[45] It was, in fact, part fairy tale, part praise of the cosmos that Volk and nature were said to symbolize, and part an embodiment of hope (equivalent to love, inward vision, and the realization of the negative nature of the outside world). But such a world view led Stehr to Germanism and élitism as well. Like Kolbenheyer and all the other writers we have discussed, he felt that the masses were incapable of higher things, that the heritage was preserved by the few. This attitude in turn led him at the right political moment to castigate Weimar as the rule of the mob.[46]

There is little doubt that Stehr as well as Kolbenheyer and Ernst were paranoiacs, who had difficulty becoming recognized writers and thought themselves constantly persecuted. Their prophecy was based on a mystical utopia, but also upon their own persecution mania. Thus they were attracted to the Nazis, who did try to perform and publish their works, even though Goebbels seems to have had his doubts about their literary ability.[47]

Although a political attitude was inherent in all these German utopias, such an attitude was made overt and explicit through the myth of the Third Reich. In the fourteenth century, Joachim of Fiore had set the tone for the eschatological counting of time, but even during the nineteenth century Fiore's three universal empires had been replaced by a more restrictive German interpretation: the First Empire of the Middle Ages and the Second Empire of Bismarck's state would lead into a Third Reich, which would finally begin to fulfill the mission of the Germanic spirit that had been kept intact, if underground, throughout the ages.[48] Such a counting of time was also related to the *Book of Revelation*, and the Third Reich concretized the unsealing of the book of the Seven Seals. But such eschatology was once again transcended by time itself, for the Reich had always been present even in a disunited Germany, awaiting its turn. For example, Werner Beumelburg, writing in 1938, praised Ulrich von Hutten because he symbolized "the German who has faith and gazes at the eternal verity of the Reich without as yet being able to realize it."[49] And Franz Schauwecker tells us at much the same time that the Third Reich is immanent in all German history, which strives toward that moment when the Volk becomes the vessel of God.[50]

The *Neue Literatur* (*New Literature*), edited by Will Vesper, attempted to create a cult around the works of Paul Ernst, perhaps one of the most interesting of these writers, who died in 1933. To be sure, that writer before his death completed his intellectual migration from socialism through naturalism to a quite reluctant and ambivalent sympathy with the National Socialists. Indeed, many volkish prophets started their literary careers with quite different ideas in mind. Paul Ernst was once the correspondent of Friedrich Engels, and Kolbenheyer's early work dealt with Spinoza. Even the first volume of his *Paracelsus* trilogy still emphasizes deistic and universalistic concepts. Yet the very pantheism of Spinoza may have facilitated the adoption of that Germanic unity of man and nature which the volkish Kolbenheyer eventually advocated. No doubt many other examples of a fairly late volkish conversion, such as Gottfried Benn's, could be cited. The pressure for such conversion was not always a result of the victory of National Socialism (Ernst and Kolbenheyer became volkish prophets long before such a victory was conceivable), but also of movements like expressionism and naturalism which could lead writers to find restfulness in contemplation of the Volk, in one's "native place." The reality of World War I, defeat, and revolution were crucial in pushing many writers to the Right.

However, in *New Literature*, Ernst was praised not for any conversion but as a prophet of the new Reich. Ernst followed that mythos through the 80,000 verses of his *Book of Emperors* (*Kaiserbuch*, 1928). (The six volumes of the book had to be printed by subscription, and a beginning was made not with German money but by donations from America and Hungary.) [51] The first Reich about which Ernst wrote could not yet break through to success; the medieval emperors were tragic figures who failed in the end. Here, as in his earlier dramas, tragedy entails the loneliness of those who want to perfect themselves through their own strength alone, who refuse to let anything external enter their lives. It was Georg Lukacs who believed that Ernst's dramas, such as *Brünhilde*, were perfect tragedies. But it was Lukacs as well who in 1916 praised Ernst as the one poet who successfully severed all links between himself and the passage of time. [52]

Lukacs retained his high regard for Ernst even as the poet wrote his *Book of Emperors* and spread his volkish message. Admittedly, unlike Martin Buber or Arnold Zweig, he refused to contribute to the *Festschrift* for Ernst's sixtieth birthday (1926) but instead sent warm greetings, though "we stand on different sides of the barricades." Ernst and Lukacs remained in touch until at least 1930. [53] This is worth mentioning as demonstrating how strong a hold such irrationalism had at one time upon that generation. Lukacs himself seemed to admit as much when he praised Ernst's importance to his own development—and here he was not merely thinking of the poet's socialist youth or his correspondence with Friedrich Engels.

Lukacs had admired Ernst as the poet who, as he put it in 1926, through his rejection of time gave voice to the greatest possibilities immanent in the age. For Ernst guides the reader to a world beyond daily confusion, and teaches him to grasp the essence of present reality: an immanent substance that derives from eternity. [54] That substance in practice was for Ernst the Volk, for Lukacs the proletariat. The same year that Lukacs wrote of his admiration, Ernst himself wrote that the Volk is nothing that exists, but something that comes into being; it is a process and not a "thing."[55] The *Book of Emperors* throws light on one stage of this process: the emperors themselves are tragic figures, but the final end is immanent here as well.[56] Ernst closes his epic with verses forecasting the time when God will stretch out His hands from the clouds and the emperor Barbarossa will emerge from the Kyffhäuser Mountain. God thus makes the immanent come true: "it will be a time when the Volk becomes the vessel of God and one master will rule the earth."[57]

Man helps only by preserving this heritage. Yet here we are not talking of all men but only one, for such a prophet "must be completely isolated and experience the Volk within himself."[58] The rejection of time, which Lukacs had so highly praised in contrast to reality, was a means to isolate a lofty volkish soul from the contamination of modernity, enabling the prophet to proclaim himself the master. Ernst probably never saw Hitler as the new Barbarossa; and during the few weeks before his death in which he was lionized by the Third Reich, he called himself cynically a "usufructuary of the revolution."[59] But others thought differently about Hitler's mission. Thus, Heinrich Anacker rhymed in 1936: "The work which took a thousand years to accomplish, which the greatest Germans merely saw through the eyes of the spirit, is about to be accomplished."[60] But here, too, it is to be accomplished through the self-sacrifice of the few, in the deed of the one: he who bound himself to the ideal of the Reich was a stranger to most of his fellow men because he transcended even himself. Few loved such a man, yet suddenly he jumped out front and took command. Perhaps Ernst dreamed of being such a man, but the one Gerhard Schumann had in mind was Adolf Hitler.[61]

For Anacker and Schumann, the Third Reich was no longer merely an inward vision but was translated into outward power— one Reich, from the Alps to the Sea.[62] The concrete aims of the existing "Third Reich" had to be integrated into a vision that was no longer as inner-directed as it had been after World War I. At that time, Moeller van den Bruck had formulated a most perceptive criticism of men like Kolbenheyer, and of the inner-directedness of such utopian literature. These writers, he wrote, wanted to console themselves for defeat in war by asserting that national values could never be lost, even if the nation itself should perish. Moeller asserted that this was self-deception; that national values could indeed perish in a national catastrophe.[63]

Moeller in 1923 broke with the belief that the eternal substance of Germanism was destined to eventual victory. Instead, he said, the spiritual goal must be reached through political action. In spite of this greater pragmatism, Moeller also proclaimed that German nationalism was fighting for the final kingdom, one whose perfection could only be reached through that which was imperfect, such as political action.[64] So Moeller affirmed involvement with the world where many previous volkish prophets had wanted to cut all such ties. But here imperfection also implies the necessity of striving and accepting defeat in order to reach a higher synthesis that will resolve all human contradictions. Moeller also thought, however, that the kingdom that was promised would never be fulfilled, and that men must therefore have the strength to "live by contraries." For Moeller, the Germanic mission meant a constant striving, and the use of political tactics, without ever arriving at the final goal.[65] Clearly, Moeller at times envisaged an apocalyptical utopia (as when he wrote that the Third Reich meant eternal peace); but for the most part, he emphasized the pragmatism of political action and the constant struggle to achieve the Reich. We must remember that the book got its apocalyptical-sounding title, *The Third Reich*, only after Moeller's original title, *The Third Way*, was rejected because of the concern that it might lead readers to feel a new and conventional political party was in the making.[66] Moeller, in fact, wanted no political parties; the political struggle was one on behalf of the unity of all Germans—a unity which he believed to be a prerequisite for the ideal of the Reich.

The Nazis took for themselves the title of Moeller's work and got rid of his pessimism about the final end. They regarded themselves as the *cognoscenti* who had preserved the ideal of the Reich when it lived on only in the hearts of a tiny minority.[67] Many poets joined Will Vesper in proclaiming that the fallen of World War I had been finally redeemed when, as a reward for their heroism, the Führer placed the new Reich symbolically upon their graves.[68] But the Third Reich was not regarded by the Nazis as the final end. Such an interpretation would have been politically dangerous, for there were obvious imperfections, and the idea of the necessity of struggle and sacrifice had to be continued—the world was hostile and enemies were everywhere. Thus the Third Reich was seen as the beginning of the end, not as the end itself. The apocalypse had dawned, but the dialectic of death and life, of time and eternity, was still operative, if on a higher level of synthesis than before. Nazi poets and festivals proclaimed that death could be challenged, while much of Nazi literature was devoted to demonstrating the unimportance of time. "A thousand years are as one day in the sight of God," Will Vesper wrote, and the men of the past were not so different from those who lived today. How could there be any difference when, according to Vesper, the blood of the Germanic ancestors flowed like a never-ending stream from the most distant times into their own? Thus the flow of time was safely imprisoned in its riverbed; and, as another Nazi writer put it, because youth were now educated through the example of their fathers, "death has lost its sting, as the flag is simply passed to the next in line." [69]

We seem to be back with the telescoping of history so familiar in earlier ages and through the Renaissance. But now such telescoping fastens onto an apocalyptical tradition and is a conscious attempt to abolish the flow of time that led to the dilemmas of modernity. The tradition of the apocalyptical dialectic moved into the second half of the twentieth century. Just as it consoled many for the defeat of World War I, so did it serve to give hope among the ruins left by World War II. There must have been others, besides the scholar Erich Peuckert, who in 1945 (with two rucksacks packed for flight) wrote that there was historical necessity in the ruin he was witnessing and that out of its dirt and foulness a new world was about to arise. Nothing is senseless. Peuckert quotes Paracelsus to the effect that God must be recognized in all His works, good or bad; a new dawn arises forever. [70] Already, in 1912, Hermann Burte had written in his *Wiltfeber der ewige Deutsche* (*Wiltfeber the Eternal German*) that "we suffer, we must suffer in order to become perfect." [71] Once more we witness a continuity between 1912 and 1945, between the beginning of our century and the end of World War II; the constant hope stated in apocalyptical terms that dawn was about to break. This dawn, as we saw, was no longer the dawn of revolution for which Ernst Bloch hoped in 1921, but meant rather a withdrawal into the eternal essence of the Volk.

The utopia was ready-made to support and glorify a volkish state as the antechamber to paradise and the framework within which deliverance and salvation would take place. The dream supported reality and reality did its best to further the dream. But, alas, reality overtook the dream as it usually does; and death, time, and history, far from being obliterated, first strangled life and then led her into a charnelhouse from which there was no exit. Like all glorious dawns, this too had been a romantic illusion. The deeper the dream, the more desperate the fall, and the emptier the movement toward redemption.

FIVE

The Poet and the Exercise of Political Power: Gabriele D'Annunzio

IDEALS OF HUMAN REGENERATION have been a part of poetic vision for many centuries. "We are selfish men: O raise us up, return to us again; And give us manners, virtue, freedom, power." Wordsworth's appeal to Milton stands within a long tradition.[1] A new man must be created, who will dissolve the present and degenerate reality. These visions belong to the literature of political utopias; they would fill a large library with their different definitions of the new man and of human regeneration. Such poetry is usually studied and analyzed for its literary style and language rather than for its political importance. The poetry and the exercise of political power seemed to exclude each other during a large period of European history. At best, as during the Renaissance, we have poets who were also politicians, but the relationship between their poetic vision and their politics seemed indirect and insignificant in determining their political action. Poets had political ideals, even in their poetry, but it is difficult to see how the poetry itself was translated into political fact. At any rate, it tended to contribute little new to the political scene and, at most, dressed traditional political concepts in poetic form.

However, during the nineteenth century the relation between poetry and politics underwent a profound transformation. The poet received a meaningful place in the creation of the politics of the times and contributed something new, essential, and original to the art of governing. The reason that poets now got their chance to be politically effective lay in the changed nature of politics itself. During earlier ages the poet, if he was interested in politics, more often than not was the servant of a dynasty, and his political deeds were confined either to glorifying the ruler, as Edmund Spenser did in his *Faerie Queen*, or to praising political morality, as in the *Mirrors for Princes*. To be sure, poets did create myths—around Queen Elizabeth, or later, Louis XIV—but such myth creation did not break through into a new and creative political approach of its own. During the nineteenth century, however, we witness an important change in the nature of politics, which gave the poet a significant place in the process of political creativity. The rise of nationalism meant a quest for the self-representation not of a dynasty but of the nation. At the same time, in western Europe the masses of people became increasingly involved in politics. As a result of these developments we can observe the growth of a new political style, which operated within the framework of myth, symbols, and public festivals. The rise of modern nationalism was accompanied by the growth of the secular religion of the nation, and it was here that the poet could find a meaningful place.

Politics became a drama, expressed through secular liturgical rites and symbols closely linked to concepts of beauty in which poetry felt at home. National festivals, often held under the stars on sacred native ground, surrounded by symbols such as the holy fire and the flag, constituted a political style essential to the building up of nations, and here the poet could make a contribution to the political expression of a growing national self-consciousness.[2] It is no coincidence that early in the nineteenth century Ernst Moritz Arndt, advocate of German national unity, combined his poetry with plans for national festivals and the erection of national monuments.[3] This is no isolated case. Later in the century, Gabriele D'Annunzio wrote about the heightening of the meaning of life attained through sacred objects, the symbols of a secular religion: instruments of a cult around which human thought and imagination revolve, and which in turn lifts these to idealistic heights.[4] Some years later, D'Annunzio connected these heights with the political regeneration of Italy. And in Germany, at the same time, Stefan George shared this ideal of renewal: through beautiful symbols and mystic festivals, the "secret Germany" would transform German politics.

The myth was all-important here, for it determined the nature and meaning of the symbols central to the new political style. As J. Huizinga puts it: "having attributed a real existence to an idea the mind wants to see it alive and can effect this only by personalizing it."[5] The idea—in our case, the nation—is no longer centered upon one person but upon the abstraction of "the people," and therefore the symbols must represent national myths. These tended to combine history and nature; supposed ancestral customs and what Schelling defined as "the universe in a festive garb, in its primeval state, the true universe itself . . . already become poetry."[6] By creating such myths and their symbols, poets were not merely glorifying a dynasty but creating a new political style, within which such myths and their symbols played a dynamic role. They could become creators of a national liturgy, and indeed some did fulfill this function. The most important of these was Gabriele D'Annunzio (1863–1938).

Poets like D'Annunzio's contemporary Stefan George in Germany never penetrated the political reality; the only German poet who succeeded in this was Kurt Eisner, leader of the Bavarian Revolution of 1918–19. But although, as we shall see, the socialist Eisner shared Schelling's ideal of nature and the universe, he never created a new political style, and the festival celebrating his own revolution was singularly traditional—an evening at the opera with music and speeches, in top hats and tails.[7] D'Annunzio, on the other hand, actually furthered the new political style during his roughly sixteen months rule of the City of Fiume (September 11, 1919, to January 18, 1921), and indeed it was from this episode that Mussolini derived the political style of Italian fascism. D'Annunzio is hardly read any more today, but he illustrates the important place a poet could take in the shaping of a new secular religion that became an all-embracing political style. The Italian poet is as important for an understanding of the nature of modern politics as any statesman or ruler, and this in spite of the fact that his occupation of Fiume was of such relatively short duration.

D'Annunzio perceived the world through myths and symbols; his mind was pictorial rather than wedded to literary forms. His style was overripe with visual and musical similes, presented to the reader in a tone of mystical exaggeration. (Theodor Herzl hit the mark when he wrote that D'Annunzio's play *La Gloria* [1899] contained a "rich pictorial world which flickers juicily.")[8] The fin de siècle appreciated this style, but what makes D'Annunzio so difficult to read today was precisely the turn of mind that led to his political creativity. It was the flamboyant, romantic, mystic, and illusionist element in D'Annunzio which determined his political style, and led him beyond traditional political thought into the kind of dramatization so crucial to modern mass politics. Visually, image is piled upon image in his works, until the reader can see the scene rising before his very eyes. These images were combined with an exaltation of action—not, at first, political action, but that inspired by narcissism and sex, cruelty and brutality, usually practiced by man upon woman. Like St. Sebastian, with whom he at one point identifies himself, the poet went out into the darkness in order to expose the scars of a night of violent love to the moon.[9] His was a world of intoxication, of illusion, of dreams. These dreams were narcissistic, to be sure, and D'Annunzio believed himself capable of all acts long before he read Nietzsche: "I stood by and watched within myself the continual genesis of a finer life wherein all appearances were transfigured as in a magic mirror."[10] This finer life was dominated by myth and symbol, with himself at the center.

While his life for a long time was obsessed with personal gratification, it soon broadened into a concern with national regeneration. The influence of Richard Wagner aided the widening of D'Annunzio's horizons. Admittedly he also personalized Wagner's myths: for example, he transposed the theme of redemption in *Parsifal* onto the violent love between the poet and his mistress. Nevertheless, he saw how Wagner attempted to elevate the German spirit by carrying his myths to the people.[11] Wagner's music drama was supposed to be a political drama, through which alone national regeneration could be achieved. It combined myth, symbol, and beauty. "The fortunes of Italy," so D'Annunzio wrote toward 1900, "are inseparable from the fate of beauty, of whom she is the mother."[12] The aesthetics of politics, so vital to the new political style, was moving to the forefront.

But what exactly was the nature of this beauty? Here the connection with political symbolism becomes evident, for the best example is provided by D'Annunzio's preoccupation with the flame—the holy fire. The symbolism of the sacred flame had grown up with the attempted self-representation of the nation, taken partly from Christianity and partly from ancient myth. Flames on hilltops, pillars of fire standing on altars erected in the street, had already been central to the German festivals celebrating the wars of liberation against Napoleon (1815).[13] The flames not only symbolized a reflection of the sun—light against darkness, warmth and growth against cold and barrenness—but also the living Volk as part of primeval nature. For D'Annunzio, the flame had similar connotations. It was the "Life giver," infused by a miraculous beauty that reflected itself in nature—autumnal gold, the flashes of the sun in the sky. The flame symbolized the "white heat" of the spirit, the nobler passions of man, the heroic, and, typically enough, the images of poetry as expressions of the human will.[14]

Thus the "Flame of Life" for D'Annunzio symbolizes both personal and national regeneration. The qualities associated with it in his mind had political connotations: the heroic passion, closeness to nature, the power of will, were all opposed to modern degeneracy and wishy-washiness. Moreover, the beauty of the flame was filled with color, and, as he wrote, color is the ornament of the world, the strenuous effort of matter to become light.[15] This ideal formed an obvious contrast to the grayness of bourgeois existence and the disputations of parliamentary government, which he hated from the very beginning. Beauty meant color and clarity of form, not compromise or inaction. D'Annunzio was close to the ideals of many other poets and writers who were to be attracted to fascism.[16] The symbol of the flame was happily chosen, for it became a political reality before the poet began his exercise of power, enabling him to fuse his vision with that of a group of committed men who emerged from the battles of World War I.

The Italian storm troopers during that war, the *Arditi*, wore the emblem of the flame on their uniform. When they organized themselves as a political group after the war, D'Annunzio's symbol of the flame came near to expressing their own thoughts. The "First Appeal to the Flame" (*Primo apello alle Fiamme*) in 1918 stressed the task of national regeneration.[17] And the *Arditi* formed the nucleus of D'Annunzio's Legion at Fiume: the "Black Flame," as they were called, symbolizing both fire and steel.

The beauty and symbolism of the flame did not stand in isolation, for in the words of St. Sebastian there was beauty also in death and suffering. But such beauty was present only to him who could profit from it through struggle and power of will. In most of D'Annunzio's writing, the theme of death and redemption is present. It is summarized in the image of Fiume as the City of Holocaust (1915): "passionate City, the sole City of the soul, all suffering and fire, all purification and consummation: a holocaust, the most beautiful holocaust, which has been offered for centuries to an unfeeling world." [18] Fire consumes and redeems; destruction and regeneration exist in proximity. Once again, this was a vision close to the war experience of the *Arditi* and to D'Annunzio's own life during the conflict. But the image also had a political meaning: the degeneracy and death of Italy meant its resurrection through heroic deeds. The paradox was later to obsess all of fascism.

The poet's political imagery and symbolism hit a common chord, not before but during and after the war. The war gave D'Annunzio his chance at political power, and also an outlet for his drive to activism, his longing to actualize the "virtue of his example." [19] As a pilot he performed many daring feats at an age when others were passing into retirement. Already in *Alcyone* (1904) he had identified himself with Icarus, flying high before crashing into the sea. Such courage was worthy of eternity. Once more, life and death are intertwined. It was the daring, spectacular adventure of the aeroplane that fascinated him rather than mere speed. It gave life a grandeur, poised over the abyss of death and darkness, which the flame also symbolized. At Fiume, he made much use of aeroplanes—not just as means of communication (others were more easily available) but in order to salute the city in a spectacular manner. The planes traced patterns in the sky and, at times, trailed flags after them.

Through the aeroplane and the flame, D'Annunzio's vision penetrated reality. Had his contribution to modern political liturgy been mostly verbal—in the form of the speeches, writings, and manifestos—he would have been small use to Mussolini, whose own bent was verbal but who showed much less interest in the outward symbolism and ceremonial needed to transform myth and symbol into political reality. Mussolini was fascinated by literature, but had little appreciation of the visual arts. (Hitler complained that when the Duce had looked at three pictures at an exhibition he could stand no more.) The opera bored him.[20] Typically enough, when Mussolini said that politics should be like art, he meant that political decisions must be informed by the creativity of the artist. He did not have a political liturgy in mind; yet he realized the importance of myths and cults. The symbols of "our eternal memories" were essential for the "beating heart of the people." It was necessary to use the older traditions of festivals, gestures, and political style in order to adapt them to the fascist revolution.[21] Mussolini was as preoccupied with the crowd as D'Annunzio (perhaps through the influence of Gustave Le Bon),[22] but he had little flair or understanding for a political liturgy that was not verbally oriented. Yet crowds had to be swayed and controlled, a dynamic had to be maintained—something that needed visual rather than merely verbal approaches. And it was the poet, not Mussolini, who first proved to be a master of this technique. D'Annunzio was obsessed with the nature of crowds long before he seized power at Fiume.

In 1900, he had written about the communication between the soul of the crowd and his own as a "divine mystery," which happened when he spoke; "there must therefore be in the multitude a hidden beauty from which only the hero and the poet can draw a flash." The word of the poet must be a heroic deed; he must create a "divine statue" out of the crowd.[23] How was this to be done? D'Annunzio turned to the theater; not the traditional theater, but the "theater of future," which was being widely discussed by the end of the century. Such a theater would eliminate the gap between actor and audience and so form both into one entity. This poet drew part of his inspiration from the theaters of antiquity and part from Bayreuth. What counted was the shared atmosphere, and this was produced by the open sky (nature herself), by music, dancing, and lyric poetry. Rhythm was also important.[24] Indeed, the theater which D'Annunzio described was to provide one of the foundations for twentieth-century mass meetings, and to become an integral part of fascist rites. This was, as he envisaged it, a national theater within which the nation would be represented both visually and verbally through its myths and symbols. It was here that D'Annunzio took a step beyond mere verbal expression to the kind of artistic synthesis the new religion of nationalism required.

The chaotic crowd became an ordered mass of people. This was essential for the effectiveness of any political rite, as important as the myths and symbols themselves. D'Annunzio, for all his flamboyance, believed in order, as his likening of the crowd to a divine statue showed. But the principle of order was, for him, an integral part of the concept of beauty itself. Even surrounded by depravity, "the intelligent man," he wrote in 1887, "raised in a cult of beauty . . . always preserves some sort of order."[25] The principal aesthetic theoreticians of the nineteenth century had held the same belief: the concept of beauty must exclude anything accidental or chaotic. Beauty symbolized an ordered universe, a healthy world, as against the uprootedness of modernity.[26] Thus it supported myths, symbols, and settings for national festivals which represented clarity of form as part of the beauty that must infuse such occasions.

Many writers who ended up in the arms of totalitarianism believed in the identity of beauty and order, which, in turn, they equated with strictness of literary form. Men like Ezra Pound, T. S. Eliot, and Charles Maurras all shared this viewpoint, maintaining that they were continuing the heritage of the ancients. Strictness of form excluded chaos in art and led to absolutism, the precondition in their mind for unwavering moral decisions.

Aestheticians like Friedrich Vischer had held similar opinions, but in the 1850s and 1860s this did not yet entail an emphasis upon harshness, struggle, and leadership, as opposed to prevarication —in art as well as in politics. D'Annunzio was the contemporary of men like Maurras or Pound for whom the amorphous mass of democracy symbolized decadent society—"sensitivity without direction," as Ezra Pound characterized that form of government.[27] The Italian poet was close in this respect to a whole generation of writers, though he went beyond them in translating such literary concept into political reality.

Communicating with the crowd, making order out of chaos, required the right setting. For D'Annunzio, such a setting abandons man to emotion and carries him away to brutality—but all within the presupposition of an ordered universe.[28] D'Annunzio's national theater never became reality; instead, another setting took its place. The "divine mystery of the crowd" always included a physical distaste for the masses, typical of D'Annunzio's élitism. The hero of La Gloria overcomes this distaste by standing on a platform above the crowd in order to "breathe freely." This, we are told, reveals the concept of power through which the tribune of the people sways the masses. A year later, this platform has become a balcony flanked by blood-red columns, preferable as a setting to a mere platform.[29] When the lord mayor of Rome asked D'Annunzio in April 1919 to address "fiery words" to the citizens, he spoke such words from the balcony of the Campidoglio, the center of ancient Rome. This experience was to be repeated in the future. It proved an effective and dramatic setting. D'Annunzio did liken this arena to the theater of his dreams. He told one of his crowds at Fiume how much it pleased him to be with the people, not in a closed theater but in the open, under the stars, in order to communicate with them and to transform their souls into an "ardent and tempestuous sky." The walls of this arena, he continued, were human, palpitating walls. Here the flame of Fiume would rise again.[30] This passage combines the preoccupation with mise-en-scène, the masses, and the image of the flame. Such appeal had a powerful effect on the "City of the Holocaust": at Fiume, speeches from the balcony of the palace became the focal point of the political rite. The balcony setting was perfected through the use of flags, which preoccupied the poet as much as the sacred flame.

For D'Annunzio, the flag as a symbol was closely associated with deeds of individual heroism. It personalized the heroic past. As early as 1915, during one of his speeches in support of intervention in the war, he had displayed a flag associated with Nino Bixio, the hero of the *Risorgimento*, and bestowed a kiss upon it with the cry: "Long live the war!" When addressing the crowd again from the Campidoglio in May 1919, he dramatically unfurled the blood-stained flag carried by Commandante Giovanni Randaccio, who fell at his side during the war. Later, he again displayed the same flag, this time with a band of mourning for Dalmatia fastened upon it.[31] The cult of the flag was a general phenomenon at the time. We know, for example, the immense pains that Theodor Herzl took to design a flag for the nonexistent Jewish state, and how important he thought this for its creation. With a proper flag, he explained, "one can lead men wherever one wants to, even into the promised land."[32] For D'Annunzio, both before and at Fiume, the symbolism of the flag was combined with the cult of the martyrs. Regeneration was once more linked to death and sacrifice. He commonly unfurled a flag on the balcony at Fiume as a part of his incantations; at times, blasts on a trumpet accompanied this rite.

Such was his political stage. But what about the distance between actor and audience, which should be abolished? This idea was adjusted to the new political setting, whether at the Capitol in Rome or in Fiume. The dialogue with the crowd became an essential part of his speeches. Rhetorical questions were the principal device: "Annexation! Is this not your will? Is it not that of everyone? Are we not vacillating today like the wind? Like a fluttering flag?" And the masses answered from below. The crowd's responses could be affirmatory, or sometimes, when he had put the question differently, a deep groan. Or the people beneath the balcony might repeat a phrase of D'Annunzio's in an almost poetic rhythm, while the *Arditi* on occasion responded by speaking as a chorus, an important device in mass ceremonial: "Whatever the Commandante wills, wherever he wills it, one for all and all for one, one against one, and one against all, all against all, in a mass!" A close collaborator of the Commandante at Fiume, Léon Kochnitzki, remarked upon the hypnotic power of D'Annunzio's prose. At one point when D'Annunzio had given a speech to his legionnaires, young soldiers and officers spontaneously produced their own confessions of faith couched in the poet's peculiar lyrical style. Here, on another level, D'Annunzio's prose itself provided the link with his audience, the *"prosa d'annunziana,"* with its exaggerated rhythms and pomposities, dominating the consciousness of hardboiled and semiliterate legionnaires.[33] But whatever the response to D'Annunzio's speeches, all present were drawn into participation.

D'Annunzio ruled Fiume not only by proclamations but by almost daily speeches from the balcony. And these speeches in turn were supplemented by other ritual occasions. D'Annunzio was fertile in inventing myths as occasions for national festivals; in common with many others at the fin de siècle, he had a fully developed sense of their importance. Men longed to escape from the banality of daily life, and this had already given impetus to public festivals in most European nations as an accompaniment of national self-consciousness.[34]

The poet used this tradition to the fullest. He mythologized the march of Ronchi, which had led to the peaceful entry of his legionnaires into Fiume; the crash of an aviator who had wanted to salute the city; even those who died a heroic death during World War I like Giovanni Randaccio. With typical pride, D'Annunzio wrote to Alceste de Ambris that during a short absence from the city he had missed three or four superwonderful (*sevramirabili*) festivals. The anniversary of Randaccio's death and the protest against the insults of the Italian government according to the poet provided the most elevated and warmest hours Fiume had ever experienced; the other evening, he added, some 30,000 people gathered "*delirio e furore.*" (No doubt the poet here was carried away, for such a gathering would have had to include most of the city's 50,000 or so inhabitants.) The sixteen months at Fiume saw a multitude of such national festivals, each replete with its own ceremonial. Thus in memory of Randaccio's death, D'Annunzio talked in front of an altar set up before his palace, and an honor guard was mounted around the flag that Randaccio had carried into battle.[35] The myth was concretized as part of political rule.

On such occasions Christian symbols were used side by side with their secular counterparts. This may seem strange in one whose writings were on the papal Index. But D'Annunzio had always used Christian imagery even if, like that of St. Sebastian, in a blasphemous manner. The "flame of Fiume" was now likened to the sacrifice of love on the Sunday of Pentecost. His entry into the city became the "*santa entrata.*" Priests participated in Fiume's ceremonials, and the Commandante went to mass. When he talked about the "religion of patriotism," he likened it to celebrations inside and outside the Church.[36] Secular symbols like the flag or the flame were linked to traditional Christianity at a time when elsewhere the secular and the Christian in national liturgy were separating one from the other. The "City of the Holocaust" was enveloped in a Wagnerian scenario—and in Wagner's kind of sentimental Christianity.

In its setting and mass participation, the political drama must be accompanied by easily remembered phrases and pithy slogans. D'Annunzio used these effectively in his rhetorical questions to the crowd. But even apart from such questions, they were needed. The poet's speeches were highly dramatic yet simple. The words addressed directly to the multitude should, in D'Annunzio's opinion, have no other aim than action, even violent action if need be.

Words as such were not enough, for as he told a crowd in 1919, words are feminine and deeds are masculine. Words must appeal to action and oppose passivity.[37] He operated with certain set slogans. To the populace, he cried, *"Me ne frega"*; to the more sophisticated: *"Semper adeamus!"* Every speech ended with *"Eia, eia, eia, alala!* (Hip, hip, hurrah!),"* a slogan he had first conjured up to encourage his men into battle during the war.[38] It became a hallmark of his political style.

This political style served to keep up a dynamic, and to disguise the growing conflict in Fiume between the undisciplined legionnaires and the victimized population. It mattered little, in the short run at least, that D'Annunzio was bored by the details of government. He had no tolerance for political discourse and debate. For a brief and unprofitable time (1898–1900), he had been a deputy in the Italian Parliament, and hatred of representative government and political parties remained basic to his thought. Yet even here his critique of parliamentarianism blended the visual and the political: "the newly elected are easily recognizable. Many have a miserable provincial aspect and look awkward in their black evening clothes, their stiff shirts, their white gloves. They glance about them suspiciously. . . ." The outward appearance, the mise-en-scène itself, characterized the political failure of that assembly.[39] Moreover, the exaltation of the crowd, and his own intoxication with it, led him to see in the acclamation of the people in the square the popular consent needed for his constitution (the Charter of Carnaro).[40] He carried through a plebiscite at Fiume, and all but ignored the working of his National Council.[41] D'Annunzio's idea of equality embraced the people as an organic whole, a kind of "mystical body" that must be led by him who symbolized virtue and beauty. He was close to fascism in his ideas here, even before Mussolini was converted from socialism.

But D'Annunzio remained silent when many *Arditi* went further and attempted to take a militant stand on behalf of the demands of manual and white-collar workers.[42] The ideal of greater social equality in the Charter of Carnaro was inspired by the former syndicalist Alceste de Ambris. D'Annunzio contributed to it clauses guaranteeing a beautiful life, and the free development of spiritual man as a gift to a world of brothers. His was also the idea of a tenth corporation among those of other professions and walks of life:

one that was to be reserved for "the mysterious force represented by the people at work and directed to higher things." He described this as an offering to the appearance of a new species of man. The common sentiment which binds such men together is a religious one, equated in the Charter of Carnaro with lyricism and, above all, with music. And music, in turn, is defined as a religious and social institution. Choirs were subsidized at Fiume, and concerts became national events. Long before this time music had always provided one crucial unifying factor for nationalism—choirs had proved indispensable at national festivals and national rites. The Charter of Carnaro defined politics once again as a lyric drama. The Italian regency of Carnaro was both social and religious. The social element was the work of de Ambris, but the religious was D'Annunzio's own.[43]

It is here, and not in the social aspects, that its true importance lies. For by "religious," D'Annunzio meant the political liturgy we have described: led by himself as the symbol of beauty and a poetic, active life, but also surrounded by other political symbols, which provided a total, all-encompassing setting. This was the new style of politics as Mussolini adopted it; the balcony at Fiume became the balcony at the Palazzo Venezia.

But Mussolini added to the national liturgy a well-developed sense of the limits of political action. He constantly dampened D'Annunzio's ardor and opposed the march on Rome which the poet planned to undertake from Fiume. For D'Annunzio, in his world of myth and symbol, with his ideal of himself as the incarnation of everything that was possible in the world, lacked all sense of political realities. His fortuitous success in Fiume must have convinced him of the fact that he was the poet-as-superman. He attempted to fight to the last, and even with Fiume under bombardment by Italian ships was proclaiming that "we belong to another fatherland [than that which undertakes such actions], we believe in heroes."[44] When it was all over and he was about to depart, he reconciled himself by proclaiming that the mantle of immortality would cover all the sacrifices that had been made.[45]

D'Annunzio now increasingly began to stress the sole importance of "the spirit," and the world of myth and symbol retreated into its own universe, separated once again from the reality of politics. He told his *Arditi* in 1922 that "we are an armed militia of faith and the spirit"[46]—and this in face of growing fascist violence against his Legion. The urge to activism was still present, but now it became transformed into a "virile patience,"[47] as he called it. To be sure, an attempted political comeback strengthened such attitudes. D'Annunzio hoped to gain power in Italy by reconciling all factions, by being above the battle, which meant not taking part in it. His mystical view of his own powers blinded him to political reality. Mussolini seized the opportunity shrewdly in order to defeat the potential rival: in 1922, the fascists of Milan praised D'Annunzio's heroism in the war, his belief in victory, but emphasized that he was, above all, "a concrete and luminous manifestation of spirituality." The poet was neutralized and his own vision turned against him.[48] D'Annunzio in the face of fascism practiced his virile patience not without ambivalence. There was always the narcissism, the desire to play a role, which shaded over into an impotent querulousness in his letters to Mussolini. But his contribution to politics had been made by 1921, and I have suggested that it was a vitally important one. The poet's conception of politics was his major contribution to fascism in Italy, and indeed to the advancement of a political style that had grown up during the nineteenth century and that he perfected.

The fact that D'Annunzio was a poet was vital. His poetic vision of the individual and the people was translated into practice. But that he was a poet also proved his fatal weakness: the world was a vision and the drabness of daily politics was excluded. D'Annunzio lost sight of possibilities, seeing only absolutes. Mussolini sensed this when he wrote that D'Annunzio was a man of genius, a man destined for exceptional situations (*ore eccezionali*) and not a man for daily politics.[49] The same could be said about many intellectuals in politics. Subsequent fascist intellectuals shared both his strengths and his weaknesses—they were obsessed with human creativity, the genuine and beautiful. The Nietzschean element remained: ". . . fascism is more than a state, a dynamo."[50] Like D'Annunzio, they combined this with a longing for order and form; but they lacked the opportunity to try out a political liturgy of their own making.

The only other writer who had this opportunity followed a different path. Kurt Eisner led the revolution in Bavaria of November 1918 and ruled for four months (until his assassination on February

21, 1919), a much shorter time than D'Annunzio. Eisner had also imbibed the atmosphere of the fin de siècle and, especially, of expressionism. He too held that the poetic vision was the reality and that the outside world gained reality only when it was suffused with an idea.[51] Eisner believed in true national festivals and became a passionate advocate of the socialist May Day, which, so he held, elected spring itself as its leader—the creator of worlds and the renewer of time.[52] Like D'Annunzio, and at much the same time, he advocated a new theater and saw in art the ennobling link between science and religion. Moreover, Eisner also believed in moral regeneration, the awakening under the open skies of the Godlike in man.[53] But here the similarity ends, for Eisner was no nationalist, nor was he occupied with his own narcissistic self. Instead, he was a Kantian socialist, who believed in the inherent goodness and morality of all men once they were freed from oppression. The poetic vision when it penetrates reality must result in social action. As an Expressionist poet and writer, he shared the ideal that expressionism was a new religion, a liberating action.[54] But the deeds needed to accomplish such liberation were social, inasmuch as the capitalist system had to be abolished. This was far from D'Annunzio's outlook, and gave Eisner the kind of concrete political and economic program the Italian poet had lacked. But it also meant that Eisner's exaltation in festivals and crowds was second to his political and social analysis. Political ritual and a political style could not take the place of praxis.

The crowd could never, for Eisner, become an object of intoxication formed by a master hand because of his belief in the innate goodness of man and man's need to control his own destiny. Eisner did form a crowd into a powerful mass at the start of his revolution, and his charisma as a speaker must have equaled that of D'Annunzio. But the crowd was for him no "mystical body," and he attempted to institute a democratic régime through the use of soldiers and workers' councils (a form of government never even discussed at Fiume). One can only imagine what D'Annunzio would have done with a "festival of the revolution," whereas Eisner simply used the framework of the conventional opera house for a speech. He was never interested in settings. No symbols or myths were created, and those that existed among the working-class movement were hardly used. The poetry of the Kantian socialist was confined to his speeches and to the originality of the placards employed for his official proclamations.

The relationship between poetry and politics was more direct in the works and actions of D'Annunzio than in those of Kurt Eisner. D'Annunzio's legacy was certainly more lasting—in Italian fascism, and indeed in the concept of politics as drama which that movement transmitted into our own time. The new political style served to disguise the absence of true revolutionary change in a time of crisis, but for D'Annunzio and for fascism it did so successfully. Men apparently prefer to participate in a drama rather than to face basic changes in their lives. This was the meaning of the political liturgy which fascism adopted, and which had grown up together with nationalism. A socialist like Eisner, though he was a poet, could not use these devices successfully, and this may have been one handicap from which most socialism suffered in the face of fascism within certain European nations.

Stefan George's ideals of national regeneration were closer to D'Annunzio's, though more restrained as a result of their idealization of Greek form. But the followers of the German poet remained a sect, and the National Socialists drew most of their inspiration from the development of political liturgy as part of the history of German nationalism. Here also the political drama with its rites and setting became the self-representation of the new state and heralded the new man it was supposed to form. Hitler seems to have believed that the Third Reich would survive through a fully formed political liturgy of that nature, for then it would not matter how mediocre his successor turned out to be; the new dictator would simply be a symbol in a cultish setting.[55]

This new politics, as we may call it, transformed the relationship of poetry to politics, and had done so ever since the rise of nineteenth-century nationalism. The poet, as the example of D'Annunzio clearly shows, was no longer solely the creator of verses glorifying the régime or the builder of utopias. Nor was his role merely extended to that of an educator and propagandist of nationalism. He could seize the opportunity to become the creator of a political style that depended upon myth, symbol, and ideals of beauty. The poet, through his vision, was well qualified to shape political liturgy, and in Europe D'Annunzio may well be only the most obvious example. Thus the problem of the poet and the exercise of political power must be analyzed not merely on the basis of actual rule but also through the contributions poets were able to make to the modern political style that fascism illustrated so well. The Frenchman Robert Brasillach was not so far off the mark when he called the fascist leaders he admired "poets of revolution," by which he meant masters of the new politics.[56] Brasillach was typical in the attraction fascism held for him, as for many people, and not just intellectuals. He saw in this movement a revolt of the senses against political philosophy.[57] Fascism too saw itself in this light, and this is why it cannot be evaluated through the criteria of formal political thought.

This very fact gave the poet a meaningful place in the movement, and indeed within all of the new politics as it had grown up during the nineteenth century. The case of D'Annunzio can help to set the signposts for an examination of the relationship between poetry and politics in the modern age. It illustrates one aspect of the relationship; the European avant garde illustrates another. Here there was less room for integration and hardly any for leadership, as the essay in Part II on Fascism and the Avant Garde seeks to show. This relationship cannot be measured merely by an examination of poetry itself, for the changing nature of modern politics was deeply involved. The aesthetics of politics with its rituals and symbols gave the poet a chance to transfer his vision to the exercise of government.

The new politics was not confined to Italy or Germany; it was France that at the fin de siècle used concepts of Caesarism, circuses, and monuments to define an approach to mass democracy which will extend the role played by the poet in the exercise of political power.

SIX

Caesarism, Circuses,
and Monuments

THE MEMORY OF Julius Caesar has faded from the political consciousness of our time. Theodor Mommsen's picture of Caesar as the statesman of genius no longer attracts us. The great ancient historian saw Caesar in the image of a "people's Emperor" who worked for the rebirth of the nation and, we might add, protected private property.[1] This was the Caesar of a national-liberal in Wilhelmine times. Mommsen provides us with a good example of how, even for ancient historians, Caesar and Caesarism became part and parcel of political attitudes which had little connection with the realities of ancient Rome.

Caesarism as a concept is important in modern times because it became shorthand for a new political constellation arising during the nineteenth century. As a result of the French Revolution, political theorists began to distinguish between two kinds of democracy: the rule of representatives and the rule of the masses.[2] The concept of Caesarism became involved with the new importance given to the masses as a political force in the postrevolutionary age. Robert Michels, writing in 1915, explained that, while monarchy is irreconcilable with the principle of democracy, Caesarism may still claim this name if it is based upon the popular will.[3] Whatever may have been the reality of Caesar's life, political theorists were now convinced that his rule was based not on legality and tradition, but had grown out of the will of the people.

A discussion of Caesarism leads necessarily to an analysis of the rise of mass democracy: if not yet within the reality of historical development, then certainly as either a fear or hope in the minds of men concerned with the trend of the politics of their time. New political instruments and new political myths were being forged in order to cope with the new élan of the masses. Here we can only suggest the nature of this new politics with which Caesarism became involved. While some historians were creating their own Caesar, others were lifting the Roman ruler out of historical reality to serve their own purposes. This essay does not attempt to write the history of Caesarism in the nineteenth and twentieth centuries; that has been done to a certain extent in Friedrich Gundolf's books on the subject.[4] Our aim is a much narrower one. We will attempt to illustrate Caesarism as a concept used to clarify the new politics which was coming into being. Historians have often dealt with the rise of the middle classes or the growth of representative government, but less with the nature of mass movements in European history. We can only proceed by a wide variety of examples over a broad time span. The selection of examples may seem arbitrary and episodic, but until more research is available, it seems best to point out some general trends and insights into the subject. Perhaps this will stimulate additional work in this much neglected field of Caesarism, mass movements, and spectacles. Because Caesarism is so much a part of this new politics, we will also have at times to leave the Roman behind us in order to illustrate the political problems and techniques which concerned those who used his name as example.

The German liberal historian Georg Gottfried Gervinus wrote in 1852 that the political movements of his age were supported by the instincts of the masses.[5] At roughly the same time, from a different ideological viewpoint, Count Gobineau attempted to analyze his own civilization, and recoiled with horror from the confrontation of élite and mass which he saw taking place everywhere.[6] The age of mass movements had begun, not as sporadic and spontaneous expressions of the crowd but as a prime factor sustaining political

parties and movements. Contemporaries of Gervinus and Gobineau believed that Europe was entering an age when the leader
would face the masses without the traditional institutions which
could mediate between the government and its people. Such men
saw their nightmare come true in the plebiscitary régime of Napoleon III. Between 1852 and 1854, for example, when Napoleon III
took over and consolidated his power, Pierre Joseph Proudhon
wrote his long and dreary work on Caesarism and Christianity.
"Caesarism" was the word Proudhon used to express his fear of
this new kind of democracy. He saw Napoleon-Caesar as a despot
who maintained his hegemony through corruption, cunning, and
terror. The multitude of people was reduced to an ignorant and
miserable mass.[7]

This was one way of looking at the new political constellation,
and it was shared by Gobineau, who saw in such Caesarism the
inevitable approach, in this case, of racial degeneration. For the
French conservative Charles Maurras at the end of the century, the
matter was still plainer: "The liberties which a hundred years of
Caesarism and Anarchy have made us lose are the liberties that
our forefathers conquered for us in days gone by under the rule of
the house of Capet."[8]

Caesarism became a shorthand term for the new politics. The
Roman ruler exemplified the symbiosis of leader and people which
left no room for traditional institutions or individualism of any
kind. But such confrontation needed its own political techniques to
go beyond the plebiscite as both Napoleons had understood it.
Such techniques became a secular religion within which Caesarism
could play the role of unifying symbol of leadership. It is necessary
for us to examine the creation of these new political instruments in
order to understand how Caesar's image could become so important. Modern terms like "totalitarianism," with which Caesarism is
often associated, are meaningless in this context. Caesarism was
never merely a matter of leader and followers facing each other.
Mass democracy and mass movements were, in this Caesarism,
opposed to representative institutions as the mediating element
between government and governed, but they could not in fact dis-
pense with such devices. The fears which such a mass democracy
engendered were fears about formlessness in political life—it was
an anarchy that demanded form. Spengler, as we shall see, went

directly to Caesarism in order to make this point. But new institutions, different from those associated with parliamentary or corporate representation, came to the fore. Historians have ignored these forms in their emphasis upon the leaders' power and their frequent use of terror and oppression.

In reality, a secular religion mediated between people and leaders, providing at the same time the instrument of social control over the masses. Public festivals are of key importance in any analysis of the nature of such democratic politics. Jean-Jacques Rousseau first put forward a theory of public festivals and stressed their purpose. He invoked the republican festivals of antiquity as the models for uplifting public and private morals. But festivals were supposed to go beyond such moral purposes; they were designed to make the people love the Republic and to ensure the maintenance of order and public peace. Festivals would be a rededication to national unity, but in order to achieve this purpose they had to be filled with symbolisms which would replace those of the Church. The Jacobins put this theory into practice: the tree of liberty, the goddess of reason, and even the early morning rays of the sun, were annexed as concrete symbols for the abstract concept of a Republic of virtue.[9]

These festivals were different from the Roman carnivals that Goethe had praised. Goethe believed that the carnivals were festivals which the people gave to themselves and which were not guided politically from above.[10] But the festivals of Rousseau and the Jacobins had collapsed. It was this tradition which was to survive and continue. Ludwig Friedrich Jahn in Germany advocated such festivals in 1810 as an expression of the new nationalism, and for him also they gave concrete character and direction to the aims of the people as a primeval political force, without any representative intermediaries to help accomplish their purpose. Festivals guided from above were also encouraged during the French Restoration in order to produce an outpouring of monarchical loyalty. But, typically enough, under a hereditary monarchy, the theory of festivals could not develop to its fullest extent.

For example, the court officials in charge of arranging "spectacles" for Charles XII held that such festivals far surpassed those of the ancients, on which they were modeled, for they were able to cater to a wider spectrum of people. They were designed to renew the link between the people and their monarch, and to make them forget, for a short time, the misfortunes and sorrows of the human flesh. Under Charles XII one of the main concerns of those who arranged the festivals was the maintenance of "decency." This concern with decorum during the celebrations was in the forefront, but little is said about the symbolism which was needed to make theory concrete. But then, Claude Ruggieri, Charles XII's pyrotechnist, had a living symbol in the king, though he may have been nowhere in sight.[11] These festivals were popular diversions rather than liturgical rites centered on a national symbol. Here the theory of festivals as part of politics is not yet fully developed; Caesarism required more than the mere maintenance of decency.

Bonet-Maury, a Protestant theologian and church historian during the third French Republic, summed up the development of festivals as instruments of popular democracy. They must lead to virtue and contentment, he said, sentiments with which Rousseau would have agreed. But above all, they must cement the national spirit in a Republic troubled by a weak executive. The liturgical element was uppermost in his mind. Joan of Arc might provide the central figure for such festivals, but so could the tombs of soldiers on Decoration Day.[12] The concrete national symbol was of cardinal importance to the ceremonies, which should be centered on it. Festivals meant emphasis upon national cohesion, not only because of the growth of the national spirit but also because of the fear of political anarchy. Rousseau had already stressed contentment as one of the results which public festivals should produce. The longing to give form to the inchoate "masses" always implied the ideal of stability and order. As we shall see, the idea of Caesarism became involved in this quest.

It is no coincidence that at the same time as Bonet-Maury was writing about festivals in France, the *Sedansfest*, celebrating the German victory over France at Sadowa, was instituted in Germany. Public festivals multiplied at the end of the century. In France, the national fête of July 14 began in 1880 with a ceremony at the statue representing the city of Strasbourg. The memory of France's defeat was to lead a resurgence of the national spirit.[13]

Typically enough, in 1897 German nobles and big business started a "national festival society." The existence of a hereditary emperor was no longer sufficient as a symbol to control the emotions of a people who were being increasingly drawn into political life. Festivals to be given at regular intervals were designed in part to overcome class differences, for people would take part in them regardless of social status. But they were also supposed to concentrate the people's political emotions upon *Reich* and *Volk*. They would stress sports and gymnastics, for many of the festival society's leaders were associated with gymnastic associations (*Turner*), which since the days of Father Jahn had always propagated a national purpose. Typically, also, other members of the festival committee belonged to the Pan-German Association. Once more this was an effort at social control through festivals which would channel the energies of the Volk into a "simple patriotism." According to the society, such a means of social and political control was urgently needed, since the public festival in remembrance of Sedan had not caught on. Indeed, the committee itself referred to Father Jahn's plea for the necessity of such public festivals.[14] Ultimately, however, the attempted creation of a "national festival" was also a failure.

Festivals could not be artificially created as part of the effort to unite the people behind their leaders. It is significant that the secular festivals of the French Revolution collapsed once the leadership had ceased to function effectively. Writing about the French Revolution, Albert Soboul quite rightly distinguished between "imposed cults" like the goddess of reason, and the spontaneous transference of popular religious impulse. As an example of spontaneity, he cited the festival of the martyrs of the revolution, which transposed into the secular realm the pomp and liturgy the Church had lavished on its martyrs.[15] Much later the Nazis promoted such a festival, celebrating the dead in the Hitler *putsch* as symbols of the movement. This distinction was understood quite clearly during the Weimar Republic, which never succeeded in creating successful festivals on its own behalf. Constitution Day was a miserable failure. At that time one writer quite correctly criticized the Republic's inability to symbolize its ideals, to create form out of formlessness. A knowledge of the spirit of the people was lacking.[16] Earlier, Péguy had made a similar criticism of the Third French Republic which, he asserted, was devoid of a mystique.[17]

Republics experienced the greatest difficulties in creating and maintaining institutions which, on the basis of a shared history, tradition, and myth, would cement together a true community. Their community was symbolized instead by Parliament. The advocates of liberal parliamentary government were as opposed to the new politics as were the conservatives whose fears we have cited earlier.

Successful festivals, as Father Jahn had realized, must embody transcendent ideals symbolized by the nation or the movement. They must link themselves with traditions still alive among the people and penetrate the unconscious. The theory behind the successful Nazi festivities is worth recalling in this context. The dedication of party flags by the leader, for example, was designed to provide a symbol penetrating the innermost region of the soul because it activated the desire to do battle.[18] Much earlier, Georges Sorel had already pointed out the importance of such myths in rousing people to action. Lofty moral convictions, he wrote, never depend on reason, but on a state of war in which men voluntarily participate and which finds its expression in well-defined myths.[19] The myth of battle fulfilled this purpose. However, the nature of the myth was not the only ingredient which could ensure a festival's success. Equally central was the conviction that everyone must be involved: there could be only participants and no spectators.

One writer at the beginning of the twentieth century summed this up: the festivals of the *Ancien Régime* were the gift of the sovereign; the plebs of Rome had its *panem et circenses*, but the entire populace is involved in Republican fêtes. He cited as example the "Ode Triomphale de la République" which was staged in 1889. Nine hundred people took part in Augusta Holme's spectacle. They represented all the arts and professions of the times, and in their midst a Marianne, symbolizing the Republic and proclaiming its virtue.[20] Yet, no more than in attempting to create a national monument (as we shall see), did the Third Republic make the breakthrough to truly successful national festivals and symbols.

The climax of the use of this instrument of mass politics comes once again in Nazi Germany. On the Nazi Party's Day of Martyrs, so it was said, every man must himself become a living symbol of the community by carrying the flag and wearing the swastika and the brown shirt.[21] Sorel's theory of the myth of battle was made concrete. We know how great were the numbers who actually participated in the Nuremberg rallies. They were actors in carefully staged liturgical rites, and this was equally true of those who appeared as a soldier or merchant in Augusta Holme's "Ode." It should be added that many of these festivals were connected with ancient folk customs: the summer solstice, the harvest festival, or the gathering of the Germanic *Thing*.

The cult element in these national festivals constituted a new secular religion. They furthered the consciousness of oneness. As Saint-Simon, himself the founder of a secular religion, had asserted: there must be no division between Church and State, God and Caesar.[22] This unity was transposed onto the nation not only through festivals as liturgical rites but also through brick and mortar in national monuments. We are not concerned with monuments to dynasts and princes but with what Thomas Nipperdey has called the national monument of a democratically controlled nation. The political self-representation of the nation, he explained, was expressed through an objectification of the ideal for which that nation claimed to stand. But the ideal made concrete explains itself through symbolisms, and these were for the most part taken from ancient mythology. The gigantic forms which were used to construct such monuments, Nipperdey wrote, were an attempt to anchor the nation in the elemental, the irrational, and the absolute.[23] The goal was to represent the nation as human destiny and as the object of a cult. Much the same could be said about the public festivals.

The heyday of the national monument came after 1870, not only because of the war of that year but also because of the accelerating influence of mass politics. The German national monument on the Niederwald in the Rhineland, for example, was supposed to celebrate the memory of the founding of the German Reich. Completed by 1878, it relied on imitation of the Greeks, now pictured in modern dress. The sword of the huge statue of Germania pointed to the earth, symbolizing the peace which had been achieved. Here also, broad popular participation in the construction of such monuments was of primary importance. The allegorical representations which surrounded the Germania were donated by war veterans' organizations and by German students through collections.[24] Such participation on an even vaster scale facilitated the construction of the most famous German national monument, that of Hermann the German (or Arnim) in the Teutoburger Forest, who had defeated the Roman legions sent to conquer the north. This monument was begun in 1838 through the dedicated efforts of the sculptor Ernst von Bandel. But his work was continually interrupted by lack of funds, and by 1846 the project was virtually abandoned. It was finally saved through a new money-raising effort seventeen years later; in 1863, Bandel wrote to the best student in each German school (Primus) asking for financial support, and got an excellent response. Finally the king of Prussia made a contribution, and after 1870 the Reichstag allocated funds. By the time the monument was finished in 1875, a broad cross section of the population had contributed to the huge figure of Arnim, with his raised sword symbolizing national preparedness. The massive pedestal on which he stood was taken in its turn to symbolize the barbaric power of this conqueror of Rome. Such symbolism parallels Oswald Spengler's Caesarism, which was also interpreted as a symbol of unity, strength, and power. The site of the monument on a hilltop, in the midst of a forest, introduced a romantic note. The German forest became the symbol of the German soul, and the hilltop was supposed to awaken association with the sacred mountains of pagan antiquity. The *Hermannsdenkmal* as a "symbol of our youthful force" had indeed captured the imagination of a large cross section of German youth.[25]

Nipperdey has also seen spontaneous popular expression of feeling at work in the construction of Bismarck towers all over Germany, a token of gratitude to the dismissed chancellor. The appeal for such memorials issued by the German student organization called for the building of towers or columns in direct imitation of the ancient Saxons and Normans, who had erected similar monuments over the graves of their heroes.[26] This too proved successful. In the creation of monuments or festivals, the role of the state was far less important than the Volk and its mystique; the people worshipped themselves and their own myths and symbols. The leaders, whether Arnim or Bismarck, were merely the focal point of the myth. Gustave Le Bon had already summarized in 1895 the theory of leadership which reflected the growth of such cults and faiths: the leader has himself been hypnotized by the ideas whose apostle he has become.[27]

In Le Bon's own country, the Third Republic faced greater difficulties in constructing a mystique for itself. The principal French national monument was the "Triomphe de la République" at the Place de la Nation, constructed by Jules Dalou between 1880 and 1899. It was, in the words of one contemporary, the first time the *"Idée synthétique de la République"* had been expressed with completeness and precision.[28] Like the German monuments, it uses the same classical tradition, the allegories of virtue and work. The Triomphe de la République is crowned by a huge figure of Marianne which could have been a Germania. But here the similarity ends. Marianne has no sword in her hand, nor is she dressed in armor. Peace walks behind her chariot, scattering in her wake fruits and flowers. Liberty pulls the chariot and Marianne is resting on a *fasci* symbolizing the law. The Republic's triumph is a triumph of peace and liberty; Jules Dalou was not a fierce nationalist like Ernst von Bandel, who had made the monument in the Teutoburger Forest his life's work. He was a former communard, a man of working-class origin who abhorred war. His monument was financed by the City Council of Paris and not by a wide segment of the populace. It symbolized not a military triumph but the victory of the Republic over its Boulangist and anti-Dreyfusard enemies. Its inauguration in 1899 was the occasion for a huge Republican demonstration of some 30,000 Parisians, mostly working class.[29]

But Dalou's monument was unable to capture and hold the popular imagination. Here, once more, it is in contrast with the national monuments on the other side of the Rhine. It proved to be the symbol of one part of the nation only; the other part worshipped at the statue of Joan of Arc. Nor did Dalou have much use for history and tradition. As he said about his proposed monument symbolizing the workers of France: "the future has arrived, that is, a form of worship which is destined to replace older mythologies." Typically enough, he sculpted the monument on the tomb of the anarchist Auguste Blanqui free of charge.[30] Apart from Marianne, reminiscent of the French Revolution, his symbols on the Triomphe de la République were contemporary: riches, peace, liberty, labor, and justice—none of them appealed to the historical memory of his audience. But then, the Republic could not very well project itself into the distant past in the manner of ancient Germans, victorious over Rome, or the Bismarck towers.

Dalou's failure documents once more Péguy's stricture that the Republic failed to project a mystique to its people. The German Republic after 1918 was in much the same position. The new political institutions of the age of the masses failed to develop as part of government policy. Such failures lead us back to Caesarism. During the Weimar Republic, the nation seemed fragmented and no instrument of cohesion seemed to be in sight. Some of those who longed for unity and who were aware of the power of the masses turned to Caesarism as a symbol of their hopes and fears. What greater contrast than that between Caesar the popular leader and the supposed degeneration of republican institutions and society? These lacked any compelling symbolism and were unable to focus attention upon a single powerful myth like the nation. But Caesarism, conceived as a theory of leadership set on a mass base, could be used to symbolize the dynamic of "the people" whom the leader both faced and represented in his person. It took its place as the idea of those who wanted to renew Germany. Such appeals to Caesarism came shortly after Germany's defeat in 1918 and the crises of the first years of the Republic. Later on, this symbol would mean little to those mass political parties which had managed to establish themselves.

It was against this background that Oswald Spengler's use of Caesarism was influential. Writing his *Decline of the West* during World War I, Spengler was obsessed with the death of old forms of political and moral life. All institutions, however carefully maintained, were for him destitute of meaning and weight. Caesarism, for Spengler, was that government which is utterly formless, regardless of any constitutional form it might claim. Caesarism seemed to be brute power exercised by a leader devoid of any moral restraints. Such a leader the people were bound to follow; their only role was duty and service. But this Caesar is not merely the feared despot of Gobineau's and Maurras's imagination. Liberties might vanish along with the high ideals of chivalry and honor, but Spengler's Caesar is still a unifying force, the only one that can transcend the decline of the West. This Caesar destroys in order to create.[31]

What he creates is a new kind of unity into which the people can integrate themselves. For Caesar does fill that formless void which at first he symbolizes. His leadership develops the "form filled power of blood and suppression of Megalopolis rationalism." For Spengler, Caesar as the unifying myth represented the same primeval and barbaric force that others saw exemplified in the *Hermannsdenkmal*. Caesarism is the force which manages to destroy existing liberal institutions and to produce a new unity of political form pointing to the future. *The Decline of the West* is, in reality, an apotheosis of the new politics in which masses and leader interact without any intervening quasi-independent institutions. Caesarism, Spengler tells us, "grows on the soil of democracy, but its roots thread deeply into the underground of blood tradition."[32] The leader works upon the most basic instinct of the people, now stripped of higher culture in an age of decline. Indeed, Spengler's Caesar is a pragmatist who knows how to manipulate the masses and to use existing society for the purpose of its own destruction. Ideally the amorphous mass will be integrated into a higher unity through the strong will of the leader who, though also a practical man, is able to activate their deeper longings. Le Bon also believed that such a leader must represent a mixture of activism and faith. His analysis of the crowd and the leader, and Spengler's vision of Caesarism, are both based on the realization that new political forms must supersede old and moribund institutions. To be sure, Spengler's reign of the Caesars opens an era of permanent civil war, murder, and rape, but from it will emerge a higher unity which he continues to characterize (in medieval fashion) as honor, chivalry, inward nobility, and selfless duty.

Many people in the aftermath of the war saw a need for ruthless leadership, but also for symbols and myths (race, in the German case) which could forge a new engine of politics. Soon after Spengler had published his *Decline of the West*, Friedrich Gundolf published his *Caesar* (1924). Here we have another approach to Caesar, coming from a source which Spengler would have thought decadent indeed. Gundolf was the leading disciple of the poet Stefan

George. George wanted to renew the German nation through an ideal of beauty and aesthetic form. His circle was intoxicated with power, but this was the poetic power of the seer who would change the nation through heroic youth, the good and the beautiful. For George, the rebirth of the nation would come from the inner strength of the soul, but this strength was quite different from Spengler's brutal vision. What George called the "secret Germany" labored to transform the nation through an élite of those who understood its meaning. The élite was held together by an eros figure, which even in outward appearance symbolized that aesthetic concern that they attempted to transform into a political force. The content of this aesthetic, this ideal of beauty, was taken from Greece. It was a classical ideal which, on another level of symbolism, we have seen operating as part of the sculpture of national monuments.

Certainly, for all their differences, the George circle shared with Spengler a concept of irrationalism, and of paganism as well. Ancient Germanic myths and Hellenism must form a new unity. For this circle of intellectuals went in for pagan rites which had something of the Dionysian ecstasy about them. Their festivals centered on living and concrete symbols of beauty (such as the boy Maximin) but with a national purpose which gave direction to this "secret Germany." George believed that the festivals of the group must be sacred occasions which, for all their paganism (such as the cult of the sun and beauty), paralleled religious observances. Indeed, by 1902 a firm ritual had developed for the admission of new adepts to the circle. This ceremonial praised a lifestyle and a life rhythm which would cement the community as the secret saviour of the Volk.[33] Such festivals are in the tradition of secret societies, but with their symbolism and their national purpose they also have links with the public festival as a political institution.

Why, then, Gundolf's preoccupation with Caesar? The longing for a leader who, as against parliamentary institutions, would symbolize a powerful myth was once more to the fore. George had also worshipped the heroic, the superman who could arrest decline because he retained the primeval human substance. This was at times defined as a substance of the blood, which derived from pagan mythology, but it was always conceived as a combination of

bodily and inward beauty. Such an individual is the potential saviour of society though society itself seems to ignore him. Caesar
was such a man. His figure, larger than life, had endured in history, and even a powerful ruler like Napoleon I still lived in its
shadow. Caesar symbolized the hero who stood beyond space and
time. It was Friedrich Nietzsche, Gundolf wrote, who broke with
the historicism of his time and reawakened to life the great world
spirits of the past among whom Caesar was the chief representative, resolving the contradictions between Hellenism and the ideal
of chivalry. Caesar becomes the symbol for a unifying force in a
fragmented world. The universal monarchy of Rome led by a
statesman of these dimensions becomes the model for a utopia, reflecting a longing for leadership. Moreover, as Gundolf was careful
to point out, Caesar was the first Roman to be elevated to godhead
not by functionaries, but by the people themselves.[34]

In spite of the historical analysis running throughout Gundolf's
books on that subject, Caesar as a historical figure has been left far
behind. Such, Gundolf writes, "are the great men of history whose
own particular purpose contains the essential ingredient which is
the will of the world spirit." Caesar has here reached his apotheosis as the incarnation of Hegel's world spirit. Gundolf quotes
Hegel himself to this purpose, but in his version Hegel's praise of
Caesar becomes a charter for the future during the Weimar Republic. That Caesar was no poet concerned with the renewal of
Rome through aesthetic concepts was irrelevant; Gundolf avoids
the difficulty by turning once more to Nietzsche, who had also exalted Caesar and fashioned him, as Gundolf puts it, into a "healthy
Zarathustra."[35]

Caesar as a historical figure had been elevated into a powerful
myth. The George circle, with its élitism and its belief in a "secret
Germany," shared with Spengler the longing for a leader in times
when existing systems of government had supposedly become
decadent. The tie between leader and led was a sacred one; the
pagan rituals so popular among the circle symbolized on their aesthetic and intellectual level what public festivals symbolized on the
popular level: a secular religion as the surrogate for traditional political institutions. Ernst Kantorowicz, the historian, himself a
member of the George circle, realized this when he wrote in the

dedicatory epistle to his famous biography of Emperor Frederick II: "interest is now beginning to stir in the figures of great rulers— now, in this age which is so un-emperor-like." [36]

But the age was, in reality, not un-emperor-like at all. The new politics as we have defined them substituted leader and led, festivals and symbols, for the traditional institutions of Europe. Caesar became a symbol for this situation both for those who feared it and for those who longed for unity outside and replacing existing political institutions. The Caesars who arrived in power after 1918 were not the embodiments of Gundolf's hopes, nor were they like Spengler's barbarians. They had to operate within a framework of historical reality, to adjust and to make compromises. But their basic techniques and the politics they exemplified were built upon the control of the masses. Caesarism is indeed a political concept which can be understood only through its involvement with modern mass politics.

SEVEN

The French Right and the
Working Classes: *Les Jaunes*

T HE EUROPEAN RIGHT has of late been receiving increased
attention from historians. The simple stereotypes have given
way to a more sophisticated analysis, which attempts to provide a conceptual framework for rightist thought and action, and
gives us a better understanding of the role of the Right in the
growth of European mass politics and mass democracy in our own
century. There is one aspect of the European Right that needs more
attention, namely, the extent to which it struck roots among the
population generally. Its social structure is usually discussed in
terms of marginal farmers, small shopkeepers, self-employed artisans, underemployed professionals, white-collar workers, and
underpaid civil servants. These are the classes said to be involved
in the counterrevolution, while working-class support is assigned
only to those industries which depended on government subsidies
and tariffs.[1] Such an analysis ignores those nations in which the
lower classes provided the principal support for what came to be
the fascist Right in the twentieth century: the peasants of the Rumanian Iron Guard or the followers of the Hungarian Iron Cross,
41 per cent of whose membership consisted of industrial workers.[2]
But even in the more highly developed industrial countries of
western Europe the Right did attempt to establish relations with

the labor movements, especially the more radical Right which can be called National Socialist.

Efforts to win working-class support began in the last decades of the nineteenth century and reached their first climax at the beginning of the twentieth. In Germany, the National Socialist movement of Friedrich Naumann made such an attempt, but its success was limited. Before World War I it is France, not Germany, that offers the best example of how the Right tried to gain a working-class following and of the success it achieved. Though conservatives were also involved, National Socialists were in the forefront. Their dynamism was due not only to their concern with social questions and their nationalist mystique but also to their anticapitalism, which they equated with anti-Semitism. National Socialists were interested, above all, in national unity, and rejected class war in favor of class collaboration without, however, approving the capitalist and bourgeois order in which they lived. Édouard Drumont (1844–1917) was a key figure in French national socialism, and many would-be French National Socialists in the twentieth century trod in his footsteps.[3] He was one of the most significant figures in the attempt of the French Right to capture the allegiance of the working classes.

For Drumont, the Jewish question was the key to French history. The Semites, mercantile, covetous, scheming, and cunning, were responsible for the existing state of national degeneration. His anti-Semitism, nourished by the Dreyfus affair, was National Socialist because hatred of the Jew was supposed to lead to a justifiable revolt of the oppressed against their oppressors.[4] His newspaper, the *Libre Parole*, was fond of featuring sentimental descriptions of the misery of the working classes.[5] Nor did he stop there. He looked favorably on the French section of the First International because it refused to deal with the corrupt bourgeoisie. His connection with the International and socialism came about through his friend Benôit Malon, a pre-Marxist socialist who was influenced by Proudhon. Malon was a committed anti-Semite and as editor of the *Revue Socialiste* opened its pages to anti-Jewish polemics. It was he who introduced Drumont to the working-class milieu of Paris. "Here," so Drumont himself tells us, "everyone received me well and complimented the author of *La France Juive*."[6]

For Drumont, socialism had become corrupt with the march of

time and the advent of Marxism. The socialist parties themselves were controlled by bourgeois and Jews. The only socialist leader for whom he now had a good word was Jules Guesde. Here was an admirable critic of the mechanism of contemporary society, even if in most respects Guesde was a fanatic who ignored human nature. Clearly, given the existing state of socialism, Drumont had to turn elsewhere if he was to become a part of the workers' movement.

However, like all National Socialists he lacked a coherent economic doctrine: the expulsion of the Jews from French life would lead to social justice, and in this process their property could be confiscated and redistributed among all those who had shared in the struggle. Since he believed that this property was immense, dominating all economic life, the redistribution would entail considerable economic change. Finance capital, which he equated with the property of the Jews, was the adversary for Drumont and for all those of the Right who attempted to organize the working classes. It was the enemy of a true national spirit.

A Boulangist, though the General himself had little use for him, Drumont believed that political change was the essential prerequisite for France's salvation. The Third Republic, dominated by Jews, must be abolished and replaced by a plebiscitary democracy governed by a strong but popularly elected "supreme ruler." Such a ruler, consulting with the people from time to time through a plebiscite, would solve the Jewish problem and create unity on the basis of a powerful national mystique. Not only Jews, but also Freemasons and Protestants would have to vanish from the French scene. Although Drumont respected Catholicism as necessary to national cohesion, he was not himself a devout believer and he despised the French Catholic clergy as weak, unable to fulfill their national function because of their ties to Jewish capital.[7]

These were the guiding ideas of the man who asserted his influence over most attempts of the Right to capture the working classes at the end of the century. He and his paper played an important part in the history of the trade union movement known as *Les Jaunes*. (The union received this name when workers who refused to strike used yellow paper to stop up the windows of their meeting place, which had been smashed by strikers. This happened in 1901 at Montceau-les-Mines.) The kind of nationalism for which this prolific propagandist stood can no longer be considered solely as an intellectual movement. It is impossible to say how many work-ers read and were influenced by Drumont's writings, but in analyz-ing *Les Jaunes* we can to some extent gauge his influence. For Dru-mont and others who shared his views managed, for a few years at least, to reach the working classes and to build up an organized following which at one point exceeded 100,000. To be sure, the effort failed in the end, but its success and failure constitute an im-portant chapter in the history of the French Right, for it did man-age to cross the class barriers that usually surrounded it in the in-dustrialized West.

The movement known as *Les Jaunes* has only begun to find its modern historian. It may seem ironic that such a movement exist-ed in France, which avoided the collapse of its Republic, whereas in Germany, where the Republic was eventually to collapse, no such workers' movement ever came into being. Recent research into Boulangism has paved the way for a better understanding of this trade union movement. General Boulanger can no longer be seen simply as a reactionary who wanted to destroy the Third Re-public. Though his movement was diverse, including royalists and reactionaries of many shades, some of its more lasting support came from men and women who desired a more fundamental so-cial reform, who were both socialist and nationalist, supporting a strong man who would respond to the longing for social change. Paris working-class districts had consistently voted for the Gen-eral, and a solid block of lower-class voters remained loyal even when the General himself had taken refuge in Brussels.[8]

The Boulangist movement was a preparation for what was to come. Most Boulangist deputies who outlasted the defection of the General and continued to vote as a political block had joined the socialists by 1892.[9] Besides these, there were others who had earlier joined "La Boulange," but who opposed the socialists and attempt-ed to build up a rightist workers' movement even before *Les Jaunes* came on the scene. These were men whose nationalism proved stronger and more extreme than that of Alfred Naquet or Georges Laguerre, future collectivists and socialists who had played a cen-tral part in the General's adventure.

Drumont himself now tried his hand at founding a workers' or-ganization. In 1890 he established the *Ligue Anti-Sémite*, a direct outgrowth of the attempt to continue a Boulangism that had collapsed in the Paris municipal elections of that same year. Drumont proclaimed the need for new trade unions, which would expropriate financial monopolies and by means of the credit give everyone a chance to become "exploiters." Hundreds of thousands of pamphlets were printed and the railway workers, in particular, were approached for support.[10] But where Paul Lenoir was to have some success with railway workers a decade later, Drumont failed miserably. While the League claimed attendances of some two hundred at ordinary meetings, the truth was different; between twenty-five and forty people were probably all it could raise on a regular basis. The most consistent working-class members were the butchers from the Paris district of La Villette, who were hired to provide security for League meetings.[11] By the mid-1890s the League was dead, or rather taken over by Jules Guérin, an associate of Drumont. He attempted more militancy, and indeed supported some strikes; but the constituency he attracted—like Drumont's—came essentially from bourgeois and clerical circles. The police may well be correct in maintaining that never more than 1,500 people altogether belonged to Drumont's and Guérin's League.[12]

It should be added that anarchists moved in and out of these workers' organizations. The spirit of revolt was in the air at the turn of the century; many men desired to break the fetters of a system that seemed to have reached an impasse. The spirit could be disciplined and controlled by socialist parties and even by syndicalism, but for the National Socialists a chaotic urge for overt violence against the Establishment was never far beneath the surface. As Drumont himself put it in 1886: "As late as 1871 I still believed that society deserved defending. Which institution, which social class is still worth defending today? The Jews," he continued, "were protected by the Freemasons [read Republic] but the workingman is shot for simply wanting to gain a few sous with which to buy bread."[13]

Though we have no membership figures, Paulin Méry's attempt to form a workingmen's organization was more important than the abortive efforts of the anti-Semitic leagues. It represents another attempt by the Right to establish links with the working classes out of which *Les Jaunes* arose. Méry (1860–1899) himself belonged to the circle of Drumont and Guérin, and like them was a former supporter of Boulanger. His *Ligue pour la défense du travail national* (1894) attacked monopoly capitalism and the Jews, while advocating a Boulangist program of plebiscites and presidential rule. Méry supported trade unionism and the *bourses du travail*. Above all, he was interested in the establishment of workers' pension funds and job security through insurance schemes. In these proposals, which he embodied in a manifesto of 1893, he was typical of the National Socialist Right.[14] Méry aligned his organization with Drumont on the one hand, and on the other with those dissident Blanquists who, drawn into the Boulangist movement, had become nationalists rather than revolutionaries.

Méry's League was not averse to industrial action, and on more than one occasion gave financial support to strikers. Together with former followers of Blanqui and Henri Rochefort, editor of *L'Intransigeant*, Méry showed special enthusiasm for the effort of the Carmaux glass workers to start their own factory: "*Verrierie aux Verriers.*" In the eyes of the police, this came close to revolutionary action against the employers.[15] Méry likened the employers to medieval lords who exploited their serfs, and equated them with cosmopolitan Jews—true Frenchmen would not act in such a way against their compatriots. He also advocated a "patriotic anticlericalism," often appearing side by side with Drumont and the marquis de Morès, who shared his anticapitalist anti-Semitism.[16]

The marquis de Morès (1858–1896) might be described as a one-man National Socialist movement. Though Drumont broke with him shortly before Morès's death, he was until then one of the closest allies and personal friends of the editor of *Libre Parole*. Drumont encouraged and took an active part in the marquis's many working-class ventures. For example, Morès was active, and indeed dominant, in the Paris coachmen's strike of 1892, which he supported financially. The coachmen themselves were at first wary of this adventurer, not long returned from North Dakota and married to a rich banker's daughter, who proclaimed that the Jews and the house of Rothschild were responsible for all exploitation. He was also active in several more strikes, so that the Paris police believed that the violent strike of food handlers in 1892 was fomented by "the followers of Morès."[17] This was the most serious side of his activities; he gained a devoted following among the butchers of

La Villette, many of whom became his own private army, hired at fixed rates to take part in street demonstrations. In working-class quarters of Paris he opened *bistros* where, in return for cheap drinks, the workers had to listen to his propaganda; this, in addition to anti-Semitism, stressed the marquis's obsessive concern with a *Crédit ouvrier* constituted by workers' pensions funds and providing credit without security, a scheme which he advocated in his speeches to the striking coachmen for whose daily bread he was paying.[18]

There seems little doubt that Morès also associated with some anarchists, financed one of their journals, and exhorted them to ever greater violence. For his own schemes were only part of a design to overthrow the existing order: for a *"revanche du Boulangisme,"* as he told Henri Rochefort in 1892.[19] He was not without organizational talent, as he had demonstrated earlier in his career when he tried to supply New Yorkers with meat direct from his North Dakota ranch, excluding all middlemen.[20] But his attempts to make inroads into the workers' movement were only sporadically successful, although they count among the precursors of *Les Jaunes*, the more so as Drumont applauded and supported them.

Men like Morès and Méry, and dissident Blanquists such as Ernest Roche, joined with political adventurers like Henri Rochefort in supporting strikes one day and depositing wreaths at the statue of Joan of Arc the next. The Blanquists had a revolutionary past; they had taken a leading part in the Paris Commune and had suffered for it. But largely through the Boulangist experience, they had moved to the Right without shedding their Jacobinism. Ernest Henri Granger, one of Blanqui's closest friends, led many of his followers into national socialism after the master's death. It was Blanqui's lack of interest in the everyday economic demands of the workers and his flirtation with anti-Semitism that explain their rightist deviation.[21]

Granger now accepted office in the *Ligue des patriotes*, with which Rochefort was also associated. They continued to support strikes and talked about the overthrow of the Republic. By the end of the century, Ernest Roche had become the real leader of these Blanquists and, while still calling for workers' solidarity, introduced an ever more strident nationalism into the movement. They, and even Rochefort, had come to share the political ideas of Drumont.[22] This section of the Right did not live in middle-class or petit bourgeois isolation, but made a genuine attempt to influence the working classes; not by standing aloof and theorizing (as Charles Maurras was apt to do) but by joining in their struggle. They did not want to make a socialist revolution; their program went no further than support for trade unionism, job security, and schemes for producer cooperatives. Yet they also wanted to overthrow the Republic for their own Boulangist ends. They envisaged a plebiscitary democracy with a strong authoritarian executive. The workers would have security and a chance to become proprietors with a stake in the country. Industry would have to accept the principle of collective bargaining. In these respects their program foreshadowed the social reformism of the 1930s, as embodied in the program of Jacques Doriot's *Parti Populaire Française*. The new society built upon national harmony would exclude foreigners and Jews, and this in itself, it was thought, would solve many of France's problems. Both Méry and Morès were dead by the time the new century opened, but the tradition they had established contributed to the formation of *Les Jaunes*.

The immediate occasion for the founding of *Les Jaunes* was the decree of July 17, 1900, establishing an administrative council for the *Bourses de travail* with the power to recognize or expel unions. Immediately the Bourse in Paris expelled unions suspected of moderation and among them that of the railway workers. Paul Lenoir, its secretary, founded *Les Jaunes* in 1901. An independent *Bourse de travail* for *Les Jaunes* was inaugurated on January 3, 1902, vowing never to yield to force.[23] Watching the event from afar, Jules Guesde thought this was merely a continuation of Méry's League;[24] he was to be disabused of this notion and to find himself faced with a more formidable rival.

From the start it formed a loose alliance with stronger and richer rightist organizations. The new movement needed finance, and this Lenoir obtained first from the conservative *Ligue de la Patrie Française*.[25] This League, seeing in patriotism a faith that would revitalize the religious spirit, attempted to imbue all classes of the population, including workers, with its own nationalist mystique.[26] In reality, it was a body of rich bourgeois, intellectuals, and journalists whose patriotism was nourished by their anti-Dreyfusard experience. Drumont initially supported this League, though later he found it insufficiently militant.

Among those attending the first congress of *Les Jaunes* (1905) were representatives of *Syndicats agricoles*. These unions were organizations of farm workers and peasants controlled by large landowners, and strongly paternalistic and religious in character.[27] Lenoir was undoubtedly grateful for their support, which had been provided long before the congress, though he himself regarded the English trade unions as the model to be imitated. As a republican he had little interest in activities directed against the Establishment, and this may well have lost him the leadership of the new movement in 1903; his gradualism could easily become a stifling conservatism, the more so as important industrialists like Gaston Japy from the north came to play an important part in union affairs.[28]

Pierre Biétry, his associate and successor, an earlier version of Jacques Doriot, had started his career as a revolutionary socialist, active in the wave of strikes which extended from 1898 to 1901. Indeed, he had led an unsuccessful march of workers on Paris in 1899, but immediately thereafter broke with his former friends and joined the Right. The reason for his break with socialism seems to have been his opposition to the concept of a general strike. To this must be added disillusionment with the failure of the strike movement. He became strongly hostile to the revolutionary socialist leadership, which according to him had captured the French unions, a development he attributed to the individualistic and liberal attitude of the employers. They had destroyed the ancient corporations that had united workers and employers before the French Revolution and had been independent of the state. As the leader of *Les Jaunes*, he advocated a nonpolitical trade unionism whose model he, like Lenoir, saw in the English trade union movement, and in the German Hirsch-Duncker unions and the Knights of Labor in the United States. By nonpolitical he meant unions not at the service of republican politicians or of the state but collaborating with the employers in collective bargaining; the right to strike was not to be contested, but the "entente cordiale" between workers and employers came first; the strike was only a weapon of last resort. What was needed was not socialists and their dreams, but men of the "métier" who would negotiate about the legitimate grievance of the workers. In this manner, workers and employers would constitute a harmonious and self-policing group independent of the state. Paradoxically, his appeal for a nonpolitical position was combined with violent hostility to the existing régime, a creature of "speculative capital" which had to be destroyed; he carefully distinguished such capital from the "working capital" of the factory owners in which, through profit-sharing, the workers could have a part. Biétry adopted the anti-Semitic anticapitalism of Drumont in his fight against the Republic, and this became an integral feature of his union. This was the man who led Les Jaunes and who had already shown an interest in Méry's organization, though he was now anxious about what it might become after Méry's death.[29]

After Lenoir had been forced out of the leadership, the membership of Les Jaunes declined, but only for a short time. The police believed that Biétry's election as deputy for Brest in 1906 made his union more attractive. The membership fell below 100,000 at the time of the break, but soon rose again to above or around that number of workers.[30] Biétry was able to consolidate the support of the Ligue de la Patrie Française and of the agricultural unions. Indeed, conservative support was eager and forthcoming. The aged royalist duchesse d'Uzès, who had helped to finance the Boulangist movement over a decade earlier, gave money to Biétry.[31] But this respectable conservative support was balanced by others who came from a more activist tradition, closer to that of Méry's movement and the Boulangist Left.

Henri Rochefort and his Intransigeant also gave support, for he was always on the lookout for movements that were both patriotic and Jacobin. Those Blanquists who had followed Ernest Henri Granger into the Boulanger camp, too, were eager to support a workers' movement that seemed to embody their ideals. Most important was the support of Paul Déroulède and his Ligue des patriotes, for this was a mass movement whose street riots the police feared even as late as 1908.[32] Déroulède's followers were soldiers in the service of an anti-German patriotism and did not shrink from the use of violence against the Republic. Such allies fitted in with the tradition of National Socialist workers' movements and were in constant conflict with the "respectable" patriots of organizations like the Ligue de la Patrie Française. The nature of the aid these organizations actually gave Biétry is not easy to determine. They held many meetings where their leaders spoke favorably of *Les Jaunes*, and sometimes sponsored the formation of branches in factories. It seems highly probable that donations were also made, though this cannot be proved. The Action Française apparently decided to offer Biétry its patronage, and provided funds from time to time. But the support of the Action Française was withdrawn when it found it could not dominate Biétry's organization.[33] In fact, the Action Française never made an effective impact on the workers' movement.

Biétry had other friends as well. His hatred of Jews and Freemasons brought both anti-Semitic groups and the *Ligue Antimasonique* into the fold. Above all, it won him the lasting friendship of Drumont, and this became one of the most important influences upon *Les Jaunes*. Biétry accepted Drumont's contention that the workers were exploited not so much by their employers as by the Jews who fomented Freemasonry and revolution. Freemasonry was synonymous with the Republic and therefore Freemasons personified corrupt politicians. For Drumont the *"solution plebiscitaire"* was a precondition for the solution of the Jewish question; he explicitly rejected monarchism as a form of government—which the country in any case would not accept.[34] Here, too, Biétry followed his friend, and the break with the Action Française may not have been as one-sided as historians of the royalist movement have pictured it. Drumont's anti-Semitic anticapitalism displaced Biétry's earlier socialism, but the association between the two went beyond their shared ideas. Biétry's co-administrator in the union, Louis Verdoz, was a close associate of Drumont and a regular contributor to *Libre Parole*. Biétry, too, was a frequent contributor, while eulogies of Drumont were common at meetings of *Les Jaunes*. Drumont also supplied the union with at least one effective national organizer. It is not surprising that Biétry took a leading position in Drumont's *Fédération anti-Juive* when this was founded in 1905.[35] While the ideology of the *Ligue de la Patrie Française* and even Déroulède's *Ligue des patriotes* was often vague and rhetorical, Biétry found in Drumont an ally whose position was carefully worked out and whose commitment to it was total.

At first the conservative influence upon the union was less important in practice than that of the more militant and national socialist organization. The Catholic social theorist Count Albert de Mun, who looked to a feudal, conservative restructuring of society, was at first under the impression that *Les Jaunes* shared his ideas, and hoped that they might become a channel for the diffusion of conservative Catholic social thought. The Paris police wondered whether the union would not have great difficulty in ridding itself of reactionary connections.[36] The speculation was premature, though it was to come true later.

The activism of the National Socialist Right always reflected a traditional image of the working class. For all their commitment to trade unionism as a force independent of the employer, and their advocacy of social reform which at times involved them in strike action, they regarded the working classes in preindustrial terms: the worker must represent an ideal which, thanks to "reds," Jews, and Freemasons, was disappearing from the modern world. Biétry had praised the corporations of the *Ancien Régime*—he believed they had been controlled jointly by workers and employers. Liberalism and socialism had destroyed this harmony. It was only logical that he should view the worker as an artisan with pride in his work and dedication to his task. This ideal workingman is best expressed in the union's literature, especially in the novels (which it may have actually commissioned in order to spread its ideals abroad). In *Les Camarades Jaunes* (1902) by Auguste Geoffroy, a prolific author of popular romances, the ideal worker dominates: a family man, a patriot, a man who loves order. By contrast, the "reds" take bribes from German and French traitors in order to stir up strikes without cause and destroy free competition. The young worker-hero of the book does not want to give up the right to strike but only to avoid unnecessary strikes fomented by foreigners and reds. The interests of the fatherland must come first, and the sins of one employer must not be held against his brethren. The possibility of industrial action is admitted, but the ideal worker symbolizes the preindustrial and traditionalist view of his class. Small wonder that the hero is happiest when he has accumulated enough money to buy a house and garden.

Leon Barracand's *Amour Oblige* (1909), another novel about *Les Jaunes*, paints a still more traditional picture, in which religion and brotherly love are more important than the class struggle. A for-

mer worker becomes an employer and shows that not all employers have hearts of stone. Barracand argues that all strikes lead to
violence. In the novel this is demonstrated when on the one hand
a good employer is murdered, while on the other, by way of ret-
ribution, the leaders of the strike are killed. The ideal is once more
the propertied worker who becomes "associated" in the employer's enterprise. (In Germany, too, the Right regarded the worker in
this light; he is seen as rooted in the native soil and endowed with
all the traditional virtues of sobriety, orderliness, and devotion to
family, virtues and hierarchies that were dissolving in modernity.)
Yet he was an industrial worker and therefore the possibility of industrial action had to be built into the picture and the sovereignty
of capital restricted in order to allow for profit-sharing, job security, pension funds, and free credit. The unity of the nation forbade
exploitation which would destroy national harmony. Rightist trade
unionism was an integral part of the national mystique. Déroulède,
for example, had himself pictured in a comic strip surrounded by
loyal workingmen toasting the fatherland.[37] For Drumont, in turn,
the workers, once more conceived as artisans, symbolized all that
had remained pure and uncorrupt in France. He blamed the horrors
of the Commune upon the bourgeoisie, the people of the Latin
Quarter, and the conservatives who suppressed it. Throughout this
episode, he contended, the workers themselves had shown moderation, they "remained human—that is to say French."[38] Thus the
ideal worker symbolized the nation.

Such a vision of the working classes made the National Socialists
doubly keen to enlist them on their side. In *Les Jaunes* tens of thousands of workers proved responsive to the call. But the novels
themselves omit one factor which, as we have seen, played a cardinal role in the life of the union: the combination of anti-Semitism
and opposition to the Establishment. The latter is present indi-
rectly in *Les Camarades Jaunes*, for it is the reds who receive government support and not the patriotic *Jaunes*. The Republic is in alliance with the reds and foreigners, though nothing is said about
the Jewish capitalist conspiracy of exploiters so dear to the hearts
of Biétry and Drumont. Yet it is clear from the meetings of *Les Jaunes* that it was this conspiracy which gave the movement its dynamism. However, unlike "La Boulange," these National Socialist
workers' movements had coherent social programs and empha-

sized the necessity of workers' solidarity through unions. They were a mixture of the old and the new, and their problem was to hold the balance between the real dilemmas that workers faced in the twentieth century and the traditional image of the workers rooted in an equally traditional fatherland.

Unionism was not usually a part of the preindustrial image of the worker. While setting out to be a trade union independent of the employers, *Les Jaunes* condemned the socialists as *"les messieurs de la gréviculture internationale,"* and opposed their own *"armée du travail"* to the red *"armée de désordre."* They wanted collaboration with the employer on terms which National Socialists had always advocated: insurance systems providing job security, interest-free credit, and pensions. These arrangements would be controlled by the workers themselves through the union. Under the influence of Japy, who had instituted profit-sharing in his factory of some 8,000 employees, *Les Jaunes* added this to their demands. The idea of transforming workers into little capitalists by giving them a share in the enterprise in which they worked had been advanced earlier by the Boulangist Left. Through profit-sharing the worker would become a proprietor and settle into that house and garden which had given Geoffroy's worker so much satisfaction. The *Jeunesse Propriétiste de France*, annexed by Biétry as an auxiliary to *Les Jaunes*, called for national reconciliation of all classes as symbolized by Joan of Arc: to make this reconciliation possible, all Frenchmen must become property owners (though it is difficult to view Joan of Arc as a *propriétaire*). The ubiquitous Henri Rochefort had his hand in this as well.[39]

Strikes were not excluded from the program of *Les Jaunes*, but they would have to be preceded by fifteen days notice to the employer to give him the chance to meet the union's terms. Compared to the tactics of the other French unions, this struck a moderate note, and it is small wonder that we find presidents of Chambers of Commerce and industrialists addressing meetings of *Les Jaunes*.[40]

The union was organized in local and regional federations, with the real power remaining in Biétry's hands. In the federations, as a concession to modernity, employers and workers were organized separately, since it was no longer possible to unite employers and workers in one body, as had been the case before the Revolution: each now bargained with the other as a separate group, but the two were linked through the federation itself. Sharing with the French Right as a whole a belief in the virtues of regional autonomy, Biétry used this as an excuse to condemn the agitation for the eight-hour day by the socialists. Such matters should be settled regionally, through collective bargaining, without state interference and with an eye on foreign competition.[41]

Union membership was extremely diverse, as the lists preserved in the police archives and the notices in *Le Jaune* show: butchers in Paris, textile workers in Lille, and weavers in Albi. In 1904 *Le Jaune*, the union's newspaper, listed the concerns in which their following was strongest: gas companies, omnibus companies, trash collection agencies, laundries, and commercial institutions. The predominance of municipal employees in this list is misleading, for among the union's adherents there were a considerable number of industrial workers.[42] Commercial employees would ordinarily be attracted to a union of this kind. (In Germany they were the backbone of a nationalist and anti-Semitic union whose outlook was far more moderate than that of *Les Jaunes*.) But they would not be found in the company of industrial workers.

No doubt many were drawn into *Les Jaunes* and left the other unions because of the failure of the wave of strikes referred to earlier. Like Biétry, many workers must have been disillusioned and hence ripe for recruitment by a new and different labor organization. Moreover, they had little choice, for French unions were syndicalist, with a built-in revolutionary *élan*. Their revolutionary pretensions probably went further than was justified by the attitude of the workers themselves, whose demands on the employers were rarely revolutionary. Unlike Germany, France did not have unions linked to a Social Democratic Party which despite its Marxist rhetoric acted with discipline and moderation. Disillusionment with syndicalist militancy and the radical nature of French unionism provided *Les Jaunes* with many recruits. At Carmaux, for example, a branch was started in 1900 by miners opposed to a strike against the company. However, some local branches were formed through insurance and credit schemes that the workers had begun among themselves in the factories. *Les Jaunes* not only encouraged such schemes but helped in their management, something other unions neglected.

The greatest attraction *Les Jaunes* held for the workers was probably its emphasis upon the transformation of workers into property owners, even if they continued to work in a factory. The support which the union gave to credit and profit-sharing plans was a part of this drive, appealing to social theories such as Saint-Simonism.[43] Workers were eager to accept the idealized picture of themselves as artisans and small proprietors. Industrialism made such hopes vain, but it took a long time for the workers to accept this fact, and some of them were drawn to the National Socialist Right in the hope that their status as proletarians in a capitalist society could be avoided.

At the head of their newspaper, *Les Jaunes* put the slogan: "Proletarians of France Unite." How many did unite under this particular banner? Membership figures given by an organization itself are not necessarily reliable, and those given by the police must also be used with caution. August Pawlowski, a commentator favorable to the union, tells us that by 1904 some 323,000 workers were organized in 204 individual unions and 20 regional federations. By 1906 his figures had dropped to 200,000, to rise again to 375,000 by 1907.[44] These figures are repeated by a recent bibliographer of French syndicalism.[45] They correspond to the union's membership claims, but the figures given by the police cut them by about one-half; they estimated the membership in 1906 at less than 100,000.[46] If we turn to a different source, the circulation of *Le Jaune*, Pawlowski's figures become still more questionable. In 1905, for example, the paper tells us that it had sold only up to 8,000 copies recently but that now it had increased to a run of 20,000.[47] This seems an astonishingly small sale for a claimed membership of well over 300,000. Clearly, unreliability is written large on all these circulation and membership figures.

Les Jaunes did not boast the militancy of a Méry or a Morès, but they did on occasion strike. In 1906, for example, they organized a strike for higher wages among the weavers of Albi, and at another factory whose owner had to call in the police. That same year Biétry himself was accused of encouraging a series of strikes in Brest. The strikes which *Les Jaunes* supported were rationalized in terms of their ideology. For example, they supported a strike by postmen in 1909 on the ground that workers deserved a share of capital which was denied them. For similar reasons, they joined with "red" unions in constant agitation for higher wages and better pension funds against the Carmaux mining company. Indeed, there they joined in strike action in 1912 and 1914, but, typically enough, these strikes were directed not at the company but at the government. They were meant to press the Chamber of Deputies into establishing an autonomous miners pension fund. *Les Jaunes* were always ready to harass the government of the Republic. There is some evidence that at times the membership got out of hand. During a textile workers' strike at Lille in 1909, the local *Jaunes* collaborated with the "reds." Biétry objected on the ground that the fifteen-day cooling off period had not been kept and, therefore, the charter of *Les Jaunes* had been violated.[48]

For Biétry, the nationalist and anti-Semitic components of his thought began to take on greater dimensions than industrial militancy. The fight against an evil Republic must take precedence. As he put it: "It is better to unite with employers against the politicians, than with the politicians against the employers."[49] *Le Jaune* featured the slogan: "Socialism is the exploitation of the people by bourgeois politicians," in this maintaining the Boulangist and anti-Dreyfusard tradition of a full-scale attack on the "rascals" who ruled France, a platform which once had served to unite an important segment of the population. *Les Jaunes* put such militancy to good use. For example, they participated with other groups of the Right in the Sorbonne riots of 1908.[50] These were directed against a professor who had supposedly insulted the memory of Joan of Arc. It was always easier for the union to join in militant political action than in industrial action directed against the bosses.

During the Boulangist episode, a precarious balance had been maintained between nationalism and the urge for social action, and this continued to be the case during the time of Méry and Morès. But after the failure of the radical unions in strike action it was perhaps no longer necessary to keep up such militancy in order to capture a part of the working class. National harmony as a prerequisite to overthrowing the Third Republic was more important than sustained militancy against the employers.

It was at this time that the anti-Semitic nationalism and opposition to monopoly capitalism preached by Drumont in his *Libre Parole* won a new and large audience among the working class, although some of *Les Jaunes* were thought by the police to have rejected this kind of anti-Semitism.[51] It is certainly true that this closer association with rightist politics came in for criticism. Biétry's abrasive personality may have added fuel to the dispute whether the union should take part in actions which lay outside the trade union sphere. Some members apparently took Biétry's advocacy of a nonpolitical trade unionism seriously and refused to follow the call to put an end to the existing régime. After all, neither the English trade unions nor the Knights of Labor combined collective bargaining with a call to political revolution. Les Jaunes, as we have seen, had joined in riots directed against the Republic. But when in 1908 Biétry lost his position as leader, his political program was retained and Les Jaunes continued to join in anti-republican street action.[52] The counterweight to such violence was provided by friendly organizations like the agricultural unions and the Ligue de la Patrie Française, deeply Catholic and conservative in character. At first Lenoir had called for the separation of Church and State, and even in 1904, Les Jaunes still denounced "Christian democrats" for fighting against their union and not against the socialists. Drumont himself, an admirer of Lamennais, condemned the Catholic Establishment for not extending its hand to the working classes, and the Christian Socialists for advocating charity without attempting to change the social system. Such opinions by men central to the leadership of Les Jaunes did not stop the police from speculating, in 1904, that Biétry might have difficulty in shedding the forces of reaction which threatened to paralyze the union. But by 1906, according to the police, there was undeniable clerical support for Les Jaunes, as well as an alliance between the union and the provincial clerical press.[53]

It was of significance in this regard that Paul de Cassagnac, whom Drumont had condemned for his inhumanity toward the poor, frequently accompanied Biétry on his visits to provincial union locals. Cassagnac was a reactionary Catholic in opposition to the ralliement of Pope Leo XIII, and a close associate of the royalist Baron Armand de Mackau. He owned the newspaper L'Autorité, and in the Chamber defended both the Ligue des patriotes and Drumont's Libre Parole against attacks from the Left and Center. Though he died in 1904, the influence of his circle strengthened a clerical and conservative trend in the union which rivaled that of the National Socialists and finally gained the upper hand. Drumont himself in those years made a half-hearted alliance with conservative Catholic forces.[54]

It is difficult to untangle the network of organizations and personal relationships which entered into every one of the ventures we have discussed. We are dealing with a closed circle of movements and personalities. Conservatives like de Cassagnac and others interacted with National Socialists like Biétry or Drumont. Sometimes we find them acting in concert, as during the birth of *Les Jaunes*; then they begin to quarrel and ideological differences become intertwined with personal rivalries. All these men had something of the cussedness of a Morès about them: lack of lasting success made them sectarians who lived by their momentary successes in Boulangism, the anti-Dreyfus movement, and perhaps *Les Jaunes*.

Within the union, the conservatives and their clerical supporters became ever more important. Militancy did not cease, but by 1908 at the latest, it was increasingly directed toward political rather than industrial action, and this must have deprived the union itself of much legitimacy in the eyes of the workers. But even political militancy was probably on the decline. Déroulède's League, always ready for street action, was by the time a faltering organization. Relations with the Action Française had been broken, and its activist royalist youth organization, the *Camelots du Roi*, could not fill the breach. It did collaborate with *Les Jaunes* in the Sorbonne riots, but such cooperation seems to have been sporadic at best. Biétry may have associated with some royalists, but neither he nor Drumont regarded royalism as a popular issue; they wanted a strong man, but not a king.[55]

The failure of the strikes at the end of the century was by now long forgotten, and for all Biétry's and Japy's efforts, the workers were not becoming proprietors and profit-sharing remained a rarity, while *Les Jaunes* became less and less militant. Moreover, the union was constantly handicapped by its ambivalent relationship to the employers. Many employers at first gave the union financial support, only to become disillusioned when *Les Jaunes* pressed their demands for better working conditions. The union's ideal of class collaboration was undermined by the needs of the workers on the one hand and by the anti-unionism of the employers on the other. The CGT was not handicapped in this way. During the first decade of the century, the unions were becoming more moderate, shedding much of their radical vocabulary while improving their organization. *Les Jaunes* were becoming superfluous through changes in trade unionism.[56] The fact that rank-and-file members collaborated with "reds" against the wishes of the leadership in the textile workers strike at Lille in 1909 may have been symptomatic of the union's decline, which must have been fairly rapid after 1908. It continued in existence until the outbreak of war, but was not heard of again after 1914. *Les Jaunes* died almost forgotten, as did Biétry himself and, for that matter, Drumont.

In its time the success of *Les Jaunes* was observed with great interest across the Rhine. The German *Gelbe* were started in 1905 among the metalworkers of Augsburg. Whether their founding was a direct response to the French union has been a matter of debate;[57] but it is certain that the French example was analyzed and discussed almost immediately, for France was regarded as the classical land of yellow trade unionism. However, the *Gelben* never adopted the anti-Semitism of *Les Jaunes* or its political activism, allying themselves with the National Liberal Party. They proceeded to encourage strikebreaking and sang the praises of unfettered free enterprise. These unions were either straightforward company unions or patriotic workers' organizations. By 1908, they had reached a membership of some 40–50,000. Their industrial action was restricted to forming savings societies and praising Japy's profit-sharing schemes. This was too mild for *Les Jaunes*, which accused them of failing to compete with socialism.[58] But in Germany, with its strong social democratic movement, this was no easy matter.

The German experiment was shortlived, but it holds some interest, for it shows what *Les Jaunes* might have become, since the same tendencies were certainly present in the French union. But *Les Jaunes* were unwilling to travel this road, and concluded in the end that the *Gelbe* were simply "anti-union." Before and even during its decline *Les Jaunes* maintained a greater distance from the employers, advocated a more extensive social program, and showed greater militancy, however misplaced. Biétry himself tried to organize unions in Switzerland and in Russia as well, without success: at least there is little evidence that they amounted to a workers' movement.[59]

Les Jaunes may well provide the most important example of a working-class movement of the Right before World War I. Thereafter the focus shifts dramatically. France never again witnessed such a large workers' movement tied to the Right. The attempt by Georges Valois in the 1920s was on a minute scale, and the Action Française had no better luck. Not until the movement led by Jacques Doriot in the thirties do we get working-class support integrated into another rightist movement. The workers in Doriot's party were accused of forming "yellow" unions, but in number and importance they could hardly compete with the *Jaunes* of an earlier day.

In Germany, the tradition which *Les Jaunes* symbolized was continued after World War I, but in a more effective direction. We know relatively little about the actual adherence of workers to the National Socialists and other sections of the radical Right. But like Lenoir's organization, the original Nazi Party was composed of a nucleus of railway workers, and many of its ideas were first expressed by working-class groups in Austria and Bohemia. Hitler gave these ideas middle-class respectability and won a vast middle-class following. *Les Jaunes* also had middle-class as well as *haut bourgeois* support, but they could not maintain it or channel it into an effective political movement. Hitler did achieve this, but it is not known how many workers he lost or gained in the process.

Research into the relationship between the Right and the working classes has not yet gone very far, but it seems clear that we can no longer make simplistic equations between the European Right and the hardpressed middle classes or petit bourgeoisie. They provided a grateful audience in some, but by no means all, regions of Europe. It sometimes seems as if the anxiety Europeans felt about the new world that industrialism had created was confined to a particular social stratum, which rushed into the arms of the Right. But workers may well have felt the same sort of anxiety and been attracted to the mixture of preindustrial nostalgia and trade unionism which this National Socialism offered. Security, national harmony, and a chance for upward mobility were combined in this appeal with dynamic action against the enemy: the Republic, monopoly-capitalism, and the Jews. The Right as well as the Left could take advantage of social dislocation and offer an attractive package to the worker. These truisms need restating, for historians have often been guilty of making a simple equation between socialism and workers while restricting the appeal of the Right to the petit bourgeoisie, dislocated middle classes, or peasantry. The Right, like the Left, attempted to become a mass movement of the people: the Boulangist coalition which included workers and even socialists was not an isolated episode. Certainly, the National Socialist section of the Right kept on trying, sometimes in combination with more conservative forces. That they failed in France and eventually succeeded in Germany does not diminish the historical importance of the attempt.

EIGHT

The Heritage of Socialist Humanism

EXILES ARE APT to be left behind by the times, forgotten in the countries they fled and ignored by those in which they found a home. For many years it seemed as if German refugee intellectuals would share this fate. To be sure, the contributions of eminent scientists and scholars were often appreciated by their hosts, for they managed to become part of the Establishment, contributing to its success and survival. The wave of German refugee intellectuals who fled from National Socialism included not only such men and women but also a sizable group who remained outsiders in exile, as they had been outside the establishment in the Weimar Republic. Their contribution as critics of that Republic had come to public notice, but once in exile they seemed to live apart, withdrawn into their own circle of like-minded friends. These left-wing intellectuals were writers or critics, and though some of them found positions abroad they still constituted a fairly well defined group within the general emigration.

In 1954, when Alfred Kantorowicz wrote about one of the most famous of this group, the novelist Lion Feuchtwanger, he lamented the obscurity into which this celebrated author had fallen—perhaps the generation reaching maturity in the year 2000 might once more appreciate such a writer and the principles for which he stood.[1] However, it is precisely the ideals represented by Feucht-

wanger and his friends which have a relevance to our times denied
to the writings of many who moved so easily from the establishment of the German Republic to the establishments of other European nations and of the United States. Even when living in isolation at the French resort of Sanay or, later, in southern California,
they were destined to provide a bridge between some of the most
fertile thought of the 1920s and the search for a new society that
has preoccupied youth in our own decade.

Inasmuch as they believed in the abolition of capitalist society,
these left-wing intellectuals were socialists. That society was corrupt and oppressive; its political institutions, such as parliaments,
merely served to disguise the suppression of human freedom and
of man's potential for development. And although they believed
that war and violence were an outgrowth of capitalist society, they
did not accept the full implications of a Marxist social analysis. The
working of society was seen as part of the operations of autonomous reason, in the belief that thinking man can grasp what is
true, good, and right. Above and beyond any social or economic
analysis of the present, there was a categorical imperative centered
upon man's dignity and his ability to control his own destiny. Man
must never be made the means but always the end of all social and
political action.

From these propositions it followed that violence must never be
used against men, and that all human institutions which restricted
his freedom must be abolished. This included the discipline a political party might enforce and the violence which might occur in a
revolutionary situation. Their attitude toward political, economic,
or social power is summed up in a phrase from Heinrich Mann's
novel *Der Untertan* (*Man of Straw*, 1911): "The use of power which is
not filled with goodness and kindness will not last."[2] There can be
no compromise with political parties or systems that use power
differently, nor can any revolutionary strategy be tolerated that
uses oppressive or violent means to bring about the socialist society. Small wonder that these intellectuals were outsiders both
within organized revolutionary movements and in society as a
whole.

We cannot follow in detail the thought and fate of all the men
and women involved, but must confine ourselves to certain outstanding examples. Lion Feuchtwanger, Heinrich Mann, Leon-

hard Frank, and Alfred Döblin will guide our discussion. It would have been easier to deal with these left-wing intellectuals as a group in the Weimar Republic, at a time when several journals expressed their point of view, in particular the *Weltbühne* and the *Tagebuch*.[3] However, after 1933 the *Weltbühne* as the *Neue Weltbühne* came under communist influence, and the *Tagebuch* as the *Neue Tagebuch* moved perceptibly to the Right. We are left, therefore, with a loose-knit group of men, writers for the most part, who shared an outlook on the world but no common journal or institutional framework.

The idealism they shared was expressed in Leonhard Frank's phrase that the "path to socialism is humanism."[4] This humanism was founded upon a belief in the traditions of the French Enlightenment. Heinrich Mann was a leader among this group, and his whole life had been committed to that tradition. When Leonhard Frank wrote the short stories published under the title *Der Mensch Ist Gut* (*Man Is Good*, 1919), he meant that man is good if he is left free to develop his own potential, or, to put it in contemporary terms, is able to control his own destiny.

Appealing as Frank's combination of socialism and humanism is, it had to confront the realities of the world in which these men lived and worked; the "objective situation," as Marxists would describe it. This is the crux of the problem, for such men wanted to change society and thought not merely as writers but as doers as well. Should force be used against counterrevolutionary elements? What about the relationship of socialism to the aspirations of the working class? And were Marxists correct to see in that class the true harbinger of the future? Moreover, a socialist society was supposedly in being in the Soviet Union: could this society serve as example? These questions were asked under the pressure of the Nazi seizure of power and the collapse of a Republic toward which such men had been critical long before the Nazi menace became a reality. How they dealt with these problems gives some indication of the viability of socialist humanism in the twentieth-century world.

In his earliest novel, *Thomas Wendt* (1919), Lion Feuchtwanger had already posed the problem arising from the confrontation of the revolution with force. The hero becomes the leader of a revolution meant to bring about a new society of freedom, but fails to carry through the revolutionary impetus. Thomas Wendt cannot compromise the respect he feels for every individual, the very goal of the revolution, in order to defeat those who oppose the socialist society. He is told by a friend: "You will always have to use force against men if you want to eradicate their ideas. You must be unjust, Thomas Wendt, for the sake of justice."[5] But Wendt cannot accept such advice. This thread of humanism runs throughout the works of men like Leonhard Frank, Heinrich Mann, Alfred Döblin, and many others. To be sure, in 1923 Mann called for a "dictatorship of reason,"[6] which would force men to shed the prejudices they had imbibed during the long darkness of Wilhelmian rule. But after this moment of despair he counseled patience, for eventually reason would prevail and the existing social system would then be changed peacefully.

Lion Feuchtwanger's most famous novel *Der Jüdische Krieg* (*The Jewish War*, 1932), which treats of the victory of the Romans over the Jews, is one song of praise for reason amidst the passions and violence of the age. Flavius Josephus, who was to write the history of that war, starts the conflict under the influence of overwhelming passion. He has abandoned reason, for the war can never be won by the Jews, and it ends with the destruction of the Jewish temple in which Josephus had served as a priest. Justus, his enemy, is correct in believing that reason must triumph if war in which all truth collapses is to be avoided. In the end Josephus himself is converted to this truth, and opposes both the barbarism of Rome and the fanaticism of the Jewish warlords.

The Nazi triumph and his own exile did not at first markedly change Feuchtwanger's outlook upon the world. In *The Oppermanns* (*Die Geschwister Oppenheim*, 1933) he describes the fate of a Jewish family in the face of the National Socialist seizure of power. The hero, Gustav Oppenheimer, lives within the world of the Enlightenment and cannot understand the political flood tide that is about to engulf him. However, the Nazi terror awakens him to the reality of the situation, and the "unpolitical" man, who had spent his time writing a book about Lessing, throws himself into the political struggle. He continues the struggle against fascism in Nazi Germany until he is put into a concentration camp and dies as the result of ill-treatment there. He comes to see that "one cannot remain silent when truth is falsified."[7] This truth is the rationality of man which is linked with freedom and tolerance. To be sure, there will be setbacks in the struggle for these ideals, but as Gustav Oppenheimer had written: "We are enjoined to labor, but it is not granted to complete our labors."

It is startling to what extent the humanism of such men survived the Nazi experience. Leonhard Frank provides another example. After a life which had meant exile both in World War I and under National Socialism, he reiterates his belief in humanity. Victory over capitalism and oppression can be won without violating the life and sanctity of the individual. But it is also typical of this ideology that he brushes aside the specific means for accomplishing this task: to work this out is asking too much of one man.[8] Because none of these men paid attention to the mechanism of change, their ideology, abstracted from reality, was bound to suffer. Reading their works before and after the Nazi catastrophe, one receives the impression that the new rational man would, by himself, solve all remaining problems.

The fact that none of these intellectuals found their way into an existing political party should not astonish us. For parties, however far to the Left, stifled the human spirit by their dogmatism, and encroached on man's control of his own destiny through the discipline which they enforced. When, in 1933, a young man asked Alfred Döblin if it were not time to join a socialist party in order to fight the Nazis, he received a negative answer. More important than any specific political commitment was the necessity to fight for humanism and justice in the world.[9] What, then, about the Nazis, who had triumphed over all such considerations in their march to power?

Germany, so the *Neue Tagebuch* wrote in 1933, was "occupied" by the Nazis, and love for Germany meant hatred of the occupation.[10] This, indeed, was the crux of their attitude: the oppressive social system had finally shown its true face and had taken over the nation against the real wishes and interests of the people. Hugenberg, the big industrialist and Von Papen, the leader of the *Junker* class, had combined to sell the nation to Hitler. All these left-wing intellectuals denied that National Socialism was a popular movement; they could not conceive that Nazi ideology was accepted by man as they had defined him. For Heinrich Mann, the meaning of exile consisted in the example which German intellectuals provided for their people. Through the patient proclamation of reason and justice they would keep alive the truth and recall Germans to their proper destiny. Feuchtwanger in his earlier works had been skeptical of the people's use of power; Thomas Wendt was the victim, not only of his own high principles but also of the masses who did not understand them. But in *The Oppermanns* he emphasizes that the "people are good," and draws a sharp dividing line between the German masses and their fascist rulers.

This optimism may have been necessary for the self-esteem of these writers; it kept them going and gave a purpose to their lives. But it grew out of attitudes that predated the Nazi seizure of power, and is also reflected in the work of intellectuals who, being closer to Marxist orthodoxy, tried to see the German catastrophe in the light of social analysis rather than merely through the spectacles of a humanistic and rational spirit. There too, in spite of the concern with facts and figures, a preconceived socialist humanism comes through loud and clear.

Franz Neumann's *Behemoth* (1942), a book which has vitally influenced Western views of National Socialism, set this belief in human rationality upon a different foundation. Starting from the sociological tradition inherited from Max Weber, he wrote that the rationalization of the labor process, essential to any industrial society, must in the end lead to rational thought and to the denial of violence. The masses in Germany had behind them a long tradition imbued with the critical spirit, which sooner or later would make them aware of the antagonism inherent in an economy that can produce in abundance for welfare but does so only for destruction. The class struggle would continue and triumph over the forces now oppressing the nation.[11] This analysis provided the facts which, as Neumann saw it, must be kept separate from the ideological framework within which National Socialism operated. He was fully conscious that liberalism had failed Germany, for injustice lurked behind the slogans of political freedom. Democratic ideals like the self-determination of peoples had consistently been betrayed by those who professed them. Ideology is defined as the verbalization of aims and goals. It is absent when events move in a direction quite different from professed aims. Thus the Nazis may be promoting cultural activities through the "Strength through Joy" movement, but as culture can exist only in freedom, no garrison state can create a demand for a genuine culture. This is the genesis of his belief that National Socialism had no ideology; it was a system which would sharpen the antagonisms of society and prepare for its own downfall. Terror was the cement of the régime, and all these intellectuals believed that by its very nature Hitler's movement could have no other cohesive force. Already during the Republic, some left-wing intellectuals had asserted that Nazism could not last because it lacked genuine contact with the true course of human aspirations.[12]

For all his social analysis, influenced by Weber and Marxism, Neumann put a concept of freedom into the very center as a prerequisite for all political thought and action. Men can determine their own destinies, and it is a perverted society, rather than some basic fault of human nature, which prevents them from doing so. Neumann was a Social Democrat, but while in exile he came to see the faults of that movement; he never made contact with communism. A true democracy must be maintained whenever possible, and this democracy he defined as putting an end to political alienation—a genuine participation by all in the making of society. But this end to alienation entails basic changes in society, indeed a socialist organization of the state. However, the final cement of such a democracy is a moral impetus—be it freedom or justice.[13] This ideal, which he reiterated at the end of his life (1953), puts him on the same wavelength as the left-wing intellectuals we have discussed. Here also we have the humanism, the belief in the inevitable triumph of rationality, and the stress upon the overriding principles of self-determination, freedom, and justice, even if such ideals were combined with a social analysis foreign to most of the writers in exile.

In the hands of these intellectuals, National Socialism became an aberration of history which would, sooner or later, right itself again. The "occupiers" could not succeed against the people. From this point of view, they contested the prominence given to the persecution of the Jews in antifascist propaganda. As one writer put it: "The emigration is not merely an outgrowth of the Jewish question." Heinrich Mann wrote that hatred of the Jew took second place in National Socialism to the hatred of human freedom. He criticized, in 1933, the dominance that the persecution of the Jews exercised over all anti-Nazi mass meetings.[14] Humanity was an integral whole, and all of it was menaced by fascism. Even Lion Feuchtwanger, many of whose novels deal with specifically Jewish themes, always connected these to the whole of mankind; the Jews were for him symbols of the travail of liberty. As he wrote in *The Oppermanns*, Jews never gave up the belief in their eventual freedom.[15]

The men whose ideals we have analyzed stood outside all political groupings and parties. But, in the end, not even their optimism about humanity could overcome their feeling of rootlessness now compounded by exile. During the Weimar Republic, such intellectuals had tried to reach out to the people and to involve themselves in some kind of political action. Some had supported the USPD (Independent Socialists) at the beginning of the Republic, others the various socialist splinter movements. There was in 1932 some talk of running Heinrich Mann for the presidency. None of this amounted to a great deal, but in exile not even this kind of activity was possible, and the attempt (in which Heinrich Mann played a leading part) to found a Popular Front of all exiled political groupings came to nothing. The result of this dilemma was a heightened urge to anchor their beliefs in some sort of political reality, to find a positive force which could be used to defeat the fascist menace. For as time wore on the "occupiers" of Germany grew stronger, while much of the Western world seemed to support their cause.

The confrontation of these men with reality took many different forms and we can only choose some examples in order to illustrate the problem. The intellectual evolution of Alfred Döblin presents one extreme. The man who had advised, as late as 1933, that one could fight for a humanistic socialism outside all established political parties began to lose faith in the socialist ideal. Later, he was to write that where he had looked for human brotherhood he found political bosses and parties. The small socialist splinter groups with which he had associated during the Republic were sects whose activities ended in disillusionment and dehumanization.[16] Döblin's socialism had been vigorously opposed to existing society and his most famous work, *Berlin-Alexanderplatz* (1929), demonstrated how in the big city, the ultimate product of capitalism, no hard and fast line could be drawn between the criminal and the noncriminal world. However, the positive side of his socialism was confused and stressed the necessity of personal conversion to a truly humane and decent life. If necessary man must sacrifice himself in order to bear witness against the injustice of the present system. Shortly before the triumph of the Nazis, he asserted that only a "new humanity" which had cut its ties with all nations could proclaim the eternal law of justice.[17]

In his earlier works, like *Berlin-Alexanderplatz*, Döblin's attitude toward the masses was ambivalent, but later he becomes more precise. In order to rouse the masses to recapture their own humanity, a leader is needed: one who by his life and sacrifice provides an example. But here, as in the works of Heinrich Mann, Leonhard Frank, or Lion Feuchtwanger, it is the human posture of the leader that counts, and any analysis of the objective conditions in the making of a revolution is omitted from the picture. Döblin shows the full weakness of this noble if ill-defined socialism. For under the stress of exile it collapsed rapidly in the search for more concrete roots. First, he sought refuge in a new realization of his Jewishness, in the arms of a Jewish Volk. Döblin became an impassioned territorialist, part of that movement which wanted to settle the Jews on the land but was indifferent to Palestine as the place where this should be accomplished. "More important than the land is the Volk." Ideas of class struggle cannot apply to Jews, who are eternal foreigners within the society where such a struggle prevails. The Jews have to normalize themselves as a Volk and gain a new security.[18]

But in all this preoccupation with Volk and security something of his old posture remains. The Jews in their own exile have been victimized by priests and by those other Jews who had amassed worldly possessions. The settled Volk will change all this; now "freedom, the urge to build and responsibility" will take the place of a past marked by cowardice and humiliation. Religion will be the cement, and this is defined as strict morality culminating in justice. Döblin never shared fully the optimistic belief in human rationality. Now his hostility to technology and science (always for him a part of the evil city) culminates in an open denial of rationalism. The Volk and its morality are inspired by the simple and direct relationship between God and man. This relationship provides the cohesive force which creates a genuine community.[19]

But Döblin did not stop at this point. His relationship to the Jews was idealistic, based upon the same idealism as his earlier socialist commitment. It proved no more lasting when confronted with the reality of political struggles among the Jews. His final conversion to Christianity took place within this context. Christ becomes the exemplification of justice and freedom, fighting to prevail in an evil world without recourse to force. The problem of revolution, force, and power, which was to occupy so many of his fellow intellectuals, had been solved. Moreover, Döblin's Christianity also gave him roots, a resting place in his wanderings. For he joined the Catholic Church, which provided him with a "halt" and a "harmonious, coordinated system." At the same time he castigated Jews who, after all their suffering, still clung to business-as-usual, while he seemed to have recaptured his old idealism within a more settled and traditional form.[20]

Döblin's evolution cannot be duplicated by others, but it shows how vague socialist humanism became under stress. The precedence given to the individual over society within this socialism proved an inadequate device against both the feeling of rootlessness and the escalating fight against fascism. However, his fellow intellectuals looked to a different east from that marking the cradle of Christianity. The Soviet Union seemed at times to be the only power willing to stand up to Hitler. On the other hand, these intellectuals had a long history of skepticism toward the Soviet Union behind them, and Heinrich Mann was only one of many writers who had signed protests against the violations of justice in that state. Moreover, they had opposed the German Communist Party as merely another oppressive institution. The growing Nazi menace had made little dent in this attitude, even though, in the presidential election of 1932, the *Weltbühne* advised its readers to vote for the communist leader Thalmann, notwithstanding the oppressive nature of communism.[21] It was a counsel of despair. After 1933, with the despair heightened, the search for positive action against the Nazi state still focused attention on communism and the Soviet Union.

Lion Feuchtwanger can illustrate the problems which these socialists faced in their efforts to come to terms with communism. As we saw, in the first years of exile he continued, and indeed deepened, his older line of thought. He now interpreted his novel on the *Jewish War* as meaning that the traditional nationalism of the

Jews must be subordinated to a broader socialism that embraced concern for one's neighbors as well as for one's own people. The Jews symbolized commitment to an ethical principle hostile to the use of force or, indeed, to territorial and racial nationalism.[22] To be sure, the two subsequent volumes of the Josephus trilogy, which were written later in exile, seem to contradict this outlook. Josephus discards his cosmopolitanism, his rootlessness, and finds his way back to the Jewish Volk in its revolt against the Romans. At the end of the last volume, however, Feuchtwanger writes that Joseph "searched for the new world prematurely. Therefore he merely found his nation."[23] Patience and self-discipline were needed in the long endeavor to create a new world (a cry Heinrich Mann was to utter as well).

However, side by side with this stress on reason, patience, and self-discipline, Feuchtwanger strikes a contradictory note. Subdued at first, this could well provide a bridge toward his later commitment to communism. Already in *The Oppermanns* he believed that arguments based upon the preservation of true humanity and civilization were insufficient to rouse the world against the German barbarians. The democracies feared bolshevism more than the Nazis, and were benefitting from the rearmament industry. Feuchtwanger fully accepted the Marxist interpretation of the victory of National Socialism. One of the characters in *The Oppermanns* accuses a German capitalist: "I know the only way you could save your rotten economic system was by calling in that lousy gang to help you."[24]

This interpretation of the Nazi seizure of power was reinforced by the belief that Germany was filled with anti-Nazis whom one could not leave in the lurch. Gustav Oppenheimer reiterates that the majority of Germans were decent people and that reason must triumph in the end.[25] Other left-wing intellectuals in exile shared this Marxist analysis of the success of National Socialism, not because they had devoted any scholarship to its investigation, but because it explained how the "occupiers" could succeed despite that rationality and goodness which Germans shared with the rest of humanity. In face of capitalist corruption, the indifference of the democracies, something more forceful than arguments based on humanity and civilization was needed. Communism and the Soviet Union lay ready at hand to fill this void.

By the time Feuchtwanger wrote his novel *Exile* (1940), communism is seen as the logical commitment of the intellectual emigration. For Feuchtwanger, the turning point came with his journey to Moscow in 1937. The book that followed is filled with praise and admiration for the Stalin régime. This praise is consistent with an attitude which had, indeed, been exemplified in many of his earlier works: that world history is an unending battle between a minority devoted to reason and an unthinking majority which, however, could be redeemed through a new society. The conformism he had opposed throughout his life, but which he found in the Soviet Union, was brushed aside, for it was based upon a justified commitment to the principles of communism, love for the Soviet state, and the hope that the Soviet Union might become the happiest and richest land on earth. What, then, about the oppression that accompanied such hopes and beliefs? The Stalinist purges are taken at face value—after all, the accused had always been conspirators and could not be expected to have changed their lifestyle.

Typically enough, his only criticism concerned censorship over literature. He could not believe that the enforcement of a "heroic optimism" was good for literary endeavor, for a novelist must be free to write what he himself feels and believes. But this is a minor drawback when compared with the building of a "practical socialism."[26] It is quite clear that this practical socialism does not always coincide with the ethical imperative, but it now becomes the *prerequisite* for the establishment of humanistic socialism. Feuchtwanger seemed to have found solid ground to which he could anchor his hopes for the future. But his commitment to the new Soviet society soon became ambivalent again. He was convinced that the future belonged to the socialism practiced in the Soviet Union. His humanistic socialism had not proved capable of dealing with the political realities, had not become a "practical socialism." But in his novel *Exile* he was unwilling to give it up altogether. "All I can do is to learn new theory but not new practice," says one of the chief characters.[27] The fundamental lines of communist policy might be correct, but heart and feeling could not "affirm them."

It can be said that the change was due to a failure of nerve, a refusal to practice that patience which he had counseled in his earlier works. However, at the end of the war he returned to his earlier self. In *Waffen für Amerika* (*Arms for America*, 1947) he reaffirmed his belief in the "slow, very slow, yet certain growth of human rea-son between the last ice age and that which is to come."[28] After the war Feuchtwanger did not contemplate settling in communist East Germany. Once again he stood between all fronts, a position simi-lar to Leonhard Frank's, who lived out his last years in Munich, almost forgotten and at war with the world. Heinrich Mann was preparing to settle in East Germany when he died, but almost against his better judgment and with a reluctance that meant a constant postponement of the journey.

Heinrich Mann has been claimed by the communist world with greater certainty than Feuchtwanger or Frank. Thus it has been as-serted that his conversion to a communist outlook was deeper and more lasting, that eventually he saw in the struggles of the work-ing classes the only hope for the future.[29] To be sure, Mann was politically active from the very first year of exile. He attempted to form a united front which the Communist Party was supposed to join. Moreover, he supported all anti-Nazi efforts. Did he, then, also depart from his ideal of reason and humanism under the pres-sure of events?

Mann attempted to take a leading part in the antifascist struggle wherever it was to be found. The Popular Front over which he pre-sided was supposed to be a broad grouping, which would take in not only the socialists and communists but also Catholics and other democratic forces. As the leader of this front, he wrote in communist journals and took part in communist-inspired organi-zations. Yet he continued to write for bourgeois liberal papers, like the *Pariser Tageblatt*, and his efforts to form a Popular Front were constantly sabotaged by Walter Ulbricht, the communist leader. In-deed, Heinrich Mann came to hate Ulbricht and the bureaucratic and oppressive movement he represented.

To be sure, Mann believed that the bourgeois world was in de-cline and had to be liquidated. But he did not deduce from this that the working classes were the sole instruments for bringing about a socialist society. Like all these left-wing intellectuals, he rejected class analysis in favor of an organic humanism in which intellec-tuals would take the leading part. Typically enough, this point of view dominated a review which Mann wrote of the poetry of Johannes R. Becher, the communist writer. Becher wrote with humor, in an easy style with a broad popular appeal. Therefore, what he called "class" must refer to the people as a whole, to all Germans. However, Mann was careful to add that belief in the healing power of social and economic change constituted a reasonable doctrine.[30] Nevertheless, concern for the spirit and consciousness of humanity must have priority over all other considerations. This is illustrated by his greatest work of that period: the novels that deal with the French king, Henry IV (1935–38). Here all social analysis is subordinated to the ideals of reason, toleration, and peace. They sound a new note, not that of class but of a militancy which permits the use of force in order to bring about the good society. However, this force is exercised by a power (like the monarchy of Henry IV), not wedded to class but committed to goodness and reason. The basic ideal is still the same as that which he had put forward in *Der Untertan* many years before.

This does not exclude a criticism of bourgeois society. Heinrich Mann, Leonhard Frank, and others anticipated in exile that rejection of American society which Herbert Marcuse was to put forward in his *One Dimensional Man* (1964). Marcuse, for all the social analysis involved, concentrates upon those cultural aspects of society which prevent man from controlling his own destiny. Earlier, Leonhard Frank had attacked the poverty of spirit (*Gefühlsarmut*) in America, putting this down to a consumer-orientated society which forces man into choices he does not want to make.[31] We have already seen that the ideological outlook of the left-wing intellectuals was shared by other critics of society, notwithstanding their commitment to Marxist social analysis. The common heritage of German idealism that had filtered through Kant united such men in the priority they gave to the autonomy of rational man over concern with the Marxist definition of objective reality.

Their leadership theory bears this out. The intelligentsia must lead society, it is the custodian of the categorical imperative. For intellectuals stand above all classes of the population, having their roots in none of them. This concept of leadership is not a product of exile, but goes back at least to World War I. During the German revolution of 1918–19, Heinrich Mann presided over a "soviet of brain workers." This soviet was supposed to provide general guidance for the other soviets of workers and soldiers. It never amounted to much, but it does show how such intellectuals attempted to become relevant to society on their own terms. Intellectuals were supposed to have a heightened consciousness of what society needed, because they were "free floating" (to use Karl Mannheim's term) and because of their rational approach to life. This is what Feuchtwanger meant when he wrote that throughout world history an enlightened minority has always battled the stupidity common to most men.[32] Both Heinrich Mann in his *Lidice* (1943) and Alfred Döblin repeat the same ideas: intellectuals as fighters for righteousness confront the masses.[33] We are back once more with concepts deriving from the French Enlightenment: mankind is redeemable but it has to be enlightened by *philosophes* before it can properly enter the age of reason. Today, when the workers seem content and apathetic, men like Herbert Marcuse have once more transferred leadership to a revolutionary intelligentsia. Perhaps new experiments with a "soviet of brain workers" will follow, and, in fact, something of this sort seemed to inspire some students during the university turmoil of the mid-sixties.

It might seem as if most of the men with whom we are concerned had been forgotten, their works scarcely read. But their obscurity is more apparent than real. These writers popularized an ideology which did seem to offer an alternative to social democracy, communism, and capitalist society. To be sure, under the pressure of exile, they seemed to compromise their principles of humanistic socialism, but this did not last. By and large they carried their trend of thought through from the Weimar Republic to the postwar world. However, the wavering of some and the apostasy of others like Döblin do throw light upon the problems which their ideals involved. The intelligentsia on the one hand, and the people with their potential on the other, would build the "Republic of Reason," as Heinrich Mann called the socialist state of the future. The idea that such a change could come about through individual example rather than violence, the constant emphasis upon the dignity of man, are beguiling as a road to utopia.

But would reason automatically solve all problems? Were the social and economic aspects of society merely mechanical problems, as Heinrich Mann believed?[34] Marxism entered into their thought, but as providing a critique of present society, rather than exemplifying the mechanism by which society must be overthrown. To the doctrine of class war these left-wing intellectuals opposed the ideal of the autonomy of human reason. They recognized the irrational forces in human history. They fought irrationalism, but their true attitude toward it was once more rooted in the tradition of the French Enlightenment. Evil was something which existed, but it was best to brush it aside, for you could not build a new society by acknowledging its extent and its depth. Thus they never understood National Socialism, for they refused to believe that millions could find a congenial home in its irrational embrace.

Socialist humanists outside Germany showed greater realism in their approach to politics. The *Partito d'Azione* (Political Action Party) in Italy was founded on very similar presuppositions and became a leading and effective antifascist organization. The ideal of one of its ideological founders, Carlo Roselli, that "the spiritual essence of liberalism can be preserved only within a socialist society," sums up the thought of the men we have discussed—provided that liberalism is connected to the tradition of the French Enlightenment and not to its evolution in Germany. Roselli also condemned communism, but he did not posit the intelligentsia as the only true revolutionary force. A strong and united proletariat was the only mechanism by which fascism could be overthrown.[35] It is astonishing that the German exiles had so little contact with this Italian antifascist movement. In spite of their urge to save all of humanity, they seem singularly Germanic in their orientation and in their pattern of thought.

The weakness of this socialist humanism should be obvious, and the so-called revolt of the younger generation has shown a similar disregard for objective reality, for similar reasons. Socialist humanism is easily catapulted into the realm of abstract philosophy and instant utopia. This heritage of German refugee intellectuals is of importance to our age. However, contrary to their own opinion, it does not belong to the mainstream of human history, which has stubbornly refused to follow the guidance of reason as they understand it. Instead, this "socialist humanism" belongs to the narrower and more constricted history of European intellectuals.

PART II

Toward a General Theory
of Fascism

IN OUR CENTURY two revolutionary movements have made
their mark upon Europe: that originally springing from Marxism, and the fascist revolution. The various forms of Marxism
have occupied historians and political scientists for many decades,
and only now is the study of fascism catching up. Even so, because
of the war and the fascist record in power, fascism has remained
synonymous with oppression and domination; it is alleged that it
was without ideas of its own, but merely a reaction against other
more progressive movements such as liberalism or socialism. Earlier scholarship concerning fascism has been singularly vulnerable
to subjective viewpoints and more often than not has consequently
been used to fight contemporary polemical battles.

In a justified reaction against the fascist stereotype, recent scholarship has been suspicious of general theories of fascism. As many
local and regional studies show, on one level it may have presented a kaleidoscope of contradictory attitudes; nevertheless, these
attitudes were based upon common assumptions. To be sure, any
general theory of fascism must be no more than a hypothesis
which fits most of the facts. We shall attempt to bring together
some of the principal building blocks for such a general theory—
there seem to be enough of them to construct at least a provisional
dwelling. Germany and Italy will dominate the discussion, as the

experience of European fascism was largely dominated by Italian fascism and German National Socialism. The word "fascism" will be used without qualification when both these movements are meant. From time to time we shall also refer to various other fascisms in Europe, but only specifically or as subsidiary examples.

We can best develop a general theory of fascism through a critique of past attempts to accomplish this task. Some historians have seen an integral connection between bolshevism and fascism. Both were totalitarian régimes and, as such, dictatorships based upon the exclusive claim to leadership by one political party.[1] Although such an equation was often politically motivated, it was not, as its opponents claimed, merely a child of the cold war.

Both movements were based on the ideal, however distorted, of popular sovereignty. This meant the rejection of parliamentary government and representative institutions on behalf of a democracy of the masses in which the people would directly govern themselves. The leader symbolized the people; he expressed the "general will"—but such a democracy meant that, instead of representative assemblies, a new secular religion mediated between people and leaders, providing, at the same time, an instrument of social control over the masses. It was expressed on the public level through official ceremonies, festivals, and not least, imagery, and on a private level through control over all aspects of life by the dictates of the single political party. This system was common in various degrees to fascist and bolshevist movements.

The danger inherent in subsuming both systems under the concept of totalitarianism is that it may serve to disguise real differences, not only between bolshevism and fascism but also between the different forms of fascism. Moreover, the contention that these theories really compare fascism not with Lenin's bolshevism but with Stalinism seems fully justified. Indeed, totalitarianism as a static concept often veils the development of both fascism and bolshevism. In Soviet Russia, for example, the kind of public ceremonies and festivals that mark the fascist political style were tried early in the régime but then dropped, and not resumed until after World War II, when they came to fulfill the same functions as they had earlier for fascism. In 1966, *Pravda* wrote that rallies, ceremonial processions, speeches, and concerts gave emotional strength to the political commitment of the people.[2] Fascism, too, did not remain static, although even some critics of totalitarian theory apparently see it as unchanging. There is, for example, a difference between fascism as a political movement and as a government in power.

Theories of totalitarianism have placed undue emphasis upon the supposedly monolithic leadership cult. Here again, this was introduced into the Soviet Union by Stalin and not Lenin. Even within fascism, the cult of the leader varied: Piero Melograni has written on how the cult of "Il Duce" and fascism were not identical, and that it was "Mussolinianism" which won the people's allegiance. In Germany there is no discernible difference between Hitlerism and National Socialism.

More serious is the contention, common to most theories of totalitarianism, that the leader manipulates the masses through propaganda and terror: that free volition is incompatible with totalitarian practice.[3] The term "propaganda," always used in this context, leads to a misunderstanding of the fascist cults and their essentially organic and religious nature. In times of crisis they provided many millions of people with a more meaningful involvement than representative parliamentary government—largely because they were not themselves a new phenomenon, but were instead based upon an older and still lively tradition of popular democracy, which had always opposed European parliaments.

Even the widespread notion that fascism ruled through terror must be modified. Rather, it was built upon a fragile consensus. Tangible successes, the ability to compromise and to go slow, combined with the responsive chord struck by fascist culture, integrated Italians and Germans into this consensus, which undoubtedly was more solid in Germany than Italy. Hitler, after all, shared a volkish faith with his fellow Germans, and his tangible successes in domestic and foreign policy were much more spectacular than Mussolini's achievements.

Terror increased with the continued survival of the régimes, for disillusionment with fascism in power could easily lead to unrest. By the time many earlier supporters woke up to fascist reality, it was too late to resist, except by martyrdom. Mass popular consensus during the first years of fascism allowed it to develop an effective secret police—outside and above regular channels and procedures[4]—as well as the special courts needed to reinforce its actions. This was easier in the Soviet Union since the revolution had destroyed the old legal framework; while in Germany and Italy, traditional safeguards paradoxically continued to exist and even to be used side by side with arbitrary action. In Germany, judges freed some concentration camp inmates as late as 1936.

Terror must not then be treated as a static concept, but as something that develops in intensity. Not only must historical development be taken into account, but also the existence and extent of a consensus, which, although differing in scope in the three so-called totalitarian nations, did exist at some time in each of them.

Despite all these caveats, both bolshevists and fascists reached back into the antiparliamentary and antipluralistic traditions of the nineteenth century in order to face the collapse of social, economic, and political structures in their nations during and after World War I. Totalitarianism was new only as a form of legitimate government: it derived from a long tradition; otherwise it would not have received such immediate mass support. Beginning its modern history with the French Revolution, that tradition continued to inform both the nationalism and the quest for social justice of the nineteenth century. Even if Jacob Talmon's concept of "totalitarian democracy" rests, as some have claimed, upon a misreading of the Enlightenment,[5] men like Robespierre and Saint-Just shared in such misconceptions. Rousseau's "general will," his exaltation of "the people," was bent by the Jacobins into a dictatorship in which the people worshipped themselves through public festivals and symbols (such as the goddess of reason), where religious enthusiasm was transferred to civic rites.[6]

The distinction between private and public life was eradicated, just as totalitarian régimes would later attempt to abolish such differences. Public allegiance, through active participation in the national cults, was the road to survival, and as, for example, the Jacobins used dress as an outward sign of true inner allegiance (the revolutionary cap and trousers instead of breeches), so fascists and bolshevists integrated various uniforms into their systems. Nationalist movements during the nineteenth century carried on these traditions, even if at times they attempted to compromise with liberal values. The workers' movement, though most of it was in fact wedded to parliamentary democracy, stressed outward symbols of unity (as in the serried ranks and Sunday dress of May

Day parades), massed flags, and the clenched fist salute. Italy was less influenced by this legacy, but it also played a part in the fight for national unity. At the turn of the century, the radical Left and the radical Right were apt to demand control of the whole man, not just a political piece of him.

Bolshevism and fascism attempted to mobilize the masses, to substitute modern mass politics for pluralistic and parliamentary government. Indeed, parliamentary government found it difficult to cope with the crises of the postwar world, and abdicated without a struggle, not only in Germany and Italy but also in Portugal and, where it had existed immediately after the war, in the nations of eastern Europe. The fascists helped the demise of parliamentary government, but that it succumbed so readily points to deep inherent structural and ideological problems—though, indeed, few representative governments have withstood the pressures of modern economic, political, and social crises, especially when these coincided with defeat in war and unsatisfied national aspirations.[7] Wherever interwar totalitarian governments came to power, they merely toppled régimes ripe for the picking; this holds good for Russia as well as for Germany and Italy. But unlike bolshevism, fascism never had to fight a civil war on its road to power: Mussolini marched on Rome in the comfort of a railway carriage, and Hitler simply presented himself to the German president. Certainly, representative government and liberal politics allowed individual freedom to breathe, but totalitarianism cannot be condemned without taking the collapse of existing parliaments and social structures into account. We must not look at a historical movement mainly from the viewpoint of our political predilections, lest we falsify historical necessity.

If some historians have used the model of totalitarianism in order to analyze fascism, others, and they are in the majority, have used the model of the "good revolution."[8] The French, American, and especially the Russian revolutions, so it is said, led to the progress of mankind, while fascism was an attempt to stop the clock, to maintain old privilege against the demands of the new classes as represented by the proletariat. In reality, fascism was itself a revolution, seizing power by using twentieth-century methods of communication and control, and replacing an old with a new élite. (In this sense, National Socialism brought about a more fundamental change than Italian fascism, where new and traditional élites coexisted to a greater extent.) Economic policy was subordinated to the political goals of fascism, but in Germany, at least, this did not preclude nationalization (for example, the so-called Hermann Goering Steel Works). By and large, however, fascism worked hand in hand with the larger industrial enterprises.

Yet a one-sided emphasis either upon economic factors or upon the proletariat obscures our view of the revolutionary side of fascism. Fascism condemned the French Revolution but was also, at least in its beginnings, a direct descendant of the Jacobin political style.[9] Above all, the fascist revolution saw itself as a "Third Force," rejecting both "materialistic Marxism" and "finance capitalism" in the capitalist and materialist present. This was the revolutionary tradition within which fascism worked. But it was not alone in such an aim; in the postwar world, many left-wing intellectuals rejected both Marxist orthodoxy and capitalism. Unlike the fascists, however, they sought to transcend both by emphasis on the triumphant goodness of man once capitalism was abolished.

Fascism retreated instead into the nationalist mystique. But here, once more, it followed a precedent. French socialists of the mid-nineteenth century, and men like Édouard Drumont toward the end of the century, had combined opposition against finance capitalism and the advocacy of greater social equality with an impassioned nationalism. They were National Socialists long before the small German workers' party took this name.[10] Such National Socialism was in the air as a "Third Force" in the last decades of the nineteenth century, when Marxism was a force to be reckoned with and capitalist development seemed accompanied by a soulless positivism: a world where only material values counted. There were National Socialist movements in France (in which former leaders of the Paris Commune, with their Jacobin traditions, joined, but also some anarchists and bourgeois *bien-pensants*), in Bohemia, and even in Germany, advocated by the Hessian Peasants' Movement led by Otto Boeckel.

In Italy, argument for the "Third Force" resulted from World War I—the interventionist struggle and the subsequent war experience seemed to transcend vested interests and political parties. There was indeed a similar reaction among a good many veterans in Germany (but not in France, which had won the war and successfully weathered postwar upheaval). Yet in Italy, unlike Germany, the "war experience" carried revolutionary implications. Mussolini was joined in this hope by the students and by revolutionary syndicalists who wanted to abolish the existing social and economic order so that the nation could be regenerated through the searing experience of war. They appealed both to the revolutionary spirit and to a sense of Italy's historic national mission as "Revolutionary Veterans." It is typical that when the Fascist Party was founded in Ferrara, it was a youth group, "Third Italy," which took the initiative.[11] In Germany and Italy—nations plunged into crisis by the war—and also among many political groups of other nations, the "Third Force" became an alternative revolution to Marxism, a retreat into the community of the nation when the world seemed to be dominated on the one hand by the mysterious power of money and on the other by the Marxist conspiracy.[12]

Yet this "Third Force" became ever less revolutionary and more nationalistic as fascists or Nazis strove for power. Mussolini broke with the revolutionary syndicalists early on and tamed his youth organization but stayed with the Futurists, whose revolutionary ardor took the fast sports car as its model rather than the nationalization of production. Hitler got rid of social revolutionaries like Otto Strasser who wanted to challenge property relationships, however slightly. Yet we must not limit our gaze to property relationships or the naked play of power and interest; such issues alone do not motivate men. It was the strength of fascism everywhere that it appeared to transcend these concerns, gave people a meaningful sense of political participation (though, of course, in reality they did not participate at all), and sheltered them within the national community against the menace of rapid change and the all too swift passage of time.

National Socialism was able to contain the revolutionary impetus better than Italian fascism because in Germany the very term "Third Force" was fraught with mystical and millenarian meaning. The mythos of the "Third Force" became a part of the mythos of the "Third Reich," carrying on a Germanic tradition that had no real equivalent in Catholic Italy. The prophecy by Joachim of Flora about the future "Third Age," which would be a kingdom of the spirit—the biblical millennium—had become an essential ingredient of German Protestantism, as had the three mystical kingdoms of Paracelsus: that of God, the planets, and the Earth. The German mystics such as Jakob Böhme believed that man, by overcoming his baser self and seeking harmony within nature, could rise from Earth to the kingdom of God—an important emphasis on "becoming" or joining the eternal spirit of the race rather than "being"; on the quest for the "genuine" as exemplified first by nature and, later, by the "Volk" itself.[13]

Moeller van den Bruck, whose book *The Third Reich* (1923) was originally entitled *The Third Way*, brought this tradition up to date for a defeated nation: the Germanic mission would transcend all the contradictions inherent in modern life, including Germany's defeat in war; Germans must struggle continually toward utopia, which he equated with the German Reich of the future. To be sure, Moeller was pragmatic in his demand for political action, his advocacy of the corporate state, and his desire to institute a planned economy (hence his praise of Lenin's new economic policy).[14] Yet he also retained the traditional elements that were so much a part of this kind of revolution, calling for the maintenance of a state authority, preferably that of a monarch, as well as of the family structure.

However, for Moeller the pragmatic was always subsumed under the messianic. The arrival of the "Third Reich" would automatically solve all outstanding problems. Such a belief was part of the "Third Force" in Germany: the purified national community of the future would end all present difficulties and anxieties, social inequalities and economic crises. Man would then "overcome" the dialectic of earthly life. Small wonder that the Nazis enthusiastically annexed the fairy tale and folk legend to their cause. However, this vision of the future was rooted in the past—it was the traditional fairy tale which the Nazis used in creating their emphasis upon the modern Volk. Precedent was always an integral part of the Nazi ideology, and of Italian fascism too—as when in the fourth year of Mussolini's government the ancient monuments of Rome were restored. For Mussolini, however, history was never more than a platform from which to jump into an ill-defined future.

Hitler and Goebbels's obsession with history reached a climax at the moment of defeat: in 1945, they clung to memories of Frederick the Great, who had been saved from certain defeat by the opportune death of the czarina Elizabeth, and to the victory of Rome over Carthage.[15] Utopia and traditionalism were linked, a point to which we shall return when discussing the new fascist man.

Ernst Bloch calls this urge to "overcome"—the mystical and millenarian dynamic—the "hidden revolution" essential to the realization of the true socialist revolution.[16] Men must hope before they can act. National Socialism claimed to represent this "inner dynamic," though it was always careful to state that the "Third Reich" stood at the threshold of fulfillment and that a period of struggle and suffering must precede eventual salvation. And indeed, in the end, this revolutionary tradition did transfer a religious enthusiasm to secular government.

While few would deny that in order to understand communism or bolshevism we have to comprehend their revolutionary tradition, fascism has often been discussed as if it had no such tradition. The revolutionary appeal of fascism is easy to underestimate in our own time; the object has been to de-mystify, and a new positivism has captured the historical imagination.

The fascist revolutions built upon a deep bedrock of popular piety and, especially in Germany, upon a millenarianism that was apt to come to the fore in times of crisis. The myths and symbols of nationalism were superimposed upon those of Christianity—not only in the rhythms of public rites and ceremonies (even the Duce's famed dialogues with the masses from his balcony are related to Christian "responses")—but also in the appeal to apocalyptic and millenarian thought. Such appeals can be found in the very vocabulary of Nazi leaders. Their language grew out of Christianity; it was, after all, a language of faith. In 1935, at Munich's Feldherrnhalle, where his *putsch* of 1923 had resulted in a bloody fiasco, Hitler called those who had fallen earlier "my apostles," and proclaimed that "with the Third Reich you have risen from the dead." Many other examples spring to mind, as when the leader of the Labor Front, Robert Ley, asserted that "we have found the road to eternity." The whole vocabulary of blood and soil was filled with Christian liturgical and religious meaning—the "blood" itself, the "martyrdom," the "incarnation." [17]

Moreover, historians have recently found that in the past, millenarianism was not simply a protest by the poor against the rich, but a belief shared by most classes;[18] not inherently psychotic or revolutionary, but a normal strain of popular piety running through nineteenth-century and into twentieth-century Europe, and common to all nations. This background was vital for the cross-class appeal of National Socialism, and perhaps, despite a different emphasis, for Italian fascism as well: the "new man," for whom all fascism yearned, was certainly easily integrated into such popular piety as it became transformed into political thought.

The "Third Force" in Italy did not directly build upon a mystical tradition, though it existed there as well as in Germany. Rather than referring to Savonarola, for example, Giovanni Gentile saw in the fascist state a Hegelian synthesis, which resolved all contradictions. In consequence, German idealism was more important in Italian fascism, derived from Gentile, than in National Socialism, though some Nazi philosophers used Hegel to prove that Hitler had ended the dialectic of history. After the Concordat of 1929, Italian fascism, seeking to rival the Church, became increasingly the religion of the state. The will to believe was emphasized, and the Italian antirational tradition was searched for precedents.[19] Yet when all was said and done, such efforts were sporadic, and some leading fascists retained their skepticism about "*romanità*" or civic religions.

While the "Third Force" is vital for understanding fascism, its importance should not be exaggerated. For fascism, it was always "the experience" that counted, and not appeals to the analytical intellect. In a play by Hans Johst, the young Leo Schlageter, about to fight against the French occupation of the Ruhr Valley, and his socialist father speak these lines:

> *Son:* The young people don't pay much attention to these old slogans anymore . . . the class struggle is dying out.
> *Father:* So . . . and what do you live on then?
> *Son:* The Volk Community . . .
> *Father:* And that's a slogan . . . ?
> *Son:* No, it's an experience![20]

It was an organic view of the world, which was supposed to take in the whole man and thus end his alienation. A fundamental redefinition is involved in such a view of man and his place in the world. "Politics," wrote the Italian fascist Giuseppe Bottai, "is an attitude toward life itself,"[21] and this phrase is repeated word for word in National Socialist literature. Horia Sima, one of Codreanu's successors in the leadership of the Rumanian Iron Guard, summed it up: "We must cease to separate the spiritual from the political man. All history is a commentary upon the life of the spirit."[22] When fascists spoke of culture, they meant a proper attitude toward life: encompassing the ability to accept a faith, the work ethic, and discipline, but also receptivity to art and the appreciation of the native landscape.[23] The true community was symbolized by factors opposed to materialism, by art and literature, the symbols of the past and the stereotypes of the present. The National Socialist emphasis upon myth, symbol, literature, and art is indeed common to all fascism.

If then fascism saw itself as a cultural movement, any comparative study must be based upon an analysis of cultural similarities and differences. Social and economic programs varied widely, not only between different fascisms but within each fascist movement. Some historians and political scientists have stumbled over this fact; for them, culture defined as "attitudes toward life" is no substitute for neatly coherent systems of political thought. They believe that fascism was devoid of intellectual substance, a mere reflection of movements which depend upon well-constructed ideologies. This has led many of them to underestimate fascism, to see it as a temporary response to crises, vanishing when normality is restored (though Italian fascism, with its twenty years in power, is surely more than a "temporary response"). In reality, fascism was based upon a strong and unique revolutionary tradition, fired by the emphasis on youth and the war experience; it was able to create a mass consensus that was broken only by a lost war.

Fascism was a movement of youth, not only in the sense that it covered a definite span of time but also in its membership. The fin de siècle had seen a rebellion of the young against society, parents, and school. They longed for a new sense of community, not for a "chaos of the soul." These youths were of bourgeois background, and their dominant concern for several generations had been with national unity rather than with social and economic change—for which they felt little need. Thus they were quite prepared to have their urge to revolt directed into national channels, on behalf of a community which seemed to them one of the "soul" and not an artificial creation. Such were the young who streamed not only into the earlier German youth movement but also into the *fasci* and the S.A., and who made up the cadres of other fascist movements. Returned from the war, they wanted to prolong the camaraderie of the trenches. Fascism offered them this chance. It is well to note in this connection that fascists were a new grouping, not yet bureaucratized, and that their supposed open-endedness made them appear more dynamic than rival political parties. The leaders, too, were young—Mussolini became prime minister at thirty-nine; Hitler attained the chancellorship at forty-four.

Youth symbolized vigor and action; ideology was joined to fact. Fascist heroes and martyrs died at an early age in order to enter the pantheon, and symbolic representations of youth expressed the ideal type in artistic form. This was the classical ideal of beauty, which had come to be the stereotype. There must have been many who, like Albert Speer's mother, voted for the Nazis because they were young and clean-cut. The hero of the Italian novel *Generazione* (*Generations*, 1930), by Adolfo Baiocchi, finds his way from communism to fascism. His final conversion comes when he sees his former comrades, now unattractive, dirty, and disheveled, taken away by the police after an unsuccessful attempt at revolution: "These are the men of the future?" Monuments to the soldiers who fell in World War I often represented young Siegfrieds or Greek youths. Indeed, this stereotype was reinforced by the war when the cult of youth joined the cult of the nation.

The war became a symbol of youth in its activism, its optimism, and its heroic sacrifice. For Germans, the Battle of Langenmarck (November 1914), where members of the German youth movement were mowed down in thousands, came to stand for the sacrifice of heroic youth. The flower of the nation supposedly went singing to their death. One writer, Rudolf Binding, asserted that through this sacrifice only German youth had the right to symbolize national renewal among the youth of the world.[24]

Benito Mussolini also declared himself the spokesman of a youth that had shown its mettle in war. While Hitler promised to erase the "shame of Versailles," Mussolini wanted to complete Italy's "mutilated" victory in the Great War. Both took up the slogan of the young and old nations which gained currency after the war as a reassertion of the defeated against the victors.

Fascism thus paradoxically built upon the war experience, which, in different ways, had shaped the outlook of Mussolini and Hitler toward the world: the former moving from a Nietzschean rather than a Marxist socialism to ideals of nationalism and struggle; the latter deepening his ever present racist world view. Above all, for millions of their contemporaries the war was the most profound experience of their lives. While some became pacifists, many attempted to confront the mass death they had witnessed by elevating it into myth. Both in Germany and Italy the myth of the war experience—the glory of the struggle, the legacy of the martyrs, the camaraderie of the trenches—defeated any resolve never to have war again. France, the victorious and satisfied nation, saw the rise of powerful veterans' movements which proclaimed an end to all war;[25] but in Germany and Italy such movements proclaimed the coming resurrection of the fatherland.

The Left in Germany and Italy, as in all other nations, had difficulty in coming to grips with this war experience, shared though it was by their own members. Social Democrats and communists sometimes paraded in their old uniforms (but without decorations), and founded self-defense and paramilitary organizations, like the Reichsbanner in Germany (which was supposed to defend the Republic). But in the last resort the Left was halfhearted about all this, and its didactic and cosmopolitan heritage, as well as its pacifist traditions, proved the stronger. The communists who were ready to discard this past found it impossible to redirect loyalty away from the fatherland and toward a Red Army.[26] To this day, few historians have investigated the Left's confrontation with the war experience, perhaps in itself a comment on the continued underestimation of this myth as a political force. Here was a political void readily occupied by the fascists.

The war experience aided fascism in another, more indirect manner. The front-line soldiers had become immune to the horrors of war, mass death, wounded and mutilated comrades. They had faced such unparalleled events either with stoicism or with a sense of sacrifice—war had given meaning to their dull and routine lives. Indeed, the war experience, despite all its horrors, catered to the longing for the exceptional, the escape from the treadmill of everyday life and its responsibilities. The political liturgy of fascism with its countless festivals catered to the same dream of excitement, of taking part in meaningful action. Typical was the expression, often repeated during the war, that death in battle had made life worthwhile.

Whatever the actual attitudes of the front-line soldiers during the war, their war experience later became for many a myth, concretized through countless war cemeteries and memorials. The cult of the fallen soldier was central to the myth of the war experience in defeated Germany and Italy, and the dead were used to spur on the living to ever greater efforts of revenge. Mussolini put it succinctly: "A people which deifies its fallen can never be beaten." It was said that Hitler offered up his conquests on the altar of the war dead.[27] The horrors of war became part of an as yet incomplete struggle for national and personal fulfillment.

The acceptance of war was aided by new techniques of communication, which tended to trivialize mass death by making it a familiar part of an organized and directed experience shared by thousands. For example, the battlefields of France and Flanders were among the tourist attractions organized by Thomas Cook and Sons. The massed and impersonal military cemeteries were faced by an equally impersonal mass of tourists, who could buy souvenir shells, helmets, and decorations. Still more important, World War I was also the first war in the era of photography. During the war, postcards, films, and newsreels showed happy and healthy soldiers, and emphasized their work of destroying farms, towns, and churches rather than the dead and wounded. After the war, tourists could photograph the trenches, but what had once been experienced in these trenches was now nicely tidied up and surrounded by flowers and shrubs.

Most people, however, were familiar with the face of war through the countless picture books that appeared after 1918. The illustrations and photos of the dead or wounded were presented as a part of a glorious struggle, a desirable sacrifice that would reap its deserved reward. One such book, typical of the genre, called the war both horrible and yet a purveyor of aesthetic values. Arms were depicted as symbols of the highest human accomplishment, armed conflict as the overcoming of self in the service of collective ideals and values.[28] Horror pictures were transcended, suffused with ideals of sacredness and sacrifice; the dead and mangled corpses of soldiers were by association equated with the body of Christ in the service not of individual but of national salvation.

Through these dual processes of trivialization and transcendence, the war experience served the purposes alike of the dynamic of fascism and of the movement's brutality. Death and suffering lost their sting; the martyrs continued to live as a spiritual part of the nation while exhorting it to regenerate itself and to destroy its enemies.

Joseph Goebbels's definition of the nature of a revolutionary, written in 1945 when Germany faced defeat, is typical of the process of brutalization begun by World War I. The Nazis, in common with all fascists, had always condemned half measures as typically bourgeois and antirevolutionary. Goebbels now defined as "revolutionary" those who would accept no compromise in executing a scorched earth policy, or in shooting shirkers and deserters. Refusal to carry out such actions marked the worn-out old bourgeois.[29] During the desperate years of the Republic of Salò, Mussolini also resorted to brutal measures, even executing pupils who refused to attend school.[30] There is little doubt that the myth of the war experience made fascist brutality more acceptable and fascism itself more attractive. Here was none of the ambivalence, shared by socialists and liberals, toward what millions must have regarded as the high point of their otherwise uneventful lives.

The crucial role which the war experience played in National Socialism is well enough known. The war was "a lovely dream" and a "miracle of achievement," as one Nazi children's book put it. Any death in war was a hero's death and thus the true fulfillment of life.[31] There was no doubt here about the "greatness and necessity of war."[32] In Mussolini's hands, this myth had even greater force because of the absence of a truly coherent volkish ideology in Italy. The fascist struggle was a continuation of the war experience. But here, as in Germany, the glorification of struggle was linked to wartime camaraderie and put forward as an example to end class divisions within the nation. "Not class war but class solidarity" reigned in face of death, wrote an Italian socialist in the last months of the war; it was not a conflict between potentates or capitalists but a necessity for the defense of the people. Historical materialism was dead.[33]

The *élan* of the battlefield was transformed into activism at home. The *fasci* and the German storm troopers regarded their postwar world as an enemy, which as patriotic shock troops they must destroy. Indeed, the leaders of these formations were in large part former front-line officers: Roehm, the head of the S.A.; Codreanu, founder of the Iron Guard; De Bono in Italy and Szalasi in Hungary—to give only a few examples. But this activism was tamed by the "magic" of the leadership of which Gustave Le Bon had written toward the end of the nineteenth century. Among the returned veterans it was even more easily controllable, for they desperately sought comradeship and leadership, not only because of the war experience but also to counteract their sense of isolation within a nation that had not lived up to their expectations.

The revolutionary tradition of the "Third Force" contained legendary ingredients essential to this taming process: stress upon the national past and the mystical community of the nation; emphasis upon that middle-class respectability which proved essential for political success. The "cult element" to which we referred earlier gave it direction by channeling attention toward the eternal verities, which must never be forgotten. Activism there must be, enthusiasm was essential; but it had to focus upon the leader, who would direct it into the proper "eternal" channels.

Here the liturgical element must be mentioned again, for the "eternal verities" were purveyed and reinforced through the endless repetition of slogans, choruses, symbols, and participation in mass ceremonies. These were the techniques that went into the taming of the revolution and that made fascism a new religion with rites long familiar through centuries of religious observance. Fascist mass meetings seemed something new, but in reality they contained predominantly traditional elements in technique as well as in ideology.

To be sure, this process did not always work. The youthful enthusiasm that reigned at the outset of the movement was apt to be disappointed with its course. Italy, where fascism lasted longest, provides the best example, for the danger point came with the second fascist generation. There, the young men of the "class of '35" wanted to return to the beginnings of the movement, to its activism and its war on alienation—in short, to construct the fascist utopia. By 1936, they had formed a resistance movement within

Italian fascism, which stressed that "open-endedness" the revolution had at first seemed to promise: to go to "the limits of fascism where all possibilities are open."[34] Similar signs can be discerned as Nazism developed, but here the SS managed to capture the activist spirit. Had it not been for the war, Hitler might well have had difficulty with the SS, which thought of itself as an activist and spartan élite. But then fascism never had a chance to grow old except in Italy; given the ingredients that went into the revolution, old age might have presented the movement with a severe crisis.

But in the last resort taming was always combined with activism, traditionalism inevitably went hand in hand with a nostalgic revolution. Both Hitler and Mussolini disliked drawing up party programs, for this smacked of "dogmatism." Fascism stressed "movement"—Hitler called his party a *"Bewegung,"* and Mussolini for some time favored Marinetti's Futurism as an artistic and literary form that stressed both movement and struggle. All European fascisms gave the impression that the movement was open-ended, a continuous Nietzschean ecstasy. But in reality definite limits were provided to this activism by the emphasis upon nationalism, sometimes upon racism, and by the longing for a restoration of traditional morality. The only variety of fascism of which this is not wholly true is to be found among the intellectuals in France. There a man like Drieu La Rochelle continued to exalt the "provisional" —the idea that all existing reality can be destroyed in one moment.[35] Elsewhere that reality was "eternal," and activism was directed into destroying the existing order so that the eternal verity of Volk or nation could triumph, and with it the restoration of traditional morality.

The traditionalism of the fascist movement coincided with the most basic of bourgeois moral prejudices. When Hans Naumann spoke at the Nazi book-burning in 1933, he exalted activism; the more books burned the better. But he ended his speech by stressing the traditional bonds of family and Volk. Giuseppe Bottai, too, had called for a "spiritual renewal," and, in Belgium, the leading Rexist Jean Denis held that without a moral revolution there could be no revolution at all.[36] Some fascisms defined the moral revolution within the context of a traditional Christianity: this is true of the Belgian Rexist movement, for example, as well as of the Rumanian Iron Guard. The Nazis substituted racism for religion, but once more, the morality was that shared with the rest of the bour-geoisie.

Almost all analyses of fascism have been preoccupied with the crucial support it received from the bourgeoisie. However, the Marxist model, based upon the function of each class in the pro-cess of production, seems too narrow to account for the general support of fascism. A common ethos united businessmen, govern-ment officials, and the intellectual professions that made up the bourgeoisie.[37] They were concerned about their status, access to education, and opportunity for advancement. At the same time they saw their world as resting upon the pillars of respectability, hard work, self-discipline, and good manners—always exempli-fied in the stereotyped ideal of male beauty already mentioned. The so-called middle-class morality, which had come to dominate Europe since the end of the eighteenth century, gave them security in a competitive world. Moreover, toward the end of the nine-teenth century, the very structure of this world was challenged through the youthful revolt against accepted manners and morals by some schoolboys, bohemians, radicals, and the cultural avant garde.

Nationalism annexed this bourgeois world (as did racism in cen-tral Europe), promising to protect it and to restore its purity against all challengers. This explains the puritanism of National Socialism, its emphasis upon chastity, the family, good manners, and the ban-ishment of women from public life. However, there is no evidence that the workers did not also share such longings: the workers' culture did not oppose the virtues of the bourgeois consensus. There was no repeating the brief relaxation of manners and morals that occurred in the years following the October Revolution in Russia.

Thomas Childers has supplied much evidence concerning the amorphous nature of the Nazi electorate. The Nazis, in the end, capitalized on the resentment felt by all classes, including the working class.[38] Italian fascism, Renzo De Felice has told us, was in large part an expression of the emerging middle classes, the bour-geois who were already an important social force and were now attempting to acquire political power.[39] This is exactly the opposite of the Bonapartist analysis, so popular among the Left, which adapts to fascism Karl Marx's discussion of the dictatorship of

Napoleon III. The middle class gave up political power, so the argument runs, in order to keep their social and economic power.

As a matter of fact, in Italy, and also in other European fascist movements, many important leaders came from the Left: for the most part they were syndicalists inspired by the war and the activism promised by the movement. Jacques Doriot, the only really significant leader of French fascism, traveled from the militant Left to fascism—a road, as Gilbert Allardyce has shown, not so different from that of Mussolini earlier. Doriot wanted a greater dynamic within French communism, and was impatient with party bureaucracy and discipline. As a fascist, he advocated "a revolution in France with French materials."[40] Nationalism became the refuge for such frustrated revolutionaries. National Socialism did not, by and large, attract former leaders of the Left. German Social Democrats and communists were too disciplined to desert so easily; moreover, they formed an almost self-contained subculture, whose comfort was not readily rejected. Revolutionary traditions, lively in Italy and France, had become fossilized dogma in Germany.

Fascism thus attracted a motley crowd of followers from different backgrounds and of all classes, even though the bourgeoisie provided the backbone of the movement and most of the leaders. Rather than renewed attempts to show that fascism could not attract the working class, at best a partial truth, the very diversity of such support needs new analysis. Most large-scale business and industrial enterprise, as we now know, did not support the Nazis before their seizure of power, and indeed looked upon them as potential radicals.[41] The Hitler government of 1933, which they did support, was a coalition in which conservatives predominated. When, six months later, the conservatives left the cabinet, industrialists compromised with Hitler, as the Industrial Alliance in Italy came to support Mussolini. But even so, the primacy of fascist politics over economics remains a fact: the myth pushed economic interests into a subservient position. Until the very end, Adolf Hitler believed that a political confession of faith was the prerequisite for all action. From his experience in World War I, he drew the lesson that man's world view was primary in determining his fate.[42] It was the fascist myth which had cross-class appeal, and which, together with the tangible successes of the régimes, made possible the consensus upon which they were at first based.

Fascist movements seem to have been most successful in mobilizing the lower classes in underdeveloped countries where the middle class was small and isolated. Spain provides one example in the West, and it is true of the Iron Guard as well as of the Hungarian fascist movement in eastern Europe. To be sure, in those countries the bourgeoisie was not as strong as elsewhere; but another factor is of greater importance in explaining the fascist appeal to the laboring and peasant classes. Here, for the first time, was a movement which tried to bring these segments of society into political participation, for Marxist movements were prohibited. The stress upon an end to alienation, the ideal of the organic community, brought dividends—for the exclusion of workers and peasants from society had been so total that purely economic considerations could for them certainly take second place.

The fascist myth was based upon the national mystique, its own revolutionary and dynamic traditions, which we have discussed, and the continuation of the war experience in peacetime. It also encompassed remnants of previous ideologies and political attitudes, many of them hostile to fascist traditions. It was a scavenger which attempted to annex all that had appealed to people in the nineteenth- and twentieth-century past: romanticism, liberalism, and socialism, as well as Darwinism and modern technology. Too little attention has been paid to this scavenging; it has been subsumed under the so-called eclecticism of fascism. But in reality all these fragments of the past were integrated into a coherent attitude toward life through the basic fascist nationalist myth.

The romantic tradition infused the national mystique, but it was also present in the literature and art supported by the fascists, especially the Nazis. It has supplied the framework for a popular culture that had changed little during the preceding century. Adventure, danger, and romantic love were the constant themes, but always combined with the virtues we have mentioned: hard work, sexual purity, and the respectability at the core of bourgeois morality. Here the novels of Karl May in Germany, with a circulation of half a million by 1913 and 18 million by 1938, are typical. They were set in faraway places—the American plains or the Orient—and combined a romantic setting with the defense of good against evil, bodily purity, law and order, against those who would destroy them. Interestingly enough, many Nazis wanted to ban May's stories because he exalted the American Indian race and pleaded for tolerance and understanding between peoples. Hitler, however, had his novels distributed to the armed forces during World War II. He once said that Karl May had opened his eyes to the world, and this was true of many millions of German youth. The virtues which American Indian heroes defended against evil European trappers were precisely those the Nazis also promised to defend. They called themselves tolerant—but the tolerance and compassion that fill May's novels would come about only after Hitler had won his battles, and eliminated the "intolerant" Jewish world conspiracy.[43]

Unfortunately, we have seen no detailed analysis of similar novels popular in the Italy of the 1920s and 1930s.[44] But both National Socialism and Italian fascism used the phrase "romantic realism" to describe realistic character portrayal within a romantic setting.[45] In Italy, such realism was expressed through the strictness of classical form. Thus Francesco Sapori could summarize these aspirations: "Live romantically, as well as according to the classical idea. Long live Italy!"[46] Sapori was a member of the "Novocento" (Twentieth-Century) group of writers and artists who wanted to create a native Italian style that was both natural and neo-classical. Though directed by Mussolini's friend Margherita Sarfatti, it was but one of several competing cultural groups in fascist Italy. "Magic realism" was their formula, created by the writer Massimo Bontempelli. Such romantic realism had already informed popular literature in the past, and provided a mystical and sentimental dimension even while proclaiming a clarity of purpose everyone could understand. Painters like Casorati in fascist Italy or Adolf Ziegler in Germany (Hitler's own favorite) provided corresponding examples in the visual arts.

Admittedly, here as elsewhere "magic realism" exemplified only one trend in Italy, while in Germany it was officially approved and furthered. But even in Germany nonapproved literature could easily be obtained, at least until the war broke out. Parallels can also be drawn between Italian and German architecture under fascism, though in Italy a party building could still reflect avant-garde style. (In Germany, among nonrepresentational buildings and even in military barracks, the otherwise condemned Bauhaus style often continued.) The Mussolini Forum was praised for the same "simplicity of style," the hard lines, displayed by the Nazi Nuremberg Stadium. The plea that architectural material must be genuine and subordinated to that "divine harmony" which reflected the Italian spirit was duplicated in Germany.[47]

Romanticism was integrated into fascism all the more easily because it had always provided the major inspiration for nationalist thought. "Magic realism" stood side by side with the romanticized view of the past: whether the ancient Germans who had defeated the Roman Legions, or those Roman ruins that were now bathed nightly in a romantic light, the kind of illumination so attractive to Italian fascism. Differences between the two political styles existed. The liturgy was not as fully developed in Italy as in Germany; and the régime was less concerned with the total control of culture. The illusion that the Italian fascist dictatorship was an innovative force in the arts could persist into the 1930s,[48] but in Germany no such illusion was ever possible. However, these are matters of degree, not absolutes. Some of the differences may relate to the fact that Mussolini was a journalist, never really comfortable with the visual expressions of fascism, while Hitler thought of himself as an architect and was not truly interested in the written word.

Liberal ideas were interwoven with romanticism. Middle-class manners and morals would lead to success (the Cinderellas of popular literature were models of respectability). But as there was no real Horatio Alger tradition in Europe, it was the "pure heart" that counted and made possible Cinderella's progress from kitchen to ballroom. Moreover, fascists everywhere accepted the opposition to degeneration which the liberal Max Nordau had popularized during the last decade of the nineteenth century.

Nordau saw the moderns in art and literature as literally sick people, maintaining that their lack of clarity, inability to uphold bourgeois moral standards, and absence of self-discipline all sprang from the degeneration of their physical organism. The Nazis, of course, illustrated their opposition to modernity by the exhibition of "degenerate art," and Hitler and Mussolini prided themselves on the clarity of their rhetoric. Fascism deprived the concept of degeneration of its original foundations: clinical observation linked to a universe ruled by scientific laws. But this was typical of such annexations—the popular and traditional superstructure was absorbed but now set upon racial or national bases.

The concept of degeneration had provided the foil to the liberal's concept of clarity, decency, and natural laws. Fascism also took over the ideals of tolerance and freedom, changing both to fit its model. Tolerance, as mentioned earlier, was claimed by fascists in antithesis to their supposedly intolerant enemies, while freedom was placed within the community. To be tolerant meant not tolerating those who opposed fascism: individual liberty was possible only within the collectivity. Here once more, concepts that had become part and parcel of bourgeois thought were not rejected (as so many historians have claimed) but instead annexed—fascism would bring about ideals with which people were comfortable, but only on its own terms.

Socialism was also emasculated. The hatred of capitalism was directed against finance capitalism only. At first glance, the opposition to the bourgeoisie seemed shared equally between Nazis and socialists, as both thundered against the moribund bourgeois era. However, fascism cut away the class basis of socialist opposition to the bourgeoisie and substituted the war between generations. "Bourgeois" no longer meant a class of exploiters, but the old and worn out, those who lacked a vibrant dynamic. The setting of the young against the old was a theme which, as we saw earlier, fascism annexed from the fin de siècle and then transferred from people to nations. Thus young nations with their dynamic fascist youth confronted the old nations with their ancient parliamentarians. This was the fascist "class struggle," and here the socialist vocabulary was employed. In this, the Italian fascists went beyond the National Socialists. Fascist students exalted the Latin, Roman, Italian revolution at the expense of the fat and pacifist bourgeois. Indeed, in Italy the lower middle class (never clearly defined) was constantly berated as being incapable of grasping the myths of nationalism and war, and as lacking any power of social interaction.[49] It is perhaps ironic that certain Italian fascists saw their adversary as precisely that lower middle class which, according to some modern historians, constituted the social basis of fascism. This antibourgeois rhetoric was undoubtedly part of the resentment that fascist leaders, usually from modest backgrounds, felt against so-called society.

Fascists not only borrowed socialist rhetoric, they also made use of some ritual examples provided by working-class meetings: the massed flags, and the color red, for example. Moreover, some of the socialist workers' cultural and sports organizations were adapted to fascist ends. The liturgy was for the most part based on nationalist precedent from the previous century, but, with typical electicism, useful socialist examples were also appropriated.[50]

Fascism absorbed important parts of well-established ideologies like romanticism, liberalism, or socialism; but it was also not afraid to annex modern technology if this could be embedded within fascist myths. Indeed, the dictators were singularly perceptive in their appreciation of technological advance.

Both Hitler and Mussolini had a passion for speed—aircraft and powerful cars provided one outlet for their activism. Hitler was the first German politician to use a plane in order to make many campaign appearances throughout Germany on the same day. Use of the latest technology was immediately linked to Nazi ideology: Hitler literally dropping from the sky, Hitler by his personal courage helping to pilot his plane through an awesome storm (this story with its obvious analogy was required reading in Third Reich schools). But Mussolini shared this passion, and in both régimes air force leaders like Hermann Goering or Italo Balbo had a special status and were surrounded by an aura of adventure and daring.

Anson Rabinbach has shown how technology was used to improve modes of production in Germany, how the program known as the "beauty of labor" turned fear of the machine into a glorification of technology through emphasis on efficiency and volkish aesthetics.[51] The newest technology was annexed to an ideology that looked to the past in order to determine the future.

Little is as yet known of how Italian fascism absorbed and used traditional modes of thought as well as the newest technology. In fact, the Italian Nationalist Association (founded in 1910), which was to be Mussolini's partner in fascist rule, combined emphasis upon industrial growth and modern technology with the nationalist mystique.[52] Nationalism, and even volkish thought, were not necessarily opposed to modernization, provided it was made to serve the ideology of the régime, which in turn justified it. That is why, for example, the Nazis supported modern technology and industrial planning, but opposed modern physics as a "Jewish science"—pragmatism was accepted, but any science resting on an abstract theoretical base had to be examined for racial purity.

Italian fascism had no such antiscientific bias. There, for example, Enrico Fermi flourished during the 1930s until the proclamation of the racial laws. In Germany, volkish thought transformed the scientist into a provincial. For example, Third Reich films praised the faithful family physician, and favorably contrasted this avuncular type to a many-sided scientist like Rudolf Virchow. For all that, Germany as well as Italy integrated technology into fascism, using it to praise and further modernization as well as to enhance the political liturgy (as in Albert Speer's use of lighting in mass festivals).

Within its basic presuppositions of revolution, nationalism, and the war experience, fascism contained two rhythms: the amoeba-like absorption of ideas from the mainstream of popular thought and culture, countered by the urge toward activism and its taming. Both were set within the nationalist myth, and the whole gave the proper attitude toward life. Fascism attempted to cater to everything held dear, to give new meaning to daily routine and to offer salvation without risk. The fact that Adolf Hitler shared in popular tastes and longings, that in this sense he was a man of the people, was one vital ingredient of his success. Mussolini entertained intellectual pretensions that Hitler never claimed, nor did he share the tastes of the people, perhaps because in Italy popular culture was diversified in a nation with stronger regional traditions and ties than Germany.

The frequent contention that fascist culture diverged from the mainstream of European culture cannot be upheld; on the contrary, it absorbed most of what had (or proved to have) the greatest mass appeal in the past. In fact, it positioned itself much more in this mainstream than socialism, which tried to educate and elevate the tastes of the worker. Fascism made no such attempt: it accepted the common man's preferences and went on to direct them to its own ends. Moreover, the lack of original ideas was not a disadvantage, as many historians have implied, for originality does not lead to success in an age of democratic mass politics. The synthesis which fascism attempted between activism and order, revolution and the absorption of past traditions, proved singularly successful. To be sure, Marxism, conservatism, and liberalism made original contributions to European thought. But they underwent a long period of gestation, and by the time they became politically important movements, they had founded their own traditions. Fascism had no time to create a tradition for itself: like Hitler, it was in a hurry, confronted with an old order that seemed about to fall. Those who did not strike at once were sure to be overtaken by other radicals of the Left or Right.

Yet fascism would never have worked without the tangible successes achieved by fascist régimes; social and economic factors are not to be ignored. But the preeminence of the cultural factors already discussed is certainly the other half of the dialectic. Without them, the ways in which the men and women of those times were motivated cannot be properly understood.

What, then, of the fascist utopia? It was certainly a part of the fascist myth. The fairy tale would come true once the enemies had been defeated. The happy ending was assured. But first men must "overcome"—the mystical ingredient of National Socialism was strong here; and in Italy, the ideal of continuing the wartime sacrifice was stressed. The happy end would bring about the "new Rome" or the Third German Empire, infused with middle-class virtues, a combination of the ancient past and the nineteenth-century bourgeois ideal. The new fascist man would usher in this utopia—and he already existed, exemplified by the Führer and the Duce. Eventually, it was implied, all Germans or Italians would approach their example.

The new fascist man provided the stereotype for all fascist movements. He was, naturally, masculine: fascism represented itself as a society of males, a result of the struggle for national unity that had created fellowships such as "Young Italy," or the German fraternities and gymnastic societies. Moreover, the cult of masculinity of the fin de siècle, which Nietzsche himself so well exemplified, contributed its influence. More immediately, a male society continued into the peace the wartime camaraderie of the trenches, that myth of the war experience so important in all fascism. The masculine ideal did not remain abstract, but was personified in ideals of male strength and beauty.

Such an ideal may be vague, as in a children's book where the Duce is described as being as beautiful as the sun, as good as the light, and as strong as the hurricane.[53] It is less vague in sculptures of the Duce as a Renaissance prince or, more often, as the emperor Augustus. In addition, the innumerable pictures of the Duce harvesting, running, boxing—often bare-chested—projected a strong and invulnerable masculinity. Yet such stereotypes were not all-pervasive in Italy; they were absent even at such events as the exhibition honoring the tenth anniversary of the March on Rome (1933).[54] The inner characteristics of this new man were more clearly defined: athletic, persevering, filled with self-denial and the spirit of sacrifice. At the same time, the new fascist man must be energetic, courageous, and laconic.[55] The ideal fascist was the very opposite of muddleheaded, talkative, intellectualizing liberals and socialists—the exhausted, tired old men of the old order. Indeed, Italian fascism's dream of an age-old masculine ideal has not vanished from our own time.

Germany shared such ideals of the male society and the new fascist man, but much more consistently. This gave the Nazi utopia a different direction from that of Italy. Volkish thought had always advocated the ideal of the "Bund" of males; the youth movement reinforced the link between the fellowship of men and the national mystique, while the war completed the task. Mussolini might talk about the war and the continuing struggle, but right-wing Germans believed that a new race of men had already grown out of the war—energy come alive, as Ernst Jünger put it; lithe, muscular bodies, angular faces, and eyes hardened by the horrors they had seen.[56] Here the inner nature of the new race was immediately connected with its outward features. Whenever Adolf Hitler talked about the "new German," he wasted little time on the inner self of the Aryan but instead defined him immediately through an ideal of beauty—"*Rank und Schlank*" (slim and tall) was his phrase.[57] There was never any doubt about how the ideal German looked, and it is impossible to imagine a Nazi exposition without the presence of the stereotype.

Racism made the difference. It gave to volkish thought a dimension which Italian fascism lacked. To be sure, as we shall see later, an effort was made to introduce this dimension into Italy with the Racial Laws of 1938, but these were largely stillborn as far as the

stereotype was concerned. The Aryan myth had from its beginning in the eighteenth century linked the inward to the outward
man, and combined scientific pretensions with an aesthetic theory
that saw in Greek sculpture the ideal of male beauty.[58] Indeed,
while the nude male was commonplace in German volkish art, the
female was usually veiled: the modest and chaste bearer of the
children of the race had to be hidden from public view. (Adolf Hitler
thought that he must hide Eva Braun from public scrutiny, while
Mussolini took no such pains about his wife or his mistresses.)

Was the fascist man then tied to the past or was he the creator of
new values? Renzo De Felice has seen here one of the chief differences between Italian fascism and German National Socialism.
For the Germans, the man of the future had always existed; even
in the past, for the race was eternal, like the trunk of a tree. The
ideal man of Italian fascism created new values.[59] If we look at the
famous definition of fascism given by Mussolini and Giovanni
Gentile in the *Encyclopedia Italiana* (1932), "fascist man" is, on the
one hand, set within the Italian patriotic tradition, and, on the
other, supposed to live a superior life unconstrained by space and
time. He must sacrifice his personal interests and realize that it is
his spirituality which gives him human values. But this spirituality
must be informed by history, meaning Italian traditions and national memories. Such an apparent paradox of standing within
and yet soaring above tradition accompanied most discussions of
the new fascist man in Italy. Man must proceed to ever higher
forms of consciousness, culture must not crystallize, and yet the
great Italian authors of the past must be studied ("These are germs
which can fructify our spirit and give us spontaneity").[60] The Universal Roman Exhibition of 1942 illustrated such principles concretely. Indeed, the new Rome built for this exhibition (Rome Eure)
was allegedly to transmit this heritage to its own day, as shown by
the effort to imitate all the Italian architectural styles of the past:
Roman, Renaissance, and Baroque. But the exhibition was also
supposed to be a signpost for the future. These intentions were
symbolized by the completion of the archaeological excavations of
Ostia Antiqua, creating access to it by means of an Autostrada, and
as the catalogue tells us, thus making the new Rome encompass
the old,[61] except that by 1942 what was supposed to be unique had
been tamed into a historical eclecticism.

In fact, the new fascist man in Italy ignored history no more than his Nazi counterpart.[62] The cult of the Roman past was pervasive; it determined the fascist stereotype whenever we do find it. But this past remained, at least until the final years of the régime, a jumping-off point for the ideal fascist man of the future. Tradition informed his consciousness, but he himself had to rise beyond it without losing sight of his starting point. Such a flexible attitude toward the ideal reflected the greater openness of Italian fascism to the new in both art and literature. This utopia was willing to leave the door to the future halfway open, while in Germany it was shut tight. The difference reflects the groping of Italian fascism for an ideology, its greater emphasis upon struggle and energy, its syndicalist and Futurist elements.

The new German incorporated the eternal values of the race, summarized in a frequently used admonition: "You yourself represent a thousand future years and a thousand years of the past,"[63] in one phrasing of this well-known Nazi attitude. The SS, the most dynamic of all party organizations, fits into this picture. True, an official SS publication tells us that the SS man should never be a conformist, and every SS generation should improve upon its predecessors. Yet the maxim that "History is human fate" meant emphasis upon racial ancestry, that the accomplishments of the past dominated the present and determined the future.[64]

Was this ideal man then to be stripped of his individuality? Was individuality not a part of the fascist utopia? For liberal democracy and for social democracy, the final goal of all social organization was the good of the individual. Did fascism really change this goal? To do so, it would have to eradicate one of the deepest utopian traditions. But it was the pattern of fascism to annex and bend to its purpose, rather than change, concepts deeply rooted in the national consciousness, and individualism was not exempted from this pattern, being at the same time retained and redefined. In contrast to unlimited economic and social competition, setting man against man, the ideal of an organic community had taken root in the previous century. The German youth movement had thought of itself as such a community, voluntarily joined but based upon shared origins. The ideal of the *"équipe"* played a similar role among French fascist intellectuals, a team spirit grounded in a common world view, exalted by the young writers grouped around the newspaper *Je Suis Partout*. It was the camaraderie of trench life, which many had actually experienced and which for others had become a myth, that seemed to provide the model for the ideal society. To be sure, they had been conscripted, but this awkward fact was ignored as veterans thought back to comradeship under fire, when each man had had to subjugate his will to that of the others in his unit in order to survive.

Fascism could all the more easily annex this idea of community since nationalism had always advocated it: individualism is only possible when men voluntarily join together on the basis of a common origin, attitude, and purpose. Fascism dropped the voluntary aspect, of course, but only as a temporary measure. Education was directed to help the young understand that *"Credere, Obedire e Combattere"* on behalf of the national community was the true fulfillment of individualism.[65] The prospectus of the élite Nazi school at Feldafing sums up this redefinition of individualism: "He who can do what he wants is not free, but he is free who does what he should. He who feels himself without chains is not free, but enslaved to his passions."[66]

Individualism under fascism then meant self-fulfillment while sheltering within the collectivity, having the best of both worlds. It is therefore mistaken to characterize fascism simply as anti-individualist, for this ignores the longing for a true community in which the like-minded joined together, each through his own power of will. The French fascist intellectuals, merely a coterie out of power, could praise the "provisional," the idea that all existing reality could be destroyed at any moment.[67] Yet for all this Nietzschean exaltation, one of their number, Robert Brasillach, not only found refuge in an "inner fatherland" but also saw in his beloved Paris a collection of small villages in which he could be at home. Between the wars the young men in the Latin Quarter wanted to be original and spontaneous, while longing for an end to intellectual anarchy.[68] Fascism gave them the means to do all that and still remain sheltered by the national community.

These French fascists expressed an *élan* typical of fascism as a movement out of power, though even here the dynamic had to be tamed. Fascism in power was often a disappointment to the young fascist activists. Although it kept much of the earlier rhetoric, once in power it inevitably became the Establishment. Indeed, Stanley

Payne's suggestion that at that point the differences between fascism and the reaction become less marked seems close to the facts, if not to the professed ideology.[69] The reactionaries, men like Francisco Franco, based themselves on the traditional hierarchies, on the status quo and, as often as not, took as their ideology the Christianity of the Catholic Church. The fascist revolutionary base, the dynamic nationalist attitudes and the prominent rhythms, were lacking. However, before the relationship between fascism and the reaction can be redefined, more detailed comparison is needed between, for example, the various stages of Mussolini's government and the evolution of Franco's rule in Spain. Here, once again, the particular national histories of those countries are of great importance.

Although national differences culminated in the distinctions between the "new fascist man" of Italy and of Germany, all fascism essentially went back to the antiparliamentary tradition of the nineteenth century in order to redefine popular participation in politics. Both such participation and individual liberty were supposedly part of a collective experience. It must not be forgotten that, in the last resort, all fascisms were nationalisms, sharing the cult of national symbols and myths as well as the preoccupation with mythical national origins. Himmler sent an expedition to Tibet in order to discover Aryan origins, while other young Germans searched for the original Aryans closer to home in Scandinavia. The Italian fascist Foreign Ministry sponsored archaeological expeditions to revive the idea of the Roman Empire,[70] while Mussolini restored Rome's ancient ruins, saying that the city was Italian fascism's eternal symbol. The Museum of Classical Antiquity, named after the Duce, was situated in the Campodoglio, in the heart of ancient Rome. Nationalism meant emphasis upon origins and continuity, however much the Italian fascist man was supposed to be a man of the future.

Racism and anti-Semitism were not a necessary component of fascism, and certainly not of those parts of the movement that looked for their model to Italy, where until 1938, racism did not exist. Léon Degrelle, the leader of the Belgian Rexists, at one time explicitly repudiated that racism which he was later to embrace wholeheartedly (to become Hitler's favorite foreign National Socialist). What, he asked, is the "true race"—the Belgian, the Flam-

and, or the Walloon? From the Flemish side, the newspaper *De Daad* inveighed against race hatred and called upon "upright Jews" to repudiate the Marxists in their midst.[71]

Even Dutch National Socialism under Anton Andriaan Mussert did not at first appeal to racism and kept silent about the Jews, an attitude the German Nazis were later to find incomprehensible. The French fascist group around the newspaper *Je Suis Partout* did go in for anti-Semitism, but even here the Germans were accused of exaggerating the racial issue, for good relations were possible with a foreign people like the Jews.[72] This state of affairs did not last. By 1938 Mussolini had turned racist, and not wholly because of German influence. Through racism he tried to reinvigorate his ageing fascism, to give a new cause to a young generation becoming disillusioned with his revolution.

It was only in central and eastern Europe that racism was from the beginning an integral part of fascist ideology. In eastern Europe were to be found the masses of Jewry, still under quasi-ghetto conditions. They were largely a distinct part of the population and vulnerable to attack. Jews prayed differently, dressed differently, and spoke a different language (Yiddish). Even if some were assimilated, enough nonassimilated Jews remained to demonstrate the clash of cultures that underlay much of the anti-Semitism in the region. Moreover, in countries like Rumania or Hungary the Jews had become *the* middle class, forming a vulnerable entity within the nation as that class which seemed to exploit the rest of the population through its commercial activities. No wonder the Rumanian Iron Guard, in appealing to the nationalism of the peasants, became violently anti-Semitic and even racist despite their Christian orientation—for they had begun as the legion of the "Archangel Michael."

From the 1880s onward, the masses of East European Jewry began to emigrate into the neighboring countries, predominantly Germany and Austria. The account in *Mein Kampf* of how sharply Hitler reacted to the sight of such strangers in prewar Vienna may well have been typical. However that may be, the facts of the situation in that part of Europe gave fascism an enemy who could be singled out as symbolizing the forces that must be overcome. Hitler built upon the "Jewish question." This led to a further differentiation of National Socialism from western or southern fascism. For

Hitler, unlike Mussolini, the enemy was not a vague liberalism or Marxism; it was physically embodied by the Jews. Building on the central European tradition of a racist-oriented nationalism, he could give to the enemy of his world view a concrete and human shape.

We have discussed Italian fascism and National Socialism as placing their emphasis upon culture. Both Mussolini and Hitler attempted to epitomize their movements, to provide in their own persons living symbols and an integrative force. Discussing the movements without the leaders is rather like describing the body without the soul. Astute politicians that they were, neither could have succeeded without an instinct for the tastes, wishes, and longings of their people; both ended states of near civil war, managing to provide economic stability and success in foreign policy. Hitler's success was the more spectacular. Between 1933 and 1936, he led Germany from the depths of a depression to full employment. Rearmament played a crucial role in this economic revival, but so did traditional investments and public works. Hitler was instrumental in the building of a powerful army, and his successes in foreign policy need no further comment. It is true, as Sebastian Haffner writes, in the only recent biography of Hitler to bring us new insights,[73] that by 1938 the Nazi régime had converted even former adversaries by the sheer weight of its political and economic success. But here again such consensus, in the last resort, rested upon shared myths and aspirations which, because of this achievement, seemed nearer realization.

Mussolini could at first claim equal success. The population had reason to be satisfied. If in Italy the Duce had not restored work to 6 million unemployed or torn up the Treaty of Versailles, he had brought order and a certain dynamic to a government that had been inert and corrupt. Moreover, Italy avoided most of the European depression. Even the conservatives, who did not want a fascist revolution, could be content with the quality of life. However, by 1938, under the pressure of the unpopular German alliance and then an unpopular war, Mussolini maintained a consensus only with difficulty.

Like many other historians, Haffner fails to recognize Hitler's success as a mass politician in the new style of politics based upon traditional emotions and myths. He therefore easily distinguishes between Hitler and a German people who, in his view, merely responded to the Führer's tangible gains. In fact, on the contrary, just because the preferences and desires of the people coincided so largely with those of the régime, the new political style won their acclaim. Gustave Le Bon had stressed that successful leadership must genuinely share the myths of the people—and both Hitler and Mussolini were his disciples.[74]

We know that real wages fell in Germany, and that the Italian workers and peasants did not materially benefit from their fascist régime. But it would seem that, to many of them, this mattered less than the gain in status. Those who have tried to prove otherwise apparently believe that material interests alone determine men's actions. Hitler and Mussolini knew that what mattered was how people would perceive their position: myth is always more important as a persuader than sober analysis of reality.

Moreover, men, and not just material forces, do make history—not just the leader himself but also the likes and dislikes, wishes and perceptions of the followers. Whenever he took an action which might upset many Germans, Hitler tried—successfully—to appear to be the pushed rather than the pusher. The local riots that preceded all new steps in his Jewish policy are a good example. His tactic of making an aggressive move in foreign or Jewish policy and then proclaiming it as his very last, confused friend and foe alike. Mussolini's policies until the mid-1930s were more modest, but he too combined gestures with patience, moving slowly in order to accomplish his ends. Yet Mussolini came to power much earlier than Hitler, and his achievement, as we have seen, was in avoiding the economic depression Hitler had to overcome. Speaking of the fascist consensus in Italy, Renzo De Felice puts it graphically: "The country was thinking more about the evils that fascism had avoided than whether it brought true benefits."[75] There was a difference between the consensus in Italy and in Germany, even though the two dictators' approaches to politics and their successful emphasis upon the myths that determine human perceptions were similar.

The desired end was different also. Mussolini's long-range objectives were traditional: to create an empire built upon the example of ancient Rome. Hitler's long-range goals were not traditional. A wide gulf divided Adolf Hitler, the provincial whose exposure to the far-out racist sects of Vienna provided his intellectual awakening, and Mussolini, who emerged from the conflicts within international socialism. Mussolini confessed himself to be influenced by some of the masters of European thought—such men as Gustave Le Bon, Georges Sorel, William James, and Vilfredo Pareto—while Hitler, also a pupil of Le Bon, was mainly taken with the thoughts of obscure sectarians like Lanz von Liebenfels, Alfred Schuler, or Dietrich Eckart, who but for their disciple's success would have remained deservedly unknown. From one perspective Mussolini may be called a man of the world, and Adolf Hitler a true believer, a member of an obscure racist-theosophical sect. But then this man who believed in secret sciences, Aryan mythologies, and battles between the powers of light and darkness, through his political genius turned such ideas into the policies of a powerful nation. Hitler's goal was both a traditional empire—"*Lebensraum*"—and the extermination of the Jews. His devotion to genocide summarized the difference between Germany with its volkish tradition and Italy with its humanitarian nationalism of the *Risorgimento*.

Because of his ideological commitment, Hitler showed a tenacity that was absent in Mussolini. This is exemplified on one level by comparing Mussolini, the bon vivant and womanizer, with Hitler, the lonely, spartan figure. But on a more important level, it may have meant that Hitler, knowing the war was lost, would nevertheless continue the conflict so that he could kill as many Jews as possible before the inevitable end. Sebastian Haffner's analysis makes sense here. Hundreds of thousands of Germans died so that Hitler could, at the last moment, kill hundreds of thousands of Jews.[76]

Mussolini was cynical about the potentialities of his own people, and even came to despise them toward the end of his rule. But while Hitler felt himself in the end betrayed by the German people, for the most part he thought in apocalyptic terms. Every action had to contribute to a "final end": indeed, Hitler himself believed in finite time—it was during the short span of his own life, he was fond of remarking, that the Aryan must triumph over Jew and find his "*Lebensraum*." The German mystical tradition asserted itself, as we saw when discussing the "Third Way," not mediated by Jakob Böhme but by an obscure and bizarre racism.

Haffner's speculation as to why Hitler kept on fighting fits better into our picture of the Führer than the usual interpretation (adopted by all other biographers as the sole explanation) that in the end he became a captive of his own myth of invincibility. It is quite possible that Hitler lost contact with reality at some point shortly before the end of the war. However, the Hitler who emerges from the recently published *Goebbels' Diaries* of 1945 does not seem to have lost control, though perhaps he realized earlier than anyone else that the war was lost.[77] To be sure, Hitler and Mussolini became isolated during the course of the war, but the consistency of Hitler's whole life makes the tenacity of his end believable as well. Mussolini changed, whereas Hitler from the end of World War I onward remained locked in his unchanging world view.

Any comparison of Hitler and Mussolini becomes difficult because of the absence of works on Hitler that in historical detail and powerful analysis correspond to Renzo De Felice's monumental biography of Benito Mussolini (four volumes between 1966 and 1974, with one more to appear). Admittedly, Mussolini had no Auschwitz and, unlike Germany, Italy had an important antifascist movement. The Duce also showed more human dimensions than the Führer. Yet the materials for a biography of Hitler exist, and are certainly as extensive as the resources that made De Felice's biography possible. But with the exception of the short and impressionistic book by Haffner, each recent biography of Hitler has merely added minor facts, without any new interpretations of note. To be sure, psychohistorians have begun to analyze the record of Hitler's life in an attempt to find new insights. Yet it is difficult to accept their contention that his mother's death by cancer determined the structure of his entire life, or that the hallucinations of Hitler, the blinded soldier, led to his hatred of the Jews. Scholarship has not really advanced beyond Alan Bullock's pioneering work, *Hitler, A Study in Tyranny*, of 1952. German historians, even of the younger generation, have avoided the figure of the Führer and concentrated instead upon the impersonal causes of National Socialism. The biographies of Hitler have been written by those outside the historical profession. Yet to write about National Socialism while omitting to confront Adolf Hitler, who was at the heart of it, means shirking a true confrontation with the past.

The building blocks for a general theory of fascism now seem to lie before us. Fascism was everywhere an "attitude toward life," based upon a national mystique which might vary from nation to nation. It was also a revolution, attempting to find a "third way" between Marxism and capitalism, but still seeking to escape concrete economic and social change by a retreat into ideology—the "revolution of the spirit" of which Mussolini spoke; or Hitler's "German revolution." However, it encouraged activism, the fight against the existing order of things. Both in Germany and Italy, fascism's chance at power came during conditions of near civil war. But this activism had to be tamed, fascism had to become respectable; for activism was in conflict with the bourgeois desire for law and order, with those middle-class virtues that fascism promised to protect against the dissolving spirit of modernity. It also clashed with the desires of a head of state who represented the old order and who could not be ignored. While Hitler was freed from this constraint by President von Hindenburg's death in 1934, Mussolini always had to report to King Victor Emmanuel. The result was that activism had to exist side by side with the effort to tame it. This was one of the chief problems faced by Hitler and Mussolini before their rise to power and in the early years of their rule.

Fascism could create a consensus because it annexed and focused those hopes and longings that informed diverse political and intellectual movements of the previous century. Like a scavenger, fascism scooped up scraps of romanticism, liberalism, the new technology, and even socialism, to say nothing of a wide variety of other movements lingering from the nineteenth into the twentieth century. But it threw over all these the mantle of a community conceived as sharing a national past, present, and future—a community that was not enforced but "natural," "genuine," and with its own organic strength and life, analogous to nature. The tree became the favorite symbol; but the native landscape or the ruins of the past were also singled out as exemplifying on one level the national community, a human collectivity represented by the Fascist Party.

Support of fascism was not built merely upon appeal to vested interests. Social and economic factors proved crucial in the collapse after World War I, and in the Great Depression, the social and economic successes of fascism gave body to fascist theories. But—and this seems equally crucial—political choices are determined by people's actual perception of their situation, their hopes and longings, the utopia toward which they strive. The fascist "attitude toward life" was suffused by cultural factors through which, as we have attempted to show, the movement presented itself; it was the only mass movement between the wars that could claim to have a largely cross-class following.

In the end, the fascist dream turned out to be a nightmare. It is not likely that Europe will repeat the fascist or the National Socialist experience. The fragments of our Western cultural and ideological past which fascism used for its own purposes still lie ready to be formed into a new synthesis, even if in a different way. Most ominously, nationalism, the basic force that made fascism possible in the first place, not only remains but is growing in strength—still the principal integrative force among peoples and nations. Those ideals of mass politics upon which fascism built its political style are very much alive, ready to absorb and exploit the appropriate myths. The danger of some kind of authoritarianism is always present, however changed from earlier forms or from its present worldwide manifestations.

Speculations about the future depend upon an accurate analysis of the past. This essay is meant to provide a general framework for a discussion of fascism, in the hope of leading us closer to that historical reality without which we cannot understand the past or the present.

TEN

The Mystical Origins of
National Socialism

AFTER NEARLY FORTY YEARS of research, the intellectual origins of National Socialism are no longer shrouded in darkness. The intensity of German national feeling itself is no
longer a sufficient explanation for the rise of National Socialist ideology. Today we are forced to realize that a more complex cultural
development gave its impress to that movement long before it crystallized into a political party.[1] At the very center of this development were ideas that were both of a national and of a romantic and
mystical nature, part of the revolt against positivism which swept
Europe at the end of the nineteenth century. In Germany this revolt took a special turn, perhaps because romanticism struck deeper roots there than elsewhere. The mystical and the occult were
taken both as an explanation and as a solution to man's alienation
from modern society, culture, and politics. Not by everyone, of
course, but by a minority that found a home in the radical Right.
As such, mystical and occult ideas influenced the world view of
early National Socialism, and especially of Adolf Hitler, who to the
end of his life believed in "secret sciences" and occult forces. It is
important to unravel this strand of Nazi ideology because this
mysticism was at the core of much of the irrationalism of the movement, and especially of the world view of its leader. Such ideas
coursed underneath the banality and respectability of National So-

cialism, though they themselves were a reaction to bourgeois society. Protest against bourgeois society and its lifestyle was widespread, but here our concern is with a specific protest against bourgeois materialism and positivism by men and women who lived on the fringes of middle-class society; eccentrics who merit our attention only because Adolf Hitler and a few other important Nazis took them seriously. This German reaction to positivism became intimately bound up with a belief in nature's cosmic life force, a dark force whose mysteries could be understood, not through science but through the occult. An ideology based upon such premises was fused with the glories of an Aryan past, and in turn, that past received a thoroughly romantic and mystical interpretation.

This essay intends to throw light on this ideology and to show its connection with later German history. An obvious connection can be seen through some of the men who participated in this stream of thought, men who later became prominent in the National Socialist movement. We are primarily concerned with the actual formation of this ideology from the 1890s to the first decade of the twentieth century. This is necessary because historians have by and large ignored this stream of thought as being too outré to be taken seriously. Who indeed can take seriously an ideology that drew upon the occultism of Madame Blavatsky, rejected science in favor of "seeing with one's soul," and came dangerously close to sun worship?

The early formulators of this romantic and mystic world view were men like Paul de Lagarde (1827–1891), Guido von List (1848–1919), Alfred Schuler (1865–1923), and above all, Julius Langbehn (1851–1907).[2] They were popularized by publishers like Eugen Diederichs of Jena, whose influence was manifest in the diverse branches of the movement. It was Langbehn who pithily summarized their common aim: "to transform Germans into artists."[3] By "artist" these men meant not a certain profession but a certain world view opposed to that which they called the "man machine." This transformation, which they felt had been omitted when Germany became unified, would convert the materialism and science of contemporary Germany into an artistic outlook upon the world, an outlook that would result in an all-encompassing national renewal. Such a viewpoint was connected to their belief in the cosmic life force, which opposed all that was artificial and man-made.

Langbehn in his *Rembrandt als Erzieher* (*Rembrandt as Educator*, 1890) supplied the key to this transformation: mysticism was the hidden engine which could transmute science into art.[4] Nature romanticism and the mystical provided the foundation for this ideology. It was no mere coincidence that Eugen Diederichs was the German publisher of Henri Bergson. He saw in Bergson a mysticism, a "new irrationalistic philosophy,"[5] and believed that the development of Germany could only progress in opposition to rationalism. The world picture, Diederichs maintained, must be grasped by an intuition that was close to nature. From this source man's spirit must flow and bring him into unity with the community of his people. Such true spirituality Diederichs saw reflected in the late thirteenth- to early fourteenth-century German mystic Meister Eckhardt whose works he had edited; later Alfred Rosenberg returned to Meister Eckhardt for the same reasons. Just as the romantics at the beginning of the nineteenth century had opposed the "cold rationality" of antiquity and had found their way back to a more genuine humanity, so Diederichs hailed this movement as a "new romanticism."[6] Thus, a search for this "genuine humanity" dominated the movement, based upon a closeness to nature for the landscape which gave man a heightened feeling for life. When Diederichs organized the gathering of the Free German Youth on the Hohen Meissner mountain in 1913, Ludwig Klages, the Munich philosopher, told them that modern civilization was "drowning" the soul of man. The only way out for man, who belonged to nature, was a return to mother earth.[7] Such ideas led naturally to a deepening of the cult of the peasant. Julius Langbehn summed this up: "The peasant who actually owns a piece of land has a direct relationship to the center of the earth. Through this he becomes master of the universe."[8]

In opposition to peasant life there was the city, the seat of cold rationalism. Indeed, this was nothing new or unique; Jacob Burckhardt had already written that in cities art became "nervous and unstable."[9] Throughout the nineteenth century men had advocated a retreat into the unspoiled landscape, away from a society rapidly becoming industrialized and urbanized. But for the "new romanticism" nature did not signify the sole source of human renewal and vitality. Mysticism played a central role in this movement, connected with the concern for man's soul as an embodiment of the cosmic life force.

Julius Langbehn cited Schiller's phrase that "it is the soul which builds the body," and added that the outward form of the body was a silhouette of its inner life.[10] The portrait painter Burger-Villingen enlarged upon this when he criticized the phrenology of Francis Gall. Gall's measurements of the skull led to serious errors, he claimed, because they comprised only the external influences of man. The important thing was to grasp the nature of man's fate, which was dependent upon his soul.[11] Thus Burger-Villingen measured the profiles of men's faces in order to comprehend the expression of their souls. For this purpose he invented a special apparatus (a plastometer), which was much discussed in the subsequent literature. Julius Langbehn wrote that researches into man's facial characteristics were a part of historical research.[12]

This remark leads into the philosophy of history of these men, which provided the explanation for the mystic development of the soul from its base in nature, through the cosmic life force. History, Diederichs wrote, is never factual but merely a thickening of the life stream of events through which, at one point or place, the universally valid laws of life become visible in reality. History could only be seen with the soul since it was the progression out of nature of the inner life substance. It was at this point that the mystic and the occult came to the fore. This belief in a life force was a kind of cosmic religion to a man like Diederichs, who referred to Plato as one of his sources.[13] Yet, in opposition to rationalism, this religion was grasped through the intuition of the soul feeling its closeness to nature.

Ernest Dacqué, whose book on *Urwelt* (the primeval world) was used extensively by all these men, coined the phrase "nature somnambulism"—an intuitive insight into those life forces that determine the physical nature of man. As man got ever farther away from nature, what remained of this somnambulism was wrongly described as soothsaying or as psychological disabilities. Yet all things creative were a survival of this nature somnambulism.[14] Paul de Lagarde put the same idea somewhat differently. Germans, though reaching into the future, should return to the past—

a past devoid of all else but the primeval voice of nature.[15] Manifestly, only those people who were closest to nature could grasp through their souls the inner, cosmic life force that constituted the eternal.

In Vienna, Guido von List set the tone for this kind of argument and fused it with the glories of an Aryan past. Nature was the great divine guide and from her flowed the life force. Whatever was closest to nature would therefore be closest to the truth.[16] List believed that the Aryan past was the most "genuine" manifestation of this inner force. It was closest to nature and therefore farthest removed from artificiality—from modern materialism and rationalism. Thus he set himself the task of recreating this past. Given the philosophy of history common to these men, they looked down upon any scholarly disciplines such as archaeology: "We must read with our souls the landscape which archaeology reconquers with the spade." Again, List advised: "If you want to lift the veil of mystery [i.e., of the past], you must fly into the loneliness of nature."[17] List's ideas were brought to Germany largely through the efforts of Alfred Schuler of Munich. This remarkable man, who never published a line, attracted to his person men like Rilke and George. His circle of admirers maintained that Schuler "saw with his soul" and could reconstruct the past by simply using his inward eye. To a small coterie of friends, Schuler lectured on the nature of the city. Urbanism was condemned and equated with the intellectuals' alleged materialism, which supposedly perverted their thought. Against this equation were those adepts whose "idealism" could only stem from the mysterious call of the blood, the true creative instinct.[18]

For Schuler, the inner life force was equated with the strength of the blood, an equation common to other writers as well. He fulminated against the shallowness of soulless men ignorant of nature and its life forces, an ignorance epitomized, he thought, in the Jewish poet Karl Wolfskehl blaspheming: "People are my landscape."[19] Significantly, Schuler believed this life force could be manipulated through spiritualism. He tried to cure Nietzsche's madness through an ancient Roman spirit rite. Klages was to lure Stefan George to a séance where Schuler would take over George's soul, transmuting it into a living receptacle of cosmic fire. George, stubbornly obdurate, was appalled by the proceedings, and after the séance demanded that Klages accompany him to a café where settled bourgeois, ordinary people, drank beer and smoked cigars.[20] In Klages's eyes he was henceforth condemned, though any historian analyzing the thoughts of these men might easily sympathize with George.

Schuler and Klages were not alone in believing the inner life force to be akin to spiritualism. Indeed, the mysticism which, as Langbehn put it, transformed science into art, was precisely this life force defined in terms of the occult. The ideology of this movement had direct ties with those occult and spiritualist movements that were in vogue toward the end of the century. Such ties were especially fostered by theosophy. The opposition to positivism in Germany fed upon movements which in the rest of Europe were regarded as "fads" rather than as serious world views. In Germany the belief in the life force or cosmic religion embodied in the blood, which all things Aryan truly represented, led to a world view that gave special status to those who were "initiates" of such mysteries.

The similarity of these ideas to the occult was noted by contemporaries. Franz Hartmann, himself a leading German-American theosophist, remarked upon the similarity of List's ideas to those of Madame Blavatsky, the foundress of theosophy. This he did by comparing List's *Bilderschrift* to Madame Blavatsky's *Isis Unveiled*. For just as List attempted to tear the veil from the true wisdom of the ancient Germans, so Blavatsky revealed the surviving traces of a "secret science" in ancient and medieval sources. Their principles, she maintained, had been lost from view and suppressed; in like manner, List claimed that Christianity had tried to wipe out the language of the ancient Germans, thus destroying their true nature wisdom.[21] List believed that this lost language could be found in the mystic writings of the Kabalah, mistakenly thought to be Jewish, but in reality a compilation of ancient German wisdom that had survived persecution. Madame Blavatsky made identical use of the Kabalah; she, too, rejected its Jewish origins, considering it a survival of true and secret wisdom.[22] Hartmann himself, attracted by such parallelisms, became one of List's leading supporters.

But we can go further than this. Madame Blavatsky's *Isis Unveiled* was concerned with a study of nature. She attempted to study nature as she thought the ancients had studied it, in relation not so much to its outward form but to its inward meaning. Thus she also saw nature as being eternally transmitted through a life force which she thought of as an omnipresent vital ether, electro-spiritual in composition.[23] This vague idea directly influenced men of the 1920s like Herbert Reichstein, who believed that the first Aryan was created by an electric shock directly out of this ether. They called their theory "theozoology."[24] Her approach was, in general, similar to those exponents of the life force we have discussed; she, too, felt that seeing with one's soul was the reality, and deplored scientific methods.

There is, however, a still closer relationship of these two bodies of thought through their use of imagery. For Madame Blavatsky, fire was the universal soul substance, and this led Franz Hartmann to state that it was the sun which was the external manifestation of an invisible spiritual power.[25] For the men we have discussed, the image of the Aryan coming out of the sun was common. The painter Fidus, so closely associated with the German youth movement, used this motif constantly. This popular painter believed that it was not enough for the artist to faithfully reproduce nature. Painting, for Fidus, was a transmission from the extrasensory world.[26] His paintings included studies of astral symbolism, as well as designs for theosophic temples. It was he who painted the official picture to symbolize the Hohen Meissner gathering. Best known, however, were his paintings, bordered by theosophic symbols, on themes such as the "wanderers into the sun"—girl and boy wandering hand in hand, surrounded by growing plants, their nude boyish bodies translucent before a blazing sun.

Eugen Diederichs was also deeply concerned with such symbolism. He founded, in 1910, the so-called Sera circle in Jena. Its symbol was a red and golden flag with the sun as centerpiece. The main activities of this circle centered in the youth movement: excursions, folk dances, and above all, the old Germanic festival of the "changing sun."[27] Here Germanic custom and spiritualist symbolism were intertwined. For Diederichs also the sun was the creator of life, a reaffirmation of the prime importance of those cosmic forces that underlay all reality.[28]

Langbehn himself maintained that "a theologian should always be somewhat of a theosophist" to compensate for the formalism inherent in his profession. He saw a similar value in spiritualism in general. His criticism of contemporary occultism was not that it was wrong, but that it was misdirected, searching through professional mediums for spirits where there were none.[29] Such a linkage between theosophy and the volkish world view will remain throughout the movement's history. This can be conclusively demonstrated through *Prana*, which called itself a German monthly for applied spiritualism and which was published by the theosophical publishing house at Leipzig. The editor was Johannes Balzli, the secretary of the Guido von List Society, founded to spread the "master's" teaching and to finance his publications. Franz Hartmann, himself an honorary member of that society, was one of *Prana*'s most frequent contributors, as was C. W. Leadbetter, the stormy Anglican curate whom Madame Blavatsky had taken with her to India and who later became Annie Besant's Svengali. Guido von List himself contributed to its pages, while Fidus provided most of the illustrations. The word "Prana" was taken to mean the power of the sun, the visible symbol of God, and "all present." This in turn was to be the sign of the "new Germany."[30]

In *Prana*'s pages we find ideas on food and medicine that were common to this movement. Medical science was universally deplored in favor of spiritual healing, and the eating of meat was said to impede not only spiritual progress but the understanding of nature and the life force.[31] Theosophists linked the flesh of animals to their undeveloped intelligence; eating meat would thus induce animal coarseness in humans. *Prana*'s writers further elaborated this idea, adding that meat could not increase life for it was lifeless and thus led to death.[32] The medical and vegetarian vagaries of Adolf Hitler were intimately linked with the mystic, Aryan ideology found in the pages of *Prana*, though *Prana* was not the only journal that reflected this mixture of thought.

That such ideas marched into the 1920s with renewed vigor can be seen in the case of Arthur Dinter, who rose to prominence as an early National Socialist in the twenties. As a National Socialist deputy, he played a leading role in the overthrow of the socialist government of Thuringia in 1924 and subsequently became the editor of the *National Socialist*, published in Weimar. His celebrated racial novel *Die Sunde wider das Blut* (*The Sin Against the Blood*, 1918) attained a large circulation. Though a companion novel, *Die Sünde wider den Geist* (*The Sin Against the Spirit*, 1921), never proved as popular, it combined the racial ideology of his first book with episodes that could have been taken directly from Madame Blavatsky. For Dinter, the racial ideas of a man like Houston Stewart Chamberlain made sense only when they were integrated with his own spiritualistic experiences. Dinter made liberal use of such theosophist concepts as the astral ether, the sun, and the idea of rebirth (Karma).[33] For Lanz von Liebenfels, another of *Prana's* favorites, the term "Ariosophy" meant a combination of such ideas with a world view centered upon the Germanic past.[34] Small wonder that the industrialist who was the principal financial contributor to Guido von List's Society was also an ardent spiritualist.[35]

This, then, was the mysticism that transformed science into art. When these men called upon Germans to be artists, they wanted them to recognize that their true soul was an expression of the cosmic spirit of the world based upon nature. Possession of such a spirit meant recalling that which was truly genuine, the Germanic past, as opposed to modern and evil rationalism. Langbehn, so often cited by his successors, felt this to be the only true individualism in a world of mass man. This individualism would lead to the creation of an organic human being in contact with cosmic forces. These forces were conceived in spiritualist terms, though Langbehn's touchstone was not Madame Blavatsky but Swedenborg. To him this mystic was the ideal German type.[36] In a similar manner Diederichs came to see the identical image reflected in Meister Eckhardt.[37]

Such a philosophy of life did not need spiritualistic mediums in order to penetrate the "secret mysteries." Indeed, for List the past came alive in the very human shape of Tarnhari, who called himself the chief of the lost German tribe of the *Völsungen*. The tribal traditions, which he related from his fund of ancestral memories, confirmed List's own researches. Tarnhari promptly produced several works of his own in which he told "family stories going back to prehistoric times." The stone of wisdom had come alive. It is symptomatic that this impressed Ellegard Ellerbeck, later one of the ornaments of National Socialist literature. As he wrote to List, "reading yours and Tarnhari's works I realize again that Ar [Aryan] lives laughingly."[38]

One idea implied in all of this must be stressed. Only he who had ties with the genuine past could have a true soul, could be an organic and not a materialistic human being. Such ties were conceived of as being inherited. The genuine spirit of the ancestors was cumulative in their progeny. For Guido von List, as for his successors, only the Aryan could grasp the "mysteries" of life which governed the world. These ideas allowed Langbehn to stress once more not only the virtue of a settled and ancient Germanic peasantry but of a hereditary monarchy as well. A hereditary monarch was not merely someone elevated from the masses like the president of a republic. In the government of the nation, such a monarch would be aided by the "natural aristocracy." This aristocracy did not derive solely from an inheritance of status; every German could be a part of it if he threw off rationalism and became again an "artist"—the organic man.[39] Such a man was Rembrandt, in Langbehn's opinion; writing his book *Rembrandt as Educator*, he hoped to influence Germans through a striking example. The end result was to be the creation of an organic state where there would be neither "bourgeois," nor "proletarians," nor "Junkers," but only "the people" linked together in a common creativity (now become possible), and united in a bond of brotherhood. Classes would not be abolished; as Langbehn put it: "Equality is death. A corporate society is life."[40]

In his first book, *Ritter, Tod und Teufel (The Knight, Death, and the Devil*, 1920), H. F. K. Günther, later to become a chief racial expert of the Third Reich, sketched such a social ideal. Human rights have today preempted the place of human duties. These duties, formerly expressed in the loyalty of the knightly gentleman to his king and generalized throughout society in the web of reciprocal loyalties between landlord and peasant, must once again become the cement of social organization. To Günther, "the community, the public good, demands that every profession fulfill the work which is its due."[41] Manifestly, such a social ideal, found in all these men, continued the impetus of romanticism. It was reminiscent of that Bavarian deputy who earlier in the nineteenth century believed that "Love" would cure the tensions between laborer and employer. In an immediate sense it was a part of the ideal of an organic society which reflected organic man. Langbehn was explicit in his insistence that true individualism could only be realized in such a social order. He considered liberal individualism a part of materialism, dissolving society into incompatible units rather than knitting it together.[42] Paul de Lagarde summarized this in one of those phrases that made him so popular: "That man is not free who can do as he likes, but he is free who does what he should do. Free is he who is able to follow his creative principle of life; free is that man who recognizes and makes effective the innate principles which God put within him."[43] (For a Nazi use of this quote, see page 188.)

Such freedom led to an organic view of man and the state. Not only was liberalism mistaken, but socialism as well. Social democracy, Diederichs claimed, was mechanistic; a true people's state was viable only if it reorganized society in a more meaningful manner, according to the aristocratic principle, the only environment in which men could unfold their real inner selves.[44] Langbehn concluded that this corporate structure fulfilled the aristocratic principle and was also in tune with the Germanic past. Significantly, this ideal urged these men to advocate only one concrete social reform: each worker should be given his own plot of land.[45] Again, the reform's justification was not sought in terms of material welfare within the framework of the movement's general ideology—factory work removed man from the all-important contact with nature.

Yet these men desired the transformation of their ideology into deeds. It is of great significance that while Diederichs used the word "theosophy" in the first prospectus of his publishing house, he came to be critical of that movement—not because it was spiritualist, but because it was too purely speculative in nature. The feeling about infinity must lead to deeds, and to his important journal he gave the name *Die Tat* (*The Deed*).[46] Paul de Lagarde had already made it plain that while something was accomplished through the understanding of true ideology, it was even more important to transform such ideals into serious practical action.[47] It was an "idealism of deeds" such men desired, deeds which helped to create a nation resting upon this idealistic foundation. Through such a concept, ideas of force came to play an important role in this ideology. For Langbehn, art and war went hand in hand. Shakespeare's name meant, after all, shaking a spear, and this for him was proof of the connection between art and war. Moreover, in German, spear (*Speer*) and army (*Wehr*) are words that rhyme. Thus in the Germanic past, true individual development had gone hand in hand with war.[48]

The lineaments of this "idealism of deeds" clearly emerge in the poetry of Avenarius, the first author of Diederichs's publishing house. Happiness was not the goal of life. What was important for the poet was the strength and wealth of the soul, and this strength depended upon the degree to which nature reflected itself within it. This whole feeling must be grounded in honesty and rootedness. But such ideals, in turn, must be sharpened through conflict with the nonbelieving world around them. Struggle becomes, therefore, a necessity. Avenarius as a poet gave due honor to the good fight honestly waged; poets must sympathize with the use of force. As one of the commentators of his poetry declared: "His is a true Germanic personality which is proud and straight, knows the bitter hate against all which is cowardly and fraudulent. Such ideas are a reminder not to let the soul degenerate through mildness."[49]

The "idealism of deeds" postulated the use of force to establish and defend a Germany based upon this romantic and mystic ideology. It was to be used not to destroy the existing social structure but to create and perpetuate the organic state. One employed force against the enemy—that materialistic and rationalistic culture which had undermined the weakened and retreating Aryan by divorcing him from nature's life force. The Jew, the creature of urbanism and materialism, typified this enemy within the gates. To Langbehn, Berlin and the Jew were the components of a conspiracy inimical to German revival, just as later a National Socialist writer exclaimed that volkish thought would triumph in the provinces, not in the cities. Berlin, above all, was the domain of the Jews.[50] Perhaps such considerations led to the anxious question in an issue of the National Socialist *Weltkampf* concerning Madame Blavatsky's Jewish origins, to which the comforting (and true) answer was given that she was of Baltic extraction.[51]

To their hatred of the Jews these men added an ambivalent attitude toward Christianity. Ludwig Klages continued a trend that derived from Guido von List, who had linked victorious Christianity to the virtual extinction of the ancient Germanic nature wisdom. He regarded it as his life's task to resurrect this wisdom. Klages believed that the course of a victorious Christianity was plotted from "a center" inimical to the Aryans.[52] Thus a universal Christian conspiracy against the truth was placed next to the universal Jewish conspiracy—a conspiracy documented by the Protocols of the Elders of Zion. With Lagarde and others, this developed into a Catholic-Jesuit conspiracy linked, so they asserted, to the Jewish world conspiracy itself.[53] Men like Diederichs and Langbehn were in a quandary, however, for they did not deem it wise to reject Christianity altogether. Protestantism as the German form of Christianity, in opposition to the Catholic conspiracy, was their solution to the problem. Their distrust of Christianity led them to reject Christ conceived as a historical figure; instead they tried to assimilate him to their concept of the life force.

This could be done, as did Schuler, by holding Christ to be merely the most important of the "initiates" into the Germanic wisdom. For List, all the great "initiates," Buddah, Osiris, and Moses, were Saxons.[54] More popular, however, was Houston Stewart Chamberlain's and Langbehn's idea of Christ as the Aryan prototype. Diederichs believed, as did Lagarde (and indeed, all of the men discussed), that St. Paul, the Jew, had made Christ into a Jewish figure, imprisoning him within the confines of theological thought. Instead, Christ was at one with the cosmic spirit, a spirit best understood not through scripture but through such mystics as Diederichs's favorite, Meister Eckhardt.[55] He spent much of his energy propagating this kind of Christianity. The chief adviser to his publishing house was Alfred Drews, who in his *Die Christusmythe* (*The Myth of Christ*, 1909), published by Diederichs, attacked the historicity of the Christ figure. Similarly, Munich's volkish publisher J. F. Lehmann spent his time furthering an identical evangelism, agitating against the theologians of the organized churches who were as inimical to the "idealism of deeds" as were the Jews themselves. Indeed, such a view of Christ rendered the Old Testament null and void; Arthur Dinter suggested that it be banned from the schools.[56]

Langbehn combined this view of Christ with the ideal of force. Germans, he wrote, should model themselves upon the medieval bishops who advanced, sword in hand, against their enemies. Such Christianity fitted into a German and mystical context, which symbolized a humanity that knew the necessity of force. "Humanity wants what is best, the fighter accomplishes what is best."[57]

Here also art and war must be combined. Yet this concept of Christianity rested on slight foundations. Diederichs, for one, realized this when he wrote that the very word Christ made him "nervous." He never tried to disguise the heathen quality of his Sera circle.[58] By fusing Christ with the life spirit of the Aryan, these men wanted to create a national religion. One of the attractions of Swedenborg for Langbehn was the fact that Swedenborg posited a separate heaven for each nation and thus recognized the importance of the national factor in religion.[59] Luther, however, was their real hero, for these men saw in him a truly national religious figure who rejected theology, so they thought.

These are the principal facets of an ideology that was to pass into the National Socialist movement. This was the "race mysticism" about which men like Günther and Rosenberg wrote. Out of this mixture of the romantic and the occult the Aryan arose: sometimes out of the sun, sometimes through a historical process, but always as a true, organic individual—a part of nature and of the life force that springs from nature. Guido von List sang of the Aryan during the ice age engaged in building his spiritual and bodily strength in the hard fight with nature, arising quite differently than other races who lived without struggle in the midst of a bountiful world.[60] For the element of struggle was always a part of this ideology; art and battle go together. This, however, was not the Darwinian struggle for the survival of the fittest, but rather the good fight of the Aryan who was eternally of the elect. The effectiveness of Dacque's book in overcoming the "English disease," Darwinism, was noted by a National Socialist journal of the 1920s. Darwinism was of one cloth with political democracy; both dissolved the organic unity of man as part of nature, and Darwinism did so through survival of the fittest.[61] The Aryan was the sole organic man, and his task was not a struggle for survival against equals, for he had none. Instead, his was an inner struggle to recapture his unique heritage and an outward struggle to rid himself of Jews and theologians. Alfred Rosenberg had this in mind when he wrote of the "romanticism of steel"; the revolution against capitalist bourgeois society could only have reality if it served the permanent values of blood in revolt.[62]

The men we have singled out for analysis were some of the chief purveyors of this thought. There were a host of others. A list of organizations sponsoring the meeting at the Hohen Meissner makes this amply clear. The German youth movement has entered this story at every turn. Undoubtedly, the *Wandervögel* were one of the prime transmitters of the movement's thought. They too rejected intellectualism for the mystique of contact with nature. Excursions brought out the "real man" as opposed to the artificial man of modern material culture. For Karl Fischer, the founder of that movement, romanticism was an expression of national feeling with an explicit racial base. Hans Blüher, the controversial historian of the *Wandervögel*, reminisced that in the movement's early days consciousness of race sufficed to join soul to nature.[63] Closely associated with the youth movement were the country boarding schools, founded by Hermann Lietz (1898). These schools, which later had a great influence, institutionalized many of the ideas we have discussed. One admirer said correctly that "in Lietz's hands the regenerating natural forces of agriculture and rural life were made to work for the education of men."[64] Lietz believed that the emphasis in education should not be on book learning but on building character through contact with the landscape of the fatherland and knowledge of the Teutonic inheritance. The end product of this educational process was to be an aristocracy of men and women who would not "bend their knees" before the Moloch of capitalism and materialism. Instead, they would stand for an ideal that represented, in Lietz's words, a "purer religious world of thought and feeling." For the sake of this ideal, such leaders would take up the fight against the "dark" instincts of the masses.[65]

This religious world Lietz saw in terms of a Christianity which, as for the others, was divorced from Christ as a historical personage. In Paul de Lagarde he saw the theologian nearest to his position. Christ must be rescued from St. Paul and emerge again as a hero image: thus young Germans could be inspired to an active, heroic life. For this task the ancient German and Grecian religious myths were more valuable than the Old Testament, which Lietz also rejected.[66] Lietz developed these ideas into an explicit racism. At first he took Jewish students into his school, but he gradually banned them from his educational system. Toward the end of his life, after the German defeat in World War I, he began to write about the necessity of freeing Germany from the "Jewish spirit" and from all those who were moved by it.[67]

Typical for Lietz's attitudes was the change he made in the English system of student self-government, a system which had originally impressed him and had, in a sense, inspired his work. He substituted for this the "family" system—each teacher was supposed to be the "father" of a small group of students. The differences of class and status were to be displaced by an "organic state."[68] This led to a break with some of his associates who believed, as Lietz did not, in the reasonableness of the majority and thus wished educational decisions to be made by students and faculty jointly. The ideal of the organic state was thus mirrored in the structure of the schools themselves. As he wrote toward the end of his life, only the organic, that which is in tune with nature,[69] will last. Here too Lietz was close to the ideology we have discussed. It is small wonder that the list of books which he recommended for reading aloud to students during the evening hour set aside for that purpose included racial-nationalistic novels and ended by recommending the books published by Eugen Diederichs. Diederichs, in turn, longed to publish Lietz's works, while Lehmann actually published books which furthered his cause, and sent his sons to one of Lietz's schools. Nor is it astonishing that one of his leading collaborators became one of the most prominent of National Socialist educators.[70]

Again, in this case, personal continuities were not as important as the furthering, indeed institutionalizing, of a cultural atmosphere. After World War I, many country boarding schools were founded, some by prominent men like Prinz Max von Baden. Their aim was a national, spiritual renewal based on the principles Lietz had set forth. To be sure, some substituted a broad non-national humanitarian outlook, while others adopted Lietz's ideas without giving them an explicit racial base. Yet the atmosphere was set; its romanticism and "idealism of deeds" colored the thought of those generations who had passed through the country boarding schools and the youth movement.

Transmitted in this way, the romantic and mystic ideology with which we have been concerned drew ever-widening circles into its sphere of influence, even if among these many later rejected National Socialism. Among those influenced were some of the best literary minds of contemporary Germany. Stefan George came under the influence of Schuler and Klages at the same time that he composed some of the "cosmic" poems of his *Der Siebente Ring* (*Seventh Ring*, 1907). Claude David has no hesitation in saying that the hand of this group of men is seen in some of Rilke's *Elegies*.[71] Still more actively involved with the movement was August Strindberg. He participated in the ancient Germanic rites which Lanz von Liebenfels, with List's assistance, performed in one of his Hungarian castles.[72] Strindberg's novel *Tschandala* took over a word which List and Liebenfels had used to designate the lower races.

In Germany the recovery of the unconscious, in reaction against the dominant positivist ideologies, laid the groundwork for the German form of twentieth-century dictatorship. This reaction combined the deep stream of German romanticism with the mysteries of the occult as well as with the idealism of deeds. What sort of deeds these turned out to be is written on the pages of history.

ELEVEN

Nazi Polemical Theater:
The *Kampfbühne*

THE THEATER PLAYED a vital part in National Socialism; indeed, it was one of Hitler's dominant passions. No German régime in the past did more to further the theater than the Third Reich. In 1936, for example, some 331 theaters, many of them recently built or renovated, played a regular season.[1] The theater was, in fact, an integral part of Nazi ideology, serving to reinforce the political liturgy of the movement. Mass meetings and the theater were intended to supplement each other. For this reason the liturgical *Weihebühne*, the "Thing theater" on which the volkish ideology was acted out, assumed special significance, presenting the liturgy of the movement through cultish plays meant to create a living community of faith. The National Socialist myth was acted out in dramatic and visual form as an act of religious worship in which masses of people participated. The Thing theater has recently been investigated[2] and there is no need to analyze it once more. However, the *Kampfbühne* (or fighting stage), the other Nazi attempt to harness the theater to their cause, has not yet found a historian, though it antedated and outlasted the Thing theater, which was created in 1933 and dissolved in 1937.[3] The *Kampfbühne* began its career in 1926, well before the seizure of power, and endured as long as the Third Reich itself.

It is necessary first to describe the diverse forms of the *Kampf-*

bühne that existed before the seizure of power. Here we shall proceed by types, as all the forms of this theater overlap chronologically. The S.A. and Hitler Youth *"Spiel-Trupps"* (amateur actors) appeared first; then, in 1931, the Gau theater, a mobile stage that played throughout each province, was created. The *NS-Versuchsbühne* (Nazi Experimental Theater) started in 1927, and in 1930 became the *NS-Volksbühne*, performing on a regular basis. Once we have analyzed these various *Kampfbühnen*, both amateur and professional, we can then set them into the historical background of the search for a national theater which, starting in the nineteenth century, became accelerated during the Weimar Republic. Finally, we must take a glance at the fate of the *Kampfbühne* during the Third Reich.

Whatever its diverse forms, the Nazis defined a *Kampfbühne* as a *"Streitgespräch"*—a polemic against the enemy. It was designed partly to "indoctrinate through fun and entertainment," and partly, in the words of one S.A. leader, to encourage "fighters for the cause to emerge from the masses."[4] To be sure, the Nazi ideology was presented to the audience, but always in a crude and polemical fashion, quite different, for example, from the majestic liturgy of the Thing theater. The first "Spiel-Trupps" were attached either to the S.A. or to the Hitler Youth, and gave themselves titles like the "Storm Troops" or the "Brown Shirts." These were enthusiastic groups of amateur actors. Little record remains of their plays, and their theatrical presentations are almost impossible to reconstruct. But as far as we can tell, these fell into two parts: fun and entertainment consisting of folk songs and folk dancing; and a "fighting part," which presented "contemporary political sketches" (*Politische Zeitbilder*). Such, for example, was the mixture of fun and action which the "Brown Shirts" of Hesse-Nassau presented as part of the Nazi propaganda program in the city of Wetzlar in 1932.[5] Sometimes such troupes seem to have used tableaux vivantes centered upon stereotypes of bankers, trade unionists, and consumers. For the most part the troupes would march on stage in closed formation, before beginning the songs, dances, and plays.

Play troupes like the "Brown Shirts" and "Storm Troopers" were often used in election rallies, especially during mass meetings in cities. Their plays were *Streitgespräche*, used to bring variety to evenings of martial music and speeches. The Hitler Youth carried their plays to such election rallies in cities, and especially to the villages, where they would perform as part of a *"Bunter Abend"* (cabaret theater) of skits, songs, and dances.

What were such plays like? For the most part only their titles have survived, and these tend toward the banal, as in *All Germans Are Brothers*.[6] I have found only one script without a title performed in Berlin by such an amateur group. Yet, for all its crudity, the play may well be typical for many others. It was performed on a bare stage in a hall belonging to the German Veterans Association (*Stahlhelm*). The stage represented the guard room of a local S.A. troop. As the play begins, shots are heard behind the stage and a dead S.A. man is carried into the room. Immediately afterwards a communist is dragged in as the probable murderer. But as the S.A. look through the pockets of their murdered comrade, they find a large sum of money and the address of a Jew. The Jew himself is then brought onto the stage, "whining in his jargon," and is shot by the S.A. as the man really responsible for the murder.[7] Through simple action and stereotypes the lesson is driven home that communists are the dupes of the Jews.

Such amateur players provided the inspiration for a more permanent play troupe made up of professional actors: the Gau theater. From 1931 onwards, such *Gau-Bühnen* presented "cultural evenings" up and down the province, which consisted of folk songs, political poetry, comic sketches, and monologues.[8] However, political plays were also performed with increasing frequency. We know more about the content of these plays than of those of the "Brown Shirts" or "Storm Troopers" because the Gau theater of Pomerania has been extensively documented for the years 1931 and 1932, though no such documentation seems to exist for other Gau theaters. For example, Walter Busch's *Giftgas 500 (Poisoned Gas 500)*, performed during these years, was a play that maintained its popularity. Its subject is described appropriately enough by the Nazi *Illustrierter Beobachter*[9] as the story of a key German invention, which Jewish greed swindled from Polish heavy industry. The hierarchy of villains will remain unchanged throughout Nazi rule—the Poles are bad but the Jews are worse. The plays performed were always highly topical. Thus the German National Party (*Deutsch Nationale Volkspartei*), always a rival of the Nazis, was satirized for its conceit and pretensions. In addition, plays directed against political Catholicism loomed large in a Polish border region. In one of these, a German Catholic priest hates the Nazis so much that he would rather sell good farm land to Poles than let it be farmed by a German National Socialist.[10] The director of the Pomeranian Gau theater maintained that all in all some 15,000 to 20,000 people would watch a play as it wound its way through the towns and villages.[11] Eventually, the *Gau-Bühnen* became a part of the "Strength through Joy" movement.[12]

The amateur play troupes and the Gau theaters traveled throughout the German provinces. But the so-called *NS-Versuchsbühne* was a traditional troupe, staffed by professional actors, which performed in Berlin in theater buildings hired for the occasion. It opened on April 20, 1927, when, to celebrate Hitler's birthday, Wolf Geyser staged his drama *Revolution* before some 3,000 spectators. It consisted of a series of tableaux vivantes which contrasted the ideal life in the future Nazi state to that in the Weimar Republic.[13] A few months later, the Experimental Theater performed Joseph Goebbels's *Der Wanderer*, which was an adaptation of his novel *Michael, Ein Deutsches Schicksal in Tagebuchblättern* (*Michael, The Diary of a German Fate*, 1929).[14] But this so-called Experimental Theater seems to have lacked success, for no regular season was attempted for the next three years, only occasional performances.

The provinces had to step in once more, and it was their pressure which led to the establishment of another *NS-Volksbühne* in Berlin in 1930. Perhaps this *NS-Volksbühne* was supposed to travel throughout Germany, but that function seems to have been usurped by the Gau theater established one year later.[15] The *NS-Volksbühne* was an imitation of the older, Left-leaning *Volksbühne* and the Christian *Bühnenvolksbund*. It performed regularly and its plays are easiest to reconstruct because they were reported by the party press.

The *NS-Volksbühne* plays were polemical, and, whether classic or modern, were conceived as *Streitgespräche* in spite of their conventional staging. Schiller's *Räuber* was one of the first plays performed, and it was claimed that here the *Räuber* had finally been staged as Schiller himself desired. The character of Spiegelberg, the enemy of Karl Moor and "leader" of the band, was brought to the fore. He became the villain, transformed into a "loud-mouthed Jewish agitator" who, while himself a coward, incites others to the craven murder of Karl Moor. Schiller's play as performed by the

NS-Volksbühne was hailed by the Nazi press as the first dawn of a new area of Aryan German art.[16] By contrast, in Piscator's performance of the *Räuber* staged five years before the Nazis' version, Spiegelberg wore the mask of Leon Trotsky, and the murder of Moor was pictured as a noble attempt to rescue freedom from the clutches of the gang. The only other traditional plays performed in those early days of the Nazi theater were Ibsen's *An Enemy of the People* and Ernst von Wildenbruch's *Mennoniten*. The Ibsen play, first staged in 1931, was intended to demonstrate the superiority of Nordic aristocracy over majority rule, and the value of personality as opposed to public opinion.[17] The *Mennoniten* was directed against the Napoleonic occupation of Prussia. It dealt with German courage and French intrigue, the chastity of the German woman and the French attempt to contaminate German blood. Waldemar, the hero of the play, could be viewed as a forerunner of Albert Leo Schlageter, who had fought the good fight more recently in the Ruhr and entered the Nazi gallery of martyrs.[18]

Historical analogies were popular in the *NS-Volksbühne* as they were in Nazi ideology. For example, Walter Flex's *Klaus von Bismarck* was part of the repertoire, a drama that attempted to show how in the Middle Ages the ancestor of the Iron Chancellor fought against the divisiveness of political parties and for the salvation of the Mark Brandenburg.[19] The *NS-Volksbühne* happily annexed such nationalist drama. If Flex's play was directed against divisiveness, others, such as G. von Noel's *Wehrwolf*, used the peasants of the Thirty Years' War to demonstrate that it was right and proper to defend national rights by violent means.[20] Finally the German struggle of liberation against Napoleon was an always popular theme; thus Joseph Stolzing's *Friedrich Friesen* invoked the wars of liberation against Napoleon. However, light entertainment was not neglected, and Ernst von Wolzogen's *Ein Unbeschriebenes Blatt* (*A Blank Leaf*), a play of "sunny laughter," was featured in the program, although with the apology that such pause in the fight rejuvenates man's energy for a renewed struggle.[21]

The party seems to have fully supported the *NS-Volksbühne*. For example, when in 1930 it played Walther Ilge's *Laterne*, a play which castigated the French Revolution, the entire Reichstag delegation of the party was present.[22] Yet the vast majority of performances in the *NS-Volksbühne* were not devoted to the historical drama or comedy but rather to contemporary plays whose message did not depend upon analogies with the past. The play written by Hitler's political mentor Dietrich Eckart, *Familienvater* (*Father of the Family*), was typical of the *Volksbühne's* didactic style. Eckart's play dealt with a tyrannical and corrupt newspaper proprietor and with a cowardly Jewish journalist who does the tyrant's bidding. Between them, the tyrant and the journalist crush a young playwright (presumably the unsuccessful dramatist Eckart himself), who has dared to expose the newspaper's corruption.[23] Walter Busch's *Giftgas 500*, already performed by the Gau theater, was taken over by the *Volksbühne* as well. The plays of a rising young playwright, Eberhard Wolfgang Möller, were especially popular, perhaps because of their more elaborate staging and the lavish use of choruses. Möller brought to the *Volksbühne* plays of Germanic worship similar to those of the Thing theater for which he wrote most of his material.[24] Möller's dramas were unique among the committed Nazi playwrights during the Weimar Republic. While the plays we have mentioned had their first and often only performances on the stage of the *NS-Volksbühne*, his works were frequently performed in regular municipal theaters even before the Nazi theater took them over. Thus his war drama *Douaumont* (the principal fortress of Verdun) was a great success at the Berlin liberal *Volksbühne* before it succeeded on the Nazi stage. Möller's themes were broader than those of most other Nazi playwrights. They were a crusade against the love of money. Parliaments were manipulated as finance capitalists, representing gold, not people. Such populism appealed to the Left as well as to the Right, even though Möller was a committed Nazi.[25]

The Nazis liked best Möller's *Rothschild Siegt bei Waterloo* (*Rothschild Wins the Battle of Waterloo*, 1932), because unlike others this one was centered on the Jews as corrupting the world through money, a racism that became central to Möller's world view. Rothschild is depicted as the "third great power" besides England and France; indeed, he is the true victor at Waterloo. Though the banker asserts that "my money is everywhere and money is friendly, the friendliest power in the world, fat, round as a ball, and laughing," in reality, it has been earned by dishonoring the struggle against the plundering and butchering French. Rothschild is told that "The dead did not die in order that you could earn money through their sacrifice, and in such a shabby way." The moral was clear: the Rothschilds were a sinister power, "which makes cripples of humanity, men into the objects of the stock exchange, profit from life and capital from blood." [26] Finance capitalism as an all-embracing menace, whether symbolized by Rothschild or the Jews in *Giftgas 500*, was a staple of Nazi drama.

What then were the historical sources of the *Kampfbühne* as we have sketched it? Was it an imitation of the Piscator theater, with its agitprop and polemics? The *Nationalsozialistische Monatshefte* in 1931 praised the Piscator stage for having had the courage to present polemical plays. [27] The Nazis paid attention to this left-wing theater, perhaps because Piscator's radicalism appealed to their populism; his unconventional staging could be applied to the *NS-Volksbühne*. However, the Piscator theater, which existed only from 1927 to 1931, was already in decline when the Nazis praised it. [28] They hardly borrowed from Piscator, in any case; certainly they did not follow the revolutionary staging or use of film, but instead placed the Nazi polemics within a conservative theatrical form. The speaking choruses are an exception here, for the Hitler Youth admitted openly to having borrowed them from the Communist Party. [29]

The genesis of the *Kampfbühne* is not linked to the Piscator theater but must rather be sought in the attempt to create a national theater, and, in the *Vereinsbühne*, a lay theater of trade and apprentice organizations.

The debate over the creation of a national theater had a long history. Gottfried Keller, for example, had been inspired by an outdoor performance of *Wilhelm Tell* during the Schiller Year of 1859 to propose the founding of a national theater, in a natural setting, which would combine choirs with folk plays. Such a theater would bring volkish mythology to life (he called his proposal the "Stone of Myth"—*Am Mythenstein*). [30] The conventional stage was to be abolished, and with it the distance that separates audience and actors. The audience should be drawn into a world of illusion which, through the immediacy of the drama, would become their world of reality. The Thing theater resulted from this pseudo-religious "Völkische drama," and such liturgical plays were staged in open-air theaters from the beginning of the twentieth century onward.

The thrust toward the creation of a national theater also affected the traditional stage after World War I. The call went out to transform the professional stage into a national theater. Its purpose was to fight so-called degenerate forms of art, which symbolized Germany's defeat and revolution. Here then was the immediate precedent for the Nazi *Kampfbühne*, both in its national purpose and in its polemical intent. Thus Richard Eisner used his older journal *Das Deutsche Drama* (*The German Drama*) after 1918 in order to advocate a national theater as opposed to the theater of the Weimar Republic. He founded an organization in 1927 and was able to sponsor some plays—for example, one entitled *Fritjof* exalting Nordic man, and another, *Andreas Hofer*, dealing with the German war of liberation against kings, bishops, and princes. However, Schiller was Eisner's ideal, just as he was the patron saint of the *NS-Volksbühne*.[31]

The *Manifesto* of Erich Brandenburg calling for a national theater in 1919 was more important than Eisner's efforts, even if lacking in aggressiveness. Indeed, Erich Brandenburg demonstrates how the postwar impulse for a national theater was transmitted into the Third Reich. His *Manifesto* called for an emphasis upon space and movement, and characterized all theater as group art. The influence of the modern dance as practiced by Rudolf Laban and Mary Wigman is of importance here; Brandenburg was captivated by "dancing choirs which make a statement," as Wigman put it. The plays performed must be dramas conceived as symbolical action, analogous to cultish rites. Brandenburg contrasted this German drama to the supposed shallowness of the French and the Italian Renaissance stage. Clearly, the *Manifesto* treats theater as a cultish rite that was capable of renewing the nation. The stage was to be extended into the audience in order to abolish the difference between spectator and performer, while the auditorium should be modeled after the Roman amphitheater.[32]

The *Manifesto* was signed by a wide variety of intellectuals, ranging from the humanist socialist Gustav Landauer (murdered before it was printed), Thomas Mann, and Richard Dehmel to Hans Blüher of the youth movement and the future Nazi poet Will Vesper. They all joined Brandenburg's *Bund für das Neue Theater* (Bund for a new theater). The Bund soon failed, and Brandenburg then pinned his hope upon the lay plays of the youth movement.[33] Meanwhile, he had refined his *Manifesto*, envisioning national drama as an instrument to fight modern mechanization and materialism. The neo-romantic tone, present but subdued in the original *Manifesto*, took over.[34] While Brandenburg took no part in the *NS-Kampfbühne* itself, as far as I can determine, he welcomed the advent of the Third Reich as the opportunity to fulfill the promise of this *Manifesto* and Bund. The time had come for a festive drama, one that would move "between masses and hero, Volk and Führer."[35] The Nazis, without mentioning the *Manifesto*, adopted Brandenburg and praised his agitation for a national stage.[36]

Brandenburg called for a national theater that would transmit its message through drama, group symbolism (such as the *Kampfbühne* used frequently), and the use of movement and space. These were theatrical forms that also preoccupied the Nazi stage. But side by side with such attempts at national theater, amateur groups continued to play as a part of the youth movement. This amateur play movement was an obvious influence on groups like the "Brown Shirts" and "Storm Troopers," and it would remain highly popular throughout the Third Reich. After World War I, the amateur play was becoming increasingly nationalistic and formalized. Whereas medieval mystery plays had captivated the enthusiasm of the prewar youth movement, now Rudolf Mirbt, prominent in the amateur theater movement, recommended dramas like Hans Johst's *Die Propheten* (*Prophets*), which contrasted the Catholic to the German man, and whose hero was Martin Luther. The symbolism and the simplicity of the staging would remain.[37]

In fact, the amateur play had already been used as a weapon of political propaganda. The Free Corps Rossbach attempted to use *Spielschaaren* (troupes of young amateur actors) directly after the war as a way to mobilize the nation against the Poles and the Republic. Gerhard Rossbach himself saw in such troupes a secret weapon in the hands of a poor and unprotected nation, a continuation of military action by other means.[38] But the Rossbach *Spielschaaren* were not imitated, even by other Free Corps, and had little influence on the professional theater.

More important were those amateur play groups that performed folk plays or folk festivals in the villages or in the countryside, known as the *Heimatspiele*, thirty-one of which were officially recognized as worthy of support by the German government after World War I. The vast majority of these, unlike the Oberammergau *Passion Play*, were not religious but either patriotic or concerned with a historical episode that had taken place in the locality. Thus, in Ahide, some two hundred amateur players reenacted the heroism and martyrdom of Andreas Hofer, the leader of the Tyrolean struggle against Italy, while other plays recreated the Hermannschlach, which the Germans won against Rome, or the saga of Wittekind. Wilhelm Tell, Goetz von Berlichingen, Andreas Hofer, and the *Niebelungenlied* provided the most popular themes for these *Heimatspiele*.[39]

Amateur plays themselves were performed through the Hitler Youth, the "Strength through Joy" movement, and the *Arbeitsdienst* (Compulsory Labor Service). Amateur actors engaged in simple productions, sometimes merely folk plays, at other times *Kampfbühnen*.[40] The Nazis were fearful that the amateur theater might lead to dilettantism and perhaps through the enthusiasm that it generated among the young escape their control; so amateur play educational camps (*Laienspielschullager*) were instituted, where lay actors could receive a minimal training for the stage.[41]

The *Heimatspiele* were viewed as a national theater in which the people themselves acted out their traditions and battles for survival. But side by side with the quest for a national theater, which extended from the nineteenth century into the postwar world, we must set the *Vereinstheater* in all its parochialism and artificiality. Eventually, the Nazis gave such plays performed by trade associations a high priority as true expressions of the Volk soul. If the quest for national theater determined the ambition and tone of the *NS-Kampfbühne*, the *Vereinsbühne* is directly related to its content.

The *Vereinstheater* was widespread and popular,[42] and it is difficult to see why it has not yet found its historian. Because we know almost nothing about it (though as the Nazis rightly claimed, every Verein had such a theater, even the *Kleintierhalterverband* or association of owners of small pets),[43] for lack of accessible records, I must confine myself to one such theater. The Verein of Catholic Apprentices, founded by Adolf Kolping in 1851, loved to perform plays that were an integral part of the educational program of the "Kolping family." The apprentice was meant to become a modest and industrious craftsman, who knew how to work, to pray, and to shun easy wealth and monetary speculation. Adolf Kolping's motto was that "Religion and work are the golden soil of the Volk."[44] But there was no Protestant harshness to this morality;

the Kolping family spent their evenings sharing play and song, and listening to popular lectures on history and natural science.[45]

The plays, like the short stories Adolf Kolping wrote, contained simple messages, such as "Thou shalt not steal," or lauded the triumph of love and devotion over a hard-hearded businessman. The villain, the enemy of all "honest work," was the speculator, the capitalist, the Jew greedy for gold and riches.[46] There is hardly a play where the Jew does not appear as the symbol of evil. If we take as our example plays performed between 1874 and 1884, we can see a hardening of the polemic and of the racism which in notable contrast to Adolf Kolping's own stories comes to pervade such plays.

Joseph Becks was the most prolific playwright of these years; a Catholic priest, he had become the president of the St. Joseph's Guild of Kolping Apprentices in Cologne. Kolping himself in his short stories had been careful to distinguish between the evil gold-loving Jew who refuses Christian conversion and the converted Jew who became a noble figure.[47] Becks no longer makes such fine distinctions.

For example, Becks's *Wurst Wieder Wurst* (*The Tom-Fool*, 1880) shows a Jew trying to cheat a master-craftsman. But the craftsman's loyal apprentices trick the Jew instead. The Jew is not only the foil; he inevitably loses throughout these plays. Becks used traditional comedy, which featured the peasant dolt as the foil. This peasant still appears in the Kolping theater, but by and large it is the Jew who takes the peasant's place, though treated with a brutality largely absent in traditional comedy. Becks constantly stresses the Jewish stereotype, and his Jews talk "jargon"—that mixture of Yiddish and German used in most anti-Semitic writing and found again in the *Kampfbühne* as well. Such plays are crude and polemical, very much like the later performances of the "Storm Troops" or "Brown Shirts." For example, a play written by a teacher called Peter Sturn, *Die Schöne Nase, oder das Recht Gewinnt den Sieg* (*The Beautiful Nose, or Justice Triumphs*, 1878) is typical. A Jew in his greed sells his nose to the highest bidder, only to finally buy it back at an exorbitant price. The content of a play entitled *Hyman Levy as Soldier* (1877) does not need elucidation.

These plays spread well beyond the Kolping families and even

Catholic circles. After World War I, the *Bühnenvolksbund* took up the heritage of this *Vereinstheater*. Founded in 1919 in order to counter the modern "immoral" and "atheistic" theater, it was supported by such organizations as those of Catholic apprentices (including Kolping), Catholic trade unions, and the Protestant Union of Commercial Employees (*Deutschnationaler Handlungs Gehilfen Verband*). The Catholics were in the forefront attempting to influence national culture in this way.[48] The Protestants were less active in exploiting the stage for their purposes. The Bund began with 700 individual and 20 corporate members; by 1928, it had gained 300 local affiliates and counted between 220,000 and 300,000 members.[49] This was almost exactly half the membership that had joined the rival leftist *Volksbühnenbewegung*.

The plays given in the first years after its founding were anti-French, antisocialist, and anti-Jewish. The morality presented was the same the Kolping theater had already proclaimed. Thus one hero exclaims: "Happy are those unemployed who have a wife to pray for them and keep them from falling into the hands of the Volksverhetzer [meaning the socialists]!" Philip Ausserer, a Catholic theologian and gymnasium professor in Salzburg, contributed a play, *Die Wiege* (*The Cradle*), in which a Jew deprives a peasant of his farm. Some plays glorified a pious peasantry,[50] always close to the heart of Catholicism. The theme of the peasant deprived of his land by the Jew was a commonplace one in all volkish literature.[51] There were other plays which showed the horror of revolution and, again through the example of a Jew, that "*Hochmut kommt vor dem fall*" (pride goeth before the fall).[52] Such themes are almost identical with those of the later *Volksbühne*.

The physical stereotypes were present as well. Thus we learn from the *Dictionary of the Theater* published by the Bund for amateur players in 1925 how to make a "Jewish mask": dark skin, sharply marked facial lines, thick eyebrows, bent nose. The "usurer" is made up in similar fashion, but as these were always conceived as old men, pale skin and deep-set eyes had to be created.[53] Yet by that time such anti-Semitic plays had largely disappeared from the repertoire. At the same point, the national Bund repudiated an anti-Jewish resolution passed by its Dresden branch and refused the pressure of younger members to haul down the flag of the Weimar Republic at one of its meetings.[54] The *Bühnenvolksbund* had made its peace with the Republic (as had the Catholic associations that sponsored it).

The Bund declined by 1928, perhaps because of the tensions between the younger and the older generations.[55] The last years of the Weimar Republic required a greater radicalization than the *Volksbühnenbund* now desired. The biblical dramas it produced and the shallow comedies (such as *The Gambler of Monte Carlo*)[56] could not meet this need. These were years when people flocked to see polemical plays hostile to the Republic or to plays like *The Three-penny Opera* where the middle classes could safely enjoy being derided and spat upon.[57] Though most people came for amusement, nevertheless this was surely one sign of the transformation of middle-class values into their own negation, something closely related to the later Nazi experience.

The building blocks of the Nazi *Kampfbühne* were laid through the debate about a national theater, by the amateur play movement, the *Vereinstheater*, and the *Volksbühnenbund*. As the *Kampfbühne* becomes an object of scholarly investigation, other building blocks will no doubt be discovered. The tradition of the *Kampfbühne* was continued into the Third Reich mainly by the Hitler Youth, but also by the "Strength through Joy" movement and the Labor Service. Baldur von Schirach in 1936 made the renewal of the German theater a special task of the Hitler Youth.[58] Beginning the following year, theatrical congresses were held. The first, in Bochum, included not only the *Kampfbühne* but also liturgical theater (in the same year in which the Thing theater itself was discontinued). Thus Eberhard Wolfgang Möller's *Frankenburger Würfelspiel* (*The Dice Game of Frankenburg*, 1936) was performed with the participation of the Hitler Youth.

This play had been produced originally for the Thing theater, and required 1,200 participants. When it opened in 1936 as a *Weihespiel* (a pseudo-religious play) to accompany the Olympic Games, the Labor Service provided the choruses and the crowds.[59] The play pictured the German Volk of peasants accusing tyrants who had oppressed it throughout history in front of seven judges; the audience was drawn into the drama as the actors addressed them directly from the stage. But the *NS-Volksbühne* was also represented at Bochum through Möller's *Rothschild Siegt bei Waterloo*, which concluded the Congress. The Hitler Youth now attempted to advance young dramatists from its own ranks, not only Eberhard Wolfgang Möller but also men like Friedrich Wilhelm Hymmen and Hans Schwitzke who wrote historical dramas very similar to those the *NS-Volksbühne* had performed.[60]

But the *Dramatists of the Hitler Youth* (to cite the title of an official publication) also included men like Paul Alverdes, of an older generation. Alverdes, for example, brought to the drama performed by Hitler Youth the memory of his war experiences. In a play written for the Hitler Youth, *Das Winterlager (The Winter Camp)*, he called for discipline and obedience to the leader, using as his example a dangerous adventure in which Hitler Youth are lost in a snow storm because they had broken the discipline of the group. However, Alverdes returns to his obsession at the end of the play when two war veterans draw the proper moral and refer to their experience in battle.[61] *Das Winterlager* was performed over the radio; indeed, the radio play provided one of the principal forums for the play groups of the Hitler Youth. But they were also sent into the countryside in order to stem the flight from the land and to help preserve peasant culture.[62] Thus the Hitler Youth took up where they had left off in their pre-1933 election propaganda. The *Spielschaaren* performed popular cabaret in the villages, consisting of singing, dancing, and folk plays, but Nazi polemics also remained part of their repertoire. During World War II they would first take a communal meal with the villagers.[63]

If little enough is known about the actual plays these Hitler Youth troupes performed, still less is known about those of the "Strength through Joy," movement, which also encouraged *Spielgruppen* in factories. Such factory groups were called the Vanguard (*Stosstruppen*) and were meant to urge their fellow workers to sing, dance, and stage plays.[64] The Labor Service in its plays does seem to have stressed what one official called the manly, heroic world view as against the attitude of a nomadic and trading people.[65] We are back to the Jewish stereotype so easily presented on the "fighting stage." Such amateur theaters seem to have been the true continuation of the *Kampfbühne*. Although the professional theater did present some of the plays of the *NS-Volksbühne*, I have found hardly a trace of those writers whose dramas were performed before the seizure of power and whom we have mentioned earlier.

This discussion is a first excursion into unknown territory. Yet it is clear that the *Kampfbühne* exemplified the thrust of Nazi ideology and in its roots points to a theatrical tradition of importance. Surely neither the *Vereinstheater* nor the call for a national stage were without influence upon the attitudes of important sections of the population. Surely, too, the polemical theater during the Weimar Republic must be seen as a whole, in its impact upon the Right as well as Left, though the actual interaction between them may have been slight. We know much about the Piscator theater because it was innovative and important in putting forward a new dramatic style, while the *Kampfbühne* was crude and primitive. However, the latter's enthusiastic S.A. or Hitler Youth play troupes may well have struck a spark because of their very crudeness and traditionalism. Nor was the *NS-Volksbühne* without an audience, though it could never rival the famous older *Volksbühne* itself.

This theater must be placed next to the Thing theater as the objectification of Nazi ideology—an important function in a modern mass movement that relied on empathy, participation, and "enlightenment." For the Nazis themselves, the theater belonged to the most elementary expressions of life, as they put it.[66] That alone makes the *Kampfbühne* worth investigating, even if it is largely devoid of literary merit.

The Nazis did innovate within the relatively new media of film and photography. Some time late in the 1920s they began to use projectors to show a rapidly changing series of photographs: "pictures without words." These contrasted, for example, slum housing to the high life of a Reichstag deputy. They were fond of projecting the so-called Jewish faces of the republican statesmen, or showing Isidor Weiss, the depty police chief of Berlin, whom they hated, in a riding outfit. This kind of kaleidoscope seems to have been a success with audiences. The Nazis also at times used photomontage, and did not disdain the newest avant-garde film techniques pioneered during the Weimar Republic.[67] However, such innovation was always embedded in traditionalism. The stream of history which the Nazis claimed was on their side had to be kept alive—the past must determine the artistic and literary forms of the present. The crude and simplistic *Kampfbühne* exemplified not only Nazi literature and art but also the Nazi historical consciousness.

TWELVE

Fascism and the Avant Garde

FASCISM CONSIDERED ITSELF an avant garde: a group of
men who were leading society into the post-liberal age. The
classical definition of avant garde as being at one and the same
time opposed to bourgeois politics and bourgeois tastes is a part of
fascist rhetoric, of that populism upon which the fascist movements sought to build their appeal. If we define avant garde as an
alternative discourse to the bourgeois consensus, then fascism
would have seen itself as such an alternative. Basic to an understanding of the relationship of fascism and avant garde is the fact
that fascism was both a new movement and in a hurry; that it had
no long period of gestation like socialism, that it was founded only
after World War I. Fascism was obsessed with the thought that it
had to claim instant success, lest the collapse of the old order benefit socialists or communists. The rawness of the movement, its
apocalyptical tone, meant at once a search for tradition and an obsession with the speed of time. Fascism stood at the frontiers of
technology and technocracy—Robert Paxton tells us that the tech-
nocrats entered the Vichy government like a conquered country.[1]
The alliance between technology, technocracy, and the authoritarian state was completed in the interwar period. But at the same
time fascism integrated itself into nationalist traditions, attempting
to harness a usable past—the Roman Empire, or the German wars

of liberation. As a nationalist movement, fascism aimed to link past and present.

The attempt to combine the technological and technocratic avant garde with a look backward to the national past was thus basic. The obvious contradictions involved would be resolved when the state of the future superseded the decadence of the present. For fascism, the post-liberal age was to substitute youthful vigor for old age, camaraderie for an atomized society. But above all, the post-liberal age would lead to the domination by an élite over nature, inferior peoples, and nations. The theme of domination is of special relevance in defining the relationship between avant garde and fascism, for it enabled fascists to champion one of the principal achievements of modern industrialism and technology, the communications revolution of the twentieth century. This revolution exemplified the sudden and frightening changes of industrialization, the new speed of time, the nervousness and restlessness castigated by so many critics of society, in a word, that degeneration which in 1892 Max Nordau saw exemplified in all of modern art and literature. Fascists, like Expressionists and Futurists, accepted the new speed of time not as exhausting but as toughening the nerves of a virile élite. They saw in the radio, the film, the motorcar, and the airplane a means of domination, an *élan vital* appropriate to the new fascist man.

But unlike the Expressionists, the most up-to-date industrial accomplishments were integrated into a glorified national past, accepted and at the same time transcended through national values. It is in this context that the airplane can illustrate the relationship between fascism and this avant garde, for here the new frontiers of technology and time became part of a new élitism, the search for a new man at the same time eternal and modern. Henry de Montherlant in 1922 summed it up well: The struggle of the airplane against nature is not so much the glorification of technology, but a means to prove one's manliness and youth.[2] Now that the war was over, aviation continued the challenge of combat into the peace. Saint-Exupéry, who did more than anyone between the wars to popularize the mystique of flying, held that man was being judged by the "*échelle cosmique*"—that as an aviator face to face with transcendent values, he could recapture his individuality in mass society.[3] Mussolini, who had written already in 1909 that the human herd could not understand the nobility of Blériot's flight across the English Channel, summed up the élitist politics of flying: "Aviation must remain the privilege of a spiritual aristocracy."[4] The pilot exemplifies the proper willpower and soul, a book about *Mussolini Aviatore* tells us, but above all he must understand the fullest meaning of the word "control." The pilot appropriates a piece of eternity, of the sky, and it is this appropriation of immutability that enables him to keep control.[5] The analogy to a political élite is obvious here.

Confrontation with the frightening phenomena of modern aviation meant emphasis upon a new aristocracy in the age of technology (so different from what Saint-Exupéry once called ants in their commuter trains). Aviation here tended to be associated with élitist and right-wing politics, though Bertold Brecht on the Left attempted to strip the adventure of flying of its mystique. His radio play *The Flight of the Lindberghs* presented this flight as the conquest of nature by man, the demystification of the world: ". . . when I fly I am a true atheist."[6] There is no appropriation of eternity here, no longing for immutability. Moreover, Brecht rejected the concentration upon the hero, because this might drive a wedge between the listener and the masses. The part of Lindbergh should be sung by a chorus.[7] Nothing could be further from the attitudes and beliefs of the living Lindbergh, and Brecht eventually retitled the play *The Flight over the Ocean*, substituting "The Flyer" for Lindbergh throughout the text. Yet it was the mystique that remained strong and that, through figures like Lindbergh, penetrated the popular consciousness. Saint-Exupéry, for all his élitism and appropriation of eternity, thought of himself as a good democrat; he nevertheless became both the mystique's victim and its popularizer. More typical than Brecht's attitude to aviation and that of other writers of the Left was the constant quest for mediation between the speed of the airplane and a harmonious universe where past and present met. It was said of Italo Balbo, Italian fascism's most famous aviator, that "through aviation he has recaptured the chivalry of old."[8]

The use of the term "chivalry" shows the association of past and present, or rather, that of technology with the eternal and immutable values symbolized by the sky. A pilot has to be "called" to exercise his profession. Typically enough, one fascist tribute to Balbo points out that he served in an Italian mountain troupe, the *Alpini*, during the war; he was therefore accustomed to dominating heights and suspending distances.[9] Indeed, the famous mass flights across the Atlantic or the Mediterranean, which he led, were supposed to educate a fascist élite and demonstrate to the world that it had conquered the challenge of modernity. But this challenge was met by integrating past and present, setting the act of flying and the speed of time within eternity—the blue skies, the mountains.

National Socialism used the same technique in accepting and modernizing mass production. Here modern industrialization did not appropriate eternity through the sky but through the nation itself, a symbol as impervious to the speed of time as the sky or the mountain. The program called "Beauty of Work," directed by Albert Speer, modernized the assembly line and the factory but at the same time surrounded the work place with national symbols, building communal halls and so-called sacred rooms in which the nation could be worshipped. Song, play, and physical exercise all became part of the work place,[10] in factories which, more often than not, continued to be built along functional, Bauhaus lines. Factories, so we are told even by a Nazi critic of the *Neue Sachlichkeit* ("New Realism") should express their function and not look like Byzantine palaces or Renaissance villas.[11] The Weimar architectural and technological avant garde was already partially integrated into the Nazi revolution.

Such a process of integration, set as it was in the context of the nationalist mystique, emphasized the activism of the movement, its dynamic when opposed to frightened conservatives and complacent bourgeois. Italian fascism, as we shall see, proceeded in a similar fashion, though here the avant garde included literature and the arts. As far as the Nazis were concerned, the architectural, technological, and technocratic avant garde was easier to assimilate than the avant garde in literature and art, which might challenge the framework within which the modern could become a part of the national mystique, dominating man and nature. No doubt the emphasis of the later Weimar Bauhaus upon form rather than content facilitated its Nazi adaptation, while in Italy the young fascist architects influenced by the Bauhaus stated that revolutionary architecture must accompany the fascist revolution.[12] There was no such talk in Nazi Germany.

Yet at first, Nazi student youth praised expressionism because it seemed dynamic, open-ended, a "chaos of the soul." But Hitler wanted no chaos, and in September of 1934, he put an end to all flirtation with expressionism.[13] The movement opposed his banal Wilhelminian taste, but he was simultaneously attempting to tame that activism which stood at the beginning of his own movement. Expressionism was outlawed at roughly the same time that the so-called *Röhm Putsch* took place, which disciplined the S.A. Now the functionalism of much of Nazi architecture was sharply distinguished from the Bauhaus, which Goebbels and the *Völkische Beobachter* had at one time admired, and which was still the style of the future in fascist Italy. Even the efforts of Mies van der Rohe to appease the régime failed, though he and others at the Bauhaus had divined correctly that rhetorical hostility was not always accompanied by the rejection of functionalism and simplicity in architectural style. Perhaps today, when we are conscious that the Bauhaus style contained as many elements of domination as of liberation, we are ready to reexamine its relationship to National Socialism.[14] Indeed, the new stadium for the 1936 Olympics had to be redesigned because Hitler objected to the large scale and functional use of glass by its architect, saying he would never enter a "glass box."[15]

The influence of the Bauhaus and the *Neue Sachlichkeit* was evident in the construction of factories and apartment houses. However, in the case of official Reich and party buildings, Bauhaus influence could easily be confused with the neo-classicism of Hitler's taste. Both, as a matter of fact, were protests against restlessness; both attempted to combine functionalism and order.[16] For example, Heinrich Tessenow, whose architectural theories almost certainly influenced Hitler, advocated simplicity of line and materials. Indeed, the clarity and decisiveness which the Nazis advocated in the struggle against their enemies was reflected in their emphasis upon simple building materials and clear lines. These were embedded in a monumental style that once more integrated modernism with symbols of domination, a linkage the Bauhaus had struggled to avoid. The official architecture—but not that of the army or air force, or even of some local party buildings—linked what had been avant garde to national grandeur and representation.

Such cooptations of the avant garde in architecture and technology were important in Germany because they enabled National Socialism to combine its self-image as a decisive and virile movement with volkish ideology. They could dominate time and space because as an élite, National Socialists had appropriated all that was eternal—the mountains, the sky, and the nation.

But in Italy, the avant garde could build upon radical and syndicalist currents within fascism that were absent in Germany. Moreover, Italian nationalism had retained certain Jacobin traditions that were of little influence in the north. That is why Italy gave more space to the avant garde than Nazi Germany, and why most of this essay looks south rather than north. While modern technology and some avant-garde architectural forms were integrated into National Socialism, as we have seen, it is difficult to extend the interaction between the avant garde and the Third Reich much further. Even in film, it was the techniques of the Weimar documentary that were used rather than the content. Music seems to be the exception to this rule. Here the avant garde found space; for example, Carl Orff wrote his famous *Carmina Burana* in 1937, and continued to compose peacefully during the war. Perhaps modern music is the most politically neutral of the avant-garde arts because its tonality is accessible only to a few, or can be tolerated if a few folk tunes are incorporated into its compositions. Here the weight of history did not strangle the contents of avant-garde art.

Indeed, it is the density of historical tradition that will determine to a large extent the space available to the avant garde. If historical consciousness and the cultivation of traditions forms the key to a régime's public thought, then whatever techniques are accepted, art and literature must look backward rather than forward. Fascist Italy, unlike Germany, made an alliance with the antihistorical Futurists and syndicalists, and in this way could possess an avant garde that deplored the weight of tradition.

Thus a group of young architects proclaimed in Turin in 1934 that as an avant garde they were joining fascist youth in the search for clarity and wisdom, in the unconditional adherence to logic and reason. Tradition itself, so we are told, was transformed and largely abolished by fascism.[17] Indeed, a member of this group, Giuseppe Terragni, in his Fascist Party building at Como (1932–36) with its cubic form went beyond the Bauhaus to the very frontiers of functionalism. At the exhibition to honor the tenth anniversary of the Fascist Revolution (1932), the hall designed by Terragni was dominated by a huge turbine ("the thoughts and actions of Mussolini are like a turbine, taking the Italian people and making them fascist").[18] Terragni did not stand alone in his devotion to fascism and avant garde; for example, Kandinski had the highest praise for the fascist Carlo Belli's defense of abstract art as the only art suitable for the "wonderful new régime."[19]

For over fifteen years, Italian fascism allowed itself to be represented by an avant garde as well as by the traditional "Roman" styles. To be sure, Mussolini's personal taste was entirely different from that of Adolf Hitler; as a man of the world, he had been exposed to a European avant garde that merely frightened the Austrian provincial. There is a continuity between the impatience with ordered society and settled social structures that Mussolini expressed as a young man and his taste for certain avant-garde art and architecture later in life. He always believed that it was movement that characterized the twentieth century: "We want to act, produce, dominate matter . . . reach toward the other end . . . other horizons."[20] Giuseppe Bottai, a former syndicalist and fascist of the first hour held, typically enough, that fascism's use of the newest technology also meant accepting the newest forms of art and literature.[21] The Futurists in their original Manifesto combined the call for rearmament and colonial expansion with opposition against the monumental in art, advocating all that was "violently modern." They were Mussolini's closest allies in the effort to get Italy to intervene in the war which, while it helped to transform Mussolini from a left-wing socialist to a fascist, did not markedly change Futurist ideals. Their Manifesto of the "Impero Italiano" (*Italian Empire*, 1923) rejected history as irrelevant: "We are the children of the Isonzo, of the Piave . . . and of four years of fascism. That suffices!"[22] Here the separation of avant-garde technology from literature and art, so obvious in Nazi Germany, evidently failed to take place.

Mussolini himself, for example, seemed to repeat Futurist ideas when at a speech in Perugia in 1927 he demanded that art must not be weighed down by the patrimony of the past, but that fascism must create a new art.[23] The response to the debate about art in Bottai's own *Critica Fascista* in the late 1920s was more cautious: the state must, as far as possible, avoid interference in artistic matters, and the corporation of artists must restrict itself to discussing the economic problems of the profession. Yet individualism should not remain unchecked. Bottai desired the liberalization of the régime in order to coopt as many diverse groups as possible into the fascist consensus.[24]

Slowly but surely, over a long period of time within Italian fascism, antimodernist forces forged ahead, trying to end the tolerance for avant-garde architecture, art, and literature. The group "*Novocento*," founded in 1922 and led by Mussolini's long-time mistress Margherita Sarfatti, proclaimed a native neo-classicism as the guarantor of order and a fitting symbol for the nation. Fascist literature must not reflect restlessness, the search for new artistic expression; instead, it must be based firmly upon the Roman tradition. Massimo Bontempelli, the principal literary figure of *Novocento*, coined the term "romantic realism," meaning a realistic character portrayal within a romantic setting.[25] The identical term became popular among Nazis as well, who rejected romantic sentimentality as denoting weakness and femininity, but at the same time retained romanticism as a "*verklärte Wirklichkeit*" (luminous reality).[26] This was the "*realismo fascista*," producing paintings of the "battle of grain" or of people listening with rapt attention to a speech of Mussolini, once again similar to those paintings that dominated so much of Nazi art.

Novocento had wanted to be cosmopolitan, to spread its myths and optimism throughout Europe. Officially, the movement was regarded with some skepticism, as the article "Novocento" in the *Enciclopedia Italiana* of 1934 demonstrates. Indeed, when Mussolini addressed their first exhibition of art in 1926, it was to proclaim that the state cannot give preference to any one artistic movement over another. Yet in that very same year he ordered the Roman ruins excavated and exhibited within the city.[27] Few could have foreseen that this command would present the greatest danger and indeed eventual defeat for the avant garde in Italy. The state was about to take sides. The *Strapaese* (or ultra-nativist) movement was a more successful attempt to produce a committed fascist literature, here through an idealized picture of village and small-town virtues. Catholic and rural, it was closely linked to the Tuscan agrarian squadristas, who had presented a nearly independent force within early fascism. Yet, typically, this volkish Italian fascism disintegrated when it had to direct its criticism to what it regarded as the undue tolerance of official Italian culture.[28] Volkish literature and art were at the fringes in Italy, not as in Germany at the center of the movement's ideology and culture. The Roman and Catholic traditions, combined with the relative open-mindedness of Italian nationalism, prevented fascism's lapse into provincialism.

More important than any single literary or artistic movement like *Novocento* or *Strapaese*, the Roman revival which had gathered momentum from the very beginnings of fascism was increasingly directed against the avant garde. Mussolini had called for the excavation of the ruins of Rome in 1926. A year earlier, the founding of institutes of classical dance, drama, and music had already documented official interest in a classical revival,[29] and still more important, the Museum of Classical Antiquity on the Campodoglio had been renamed the "Museo Mussolini" (1925). What could better demonstrate the Duce's association with antiquity than this museum, the only one that bore his name, standing as it did in the capitol of ancient Rome?

But it was the construction of the Forum Mussolini in 1932 that proved the most spectacular symbol of the close connection between past and present. The Duce joined the ranks of such builders of Rome as Pope Urban VIII; he immortalized himself by imitating antiquity. The forum, which was to hold 200,000 people, was surrounded by classical statues symbolizing bodily perfection, and it contained a Roman amphitheater as well. By that time, the Italian Architectural Association (which earlier had taken Mies van der Rohe and Le Corbusier as its models) was beginning to advocate monumentalism and the imitation of classical styles.[30]

This neo-classicism was the result of a conscious search for a national fascist style. Marcello Piacentini, the dominant architect of the 1930s, rejected Mies van der Rohe as being too intellectual. The quest for what he called simple and tranquil lines must lead back to regional traditions, either Renaissance or classical.[31] Piacentini's columns and arches (including his Arch of Triumph at Bologna) led to an eclecticism of style most clearly illustrated by Rome Eur (Esposizione Universale Reale), the so-called Universal Exhibition of 1942 (which can still be seen today coming into Rome from the airport), whose buildings represent a mixture of past Italian styles.

Modernism and the avant garde were in retreat but not yet defeated; Terragni was asked to design a building for the exhibition in his functional style. What happened in architecture can also be traced in literature, where works close to the *Novocento* and *Strapaese* dominated.

The conflict between the ancients and moderns in fascism illustrates the constant search for clarity within the movement, the attempt to find an artistic and literary equivalent to the designs of modern technology while maintaining the uncompromising struggle against all enemies, and then to combine this clarity and dynamic with ideals of law and order. The Forum Mussolini, like so many National Socialist representational buildings, combined the use of clear and simple materials with grandeur defined as the monumental pointing back to a secure national past. The Futurist critique of Nazi art as being static, like photography, was in reality a criticism of fascist neo-classicism as well.[32] Like so many early fascists, the Futurists had believed that fascism was a movement whose dynamic would carry it into uncharted spaces. Their poetry and Terragni's architecture were designed to occupy such spaces and at the same time to point forward toward the unknown. But fascism would not follow; as a political movement and as a government, it could not enjoy a wild ride into wide open spaces but was forced to retain control.

Admittedly, in its "second stage" after the war, Futurism absorbed a dose of mysticism that could have been used to tame the movement but that in actual fact was never strong enough to fulfill this purpose. However, even Terragni abandoned his avant-garde modernism when it came to designing memorials to the fallen soldiers. Here, at the very center of the national experience, reverence meant homage to tradition.[33] And this is hardly surprising. Nationalism has always emphasized continuities rather than a leap into the future. The traditionalism of fascist thought was in conflict with Futurism, but it was Marinetti and his group who were banished to the side-lines. The conflict between ancients and moderns is well summed up by the Manifesto which the leading composers of fascist Italy, all of them devoted to traditional modes of composition, issued during the 1920s. Ottorini Resphigi, among others, warned against the "biblical confusion of Babel" that was being brought on by the "continual chaotic revolution in music." It was important to recognize that the past was linked to the future, that "the romanticism of yesterday will again be the romanticism of tomorrow."[34]

But that time was not yet, however much this search for order and harmony appealed to intellectuals like Gottfried Benn, Ezra Pound, William Butler Yeats, or T. S. Eliot. Rejecting neo-romanticism as false sentimentality, they saw fascism as a bulwark against disorder, the "formless wobble," as Ezra Pound called it.[35] These writers, among them some of the most important literary avant-garde figures of Europe, searched for immutable forms and found them in the political discipline of fascism.[36] Gottfried Benn, for example, in his speech in praise of Stefan George (1934), called the feeling for aristocratic form the way to transcend the present—through strictness and discipline (*Zucht*) of form, the "German will" triumphs over nature, science, and technology. The state satisfies the longing toward form, and only then should art follow.[37] This avant garde of writers was integrated into the fascist state through its desire for order and unambiguous literary form; Benn himself saw such form as expressing a spirit analogous to commands given the Nazi battalions.[38]

When Benn welcomed Marinetti to Berlin in 1934, he praised form, order, and discipline once again, as against so-called chaos. The avant garde is not mentioned; instead, the leader of the Futurists is approved for having given fascism the black shirt as the color of horror and death, its battle cry "*A noi,*" and the fascist hymn, The Giovinezza. Those who had once been of the avant garde—not only Benn but also Ezra Pound, for example—ignored the fact that an avant garde of Futurism continued to coexist alongside Italian fascism. Marinetti was not mistaken, from his point of view, in despising the Nazis and the kind of fascist discipline that Benn thought essential for true and eternal art. The Futurists continued to oppose neo-classical and romantic styles, along with the accompanying political turn to the Right symbolized by the racial laws. Thus Marinetti, as well as Terragni, took a strong stand against racism while remaining loyal to fascism—the fascism of their dreams.[39]

All these tensions within Mussolini's Italy are exemplified by an ideal that was constantly on fascist lips: that of the "new man" whom the movement was to produce, who was its goal and its hope. Mussolini in particular was content to let the new fascist man symbolize the hopes and dreams of the movement. Was such a man to be tied to the past or would he be the creator of new values? Would he be the leader of an avant garde? Renzo De Felice has told us that the new fascist man was indeed a man of the future, that while the "new man" of National Socialism felt suffocated by modernity, in Italy the future was considered open-ended.[40]

But whether in Germany or Italy, the "new man" continued a stereotype that had its roots in nineteenth-century nationalism. This was based upon an ideal of male strength and beauty, upon an aggressive virility, an *élan vital*, which we have seen attributed to the pilot who dominated the skies. The new fascist man was supposed to be the very opposite of muddleheaded and talkative intellectuals, of the exhausted old men of a dying bourgeois order. The antibourgeois rhetoric and imagery was strong here, yet symbolized by an ideal type, who himself represented bourgeois respectability, order, and domination. However much the new fascist man soared off into uncharted spaces, his ancestors were those youths who had fought the battle between the generations of the fin de siècle. Like all of fascism, he was a part of the bourgeois antibourgeois revolution, of a play within a play. He was a member of that spiritual aristocracy of aviators of which Mussolini had spoken, those who simultaneously confronted the new speed of time while appropriating a piece of eternity in order to keep control. The literary and architectural avant garde was supposed to proceed to new frontiers, while still keeping in mind the nation's need for immutability. If immutability eventually triumphed with the Roman revival, even earlier the difference between Terragni's cubic party building and his traditional monuments to the fallen seem to bear this injunction in mind.

Within this pattern of thought, Italian fascism was certainly more open to the future than German National Socialism; the new man of the south had avant-garde features lacking in the north, where the ideal German was the ancient Aryan whom Hitler had roused from centuries of slumber. Mussolini was much more ambivalent. In his famous article on fascism for the *Enciclopedia Italiana* of 1934, Mussolini described the new man as, on the one hand, restrained by the Italian patriotic tradition, and on the other, transcending space and time. Man must proceed to ever higher forms of consciousness, culture must never crystallize; and yet the great Italians of the past "are the germs which can fructify our spirit and give us spontaneity." [41] When all is said and done, Mussolini did leave the door ajar to the future, while in Germany nationalism and racism blocked all exits. Neither Mussolini nor many of his followers gave up the idea that fascism, while rooted in the past, was not destined to cling to these roots. Nevertheless, however uncharted the new spaces, they were to be controlled and dominated by a national stereotype, rooted as a matter of fact in the imagery and the ideals of the attempted revolution of bourgeois youth at the fin de siècle.

The very nature of fascism as a successful modern political movement was bound to restrict the space within which the avant garde could live and flourish. Fascism was a nationalist movement, a mass movement, and a movement of youth. The opposition of nationalism to the avant garde must be evident: emphasis upon the past must necessarily be in conflict with the denial of history. To be sure, in Italy the opposition between nationalism and avant garde seemed muted as Futurists joined the interventionist battle, and as the early fascist movement stressed the immediacy of the war experience and the dynamic of youth. But it was only a matter of time before preoccupation with the heritage of antiquity pushed Futurism to the fringes of the movement. Yet where fascists had little chance at political power, ideas of youth, virility, and force could assume greater importance than national memories. The rejection of history could be combined with a fascist commitment.

Drieu La Rochelle is perhaps the principal example of such a fascist. He was not attracted to integral nationalism; his fascism was based rather upon the philosophy of youth and force exemplified by a virile élite. [42] La Rochelle's fictional hero *Gilles* (1939) was not converted to fascism by an appeal to France's glorious past, but by the attraction of a spiritual renewal based upon the values of virility, authority, discipline, and force. [43] While Italian fascism was certainly attracted to all these ideas, it was, after all, a nationalist movement; moreover, it attained power in coalition with the Italian Nationalist Party, which occupied the traditional Right in Italian politics.

The incompatibility between the avant garde and political mass movements needs no elaboration. More than ever before, mass movements between the wars felt the need to stress traditional values, a happy and healthy world based upon the national past. The avant garde wanted to lead the masses, but it was doomed to failure and frustration. Fascism did have a place for the creative artist, but his role would be to create a setting for its political liturgy or to popularize the movement and recapture the supposedly glorious national past. Its model was Gabriele D'Annunzio—the power of artistic creativity harnessed to nationalist politics, helping the "First Duce" rule Fiume.[44] Even if the avant garde was able to function in fascist Italy, even if Mussolini himself liked much of what it produced and had to say, the inner logic of fascism as a nationalist mass movement was bound in the end to restrict the space of human creativity.

Not only did fascism exalt youth but its leadership and followers were much more youthful than those of the established political parties. The avant garde at the fin de siècle was also youthful as it hurled itself against the manner, morals, and culture of its elders. That revolt, as the years wore on, tended toward a certain rudeness and virility, and also, strengthened by the war experience, found itself attracted to various nationalisms. The war which furthered the nationalization of the masses also tended to further the nationalization of bourgeois youth. Marcel Arland, writing in 1924, declared that the *mal de siècle* was a superficial sophistication and wit, which made it natural that youth should appear rude in the midst of such grace, violent amid such sweetness.[45] Fascists like Drieu La Rochelle mobilized this rudeness and violence on behalf of right-wing causes.

The French situation differed markedly from that of Germany after the war. The victorious Third Republic was able to coopt much of the nationalist space in politics, retaining, for example, the loyalty and even affection of its largest war veterans' associations. Thus it undercut that integral nationalism which the fascists appropriated successfully in Germany and Italy. Here some French fascists could base themselves principally upon the exaltation of youth, virility, force, and camaraderie, the "équipe" of which they were a part. Typically enough in Germany, the Bund, which was the equivalent of the "équipe," was filled with nationalist and even racist content. The thought of a leading French fascist like Brasillach, though he felt nostalgia for the historical past, often lacked this proper nationalist dimension.[46] This enabled such French fascism to provide some space for the vanguard, as Le Corbusier, for example, collaborated in *Plans*, a journal mildly fascist in character.[47] The *élan* of youth led to brutality but also to a certain openness toward new artistic forms and content. The originality of style and tone of a Louis-Ferdinand Céline cannot be found in the literature of the extreme Right either in Germany or Italy.

Céline did identify himself with fascist and racist politics, and the books which he wrote before and during the war reflect this commitment. Admittedly, these books were a theater of the absurd, filled with irony and self-contradictions. Here virulent racism and fascism were in the hands of a true avant-garde writer, who integrated them with novelty of style and thought. The task is not, to my mind, to explain away Céline's politics, to underestimate, for example, the seriousness of his attempt to found a fascist party, but rather to explain how French fascism could stand this embrace. To some extent Céline wanted order and certainty in the world, and that is why in *Bagatelles pour un Massacre* (1937) he constantly praised the honesty of Adolf Hitler, who had dared to act out his ideology in contrast to hypocritical French politicians. Like Pound or Benn, fascism gave him the comfort of clarity; but unlike these other writers, he did not long for a strict discipline of literary form. On the contrary, he seems to have despised it. When all is said and done, here a youthful and ahistorical fascism was interacting with a genuine avant garde, and the case of Céline, unique among writers, must be put side by side with that of Futurist painters and architects in Italy.

For the most part, the relationship between fascism and youth was determined by the nationalization of bourgeois youth. The German youth movement shared with the avant garde the urge for simplicity, for the genuine, and a hatred of the academic in art and literature. But it found its inspiration in medieval dances, folk songs, and folk music. This search of youth for the beautiful was not functional but based upon the artistic forms of the past. Even those on the left of the youth movement, men who later joined the Communist Party like Alfred Kurella and Karl Bittell, remained romantics. Kurella admired the Stefan George circle,[48] and though George's own poetry might perhaps qualify as avant-garde, the classicism of the master and his disciples was meant to bring about the triumph of the "secret Germany"—a concept close to the élitism of the majority of the German youth movement, who regarded their own nationalism as the wave of the future. If we look at the writers and artists who came from this movement, those who worshipped at the altar of the fatherland by far outnumbered avant-garde artists like Max Beckmann or Expressionist writers like Kasimir Edschmid.

Though some members of the youth movement called themselves anarchists,[49] the majority followed the radicalization to the Right of German bourgeois youth already discernible at the fin de siècle and gathering strength after the war. As we saw, in France this was not the case to the same extent, and in Italy many of those who glorified youth were attracted to the Futurists. What proportion of bourgeois youth was attracted to left-wing causes in Italy before the victory of fascism remains to be investigated. Certainly here, as in France, the vast majority of veterans supported parliamentary democracy. Mussolini was specifically excluded from the electoral lists of veterans' organizations in the election of 1919, and suffered a shattering defeat.[50] But it may have been precisely the younger veterans who supported the Legionari Dannunziani or the Fasci di Combattimento. Mussolini called them the "marvelous warrior-youth of Italy."[51]

Fascism wanted to lead beyond liberalism and to find alternative methods of discourse, and yet it was dependent upon the bourgeois consensus. Its members were attracted to Futurism and Expressionism, but both these movements were, like fascism itself, antibourgoeis revolutions, which were profoundly indifferent to social and economic change. To parody the Expressionist dramas of Walter Hasenclever and others, bourgeois society was not likely to die from an unloaded pistol or from fright. Italian fascism maintained the idea of a permanent revolution that had been close to Mussolini's heart ever since his days as a left-wing socialist. But this permanent revolution, though complicating the relationship of fascism to history, was supposed to be a moral revolution, a quest for higher forms of consciousness based upon political domination. "Fascism is a revolution which, contrary to all others in history, perpetuates its political conquests through a continuous moral renewal."[52] The avant garde fitted these aims of fascism. Its crime in fascist eyes was not that it escaped the confines of complacent bourgeois society, but those of nationalism and the political necessities of a modern mass movement.

Yet, if we define modern technology and modern functionalism as part of the avant garde, its link to fascism becomes meaningful. Here Italian fascism was more portentous than National Socialism in unleashing a victorious revolution. Eventually, no analogy to medieval chivalry or ancient Rome could tame the speed of time, the new technology, and the dynamic that accompanied the victory of the new over the old. Fascism prided itself on controlling and dominating this rush to the future, yet it was not destined to play the pilot in the long run; instead, the modern state and its impersonal bureaucracy would fulfill that function. Mussolini, not Hitler, had paved the way when he exalted the Italian state rather than the Italian Volk. Modern technocracy would eventually displace fascism as the instrument of domination.

Though it seems today that the modern impersonal state determines the rather wide limits within which the avant garde can function, this might prove deceptive. For in time of renewed crisis, with the new age of scarcity that is upon us, the modern state may well once more need the support of nationalism, mass movements, and the worship of youth in order to retain control. The apparatus of modernity alone—lacking an ideology to connect past and present without seeming to appropriate a piece of eternity— may no longer suffice.

There will always be an avant garde, but its living space will always be restricted in the future, as it is in the present and has been in the past. The avant garde in and out of fascism is only tolerated as long as it remains within its charmed circle, as long as it does not ally itself with other powerful groups of society and so present a menace to the prevailing consensus. As we saw, there was fear that Mussolini might make such an alliance, but even when he praised the avant garde he was already preparing a Roman revival. Such a statement about the restrictions imposed upon the avant garde can surely be made about all that our society regards as unusual, abnormal, or disquieting. Like Swann and Charlus at the court of Proust's Guermantes, eccentricities are tolerated just so long as they remain amusing.

PART III

THIRTEEN

The Secularization of
Jewish Theology

THE RELATIONSHIP of Judaism to modernity was part of the process of Jewish emancipation whose crucial period spanned the first decades of the nineteenth century. The secularization of Jewish theology took place as that generation of Jews' perception of "modernity," was absorbed into the fabric of Jewish piety—accomplished through the adjustment of religious liturgy and religious thought to encompass the new cultural and political trends of the times. Thus the Enlightenment, nationalism, romanticism, and middle-class values penetrated to the very core of Jewish religiosity and eventually helped to define it. Just as Christianity through casuistry had adjusted itself through the ages to take in new exigencies and to meet new situations,[1] a young generation of rabbis followed suit at the beginning of the nineteenth century. But they did so much more suddenly and abruptly precisely because of the new fact of Jewish emancipation.

No religion can escape casuistry, for it has to cope in one way or another with the relentless onslaught of modernity. The newly emancipated Jews did not have much choice: they could attempt to complete their assimilation by the absorption of those forces of their environment which they perceived as "modern," and these were secular rather than religious in nature; or they could have fought to remain ghettoized (as indeed a small minority tried to do), which was surely not a viable alternative at the time. The secularization of Jewish theology was part and parcel of the historical context in which our forefathers found themselves. If I concentrate on the confrontation of Jews with modernity and on German Jews in particular, it is because here, as if in a laboratory, we have an excellent example of the problems and dangers inherent in such a secularization and modernization of religion.

Jewish as well as Christian casuistry absorbed the newest trends of the time into a generalized piety. This it seems to me is the true history of secularization, rather than the much discussed conflict between religion and modernity. But this casuistry raised an additional problem of importance: once one "modernity" had been absorbed, could this be discarded when the next "modernity" came along? Jewish reform, eventually, found that it could not do this, which was one of the basic reasons why so many young German Jews in the twentieth century turned to "secular religions" closer to their own desires, such as Zionism or socialism. Aspirations that were new and exciting for the recently emancipated generation of Jews at the beginning of the nineteenth century seemed stale and reactionary several generations later. The substance of religiosity, which had been secularized by the social and political values of the age of emancipation, could no longer be recovered and made relevant for a new age. That, too, is part of the story of the encounter of religion with modernity.

Jews were emancipated at a time when the Enlightenment coexisted with Romanticism and both with the pietistic heritage of the eighteenth century. In 1813, Rabbi Joseph Wolf quite typically combined the appeal to reason with an appeal to a sentimental piety. The "sun of the Enlightenment," he preached, "had finally pierced the fog which had for so long surrounded our existence." This happy circumstance now made it possible for Jews to discover the depth of their spiritual being. Not the intellect, but their very soul had become the center of Jewish religiosity.[2] The religion they discovered was described by the German word *"Erbauung"* (edifying) which, as Alexander Altman has told us, meant the pietistic cure of souls, adapted to Judaism from pietistic Christianity. Indeed, in 1832, Leopold Zunz referred to those sermons he wanted to see introduced into the Jewish service as "sermons of edification" (*Predigten oder Erbauungs-Vorträge*).[3] The increasing proximity of this

Jewish to the pietistic Christian religion was perceived with much pleasure at the time. Hirsch Traub, for example, rejoiced in 1825 that he had lived to see the end of the Jewish dark ages and was witnessing a time when the hearts of people of differing religions could find each other.[4] The emphasis in such rabbinical sermons was always on the heart, on seeing with the inner eye (*Anschauen*), and it reflected the Romantic period in which they were set. The constant analogies to nature are part of the absorption of the general German intellectual climate. The rising sun, the mountains and valleys, rather than the law, were frequently taken as the principal evidence of God's presence in the world. This in turn was linked to a predominance of the human senses; it is there that God is present, as one preacher remarked.[5]

Such piety was bound to find expression in Jewish religious service. It was only logical that *Sulamith*, the paper devoted to the Jewish enlightenment, should in 1908 contrast true faith with ceremonial and rote learning (a criticism that also castigated repetitive prayer). Religious ceremonies must appeal to the senses through their disciplined beauty and decorations; moreover, all religious ceremonies must contain something mysterious.[6] This is the Christian "beauty of holiness" transferred to the Jewish religion, which had never known a baroque. It seems ironic in retrospect that so many Protestants accused the Jews in Germany of clinging to a legalistic and ceremonial religion, the kind of faith most Jews themselves in fact rejected on behalf of a newly found piety. Jewish reform paralleled the pietistic reform which Friedrich Schleiermacher introduced into the Protestant Church in Prussia. Indeed, Schleiermacher and the young rabbis used to listen to one another's sermons.[7]

Such pietism emphasized the "religious community" rather than the congregation, and Schleiermacher believed in the vital interplay of personal piety with the Christian community. He wrote that Protestant liturgy must aim to create a feeling of the grandeur and importance of the ecclesiastical fellowship. Schleiermacher objected to placing prayers for the king and his dynasty at the beginning of the service; instead, he pleaded that prayers for the community of the Church should be substituted.[8] This emphasis had warrant in the Protestant tradition, but it was also a response to the growing alienation of so many in times of revolution, war, and industrialization. From our point of view it is especially significant that the concept of a religious community was supposed to give a more precise direction and definition to the generalized piety. The young rabbis followed suit, not because of the tradition of the Kehilla, which they deplored, but because they also had to give some specificity to the Jewish piety, which arose from the soul or from the senses.

What, then, was needed to cement such a community, to give it a more concrete meaning? Typically enough, following reform Protestantism, Rabbi Moses Mannheimer called for an emphasis on art (the "beauty of holiness") and common song in hymns shared by the congregation. The voices of "lamentation and complaint" must from now on be banished from the temple.[9] In the Jewish religious service, this meant that hymns must retain their ancient Jewish content while submitting to new and modern forms, as a Württemberg song book for Synagogues put it in 1834. The Jewish content was based upon the Psalms which, as we shall see, could and often were given a relevance to the present. By "form," such books understood the German language and choral music.[10] In religious services, such a division between form and content was bound to work to the detriment of the latter, for it is the form of the service which symbolizes the content. Form was openly subjugated to new trends such as the German language and style, but the content was bound to follow. Language was thought crucial in forming consciousness, and indeed, language had already been used by rabbis steeped in Herder's thought in order to prove the unity between Jews and Germans.[11] Language, after all, was crucial to the process of assimilation to a nation and culture not only for Jews but for all the awakening peoples of Europe.

The hymns themselves were described as songs of edification, meant to inculcate obedience to a secular authority and to exhort the congregation to industriousness, moderation, and contentment.[12] Clearly, the hymns that penetrated Jewish religious service carried with them the freight of many secular ideas popular at the time. For both Jews and Protestants, these hymns served to cement a pietistic community and to propagate ideas that could give it body while edifying the soul. For Jews as for Christians, the newly found love of song left the house of God to become part of social life. Jewish choral organizations were founded in the 1840s and 1850s when most male choirs were instituted in Germany, and attained almost universal popularity;[13] these Jewish societies also mixed religious, secular, and patriotic songs.

Yet the religious community was not to be based merely upon the outward emotional expression of an inner piety. It needed greater discipline now that past traditions had been questioned. There was a good reason why Schleiermacher partially defined his religious community in terms of a moral attitude[14] that was coming to dominate European life as it had not done before, an attitude we are apt to characterize as middle-class morality. The gospel of work, ideas of restraint, moderation, and loyalty to one's profession, penetrated this religious community in order to help define it. The identical process took place within Jewish piety, and here it also served in part to discipline a largely voluntary religious community held together by a piety largely devoid of specific Jewish theological content. Rabbinical sermons during the first decades of the nineteenth century appealed, as we saw, to reason and above all to sentiment; however, they are also filled (as are the hymns) with exhortations to work and moderation, "leading a quiet and settled life," as Ludwig Philipson put it in 1834. He added to this catalogue the virtues of grace and friendliness.[15] Of course, such sermons and hymns can also be seen as attempts to direct the Jew away from his stereotype and to fulfill the conditions of emancipation. But in the final resort, virtues taken from the secular world penetrated to the core of Jewish piety. Gotthold Salomon in 1837 summarized the essence of this morality succinctly: Without self-restraint, no human greatness and no virtue is possible.[16] Salomon here was referring to the modern *Anstand* (a cross between codes of good behavior and decency) rather than to the traditional exhortation to conquer the passions according to the *Sayings of the Fathers* (IV:I). Middle-class values, making their mark against those of the aristocracy, were an easy substitute for a ruptured tradition. They served to give body to pietistic feeling and to discipline the religious community. This system of values fulfilled much the same function in Schleiermacher's Protestantism. Religion, so Abraham Asch declared in 1813, provides the foundation for the state and for bourgeois well-being.[17] The secularization of Jewish theology could hardly find better expression.

But this middle-class morality (what Harold Nicolson called

"good behaviour")[18] was not the sole secularizing element meant to give more precise definition to the concept of a religious community. The rise of a new national consciousness accompanied the Enlightenment, romanticism, and the dominance of middle-class values. For Schleiermacher, the struggle for national liberation was an integral part of the Christian moral universe:[19] Jews not only lived through the euphoria of the German Wars of Liberation shortly after their emancipation but had concrete reasons to support the German kings and princes who entered the battle. And Jews are happy, David Fränkel wrote in 1807, when they are viewed as subjects of the state and not solely as Jews; then they are regarded as fellow human beings and not as "trading-Jews" or "court-Jews."[20] The Berlin Jewish community called out to its volunteers in the war of liberation: "O heavenly feeling to possess a fatherland: O what an enchanting thought."[21] Such patriotism was a logical consequence of emancipation. But it did raise the problem of tradition once more, for the Jews after all had possessed a nation of their own in the past, and this biblical fact could not easily be ignored.

The rabbis at the time attempted to make an unusable past into a usable present. They liked to cite some of the Psalms (for example, Psalm 45, verses 4 to 7, on the divine anointment of King David)[22] as biblical examples of present relevance. At the accession to the throne of Frederick William II of Prussia, the prayer recited in the synagogue reminded Berlin Jews that Jeremiah had commanded them to pray for the welfare of the towns into which they had been scattered. Now Jews were called upon to pray with still more intensity and loyalty for a king whom God Himself had chosen.[23] The virtues of King David were said to have been transferred to the king of Prussia embattled against Napoleon, just as the biblical king's example must inspire Jewish volunteers faced by a French Goliath in the Wars of Liberation.[24] Salomon Plessner, the rabbi of Posen and defender of Jewish Orthodoxy, summed up the basic principles involved in such a use of the Old Testament, which was not confined to religious reform, very well when he said that Jewish messianism must be postponed indefinitely on behalf of the benefits of citizenship.[25] Again during the Wars of Liberation, to cite an extreme case, Abraham Asch felt himself uplifted by the example of the ancient German Arminius, who had defeated the Roman legions, just as his forefathers, the ancient Jews (so he tells us) were inspired by their own heroes. Here Arminius has become the new and relevant David.[26] But such analogies were not confined to the Wars of Liberation. They were also used, for example, to encourage Jewish volunteers at the beginning of World War I. And while the German Jewish Establishment used the Jewish past in order to glorify a Germanic present, the Zionists later linked the struggle of the Maccabees and the heroism of Bar Kochba to Jews doing their duty as German citizens during World War I.[27]

Jews had done their duty in national wars ever since the struggle against Napoleon; indeed, it was thought singularly fortunate that Jewish emancipation coincided with those patriotic wars, which might serve to complete the process. It is typical of the turns and twists of emancipation, which may seem strange to us more than a century later, that the form of the newly introduced military decorations threatened to redivide Jews from Gentiles during the welcome struggle for German unity.

Could and should Jews wear military decorations in the form of a cross? While some Jewish volunteers were among the first to receive the Iron Cross, the highest decoration for bravery founded by Frederick William of Prussia in 1813, others were denied such a deserved honor because they were Jews. At times there were complaints from Jews who coveted the Iron Cross but were given written commendations instead in order to spare their religious sensibilities. It was rare to have graves even of fallen Jewish soldiers marked with a cross, although there are instances of this during World War I as well.[28] We shall discuss the acceptance of this Christian symbolism further in the next essay. Meanwhile, most Jews were eager to accept the Christian symbol as a mark of equality and civil pride.

Johann Gottfried Herder also played a role in helping to adjust the Jewish past to the Jewish present. Eduard Kley, the famed Hamburg reform rabbi, repeated in 1819 Herder's axiom that language unites a people and leads to the unity of their hearts and feeling. The Jews, Kley stated, had ceased to be a Volk after they had lost their own language. But the revival of religious piety after emancipation produced a new language for the Jews, which because it was German, united them in heart and feeling with their new fatherland.[29] Surely this is a curious but telling use of Herder. Leopold Zunz saw in what he called "the corrupt language of the ghetto Jews" the symbol of the superstitions and Talmudic dialectic that had destroyed true Jewish religiosity. He called in 1832 for the freeing of ancient customs from abuse, by which he meant the reform of Jewish service and preaching and an end to the disorder in worship, the lack of reverence and attention.[30]

In fact, what Zunz called "abuse" was dangerously close to the continuity of the Jewish tradition, and what he called the "restoration of ancient custom" had suspiciously close ties to the German idealism of his time. Zunz agreed with the definition of traditional Jewish worship we find in Campe's Dictionary of 1810, a typical product of the Enlightenment: a "Jew-Shul [*Judenschule*] where people mumble in an unlovely way."[31] In common with all the rabbis we have discussed, Zunz held that Judaism was based on "*Erbauung*," and he regarded as abuse everything that ran counter to a religion of piety and edification. Patriotism was a fact of the times, and Jewish piety must absorb it along with the other secular elements we have discussed at the expense of continuities of liturgy and religious thought. To attempt to transform a faith that was supposed to be eternal into a usable present was bound to affect the core of traditional piety.

It matters little for our argument that Jews had good and practical reasons for absorbing the principles of secular obedience and patriotism into their own religion. That they did so helped to define the religious community alongside general middle-class attitudes toward life. But while Protestantism could go ahead and make such fusion ever more perfect, this was not so easy for Jews. There was a Germanic Protestantism of various shadings long before the notorious "German Christians" of National Socialism. The German Jews who would have liked such a perfect fusion, to be called the "National German Jews" (*Nationaldeutsche Juden*), were always a small although not uninfluential minority linked to the most radical of Jewish religious reform.[32]

Jews did diverge from the course of Christian pietism through their acceptance of the spirit of tolerance and pluralism, which had been important in their emancipation. Nationalism as well as middle-class values also informed their concept of religious community, but these were joined by liberalism. When the Jewish publication *Sulamith* stated in 1811 that intolerance was the enemy of every religion,[33] it would be difficult to find such a thought repeated among the Christian churches; certainly it did not determine Schleiermacher's own attitude toward Jews and Judaism. That religion teaches "liberal thought and humane actions"[34] is not a sentiment typical of the Christian piety we have discussed; a liberal Christianity did indeed exist, but it was weak, and as liberal Protestantism hardly lived up to *Sulamith*'s call for tolerance, as Uriel Tal has shown.[35] The secularization of Jewish piety had this special dimension, which would not only distinguish Jewish from Christian religious thought but also serve eventually to isolate the Jews in spite of their desire for a unity of heart and spirit with the fatherland.

This liberalism did not obviate the problem of Judaism and modernity, instead, it aggravated it. Cesar Seligmann, one of the leading liberal German rabbis, summed up the function of liberalism as a solvent of faith, together with the other secular factors we have mentioned, when he looked back over the nineteenth century from the vantage point of the first years of the twentieth. Since emancipation, he wrote, political and economic ideas had taken the place of the Jewish religion: "from a martyr, the Jew has become a bourgeois."[36] The term "bourgeois" for him encompassed liberalism, as well as patriotism and the industrious, quiet, and settled life. But was he correct when he saw a better future ahead for Jewish religiosity in the founding of the Association for Liberal Judaism (1908)? Perhaps he envisaged a better future because he believed that the trend toward such secularization could be reversed. In reality, however, the process was not one of replacement but of absorption, of casuistry. The reversal therefore proved impossible. Certainly, the universal moral mission of Judaism that Seligmann stressed, as it had been stressed ever since emancipation, was not a good substitute for theological precision. Walther Rathenau, not an unperceptive observer of his times, wrote in 1912 that "the present cultivated Jew is in my opinion less dependent upon religious dogmatism than any other man of culture."[37] Typical of the very Jews he was writing about and of whom he was himself an example, he meant this as a compliment; yet from our point of view it provides additional testimony to the problematic religiosity which stands at the center of our analysis.

It was surely symptomatic that in honor of a meeting of the Association for Liberal Judaism in 1912 the Posen municipal theater performed Lessing's famed *Nathan the Wise*.[38] Lessing's play was a reaffirmation of rationalism, pluralism, and tolerance in the best liberal tradition, but it was also based upon the principle that all religions are essentially alike, that men's hearts find each other regardless of religious confession, as Hirsch Traub had exclaimed with such joy. Religiosity was stripped of its theological content on behalf of a generalized virtue all men could share. It was certainly flattering for Jews to rediscover themselves in *Nathan*, but what was Jewish about this rich merchant except his stereotyped wealth and profession?[39] At the time, however, Jews did not ask themselves this question.

If *Nathan the Wise* came to symbolize their liberalism, which aspired to a more perfect toleration, Georg Hermann's *Jettchen Gebert* (1906), the most famous novel of German-Jewish life, drew a picture of assimilation accomplished and of the ideal bourgeois life. Nothing distinguishes the Geberts from their Gentile middle-class neighbors except for some of their names; that was the very attraction of the book. Still, when Jettchen Gebert wants to marry Dr. Kössling, all sorts of objections are raised to prevent the match— his poverty, his lack of a stable profession, his family background, and only as a last resort the one that really mattered, namely, that he was a Christian. For the Geberts took pride in being respected as Jews in the community, never having given in to the temptation of baptism. That is the total content of their Jewishness. The secularization of Jewish theology meant, in the last resort, a negatively defined Jewish identity, which could be held together by the fight against anti-Semitism (as a community leader put it in the 1920s), or by the Geberts' nebulous family pride.[40] Moreover, religious feeling itself had become identified with "*Anstand*," or the proper bourgeois morality.[41]

The *embourgeoisement* of Jewish piety went hand in hand with the absorption of liberalism, and of nationalism as well. This "*Trotz-judentum*" (Jewishness out of spite) as it came to be called, was set within an ideal of life that was shared by most Germans and that, in reality, determined the course of Jewish piety. *Jettchen Gebert* sums up this ideal: life should be lived in "the most beautiful uneventfulness," and in excellent harmony.[42] It is surely significant that one of the best and clearest statements of a bourgeois utopia in the entire German language comes to us from Georg Hermann, who had assimilated into it so successfully—and who was to perish at Auschwitz.

As programmatic statements, both *Nathan the Wise* and *Jettchen Gebert* fitted in well with Seligmann's own attempt to define Jewishness. This, Seligmann wrote in 1927, is not a sterile worship of past tradition or merely an attempt to maintain a feeling of honor. Jewishness is, rather, a feeling which we cannot control—"Why does the sun shine? Why does the tree grow?" (Again, nature analogies are summoned to the rescue of a religion that has dwindled into generalized piety.) Seligmann coined the much quoted phrase of the "will to Judaism." In the last resort, he called Jewishness a communality of blood, a feeling of tribal kinship, but he found his meaning summed up in the concept of a "Jewish heart." [43] Jews— he asserted on a different occasion—were solely a religious community; in all other matters they shared a common "soul" (as he called it) with that of the people among whom they lived. [44] Apparently there was a distinction within each Jew between his Jewish heart and his German soul, but this very confusion illustrates once more that secular ideas now determined the direction of a piety that had become vague and ill-defined.

This last example is meant to illustrate a continuity of thought which, though far from consistent among German Jews, was inherent in the attitudes of the German-Jewish religious Establishment. The relative success of the reforms that came after emancipation is without doubt related to the peculiar social composition of the vast majority of German Jewry. They were, by and large, well-to-do members of the cultured middle classes. Such a shared social status was unique among minority groups, and this uniqueness reflected itself in religious terms as well. Above all, the crucial relationship between popular piety and religious reform that served to continue tradition never arose at all in this context. Popular piety depends upon continuities, upon what reformers usually called superstitions. Popular piety is essentially rooted among the lower classes of the population; it is there that we find resistance to changes in religious customs and liturgies most widespread. But among a religious group that was wholly middle-class in nature, such conservatism did not operate. Of course there were exceptions among the Jews in Germany who clung to the old ways, but by and large emancipation and the opening to modernity which it offered were enthusiastically received. Within Christianity, those who advocated a too radical break with the past were apt to remain sects without a religious future. But in the German Jewish reform which we have analyzed, continuities and the security of immemorial custom and liturgy were roughly pushed aside. We confront a unique situation: a religion which could successfully cut much of its link with the tradition of its own popular piety because of the coherent social composition and cultural ambitions of its members. The vast majority of German Jews were not only bourgeois and patriotic but also, let us remember, cultured in the German sense of the word *"Bildung."*

When immigrants from eastern Europe streamed into Germany during the last decades of the nineteenth century, they came to symbolize for some young German Jews the ties with a Jewish tradition absent among their own parents. Gustav Landauer in 1906 voiced just such a search for rootedness. "When I was a student," he wrote to Martin Buber, "I underwent the profound experience which meant that within that lack of roots usually called radicalism . . . I suddenly found a new peoplehood . . . I took refuge from the heartless world of the bourgeoisie in the workers' movement, adopting it as my own Volk. I never thought that in my mature years I should still find something like a second home in an aged people." [45] The newly revealed existence of this Jewish people ended Landauer's loneliness.

Young German Jews at the turn of the century were apt to turn to Zionism or socialism in order to find a home within a cohesive community. The *Bildung* of German Judaism seemed sterile to them; they were inspired by Theodor Herzl or Karl Marx, but no longer by Wilhelm von Humboldt, Schiller, Goethe, or Schleiermacher of a more distant time. They found a generalized piety, which lacked clear definition, unsatisfactory, and the secular elements that gave it direction now seemed reactionary. The conflict of generations was a general phenomenon of that time, and young Jews followed a path quite similar to that of other young Germans. But from our point of view, the generational clash among Jews exemplified one aspect of the problem of the relationship of religion to modernity mentioned earlier in our discussion: a modernity once accepted can lock into positions that later may appear archaic, lacking a dynamic of their own.

German Jewry was apt to use outdated responses to emancipation, in order to confront a new crisis a century and a half later. A religious piety that had been infiltrated to such an extent by nineteenth-century ideals and values could no longer understand or respond effectively to the anxieties of the twentieth-century world. Neither the left-wing ideals that motivated the responses of a large section of German-Jewish intellectuals nor, at that time, the Zionist ideas could find a home in Jewish religiosity comparable to those earlier secularizing forces we have discussed. German Zionists and Jewish socialists had already rejected the religious Establishment and found their own better defined and more meaningful communities. But the question deserves to be raised, whether the defection of some of the best and most vital minds of the time is connected to the failure of a religious system of thought to cope with one modernity after it had absorbed another. The "sun of the Enlightenment" seemed to have set.

It is the task of the historian to pose problems although perhaps not to solve them. Conceivably, even if Zionism and socialism had been absorbed into Jewish religiosity, as seems to have happened to Zionism in our time, the problem of religion and modernity would still beg solution. For such ideals can become externalized or part of a rhetorical formula when they exist side by side with the forces of secularization we have been discussing. The hunger for myth has not lessened in our time, and it is doubtful whether a secularized religion can satisfy these needs. It may well be relevant to recall that it was the Chassidut of Martin Buber who just before World War I awakened the great enthusiasm of so many young Jews because here they found a connection with popular piety, the Jewish tradition, without the supposed ceremonialism or the dialectic of Jewish orthodoxy. For example, the young Georg Lukacs suddenly discovered to his joy that he might have been of Chassidic descent; and Lukacs, in 1911, desired nothing more than to read a complete edition of Chassidic tales.[46] He was not alone in feeling the impact of Buber's work, which, as a viable alternative to liberal Judaism, might make a new and truer community possible. From an attentive reader of the legends of Rabbi Nachman and the Baal Shem, Walther Rathenau developed (for a short period) into an avid student of Hebrew. This Jewish tradition seemed to him to provide an answer to the "why" of life.[47] The reaction of a cynic like Maximilian Harden was not much different as he heaped praise on Buber's reinterpretations of this Jewish past.[48]

Both Rathenau and Harden soon reverted to that Jewish self-hate which characterized their complex personalities. But the great impact of a new kind of Jewish nationalism is obvious, the more so as it paralleled the changing nationalism of Germany itself. Perhaps the reception of these legends was facilitated by the contemporary revival of interest in the German mystics as the true harbingers of the Volk. Both Buber and Landauer had studied their works. However that may have been, for our theme this new if often fleeting feeling of Jewish Volkdom demonstrates the void left by the evolution of the Jewish religious Establishment.

It seems that if the connection with tradition, with popular piety, was so largely ruptured and secularized by the religious Establishment, its eventual restoration on the basis of myth and community had great appeal to a new twentieth-century generation. Not because the social composition of German Jews had changed—for it had not—but because of an intense longing for community, which reform Jewish religiosity could no longer satisfy.

FOURTEEN

The Jews and the German War Experience, 1914-1918

THE ROLE of the German Jew in World War I has been analyzed often—the hope that the "spirit of 1914" would lead to a more complete union of Germans and Jews, and an end to the discrimination and suspicion which dogged Jews even in wartime. There were those German Jews who recalled Gabriel Riesser's remark that only blood spilled in the struggle for fatherland and liberty would lead to emancipation,[1] and there were other German Jews whose faith in such baptism of fire decreased in the course of the war. It is time to go beyond such attitudes in attempting to illuminate certain fundamental problems in the German-Jewish dialogue which the war laid bare and which cannot be subsumed under the familiar dichotomy of assimilation and anti-Semitism.

The war provides us with a glimpse of the position of the Jew in Germany under extreme conditions. The life of soldiers in the trenches must be our concern, a unique world not only isolated from the normalcy of home and family life but also at war with its military surroundings, such as the base camp or the regimental headquarters. Typically enough, at the end of the war a guide for returned veterans was published (1918) "because for the most part veterans are completely alienated from bourgeois existence";

through their overwhelming war experiences they have lost any sense of the so-called necessities of life.[2] Soldiers at war had indeed left the ordered society they knew and had to make a new life for themselves in the trenches, largely underground and exposed to constant discomfort, danger and death.

From the winter of 1914 to the spring of 1918 the trench system was fixed, belligerents' positions moving only a few yards or miles over terrain covered with the bodies of dead and wounded combatants. This new "world of myth," as Paul Fussell has called it, had its own rules, superstitions, miracles, legends, and rumors.[3] The personal issues at stake were indeed momentous: the expectation of death, injury, and disease, and yet there was also a certain exaltation in battle and in that camaraderie which was vital for any survival at all.

The war experience created patterns of thought that were to last into the postwar world. Myths and symbols, cults such as that of the fallen soldier became central to the self-understanding of the nation. The necessity of transcending the horror of trench warfare created a new world of myth, which affected German Jewish relations in a multitude of ways. Jews had to take part in this world, though it demanded a still more thorough assimilation. A new ideal of manhood grew out of the war, providing a stereotype that was not new but that became more firmly rooted as a German ideal. The Jew was to become the foil not only of this ideal of manhood but also of the myth of the front-line soldier.

War, one combatant wrote, "compresses the greatest opposites into the smallest space and shortest time."[4] Rainer Maria Rilke was not unique in viewing the outbreak of the war as a new release of primeval energy, an intrusion of supposed reality into the realm of illusion.[5] Rilke wrote under the spell of the "spirit of 1914," but while he himself grew disillusioned with war, others fled from reality to myth. With heightened sensibility a new appreciation of nature rose from the mud of the trenches, together with all sorts of superstitions, prophecies, signs, and portents. All of these reactions to an unparalleled confrontation with the horrors of war were integrated into myths and symbols that would explain the present and give hope for the future.

At this point, Christian patterns of belief gained new vitality, not only as safeguards against danger but also in making the close proximity of death to life bearable. Christian belief under such circumstances tended to be neither Protestant nor Catholic, but rested upon shared myths and symbols. The difference between Protestant and Catholic troops in the reception of the war experience remains to be examined, as military units from Protestant and Catholic German states fought separately from each other. The sources for this essay are Protestant rather than Catholic. However this may be, the war became infused with Christian meaning and vocabulary.

The initiation into the world of the trenches was so momentous that it became natural to speak of the "baptism of fire."[6] Death was so close, with bodies all around, that it made men think about Christ's passion and resurrection, an analogy basic to the cult of the fallen soldier. The one celebration in the year that seemed most meaningful was Christmas, a symbol of peace, family, and home, for one moment breaking the isolation of the trenches. These basic patterns of myth and symbol will occupy us, for they are relevant to the place of the Jew in the war and to the peace that was to follow. As we shall see, many Jews accepted the structures of Christian mythology without their specific religious content.

Christian analogies were everywhere. The most popular writer of wartime Germany, Walter Flex, stated in 1914, that "the sacrifice of the best of our people is only a repetition willed by God of the deepest miracle of life . . . the death of Christ."[7] Ludwig Ganghofer, another best-selling author, likened Germans to the Three Kings who are led by the star to Bethlehem.[8]

We must focus upon such Christian themes, which informed the new "world of myth" of the trenches, for without realizing their impact the Jewish position cannot be understood. Moreover, in order to make our point we will deal with detail, even with trifles, the perception of which dominated the daily life of the trenches. The trench experience was taken as representative of human experience.[9] Of course, it needs stating that we are dealing here with only one major theme of the war experience, but one that throws an important light upon the position of Jews in Germany. After we have analyzed these themes and their consequences for Jewish integration, we will have to evaluate whether the attitudes of some important Jews toward the war did not in fact differ from those of non-Jewish Germans, even if Jews by and large accepted the new world of myth trench warfare created. Finally, the adversary habit of mind and the stereotypes the war advocated helped to transform apparent differences between Germans and Jews into a racial reality by the end of the Weimar Republic.

Mass death was central to World War I, a new experience for most Germans and therefore a reality difficult to confront. The only possible confrontation was to transcend it, and this was done by the analogy of death for the fatherland to the passion and sacrifice of Christ. This was not new but strengthened a tradition going back to the wars of liberation against Napoleon. German poets had likened these wars to a German Easter and later Christ's holy blood was harnessed to German legend in several of Richard Wagner's operas. The Holy Grail was said to be in the custody of the German Volk. When Walter Flex called World War I the "Last Supper," he was refurbishing this tradition. Now it was projected upon the fallen comrades and on one's own imminent death: "Christ's wine consists of German blood." [10]

One memorial book may stand as exemplary for a great many others: the fallen have found no rest, they return to earth in order to rejuvenate the Volk. "To fight, to die, to be resurrected that is the essence of being. From out of your death [in the war] the nation will be restored." [11] Such sentiments are not merely typical of the Right, but can be duplicated from the official guide to war monuments issued by the Weimar Republic. [12] Clearly, a Christian theme became symbolic of sacrifice for the nation. Moreover, Germany was not unique in proclaiming such a synthesis: across the Channel August 4, 1914, which marked England's entry into the war, was often depicted as the nation's crucifixion and resurrection. [13] Life and death became united, linked by the *Imitatio Christi*, pictured after the war through the "cross of sacrifice" in military cemeteries or even in frescoes showing the fallen soldier resting in the lap of Christ. Decades of secularization had not markedly affected the symbolism and the iconography surrounding heroic death. It was still the saviour who drew death's sting.

That sometimes Jews were buried under crosses on the battle field becomes meaningful in this context, and so does the fact that one Jewish officer immediately connects his presumed death with the plain wooden cross under which he will rest, and this in a poem published in a Jewish wartime pamphlet.[14] Moreover, even where Jewish graves were marked with the Star of David, they were apt to rest in the shadow of a giant cross of sacrifice or in that of a chapel which stood as a symbol of the resurrection of Christ. Soldiers' burials were roughly the same in all warring nations. For example, the United States Monument Commission also at first automatically placed crosses on the graves of Jewish soldiers. When eventually the Star of David was substituted, one American Jewish leader protested against this "mischievous act." Matters of faith were irrelevant as ". . . Jews and Christians fought shoulder to shoulder, actuated by the same patriotic impulse."[15] The cross became a national symbol for a war that was regarded as holy by all combatants. War graves became part of this myth; for Ludwig Ganghofer traveling along the front, individual graves with their crucifixes were not places of death but "verdant temples of resurrection."[16]

We are apt to take Jewish acceptance of certain Christian symbolism for granted, as we mentioned in the last essay—the Iron Cross of valor if not the cross over the grave. But this was not always the case. During the Wars of Liberation the Prussian government, hesitant to offend Jewish sensibilities, sometimes withheld from Jews the Iron Cross or the Louisen Cross, the medal of valor for women on the home front. Thus a Jewish banker's wife merely received a medal instead of the decoration, whereupon she protested that she was proud to wear a cross. For, in any case, eventually she would be buried next to her son who had fallen in battle—and whose grave was marked by a cross.[17] As late as 1853, Carl Meyer Rothschild received the Prussian Red Eagle in a form especially designed for Jews which substituted a round base for that in the form of a cross.[18] But such times were past. The common war experience meant accepting a shared symbolism.

To make such a statement does not deny that for the most part Jews tried to make use of their own religious symbolism in order to confront the war. In fact, during the Wars of Liberation, Prussian rabbis had already justified enlistment through the use of biblical analogies. Following this tradition, in the Great War, Russia became Goliath, while the president of one German-Jewish community proclaimed that "German courage and the heroism of the

Maccabees are one and the same." [19] We shall discuss Jewish reservations about the war, which sprang from a still vigorous ethical tradition, later in this essay. But here it is important to point out that the shared camaraderie of the trenches did mean a further assimilation.

After all, the Jewish soldier was a part of this comradeship, even though Julius Marx believed that this was only true during times of danger. [20] We have no concrete knowledge of what such comradeship actually meant to the front-line soldier. To be sure, officers wrote about it, writers like Walter Flex, and propagandists behind the front. But there is no survey in Germany such as that taken in France in 1917, and even in this case only some fifty soldiers replied and attempted to formulate the meaning of wartime friendship. Often this was assumed to be instinctive, based upon common affinities, and these in turn were thought to be both products of a shared hatred of the enemy and also of shared traditions reaching back into the past. Religion and regional ties usually defined such traditions. [21] This survey comes to us from the Right, from admirers of Maurice Barrès, and must be viewed with suspicion; but in Germany, glorification of shared hatreds and common religious and volkish ties was carried into the postwar world. For the National Socialists, but not for them only, this Bund of males was the cell from which all states have their origins. [22] The postwar tendency to endow the war with dramatic unity was especially effective in making the myth of the camaraderie in the trenches symbolic for the fate of the entire nation.

The immediate symbol of the wartime camaraderie was the military cemetery: linking the living comradeship of the trenches with the fallen comrades. Already in 1915, the distinction was made between bourgeois' and soldiers' cemeteries. Bourgeois' cemeteries are materialistic in the boastfulness of their monuments; in soldiers' cemeteries, "gravestones through their simplicity and uniformity lead into a serious and reverential mood." [23] The camaraderie in life is continued in death. The historical background of this kind of cemetery cannot concern us, except to mention that it owes something to the classical revival of the eighteenth century, and that the simple row graves date from the quest for equality in the

Enlightenment and during the French Revolution. But now a myth grew up around the simple, uniform graves with their serried crosses: they symbolized Germany. As we read in the previously cited war memorial published by the Republic, it is from these graves that the fallen are said to rise and visit the living in their dreams in order to command them to continue the battle. War cemeteries are the symbols of war turned to stone.

Uniformity was crucial here, and so were the walls that enclosed the war cemeteries. They were meant to form a sacred space, analogous to a church, centered upon a cross or a chapel. Jewish cemeteries did not of course entirely follow this plan, though the separately enclosed space was kept and so were the row graves. Instead of crosses, these resting places sometimes adapted another German tradition that had become an alternative to crosses of sacrifice, if not in military cemeteries, then in war memorials. Huge boulders, symbols so it was said of primeval power (*Urkraft*), exemplifying reverence, exaltation, and iron force. These, so we are told, had been used by ancient Germans to represent an *Ehrenmal*. Jewish cemeteries were, at times, centered upon such a boulder; in the Jewish cemetery of Nuremberg, it took the form of an altar.[24]

The iconography of death in war was similar among Jews and Gentiles, though of course there were no crosses or chapels of resurrection among the Jews. Yet, more often than not, Jews and Gentiles were buried in a common cemetery in Flanders or in the East. Sammy Gronemann tells of the difficulty of persuading a Jewish parent that his son should be torn from his comrades and buried separately in Jewish soil.[25]

The war produced one new form of military cemetery—the *Heldenhain* or Heroes' Wood, first proposed in 1915. War heightened the sense of nature: from out of the trenches soldiers stared at a ravaged no man's land, and looked for an enemy they could never see. But what they did see were the woods of Flanders, which seemed to suffer much like themselves. "The Murdered Wood" is the title of a story in *Die Feldgrauen* (*The Field-Grey*), a journal written by soldiers at the front. "This wood, battered and beaten like myself, nevertheless lives on"[26] Walter Flex's *Wanderer Between Two Worlds*, that most famed of war books, is filled with descriptions of nature. For Flex, nature is a means of transcending the war experience; for example, fields full of flowers directly behind the trenches are reminders of beauty and hope. Here typically enough, nature is Christianized, as it were, and Flex's hero reads the New Testament even as he admires "a breath of religious spring."[27]

The image of the crucifixion was very much a part of the Belgian and Flemish landscape: the numerous calvaries visible at the crossroads. Paul Fussell has pointed out the role that these calvaries played in the imagination of British soldiers, who coming from a Protestant country were much impressed. The sacrificial theme, in which each soldier becomes analogous to the crucified Christ, was not confined to English war poetry.[28] Walter Flex spoke to his friend Wurche for the last time in the shadow of just such a calvary; a few days later, Wurche was killed while on patrol.[29] The heightened feeling for nature was infused with such Christian symbols, which seemed an integral part of the countryside.

The Heroes' Wood however, while linked to the heightened sensibility toward nature in wartime, was based upon the tradition of the Germanic landscape with its sacred trees and forests. "Emperor's oaks" (Kaisereichen) had already been planted as a thanksgiving for the victory of 1871. The renewal of a Germanic nature was now seen as symbolic of the resurrection of the dead. The German wood itself should form the sacred burial space. Field Marshal von Hindenburg in praising this new concept of burial wrote about the "German tree, gnarled and with solid roots, symbolic of individual and communal strength."[30] "Oaks of honor" were common in Jewish as well as Christian military cemeteries. The Heldenhaine were ecumenical, fusing Germanic and Christian symbolism for all of those who had made the ultimate sacrifice.[31]

A common mood united Jews and Gentiles, but it was a mood subsumed under Germanic and Christian symbolism. Sermons preached on days of mourning by Christian ministers and rabbis might well be compared. Such a comparison made on a very limited scale emphasized once more a joint approach to the fallen heroes. The day of mourning was conceived as a festival: a worthwhile death has climaxed a worthwhile life in the service of the fatherland. Such themes are hardly surprising. But some sermons of Jewish chaplains show a confusion of Christian symbolism and Jewish identity, especially as services at the front were sometimes held in churches. Thus Bruno Italiener was carried away when he praised the combination of organ music, bright light falling through the Church windows, and the power of ancient Germanic song. In such a moment, he said, there exist no Jews, Catholics, or Protestants, but only Germans.[32] Ecumenical cooperation between all faiths was the rule during the war, *communio sanctorum* as a Protestant court preacher called it,[33] but here such a community is found within a specific Germanic and Christian context.

Christmas in the trenches became the festival that best symbolized the longing for an end of isolation, for home and family, for camaraderie and a return of the fallen. It is curious that this festival has never been analyzed, though "war Christmas" became a chiché in both world wars: it was accompanied by an outpouring of poetry and prose claiming to be symbolic of the true national spirit. Christmas was a festival of peace, a "secret armistice," as it was called, which in the first year of the war did in fact become real, as enemies met in the no man's land between the trenches. But when such fraternization was stopped (in 1915 anyone repeating such fraternization was ordered shot), Christmas in the trenches still mimicked times of peace—the decorations, the Christmas tree, presents from home, and the festive board. "Everyone's face lit up at the thought of home." Yet a short sermon by an officer was supposed to exhort the men, to strengthen their will to fight in the realization that peace can only be attained through war. Moreover, once more thoughts of home were mixed with memorials to the fallen.[34] Walter Flex, that great myth maker, in his "Christmas Fable" has a war widow drown herself and her son. They are restored to life through an encounter with the ghosts of dead soldiers: "Christmas night the dead talk in human voices."[35] Flex likens the fallen to the angels who brought the news of Christ's birth to the shepherds—a repetition of the motif that Ganghofer made symbolic for the role of Germany in the war. Small wonder that a rabbi justified his leading such a Christmas celebration: it also symbolized to him a camaraderie that knew no barriers of faith, it was a festival symbolic of German unity and the bonds of friends and family back home. His rejection of the belief that the saviour was really born on this day was of little importance, he tells us, compared to the wartime meaning of Christmas.[36]

We might see in the war Christmas, as in the other symbols and myths discussed, a secularization of Christianity; an ecumenicism that was so broad as to lose its specific Christian relevance. It is indeed possible that the references to Christ and Christianity were rhetoric, a shorthand for dilemmas and longings shared by everyone at the front. Certainly they could become form without content, as, for example, in the constant Nazi use of Christian vocabulary that transferred terms like "apostles" and "evangelical" to their own substitute religion. But there was no such substitute religion in the trenches; worship of the nation was expressed through the passion and resurrection, the national landscape was replete with Christian symbolism. As the Christian metaphors of war were transferred into the postwar world, nationalism increasingly took the lead in a badly defeated and disorganized nation.

Yet if it had not been for the crisis that followed the war, Jews might not have been affected by the mood and piety we have analyzed. As it turned out, the details and even the trifles that have concerned us opened a deep gulf between Germans and Jews because they operated on the level of myth and symbol, within an extreme human situation. The Volk community, the camaraderie, were wrapped in a Christian analogy, which had to be accepted. Not all Jews went so far in their acceptance of this as Walther Rathenau. During the war, he wrote that he was taking his stand on the Acts of the Apostles. But this did not prevent him from going his own way and remaining a Jew, just as his pious Christian friends believed in religion without dogma. "I want a Christian state," but without state power or a state Church.[37] In fact, many important Jews attempted to disentangle themselves from the German mood, or at least to mitigate its effects.

Amidst all the enthusiasm there were reservations. One need only read Leo Baeck's sermons or his official reports as field chaplain to the Jewish community, to feel his love of peace and hatred of all wars.[38] For Leo Baeck the war was a necessary evil, and there can be no greater contrast between his thoughts and those of most Protestant chaplains. Chauvinism of any kind is rejected by Baeck, but accepted by nearly all of his official Christian colleagues. The ethical ideals of Reform Judaism held fast in this case. On the home front, where on the one hand enthusiasm ran high but on the other hand voices of dissent did exist, some, though by no means all Jewish publications, were remarkable in their outspokenness. Not only did Leo Baeck's reports and articles in the *Gemeindeblatt* bear witness to this fact, but so too did certain Zionist papers. For example, after first sharing the "spirit of 1914," the *Jüdische Rundschau* emphasized that the war proved the importance of nationalism, but immediately qualified this statement by referring to the brotherhood of man.[39] Robert Weltsch clung to his ideal that the nation was but a step toward the unity of mankind. In the midst of the myth of the fallen soldier, the *Herzl-Bund* of young Zionist merchants stressed the awfulness of death and war, and the burdens that they impose upon life. In the halcyon days of the "spirit of 1914," even as it defended the Jews against the charge of cowardice, *Ost und West* exclaimed that the moral grandeur of a people is not only revealed in war, but above all in the solid accomplishments of peace. This is certainly a unique dissent in the chorus of German voices.[40]

To be sure, all Jewish papers exhorted young Jews to do their best and called upon them to volunteer for the colors. Yet there is enough meaningful difference that we can talk, even if not consistently, of an ethical imperative that remained intact. If Jews were prone to accept Christian metaphors because ideas and rituals taken from the non-Jewish environment had penetrated to the heart of Judaism during the process of assimilation, as we saw in the last essay, so the ideals of the Enlightenment lasted longest among the Jews. The *Israelitische Wochenblatt*, as early as September 1914, warned against "unhealthy chauvinism" and appealed to reason instead.[41]

We can cite as additional evidence for the attitude of large parts of the German-Jewish and Zionist Establishment their rejection of Ernst Lissauer's hymn of hate against England. This poem became for some time the most popular war poem in Germany. It received praise from the emperor and the crown prince of Bavaria, but not from many of his fellow Jews. When Binjamin Segel surveyed sixty important Jewish personalities they unanimously rejected the *Hassgesang* as un-Jewish.[42] *Ost und West*, once more in the forefront, wrote a whole article against Lissauer entitled "Education in

Hate." Jews generally, it asserted, have rejected Lissauer, toward whose poem one can feel only revulsion and horror.[43]

Here, then, there was no easy acceptance of the new world of myth of the trenches, and this in spite of the acceptance of the common mood. This persistence of ethical attitudes, of a refusal to join in the symphony of hate and the deification of the nation, separated some important Jews from most Germans. Once more we face a phenomenon that will continue into the postwar world, when Jews in their liberalism and cosmopolitanism will face ever greater isolation in a Germany where the war experience led to a heightened chauvinism. This alienation worked hand in hand with the covert rather than overt exclusion of Jews from the *communio sanctorum* of the embattled fatherland.

At the same time, the war led to several other attitudes that were to prove dynamic in destroying the precarious German-Jewish relationship. The hatred Leo Baeck rejected dominated the war. The adversary relationship led to a state of mind that craved an enemy, and that was ready for the politics of confrontation in postwar Germany. The crises of the Weimar Republic took the form of an undeclared civil war, which the Nazis eventually exploited and won. The Jews became the real victims of the continuation of war in peacetime. Just so, the war deepened an already present German stereotype of manliness. This "totally new race," as Ernst Jünger called it,[44] which emerged from the war, was to take the Jew as its foil.

Eventually, all the ideals we have discussed—the glorification of sacrifice and the reward of resurrection, the exaltation of simplicity and equality as the essence of comradeship, and the love of home and of nature—were turned against the Jews. What started as Jews coming to terms with national Christian myth and symbols ended with the expulsion of the Jew from participation in the national myth. He became the enemy who had to be destroyed.

II

The hatred of the enemy in wartime needs no documentation. To be sure, there was at times respect for the adversary as well as fraternization during the first war Christmas. Whatever the soldiers may actually have felt, the barrage of propaganda and the loss of their comrades can hardly have left them without moments of hate. As the entire war experience was constantly lifted into a world of myth and symbol, so the adversary relationship was transformed into a general principle of life by influential writers and poets. Ernst Jünger was the most famous of these, and his war diary *In Stahlgewittern* (*The Storm of Steel*, 1919), which sold 244,000 copies in twenty-six editions, and which was translated into seven languages,[45] put it bluntly: "For I cannot too often repeat, a battle was no longer an episode that spent itself in blood and fire; it was a condition of things that dug itself in remorselessly week after week and even month after month."[46] This was a total confrontation for, so we are told, "War means the destruction of the enemy without scruple and by any means. War is the harshest of all trades, and the masters of it can only entertain humane feelings so long as they do no harm."[47] Such passages seem to anticipate the Nazi future, and indeed Hitler greatly valued *In Stahlgewittern*. But then the book was received with universal praise by the *Tagebuch* on the moderate Left as well as from the Right where the welcome was warmest.[48]

Jünger revised his book from edition to edition during the Weimar Republic. It is not without significance that he now omitted the beginning of his diary and took the acceptance of war as a necessary and higher reality for granted. Within the diary itself, personal experience is changed into the shared experience of comradeship in the trenches and in battle.[49] Such an emphasis upon camaraderie brought Jünger's work into line with many other books about the war, but also reflected the search for a new nation that would restore German power and glory.

Jünger, despite his rejection of the Nazis, must have approved of the words Joseph Goebbels addressed, in the midst of the victories of World War II, to the dead of World War I: "Germany is beginning to glitter in the dawn of your sacrifice." Already in 1928 he had written that the young Nazi movement was led by the fallen soldiers.[50] Not only the Nazis annexed the myths of the war and its aggressive attitude of mind. The political Right under the Republic fed and grew fat on it, while much of the Left proved unable to cope with the war experience although it also dominated the lives of its followers.

Jünger did not stand alone. War novels and war poetry echoed the constant refrain that Germans must remain hard as steel, that sentimentality, even during Christmas, must not sap the fighting spirit. It is no accident that these hackneyed sentiments dating from World War I were repeated by Himmler in the midst of World War II. Telling his SS execution squads in 1943 that they must know what it means to see a hundred Jewish corpses lie side by side, or five hundred, or a thousand, he continues: "To have stuck this out . . . to have kept our integrity, that is what has made us hard." [51] This comparison does not telescope history, but tells us about one consequence of World War I: the adversary relationship, the acceptance of mass death, led to an ever greater brutalization of the human mind.

This brutalizing effect was noticed in the first year of the war by a psychologist who otherwise fully shared the "spirit of 1914." "The marvelous enthusiasm, heroic courage, and willingness to sacrifice . . . which sprang from a shared devotion to the fatherland," wrote Otto Binswanger, "have been sadly perverted into degrading . . . feelings of cruel hate, of lust for revenge and desire to ruthlessly exterminate the enemy." [52] The confrontation politics of the Weimar Republic continued this trend. Yet such brutalization was not merely the product of the enthusiasms Binswanger cited, but also of the efforts to transcend the horrors of war through the myth of the fallen soldier and the other myths and symbols we have discussed. They made it easier to confront mass death—not merely for soldiers to face their own death, but also the task of killing the enemy.

The contrast between "we" and "them" was used as the spearhead for the postworld war attack against liberalism. Liberalism, so Jünger tells us, relativizes everything on behalf of its business interests, and the political philosopher Carl Schmitt praised decisiveness without giving quarters, which alone was said to be worthy of the sovereign state. [53] Such attitudes gave solid support for the onslaught upon the Weimar Republic's ideals of freedom and pluralism. That the Republic and its Jews as well were victims of such antiliberalism needs no demonstration. Jewish existence had always depended upon the pluralism and liberalism of society. That such an onslaught was made in the name of the war experience gave it a frightening dimension. That the Republic was watering down the myths of the war was one of the most fundamental accusations made against the freedom and tolerance it championed.[54]

The veterans' organization *Der Stahlhelm*, for example, opposed the Republic in order to transmit the "spirit of the front-line soldier" to future generations.[55] According to the *Stahlhelm*, the new nation was to be built upon the "camaraderie of the trenches." Yet the Jewish soldier was now excluded from such comradeship. As Jews formed their own veterans' organization, the cooperation between all faiths that had taken place on the front collapsed—Christianity had become too Germanized, an integral part of the *Volksgemeinschaft* embattled against the enemy. It is all the more significant that the *Stahlhelm* leader, Franz Seldte, was no passionate anti-Semite. His novel *Vor und Hinter den Kulissen* (*In Front of and Behind the Scenes*, 1931) praised one Jewish officer as an exemplary German patriot, modest and of pleasing appearance. At the same time Seldte demanded a clear-cut division between German and Jew.[56] While he regarded the Jews as a separate people, many of his followers came to regard them as a separate race as well. In 1932, when it was revealed that the *Stahlhelm's* deputy leader had some Jews in his family tree, a veritable storm broke over Theodor Duesterberg's head in spite of his own unquestioned volkish allegiance. In vain Duesterberg gave his word of honor that he was not related to any Jews himself or through his children, that he never borrowed money from Jews, nor had Jewish clients.[57] Nothing can demonstrate more clearly how exclusive the *Frontgeist* had become: a clean separation between Germans and Jews was now part of the "spirit of the trenches," in spite of Seldte's noble Jewish officer, or the *Stahlhelm* delegations which appeared at memorials to the Jewish fallen.

Such a separation might have been inherent in the mythology of the war, but it became explicit only after the war. To what degree the Jewish war veterans' association attempted to reestablish the lost comradeship, and to what extent it attempted to revitalize a shared myth once more—now volkish rather than Christian— must be left to further research. But it is possible to trace the German-Jewish dialogue based on shared Germanic and Christian myths,[58] just as it is possible to trace the ethical imperatives which separated important Jewish leaders like Leo Baeck from the commonly accepted war experience.

Hatred of the enemy, the adversary relationship, became a total commitment for important and powerful segments of the population. Hans Oberlindober, the leader of the disabled veterans' organization, wrote that though World War I was finished, the war against the German people continues, and that 1914–1918 was merely its bloody beginning.[59] The politics of struggle, of clear and unambiguous decision making, was thought to be the consequence of facing an enemy, foreign or domestic. Great revolutions are decided by blood and iron, wrote Oswald Spengler, without the kind of hesitancy about violence that characterized many left-wing revolutionaries as well as many republicans. The German revolution, he continued, must go forward until the nation becomes once more a community like that of the trenches. Typically enough, Spengler believed that such politics was the politics of power, the only politics that counts. Power belongs to the whole nation; the individual is merely its servant.[60]

Those who wrote about the trenches often stressed the primitivism of such a life, glorifying it as the breakthrough of elemental forces that had slumbered within an artificial civilization. The rage of which Jünger and others spoke as they went over the top was exalted as an ecstasy that revealed the true nature of man. The myth of the storm troopers existed during the war and was not merely a creation of the postwar world. Such men were endowed with certain characteristics, so it was thought, which went beyond mere courage and the will to fight. Contemporaries believed that this stereotype was new: the iron hard man of decision, slim and lithe, with fair skin and clear eyes. In reality this was a stereotype present in European aesthetic consciousness ever since the eighteenth century, sinking still deeper into the German mind through its reaffirmation during the war.[61] Such stereotypes were not confined to Germany. In England, Siegfried Sassoon described George Sherston's friend, the young officer Dick Tiltwood, in almost the identical terms with which Walter Flex characterized his hero Ernst Wurche: "He had the obvious good looks which go with fair hair and firm features, but it was the radiant integrity of his expression which astonished me." [62] *Wanderer Between Two Worlds* began with a description of Wurche, student of Christian theology, whose outward appearance mirrors his inward beauty. Wurche's integrity is symbolized by his light and clear eyes, his good looks, and slender well-proportioned body. [63] When Sassoon followed up his description of Tiltwood by writing that "His was the bright countenance of truth . . . incapable of concealment but strong in reticence and modesty," [64] without knowing it, he was duplicating the ideal of that manliness Walter Flex popularized in Germany.

Wurche, however, loved nothing better than his naked sword, and rejoiced in battle. If the English ideal type included vulnerability and innocence, as Paul Fussell tells us, [65] the German model was hard, wise, and invulnerable. There exist vital differences in national traditions, which surface in times of deep stress and anxiety. Dick Tiltwood is not particularly religious and his patriotism was tempered by his gentleness. Wurche, who reads Goethe and the New Testament even while rejoicing in his sword, is reconciled to a heroic death as part of his joyful duty to the fatherland and to his men. And so is Otto Braun, the *Frühvollendete* (one who dies young) who, unlike Flex, cannot be counted on the political Right. The body, so he tells his war diaries, must become hard, steely, grave, and austere, pregnant with future deeds and manly beauty. For Otto Braun, this ideal warrior corresponded to the stereotype of Greek beauty that had formed the Germanic ideal ever since the eighteenth century. [66]

Ernst Jünger once more summed up this stereotype in all its mixture of brutality and beauty, so common in Germany. "This was a totally new race, all energy . . . slim, lithe and muscular bodies, finely chiseled faces. . . . These were men who overcame, natures of steel, ready for any struggle however ghastly," and Jünger thought that such a struggle was a permanent condition of life. The foils of this hero were the philistines, the bourgeois and the liberals, the "retail merchant and the glove-makers" as Jünger characterized them. [67] It was the Jewish stereotype that became the foil of this manly ideal. For like the new race of which Jünger spoke, the Jewish stereotype had over a century of history behind it and was quite ready for use. Werner Sombart's contrast between merchants and heroes (*Händler und Helden*, 1915) projected the opprobrium of the antiheroic upon the English enemy, but it was easily transferred back to the Jew. It is not necessary to cite further proof that the Jew was excluded from this heroic ideal.

The specific monuments to the fallen that we find in the Heroes' Woods often present the dying young Siegfried,[68] a figure thought especially effective when juxtaposed against the darkness of the trees. We have already mentioned earlier the role played by massive boulders as war monuments, but in this case the symbolism was not so limited that Jews could not follow, in spite of the frequent references to ancient Germanic tradition. Young Siegfried was another matter. The emphasis in such monuments was on simplicity and youth. Simplicity, as we have already seen, was thought essential for military cemeteries because it was said to reflect the manliness of the comradeship of the trenches. Greek ideas were operative here, reinforced by the stress on youth. The young hero was modeled on Greek sculpture, whose concept of beauty had determined the German stereotype ever since J. J. Winckelmann wrote in the eighteenth century. In 1931, looking back over the war memorials of the last decade, Karl von Seeger was moved to wonder about the persistence of the ideal of Greek art. The "naked, lithe, muscular youth, filled with spirit and will, still represents our ideal of humanity."[69] The eros that was always part of the camaraderie of the trenches was worshipped as youth. Poetry and prose were filled with admiration for "youthful steps" and "youthful exuberance." Much of the best English war poetry was also erotic, with its delight in blond and tender youth, but in Germany this kind of eroticism became politicized. Such heroes' memorials, so we are told in 1915, are symbolic of the eternal youth of the people, Siegfried was a young Apollo, and so was Germany.[70] The struggle between young Germany and the old nations of the West was popularized by Moeller van den Bruck, but it subtly drew much of its strength from the image of heroic youth during the war. The Jews were considered an old people, and the Jewish stereotype was consistently one of age, not of youth. In German literature, even young Jews usually have old faces.[71] This Jewish stereotype is once again a part of a long tradition that cannot be analyzed here. The epithet "old" had become attached to the image of the Jew, but now this confronted a nation which adopted the symbol of heroic youth.

Not only did the Germanic stereotype receive renewed impetus through the war experience, but also the ideals of simplicity and modesty that were a part of the myth of camaraderie as symbolized in the resting places of the fallen. Once more the Jewish stereotype ran squarely counter to this ideal. The Jew as arrogant and showy was a myth over a century old by the time of the war. But now it was heightened by the supposed qualities of the front-line soldiers so contrary to what the Jew was meant to represent. Finally, the concept of beauty and eros that symbolized the ideal German confronted a Jewish stereotype that was its opposite: small and puny, ill-proportioned and with shambling gait. The clash of stereotypes is well enough known, but the war gave it a dimension unknown before this time. To be sure, without a long tradition behind them neither stereotype would have acquired the force given to it by the war and the defeat that followed. The commonplaces of anti-Semitism received a new importance when transposed upon the myths and stereotypes of the war.

Germany saw itself defending European civilization. The myths and symbols we have discussed were thought to be specifically German. Germany in turn was the guardian of Europe, and more than that, God's instrument to pass judgment upon the world. As Klaus Vondung has shown, ideas of the Jewish and Christian apocalypse became one means of interpreting the war: Germany is lifted from an instrument through which God judges to the executor of the Last Judgment. Jewish war sermons, at times, echoed such thought.[72] Through this self-appointed task, some racism penetrated the war experience, directed not so much against Jews but against blacks. The Entente was accused of importing inferior races to Europe in order that they might fight God's chosen people. Such racism strengthened German feelings of exclusiveness and mission, which later flowed into Weimar racism and anti-Semitism. Indeed, when the Entente used black troops to occupy Germany after the armistice (1919–20), the cry that culture was being raped coincided with the first and as yet merely social restrictions against the Jews because of their race.[73] Walter Bloem, writing in 1916, had already likened the black and colored troops used by the

English to Hagenbeck's famous circus.[74] War literature and war memoirs show a special hostility to blacks, and no fine distinctions were made between the Moroccans, Indian Sepoys or Africans from Senegal. Stefan George, from his ivory tower, pontificated against the *"Blutschmach,"* that is, the destruction of the white by black and yellow races.[75] The war not only furthered the stereotype of the German hero but also encouraged racial myths. France and England were not yet seen in racial terms, but the war helped Germans see the world as a struggle between races. By 1939 it was the Jews who also became the victims of this inheritance of the war.

German Jews like Leo Baeck shared a common German tradition but bent it to different purposes. They continued to combine German idealism with the heritage of the Enlightenment. Leo Baeck, with some justice, blamed the Lutheran tradition for the worst in German thought and thus connected it with the destructiveness of the war. The Lutherans had created a paternal police state, a tradition Baeck contrasted to that of the Prussian Enlightenment. This Enlightenment put the state in the service of morality and attempted to improve all that was human. Significantly, looking at the destruction of the war, he added in 1919: "Prussian idealism with its optimistic belief in the future of all mankind has retained a home within the Jewish communities."[76] Historically that was a true observation, and one that helps to explain Baeck's own attitude toward the war, the more so as he saw such Enlightenment as part of the essence of Judaism. But this mixture between German idealism and the Enlightenment also influenced Zionists like Robert Weltsch who wanted to give nationalism a human face.

To be sure, most German Jews succumbed to the almost irresistible temptation to share to the full the German war experience. But after the war, many had a rude awakening and recaptured the liberal and Enlightenment tradition. At that time, Establishment figures like Baeck had more in common with the left-wing Jewish intellectuals than they might have cared to admit. Both believed that man must be the end and never the means, and that war perverted the inherent virtues of man. It must be left to another time and place to show the similarity of thought between Baeck and the young Lion Feuchtwanger, between Robert Weltsch and Kurt Eisner, between such Jewish leaders and that socialist humanism discussed in a previous essay. All that needs to be stated here is the existence of a certain German-Jewish tradition, widely shared among Jews of different political persuasions, retaining ideals the war experience had helped to defeat. It is hardly surprising that so many Jews were willing to pay a high price in order to complete the process of assimilation, even if it meant accepting foreign and inherently hostile myths and structures of thought. But that a quite different German-Jewish tradition existed, which though it thought of itself as loyally German, opted to stand aside—this should fill us with wonder.

FIFTEEN

German Socialists and the Jewish Question in the Weimar Republic

IT HAS BEEN ASSERTED that in the final phase of the Weimar Republic, the Jewish question played a minor role in the propaganda and journalism of the Left.[1] This statement could be extended to cover the whole period of the Republic, for while leftist thought on the Jewish question varied in the emphasis given to it, the theories on which it was based remained much the same from the end of World War I to the Nazi seizure of power. But while, as we shall see, there is some truth in the contention that the Jewish question played a minor role in leftist thought, it did so only as the peak of an iceberg that determined the attitudes of the Left toward the Jewish problem. That problem was an integral part of a general theory about man and society, and as such it was highly significant during the Republic, and is of topical interest even today. Not only does an analysis of the Jewish question in this context throw some light upon a much-neglected phase of socialist theory and action, but it also affected the position of German Jews embattled against rightist anti-Semitism.

What sort of Left should concern us here? The Social Democratic Party, obviously, and the communists as well. But in addition we must pay some attention to the left-wing intellectuals, most of whom were themselves Jewish. But before we analyse these various positions on the Jewish question, we must be aware of socialist

284

theory as it had been elaborated earlier, for all discussions on the Jewish question during the Republic originate in prewar socialism, a necessary background to which they had to relate.

I
———————

The foundations for modern German socialist thought on the Jewish question were laid by Karl Kautsky. This "pope" of the prewar *Sozialdemokratische Partei Deutschlands* (SPD) set the tone for discussions about Jewish assimilation and Zionism even when, after 1914, he himself had fallen out of favor. The "German" must be emphasized here although, as we shall see, Kautsky's analyses of the Jewish question were spread beyond German-speaking countries by such men as Lenin and Stalin. In France, however, as George Lichtheim has shown, the foundation for a hostile socialist view of the Jewish question was laid as early as the decades following the French Revolution. Edmund Silberner has demonstrated the existence of German socialist anti-Semitism up to World War I, but its direction was different from that of many French socialists. The Marxist tradition prevailed in Germany, but not in France, where the anti-Jewish attitudes of men like Fourier and Proudhon could have greater scope.[2] We should be careful, then, with the use of the word "anti-Semitism" for, in Germany at least, what might be regarded as hostility toward the Jews was always part of a larger socialist doctrine which, whatever its immediate effects, looked toward a future society where all mankind would live in peace and equality.

Karl Marx had been the first to deal with the Jewish question, but it was Kautsky who produced its modern socialist formulation. His first important contribution to the Jewish problem was an article, written in 1903, called "The Massacre of Kishinev and the Jewish Question." Here, as in his later writings, his ideas were based on Karl Marx's pamphlet on the Jewish question written half a century earlier. Kautsky accepted the thesis that Jews, through the evolution of their history, had become the representatives of the worst aspects of capitalism: the fetishism of goods, love of money and devotion to commerce. Judaism as a religion was merely the objectification of commercial transactions.[3] Kautsky's own contribution to this analysis did not change its fundamental direction but provided an updating of Marx's mid-nineteenth-century tract. Jews are an urban people—Kautsky again and again emphasizes this point—and as city dwellers show all the peculiarities of their milieu, not only in trade but intellectually as well. In his later book, *Rasse und Judentum* (*Race and Judaism*, 1914), he attributes the negative, critical, and "dissolving" (*zersetzend*) spirit of Jews to this milieu.[4] Both Marx and Kautsky continued a tradition begun in the Enlightenment of the eighteenth century. The Jew who was faithful to his Jewishness was wholly corrupt, an evil force in society, who must be reeducated to shed his Judaism and enter the age of progress and enlightenment. Marx did not stress the reeducation of the Jews, but believed that Judaism would end only with the fall of capitalism. Kautsky, for whom a revolution was far in the future, was closer to the Enlightenment when he wrote that the Jewish masses have to be enlightened in order to counteract their Judaism. For both Marx and Kautsky, the Jews' supposed lack of humanity was of crucial concern. Jews were alienated from their own humanity by their intimate involvement with capitalism and with their religion. Eugene Kamenka has stressed the young Marx's preoccupation with human dignity, which was at its height at the very time he was writing his tract on the Jewish question. Emphasis on human dignity, coupled with opposition to servility, was deeply entrenched in the socialist tradition: the Jew seen as an urban merchant, linked to the ghetto both physically and spiritually, typified a state of dependence that perpetuated the feudal Middle Ages within the dialectical progress of mankind.[5]

The "vanishing of Judaism" is a phrase of Kautsky's that was to be repeated by many socialists. It means not only the vanishing of the Jewish religion but also an end to the "Jewish peculiarities" of devotion to commerce and the "negative" spirit.[6]

Kautsky always looked at the Jews from the standpoint of Western culture to which the socialists, despite their revolutionary vocabulary, were deeply committed. The enlightenment of the East European Jewish masses would serve to elevate them to the plateau of Western culture, a viewpoint which Kautsky shared with his liberal contemporaries. Jews everywhere must become "modern people," as he put it in *Rasse und Judentum*, and he fully accepted the stereotype of the ghetto as it had grown up in the nineteenth century.[7] Moreover, physical factors were taken into consideration, and

Kautsky (though he attempted to minimize them) wrote with enthusiasm about the necessary infusion of fresh peasant blood to strengthen the physical constitution of Jewish city dwellers. Finally, Jews are always "strangers," and thus it seems only logical that they cease to be strangers by intermixing with the local population.[8]

Given these premises, the rejection of Zionism was a logical consequence. For Kautsky, the Zionist movement merely reinforced "Jewish peculiarities" and Jewish isolation. In his own mind, that movement was connected with the ghetto and the commercialism of the "medieval" Jewish religion.[9] Kautsky never changed his mind on Zionism or, indeed, on the Jewish question in general. At the very time when his own star was being eclipsed in the socialist movement, his analysis of the Jewish question received new impetus. For the article on the Kishinev massacre was received with enthusiasm by Lenin. He not only reprinted it in *Iskra* but based his own analysis of the Jewish question largely on Kautsky's earlier article. Stalin, in turn, took over the argument in his own work on nationalities, which stated that Jewish nationhood and nationality must be denied,[10] and had Lenin's full blessing. Surely, given his premises, Kautsky was correct in asserting that Jews must not merely move from one medieval ruin (capitalism) to another (Zionism). Their disappearance would not be a tragedy, like that of the Red Indians or the Tasmanians; instead, it would lead to greater strength, well-being, and prosperity.[11]

From a socialist standpoint, such ideas were fully justified. The end product of socialism was to be a new man, a new humanity, encompassing Jews as well as all mankind once capitalism had been abolished. "Where the Jew is regarded as free and equal he vanishes." Socialist theory was reinforced by Lamarckian theories of biological evolution. The materialist and environmental explanation of how life on this planet evolved helped to explain how Jews could shed their "Jewish" characteristics with the triumph of socialism.[12]

Jews were destined to a process of denationalization. Kautsky had already added to his other arguments in the "Kishinev Massacre" the fact that Jews had lost their own territory hundreds of years ago. Moreover, ever since 1887 Kautsky had clung to the idea that a common language is necessary in order to make a nation. The importance of language he traced to economic roots.[13] Obviously the Jews had no such recognized common language to offer, for they spoke not only Yiddish but also, for the most part, the languages of the host nations. Historical claims to Jewish nationality could not be accepted as valid by socialists. Austrian Marxists like Otto Bauer agreed with Kautsky's arguments. More important still, Lenin and Stalin were ready to grant autonomy to other suppressed nationalities, but not to the Jews, who were not granted separate political rights. They applied Kautsky's theories to the Jewish question—an analysis that did not apply to other peoples either in the Soviet Union or elsewhere.

These views on the Jewish question and Jewish nationality remained the prevailing opinion among socialists until the end of World War I. When, for example, in 1916 the Zionist labor movement, Poale Zion, was finally admitted to the Second International, it entered as a national organization of Palestinians and not as a representative of proletarian Zionist Jewry.[14]

Kautsky's major work on the subject, Rasse und Judentum, first published in 1914 and republished in 1921, added nothing new to his original analysis. It apparently did not sell well, and in spite of Kautsky's repeated urging was not republished again.[15] The reason for this failure may lie in Kautsky's own increasingly isolated position within socialism. The Social Democrats were having a change of heart about the Jewish question, as we shall see, and the communists were publishing their own literature, which derived from the early Kautsky but ignored the old Kautsky who had refused to join their party. Certainly the subject itself never lacked interest in Germany.

Disappointed, the ageing socialist published a new article on Zionism after the Palestine massacres of 1929.[16] These events seemed to him to confirm his analyses of Zionism; not only was it a movement of the Jewish petty bourgeoisie, as he had held in Rasse und Judentum, but it had proved to be an unrealizable utopia. The Jews in the Holy Land were the victims of the Zionist movement, closely linked with the imperialist aims of British policy. Yet here Kautsky seems to be weakening. The blanket condemnation of Jewish nationalism is replaced by the statement that Zionism is attractive as a solution to the persecution of Jews, but that Palestine is not the land where this can be accomplished. It is too small and not fertile enough. Moreover, Islamic culture predominates and the

Jews are Europeans. One wonders what has become of the mass of primitive Jews who must first be raised to the level of Western culture. Kautsky now admires the Zionist pioneers, but deplores their useless sacrifice. All this does not prevent him from repeating almost word for word his earlier analyses of the Jewish question.

With the passing of time, Kautsky seemed to be weakening in his polemics and in his hopes. At the same time that he wrote his article after the Palestine massacres, he received a circular letter from Ben Gurion and Eleazar Kaplan asking him to join in founding a united socialist party in Erez Israel. There is no record of his reply. It is certain that in 1937, by now an exile, he was on very friendly terms with Berl Locker of the General Federation of Jewish Labor in Palestine.[17] Kautsky must have felt deeply the Nazi onslaught upon the Jews. But for all the scattered evidence of a certain new ambivalence in his attitude, there was no fundamental change in his outlook. Indeed, the muted tone of the article of 1929 may have been due to quite a different factor. Kautsky realized sharply that the socialist consensus on the Jewish question and Zionism was dissolving. He wrote this article, at least in part, in order to put an end within socialism to divided attitudes about this "romantic and reactionary Utopia."[18] That this division affected his own Social Democrats must have been especially painful to him. That the communists continued his line of thought on the Jewish question must have seemed equally distressing to one who hated the "Bolshevist terror."

II

Under the pressure of growing anti-Semitism and reaction, many Social Democrats began to have a change of heart. Anton Fendrich, a party publicist after 1918, may have been at least partially correct when he wrote, in 1920, that Marx's work on the Jewish question had always been rejected by those Social Democrats who were capable of a greater spirituality. For Fendrich, Social Democrats rejected the bitter judgments heaped upon the Jews by Marx, the convert and missionary. But he also believed that Germans and Jews must be united through the emergence of a new species of man.[19] Indeed, it must have seemed after the war that Marx's Jewish stereotypes would play into the hands of the racists. Anti-

Semitism was on the rise, and this was clearly connected with the thrust of the Right against the new Republic. At that moment, shortly after the end of the war, social democratic criticism of the traditional Marxist analysis of the Jewish problem started. The communists never followed the Social Democrats along this road, and instead published a new edition of Marx's work on the Jewish question. Within social democracy a different trend was to emerge, which not only liquidated Marx's own standpoint but also the older socialist attitudes toward Zionism.

For example, Paul Kampfmeyer, one of the chief social democratic writers against anti-Semitism, sought to demolish the idea that Jews were wedded to the spirit of usury and materialism. After all, he wrote, Marx himself, although he was a Jew, had nothing of this spirit. His system originated in the philosophy of German idealism: for him the negative Jewish spirit did not exist. Marxism was flexible and German. Typically enough, Kampfmeyer was influenced by Ferdinand Lassalle as much as by Karl Marx. He condemned the "Bolshevist terror" and the soldiers' and workers' councils that had sprung up briefly during the German revolution of 1918. Red terror, he held, always ended in white terror. Though his patriotism made him condemn the Treaty of Versailles and see in the French a continuing "enemy," his defense of the Weimar Republic and of the Jews was straightforward and unambiguous.[20] Such a defense by the Social Democrats could be combined with a stress upon the "German" nature of social democratic Marxism as well as with a rejection of "materialism." (It should be added that much of the material the Social Democrats used in combatting anti-Semitism stemmed from Jewish sources.) These arguments were often repeated by Social Democrats in the early postwar years, usually combined with an appeal to the solidarity of the oppressed, though it must be added that at times the physical stereotype was accepted only to be brushed aside in the name of a common humanity.[21]

Eduard Bernstein, the revisionist, played a leading part in changing the accepted picture of Jews and Zionists. During his youth, the normal world had seemed to him non-Jewish, and the Jewish world abnormal. Just before the war he had also condemned Zionism as an ecstasy that would pass, though it had found its way into the heads of some socialists who he felt should have known better.[22] Bernstein was, no doubt, encouraged in this stand by his general aversion to nationalism, though this was never without ambivalence. World War I and its aftermath changed his views; and Kautsky was right in deploring the fact that the war had given Zionism a new beginning.[23] But, typically enough, in revising his stand on Zionism, Bernstein also liquidated Marx's and Kautsky's picture of the Jews as a whole. For though the earlier socialists (and later the communists) attempted to distinguish between Jews and the reactionary Zionist utopia, their viewpoint toward Zionism and the Jews proved to be organically linked.

Bernstein's bridge to a reevaluation of his position was the Austrian view of the nationalities question elaborated by Karl Renner and Otto Bauer. For Bernstein, nationality had always been a sociological fact which socialists could not ignore. Now he held that the concept of national autonomy surpassed ideas of socialist centralism in their democratic potential. Jews should, if they so desired, be granted "Jewish nationality" within individual European countries, a situation that might eventually lead to the establishment of a Jewish state. This argument was in line with much of the ideas of the Zionist movement, as was his contention that all nationalism was only a step toward the organization of humanity as a whole.[24]

Bernstein became an ardent champion of Zionism: "a free human community on free soil."[25] He aided the Poale Zion in its quest for entry into the Second International. Salman Rubashow (Zalman Shazar, former president of Israel) wrote that when Kautsky made accusations against this Jewish proletarian party, Bernstein came to its defense.[26] As late as 1930, the secretary of the Socialist Committee for a Labor Palestine asked for Bernstein's support in the executive of the Socialist International against attacks by Otto Bauer and Victor Adler.[27] Obviously Bernstein was an important contact for the Poale Zion. In gratitude, Rubashow linked together what he considered to be "three great Jews": Lassalle, Marx, and Bernstein.[28] Bernstein's sympathy for Zionism also led him to adopt a positive attitude toward the masses of East European Jewry. Contrary to Marx or Kautsky, Bernstein considered these Jewish masses, still involved in their ghetto, on the whole just as "moral" as the Germans.[29] He carried his regard for the downtrodden masses to its logical conclusion. Certainly a defense of the

ghetto Jews runs through some, but by no means all, social democratic literature. It enabled socialists like Bernstein to engage in a
straightforward defense against the forces of anti-Semitism, for
most social democrats refused to concede the reality of a Jewish
stereotype.

The close relationship between such men of the SPD's moderate
right wing and Jewish efforts at self-defense should not be surprising. Arnold Paucker has documented this fact, and has shown
how the social democratic press consistently used material given to
it by the *Centralverein deutscher Staatsbürger jüdischen Glaubens* (CV),
the Jewish defense group. This did not hold true for other German
political parties. Typially enough, this relationship dated only
from the end of World War I, and became increasingly more intimate after the elections of 1930.[30] The change of heart on the Jewish
question encompasses not only Zionism but also collaboration
with Jewish non-Zionist and anti-Zionist efforts at self-defense.

Bernstein's views were shared and forcefully expressed by men
important in the Socialist International, like Paul Löbe, Camille
Huysmans, and Émile Vandervelde. Löbe, the Social Democratic
president of the Reichstag, admitted that the Social Democrats had
been critical of Zionist experiments. But by 1929 he believed that
Zionism was of the greatest significance for international socialism. For unlike the bolshevik régime in Russia, Zionist socialists
attempted to bring about a new society without the use of force.
Others also took the opportunity of the 1929 Palestine riots in
order to proclaim their support.

The French right-wing socialist Renaudet republished Kautsky's
"Die Aussichten des Zionismus" in his journal *La Vie Socialiste* in
1929. Both Huysmans and Vandervelde answered Kautsky in that
same issue. Huysmans, while stressing the fertility of Palestine,
also broke a lance for utopias in general. Vandervelde believed that
Zionists did not practice traditional colonization, but that between
fellaheen and Chaluzim there was a community of interests directed against all capitalists.[31] Vandervelde was sent to Palestine by
a Zionist committee; in his book *Le Pays d'Israël* (1929), subtitled *A
Marxist in Palestine*, he not only repeats his faith in the building of a
socialist state in that country but also praises "one of the most
wonderful idealistic efforts of our time." The failure of assimilation
and the continued oppression of Jews was evidence of the need for

a Jewish state. The vitality of the Zionist ideology was proof against the bolsheviks (and Kautsky, it would be safe to add) who believed that economic considerations placed a primary role in solving the Jewish question.[32] It should be added that it was Huysmans, the secretary of the Second International, who sponsored the admission of Poale Zion into that organization during World War II.[33]

Clearly, an important cadre of social democratic leadership, then, was pro-Zionist after the war, taking a firm and unbending stance against all anti-Semitism. These men stood, for the most part, on the right wing of their respective parties, for their attitude implied a break not only with Marx's own view on the Jewish question but with orthodox socialism as it had developed since Marx's death. Their attitude on the Jewish question was part of a more general revisionism, which tended towards gradualism, while those who moved further to the left put their faith in revolution and in the ideal of the new man. Revolutionary socialism desired to put an end to Jews and Judaism. We shall come back to such movements, but even for social democracy the path was never as straight as men like Bernstein would have it.

In 1933, Kurt Blumenfeld, a leading German Zionist, declared that hardly any Jewish Social Democrats were being appointed to public positions. To be sure, he made this statement with respect to every German political party, and at a time when Hitler had just become chancellor in a coalition government. Blumenfeld concluded that now Jews would have to become conscious of their Jewishness and keep their distance from the German world.[34] For all his obvious partisanship, there is truth to his contention. Nevertheless, the Social Democrats never tried to beat the Nazis at their own game by adopting a nationalist stance, as the communists did during the last years of the Republic. The pressures upon the Social Democrats were more subtle, and they resisted them as best they could. The obvious successes of the German Right in their use of anti-Semitic actions and slogans put the Social Democrats ever more on the defensive. It had already been said in some of their pamphlets that Marxism could not be a mere "Jewish" concept because Engels, after all, was a Christian.[35] For example, the SPD police president of Berlin, Albert Grzesinski, instituted legal actions against those who "insulted him" by spreading the rumor of his Jewish descent. As Grzesinski wrote to the editor of the *Vor-*

wärts (who was Jewish himself): "by spreading the rumor that he was the product of an affair between his servant-girl mother and the Jew Cohen, the rumor-mongers were insulting his mother and presenting him as a *Judenstämmling*."[36] By 1932 it was no longer desirable to be considered a Jew, at least for anyone in a public position. Though the SPD fully supported Grzesinski's Jewish deputy, Bernhard Weiss, they too could not escape the influence of a growing anti-Semitic atmosphere. Indeed, the anti-Jewish stereotype surfaced from time to time in the socialist press.

Another factor may well have entered here, one that is difficult to document properly. The relationship between the SPD and its intellectuals was both stormy and full of strain; these intellectuals were for the most part Jews. Was this important in weakening the social democratic attitude on the Jewish question? As far back as 1894, August Bebel had felt that Jews "undoubtedly" lacked tact when dealing with the Christian world, that they were apt to be brilliant and pushing. He had put this forward in a speech arguing against anti-Semitism in which he offered arguments lifted in part from Marx and leaning on Kautsky.[37] When Kautsky himself spoke about the "negative spirit" as one of the Jewish "peculiarities," he may well have had the party's troublesome intellectual critics in mind.

The tension between party and intellectuals came to the fore at the SPD Party Congress of 1903. At that point, the leadership suggested that intellectuals might undergo a special probationary period before being admitted to full party membership, in order to test their ability to become integrated with the working classes. This integration was supposed to be proven through their loyalty to party dogma and leadership.[38] Much later, at the Party Congress of 1931, young comrades who revolted against the leadership's lack of militancy were at once likened to those intellectuals who constantly criticized the party.[39] Hugo Marx, who tried to found an *Intellektuellenbund* (League of Intellectuals) within the SPD, saw his hopes dashed and the council dissolved by the beginning of the 1930s.[40] Fritz Naphtali reflected the official party position when in 1930 he called for an end to such leagues. He held that the intellectual needed contact with the worker, and the worker needed a sense of the cultural dimensions of his struggle.[41]

Naphtali was more polite toward intellectuals than Bebel had been. However, in no case did anyone in the party officially link intellectuals and Jews. In fact, both Hugo Marx and Naphtali were Jewish, but it could perhaps be proved that Marx was more representative of the articulate Jewish party membership. Here Theodor Lessing, the maverick philosopher, was closer to the mark when he characterized the League of Intellectuals as crucial, for the party had to be provided with a conscience.[42]

The effect which these strained relationships had upon the general attitude toward the Jewish problem can only be surmised. Those who wrote about the failures of the intellectuals in the party do not mention this particular aspect of the problem. Among the workers themselves, the matter may well have been different and more clear-cut. Hans Jaeger reports that when giving a course for workers on behalf of the Communist Party at the beginning of the 1930s, he was asked, "What are intellectuals? Are they [the same] as Jews?"[43] The problem posed by Jews as socialist intellectuals may well have been one dimension of the pressures put upon the party's posture as a bulwark against rightist anti-Semitism. Certainly the existence of the left-wing intellectuals who constantly criticized the party from without, and who were overwhelmingly Jewish, must have added to this tension. The young radicals within the party were, in 1931, likened to these intellectuals who gathered around the *Weltbühne*, a journal to which we shall return.[44]

Yet the problem posed by intellectuals was only one factor in the party's situation at the end of the Republic, and certainly not the most important. The anti-Semitic dynamic of the Right collided with a party that refused to move off center. SPD support of the Brüning government was combined with an official optimism about the ineffectiveness demonstrated by the Nazi movement. The Nazis would not succeed, said Rudolf Breitscheid, a member of the party directorate, to the Congress of 1931, because they rested their appeal upon a slender theoretical foundation directed toward the lower human instincts of hatred and envy. The Social Democrats never descended to these depths, but while this gave them moral strength in retrospect, it also blinded them to the real Nazi menace. The Brüning government, in their eyes, was supposed to prevent a coalition between the bourgeoisie and the Nazis;[45] their

revisionism made them believe in the strength of middle-class liberalism, and they ignored the fact that National Socialism was, in
large measure, a bourgeois movement in the first place. The result
of their political analyses was the need they felt to survive this crisis and wait for better times to come.

Social Democrats had an abiding faith in the strength of their organization, exemplified by Friedrich Stampfer in his funeral ora-
tion for Eduard Bernstein. Even in 1932 he held that the "disorganized mob" of Nazis would never be able to conquer the firm
organization of the traditional German workers' party.[46] We shall
see later that the left-wing intellectuals also had an abiding belief
in the strength of the working classes in face of the Nazi menace.
However, for them this faith was founded on the strength of socialist belief as it existed in every worker, and not upon a glorification of
party organization. The very organization of the Social Democrats
may have dulled their revolutionary and militant fervor.

How typical that Rudolf Hilferding, the economic expert of the
SPD, sounded a warning against stupid adventures that would
only breed nervousness within the party—though he saw his
party hemmed in between communists and Nazis. Julius Deutsch,
the founder of the *Republikanischer Schutzbund* (League for the Protection of the Austrian Republic), attempted to persuade Kautsky
to take violent action. But he, too, was resigned; the large majority
of party members was opposed to revolutionary Marxist action
and would do everything possible through democratic means.[47]
This was written in Austria in October of 1933, and the Nazis had
been in power in Germany all that year. Survival for the Social
Democrats never meant entering into competition for the nationalist masses, as the communists attempted to do. But it did mean the
use of "discretion," both generally and as far as the Jews were concerned. Such discretion could have been made easier through the
general anti-Semitic atmosphere of the times, the underestimation
of the Nazi menace, and by the party's own internal problem with
its intellectuals as well.

When all is said and done, the attitude of the Social Democrats
toward the Jewish question and toward the defense of the Jews
was firmer than that of other socialists. They had largely succeeded in liquidating the heritage of Marx's *Jewish Question*, and
Kautsky's became an increasingly lonely voice within his party.

The Communist Party continued the older tradition, and was here indeed the inheritor of orthodox Marxism.

III

This continuity with Marx and Kautsky was established almost immediately upon the founding of the *Kommunistische Partei Deutschlands* (KPD). The party could not very well republish the works of the "renegade" Kautsky on the Jewish question, and so they returned to Marx instead. Marx's *Jewish Question* appeared under party auspices in 1919. Its behind-the-scenes sponsor was Ernst Meyer of the central committee of the KPD and editor of the *Rote Fahne*—a man destined in a few years to become one of the most influential and durable German communist leaders. The publication rights of the pamphlet belonged to the literary estate of Franz Mehring, who had edited it as part of his edition of Marx's collected works. Mehring had joined the communists in the last year of his life (1918) and consequently left his literary estate to the party. Meyer had no trouble, therefore, in asserting the party's rights to the book, much to the chagrin of Kautsky, who wanted to republish it himself.[48] Kautsky, as we have seen, republished his *Rasse und Judentum* instead, two years later. The fact that Meyer was in such a hurry to bring out Marx's pamphlet once more is in itself interesting. Both Meyer and Kautsky, for all their enmity, had the same goal in mind. The traditional position on the Jewish question had to be reaffirmed at a time when, as we have seen, some socialists were beginning to depart from the orthodox line.

Stefan Grossmann, left-wing writer and himself a Jew, wrote the preface to this edition of Marx's *Jewish Question*. The technique of using sympathizers who were not party members for such tasks in order to give them a wider audience was to become standard procedure. The Rowohlt publishing house which published the pamphlet was not one of the party's many enterprises. Grossmann stressed that Marx was neither a friend nor an enemy of the Jews, but rather the herald of a new world. Moreover, those who wrote insultingly about the "Jew Marx" could now judge for themselves Marx's own critical attitude toward the Jewish question.[49] The Jew was never to be defended as a Jew—that approach to the Jewish question was now set for the future.

The traditional socialist arguments continued, together with the contention that for the workers it made no difference whether the means of his oppression were in Jewish or in Aryan hands. This could lead to a laudable emphasis upon equality, which required all Socialists to fight anti-Semitism regardless of the existence of the Jewish capitalist stereotype. For example, the *Rote Fahne* wrote in 1932: "When the Nazis sing in the streets that Jewish blood will drip from the knife, they mean by this not only the blood of poor Jewish proletarians but also the blood of the working classes. That blood will flow in the mutual interest of German and Jewish capital."[50] Whenever Jewish firms are mentioned in the communist press, they are described as capitalist, and nothing is said about their Jewish stereotype as encountered in Marx's own writings. But communist attitudes were not so simple or straightforward. The traditional view of the Jewish question exemplified by Marx and Kautsky became enmeshed in the struggle against National Socialism. Moreover, the attempted solution of the Jewish question in the Soviet Union was bound to have a crucial effect upon the German party. These factors were to keep the traditional socialist attitudes alive and even to deepen their portent.

On a rather superficial level in the struggle against the Nazis, the *Rote Fahne* was fond of featuring every occasion when Jews seemed to support National Socialism or when National Socialism flirted with the Jews. Thus, for example, it claimed that a wildly anti-Semitic Nazi had turned out to be of Jewish ancestry.[51] Such glosses served the purpose of making the Nazis look ridiculous rather than providing an anti-Semitic thrust. But this dividing line was easily crossed in the effort to show that Jewish and Aryan capital were identical and that therefore the Jewish problem as stated was irrelevant. "Nazis support Jewish capital" appeared as a headline in the *Rote Fahne*,[52] while *Der Rote Aufbau* went even further: it asserted that there were many Jewish capitalists among the financiers of National Socialism, while numerous Nazi leaders carried names that pointed to Jewish descent or were shown to be the offspring of mixed marriages. When this could not be proved, then physical appearance makes the point, and Goebbels was cited as an example. Kurt Kersten, who wrote this piece, was quick to end by asserting that ideas of racial purity are nonsense.[53]

To be sure, "Hitler was the saviour of rich Jews,"[54] but communist analyses went beyond such a claim in order to link Jews and National Socialists more intimately. They thus accepted the stereotype (at least for non-proletarian Jews) of physical appearance (though this seems rare) to the point of castigating the "Jew editors" of the *Völkischer Beobachter*.[55] It must be stressed, however, that such accusations were the exception rather than the rule. Yet emphasis upon the class struggle meant the linkage of Jews and Nazis, on the surface deadly enemies, but in reality joined in the common struggle of all capital against the new order. "Jewishness" was irrelevant in the face of this overriding consideration.

These ideas were deepened through the sporadic efforts of the party to compete with that nationalism which the Right exploited so well. This competitive course was adopted in 1923, when Karl Radek advocated an alliance between communism and German national aspirations. In a famous speech, Radek praised the good patriotic intentions of Albert Leo Schlageter, the Nazi martyr executed by the French in the Ruhr. He was lauded as a truly courageous soldier of the counterrevolution, who should have joined the working classes in fighting French imperialism. Radek also dealt with the Jewish question in his advocacy of the new party line. The union of the workers with the nationalist petty bourgeois masses would end the rule of both "circumcised and uncircumcised capital." Jewish capital would opt for fascism in this struggle, and "we will witness how Messrs. Warburg, Litwin and Bosel pin on the Swastika." Anti-Semitic propaganda was considered stupid by Radek because it did not distinguish between Jewish capitalists and Jewish workers.[56] Unfortunately there were very few Jewish workers in Germany. Nationalists could easily focus their notions of the Jew upon the Jewish capitalist classes, and indeed for them the figure of the "Jewish banker" played a leading role.

The nationalist course of the party in 1923 was not as dangerous as the resumption of that course after 1930. By that time it was explosive stuff, for an increasingly dynamic, chauvinist anti-Semitism also concentrated on the Jew as the exploiter of the masses, though, in this case, he had a monopoly of exploitation. In a speech of 1930 the communist leader Heinz Neumann called on the Nazi masses to join the communists in a common struggle and not to continue the "fratricidal war,"[57] but the new nationalist course was never quite as blatant. The conversion from National

Socialism to communism of Lieutenant Richard Scheringer, who had been imprisoned for spreading Nazi propaganda in the army, was exploited to the fullest extent. Here was a patriotic officer whose phrases of "national and social liberation" were backed up by an unblemished nationalist past.

When Scheringer came to deal with the Jewish question in 1931, his nationalist past was easily adjusted. For the new communist convert, the Jewish question, the "Jewish spirit of commerce and usury," was part of the capitalist *hubris*. But Scheringer also struck a different note when, at the conclusion of his analyses of the connection between Jews and capitalism, he stated that "no Jew had a seat in the Central Committee of the Communist Party." However, there were nine "representatives of this race" in the nationalist and anti-Marxist Scherl publishing house.[58] Where Scheringer adopted an almost apologetic tone in his claim that no Jew sat in the Central Committee, the communist mass circulation newspaper *Welt am Abend* in that same year reacted against a Nazi accusation of Jewishness with unrestrained fury. Not a single Jew sat in its editorial office, the paper claimed, and among their collaborators not one had the "terribly Jewish" appearance of Goebbels.[59] Such remarks must be seen in the context of polemics against Nazi attacks, and on this level such a reply is not much different in technique from those put forward by some Jewish organizations. If Jews were pictured as bad, they countered with examples of Jews who were moral; if Jews were said to be "un-German," stories were published of Jews who had sacrificed their lives in war. Thus if communism is said to be "Jewish," it was asserted that there were no Jews in the Central Committee or working for the *Welt am Abend*. Even the Social Democrats, as we have seen, at times succumbed to this technique of reply: Marx did not have the "Jewish spirit," or it was the "Christian" Engels who systematized socialist doctrine. Such counterarguments were inevitable once the Nazi contentions were accepted at face value and taken seriously. The arguments put forward against them therefore had to depart from anti-Semitic premises in putting forward examples that might defeat Nazi contentions. The Nazis were successful in forcing their adversaries to argue within a framework they themselves had laid down, however absurd this may have seemed to these who opposed them. This factor was one of the chief purveyors of the anti-Semitic atmosphere of the time, whose importance has already been noted. Much of the defense against National Socialism seemed, however reluctant, to accept the fact that Jews were a special and problematic element within the German population.

The communists went further in this direction than other organizations, not only in order to reply to Nazi polemics but also to capture the nationalist masses for themselves. They did emphasize Germany's exploitation through French and British imperialism, but the Jewish question was involved as well. No doubt, traditional socialist theory made it easier to adopt such a posture as all matters specifically "Jewish" fell under a blanket condemnation.

Alfred Kantorowicz, then a young communist literary critic, summed up the party's attitudes toward the Jewish question as discussed up to this point. Writing in 1932, he asserted that the Jewish problem would be solved when the specifically "Jewish," and therefore parasitic class of *Luftmenschen*, of unproductive capitalist middlemen, was made productive—when the Jew ceased to be merely a capitalist merchant. This feat had already been accomplished in the Soviet Union; there innkeepers, middlemen, and usurers had become peasants and soldiers.[60]

Kantorowicz's proposed solution already existed, and the impact of the Soviet Union upon communist attitudes toward the Jews was of decisive importance. It meant the acceptance of Lenin's and Stalin's contention that the Jews, unlike other territorial minorities, were not a nation with claims to separate political rights. But it also meant a concern with the Jewish settlement at Birobidjan, then new and attracting worldwide interest and attention. From this point of view, the traditional rejection of Zionism was kept and, in fact, deepened; there could be no change of heart on this question.

Willi Münzenberg put his enormous organizational talents at the disposal of propaganda on behalf of Birobidjan. The organization he created for this purpose became the leading communist forum for the discussion of the Jewish question. Moreover, its scope was soon broadened beyond a concern with Birobidjan or anti-Zionist polemics, to encompass agitation and propaganda on behalf of all the political aims of the party. OZET (Society for the Rural Placement of Jewish Toilers) was originally founded in 1924 in the Soviet Union in order to attract settlers for Birobidjan and the short-lived

Jewish settlement in the Crimea.[61] The German branch of OZET, *Geserd* (a Yiddish term for OZET), was founded in 1928. Its sponsors were largely fellow travelers rather than party members and included many Jews. This, as we have noticed earlier, was in accordance with the technique of broadening the appeal of such organizations by keeping party control in the background. No doubt the general enthusiasm for the Soviet Union played a large part in the support *Geserd* received. For example, Ernst Toller's words of greeting to the organization praise the Soviet Union but never mention the settlement idea. But for others like Kurt Hiller the Soviet Union seemed to provide a meaningful alternative to Zionism at a time of heightened Jewish persecution.[62]

Geserd published some literature, but above all it sponsored public discussions and courses for workers. The topics generally concerned communism versus Zionism but later, in the years after 1930, were also addressed to the general struggle against fascism. The Soviet Union itself asked with some interest what the *Geserd* groups were doing within the general framework of antifascist activity.[63] Nevertheless, the Jewish question was the foremost reason for *Geserd's* existence. Otto Heller was appointed secretary of the organization, undertaking many lecture tours on its behalf. Heller had studied at the University of Prague, the son of a wealthy accountant. Once he had left the university, he joined the Communist Party and became the editor of a local party newspaper. He left Bohemia for Berlin in 1925, and there he caught the eye of Willi Münzenberg. He wrote for the *Welt am Abend* until he was dismissed in the late twenties for some disagreement with the party. Yet Münzenberg continued to befriend him, making possible Heller's trips to the Soviet Union and consequently his glowing reports about conditions in the workers' and peasants' state. Münzenberg undoubtedly suggested his appointment as secretary to *Geserd*, which must have been attractive for Heller who was himself Jewish. He was killed by the Nazis in Mauthausen in 1945.[64]

Heller's real "fame" came in 1931 with the publication of his *Der Untergang des Judentums* (*The Vanishing of Judaism*). The book has been called, with some justification, a "breviary" of *Geserd*,[65] but it also became an instant classic the day it was published—the only full-length German communist book on the Jewish question. Part of its contents should be familiar to us: Jews as Jews are always in tune with capitalism; their fetichism of goods is not an inborn trait but derives from their milieu; not only is trade their way of life but they have also acquired other undesirable characteristics: they are a nervous people who gesticulate; the Jewish religion springs from the necessity of inventing rules for the pursuit of commerce; it is a "dead ceremonial religion."[66] The social democratic journal *Die Gesellschaft* was largely justified when it fulminated against such "Communist Marxism," which lacks any originality.[67] After all, Kautsky was associated with that journal. But Heller's plagiarism was confined to the first part of the book. His solution of the Jewish question had to go beyond the advocacy of assimilation in order to take into account the Jewish settlement in the Soviet Union.

Heller did this by confining his advocacy of assimilation to western European Jews. The eastern European Jewish masses have different needs, he said, though these cannot include the assertion of a nonexistent Jewish nationality. This led him into some mental gymnastics. Birobidjan was not a Jewish state but a proletarian settlement, where Jews could practice their culture and their language (Yiddish). Because it was in the Soviet Union, it was a living culture, not a dead religion, and served to assimilate the Jewish to the Russian proletariat. We might add that, in contradiction to such proletarian assimilationism, *Geserd* propaganda itself now and then stressed the importance of Jewish nationalism. For example, with reference to the Birobidjan settlement, they quoted Lenin as saying that nations are all-important and nationalism is a necessity.[68] As for Heller himself, it soon became evident how tenuous his construct proved to be. The Jews in the West were to be assimilated, and yet the masses of eastern European Jewry were to retain their own culture without sliding into nationalism, which for Jews was one more manifestation of capitalist repression. Heller called Zionism a movement of the petty bourgeoisie, a movement that sought to compensate for growing class differences. For him Zionism had no connection with anti-Semitism, but instead was part of the universal capitalist conspiracy. While in Palestine Jews who are exploited go from the land to the cities, in Birobidjan, though the Jew still gesticulates, "his hands are heavy from manual work."

It is worth noting that a year later the same Communist Party publishing house which brought out Heller's book, republished

W. I. Lenin on the Jewish Question (1932). Lenin's prewar polemic against the Bund ("General Jewish Workers' Union" in Russia and Poland) for its advocacy of Jewish nationality and opposition to assimilation still seemed relevant to the party's position on the Jewish question at that time. We have seen how, earlier, the party had republished Marx's own tract on that problem. In the preface to this short collection of Lenin's writings, the publisher pointed to Heller's work as showing concretely how the Soviet Union had managed to solve the problem of the Jews.[69]

Heller repeated the theses of his book in lectures throughout the German-speaking countries, and in books and articles about his further travels in the Soviet Union. The newspaper *Die Welt am Abend* published long excerpts from *Der Untergang des Judentums* for its mass readership, contending that here, for the first time in contemporary literature, the Jewish problem had been analyzed from a Marxist standpoint[70] (thus choosing to ignore Kautsky's work). The Jewish reaction to the book was not as hostile as might be imagined. The official Jewish paper, the *C. V.-Zeitung*, gave it large coverage, and while it had no objection to Heller's anti-Zionism, it did strongly object to the idea of a vanishing of Judaism in the West. Above all, it disagreed with Heller's materialism. This criticism was one of the main objections to the communist point of view raised by the anti-Zionist liberals. Alfred Wiener, the Syndicus of the CV (the central organization of German Jews), asserted that the CV's attitude toward communism was largely influenced by the communist warfare against religion. The CV always refused to collaborate with the communists, in spite of sporadic exchanges of anti-Nazi material. In 1932, for example, the CV declined to make a financial contribution toward the creation of an SPD-KPD united front against Hitler.[71] The German organization to combat anti-Semitism, the Verein zur Abwehr des Antisemitismus, raised similar objections, but concluded that "the book is not as frightening as its title."[72] Jewish liberals, involved in the struggle against the Nazi menace, showed a certain ambivalence here as they had done in their relationship with the Soviet Union.

The Zionists reacted with greater vigor, as might be expected. They had good cause to do so, for communist attacks on Zionism did not stop with Heller's book or the activities of *Geserd*. In 1932, a party publishing house produced a novel in its popular "red series" glorifying the heroism of a young Arab in the 1929 uprising against the Jews and the British in Palestine. The young hero leads the revolt, even against the advice of the Grand Mufti (not known for his love of Zionism). The *Day of the Fellahin* by Hadad (himself a Jew) served to popularize communist theory and give it an added edge.[73] Where Kautsky had been disappointed to find his prophecies about Zionism fulfilled in 1929, this book praised the uprising and glorified its leader. Once more it must be stated that such attitudes toward Zionism were not irrelevant to attitudes toward Jews in general. Otto Heller expressed this well when he stated that the Jewish question regarded from the standpoint of the Jews was without interest to him.[74] The main Zionist response to Heller was a book by Eli Strauss devoted to a point by point refutation of his theses.[75] But for all such "self-defense," Felix Weltsch was undoubtedly closest to the mark when, in the *Jüdische Rundschau*, he stressed Heller's basic indifference to any "Jewish" concerns. Party dogma and the Soviet Union were for him all that counted.[76]

It became impossible to remain even a fellow traveler and support the Zionist cause. The case of the Jewish journalist Arthur Holitscher is instructive in this regard. Shortly after the end of World War I he sang the praises of Zionist Palestine; once again, the war had strengthened a Jew's feeling of his identity. By 1928, he could recall how he had known three great movements for man's liberation: bolshevism, the Chinese liberation movement, and Palestinian Zionism.[77] However, by that time he was a firm supporter of *Geserd*; Zionism had lost its heroic phase and was doomed to failure. Unlike Zionism, the Soviet Union had managed to maintain its socialist and proletarian impetus, while in Palestine capitalism and the "barren" Jewish religion had triumphed.[78]

Holitscher constantly looked for heroics and for a mystical spirit that could sustain the approaching new world. He was not a party member, not even an orthodox communist, but thought of himself as an intellectual in the service of the proletarian ideal. Unlike other left-wing intellectuals, to whom we shall return, he accepted work in party front organizations and consistently glorified the Soviet Union. For this kind of Jewish left-wing intellectual, commitment to communism meant ever closer adherence to the party line

and, therefore, a necessary (though perhaps deeply felt) repudiation of a momentary enthusiasm for the resurgence of Jewish
nationality.

Communist attitudes toward the Jewish question back up the
recollection of Hans Jaeger, a party lecturer during the last years of
the Republic, that communists were not deeply troubled by anti-
Semitism.[79] It must be clear from our analysis that such a lack of
concern was built into their socialist theory. This is why communists could side-step the issue of anti-Semitism in their flirtation
with the nationalist masses. Jaeger, who was also a member of the
KPD "anti-Nazi" commission, documents the manner in which the
party tried in the last years of the Republic to de-escalate the struggle with the Nazis. Communists and Social Democrats equally un-
derestimated the strength of the enemy.[80] For the *Rote Fahne*, in
1930, the resurgence of fascism did not mean a decline of the proletarian movement. It was, instead, the inevitable sign that a revolutionary situation was in the making.[81] This mistaken assessment
of National Socialism must be joined to their attitude toward the
Jews in order to understand the full dimension of the communists'
relationship to the Jewish question.

Those groups that broke with the established socialist parties in
order to advocate greater militancy against fascism paid little attention to the Jewish question. The "KPD-Opposition," led by Heinrich Brandler and August Thalheimer, was preoccupied with pre-
venting the masses from drifting to the Right. The economic crisis
of capitalism, which seemed decisive, could only be overcome by
immediate militant and revolutionary action. They did believe that
a Jew like the president of the powerful Danat Bank (Jakob Gold-
schmidt) would join the advocates of a Third Reich in order to preserve finance capital. But they also regarded anti-Semitism as the
lowest form of reaction, exemplified by czarist Russia. The "KPD-
Opposition" held that the Communist Party had abdicated the
leadership of the proletarian masses through its flirtation with nationalism. They republished Trotsky's attack upon "national communism" which, so he charged, had substituted Scheringer for
Liebknecht.[82]

The "Red Fighters," who had been driven out of the SPD in 1931,
to a large extent shared the ideology of the "KPD-Opposition,"
though the two were fighting each other. Here also, revolution

was the call of the hour and no compromise with any part of the fascist movement was possible. They, too, accused the communists of having accepted the nationalist ideology. Neither communists nor Social Democrats were any longer the allies of the proletariat, but instead based their ideas upon the petty bourgeoisie.[83] As we have seen, the "Red Fighters" had some truth on their side. For such groups a truly revolutionary and proletarian thrust against the existing order, meeting force with force, made the Jewish problem irrelevant within the framework of the struggle.

Within the established socialist parties, the Jewish problem did play a part. For the communists, in particular, it was an integral part of their outlook on man and society. Both Social Democrats and communists had to face the Jewish problem, and the way in which they did this influenced the kind of support Jews could expect from them during their period of crisis.

I V

The Communist Party was hardly a reliable ally in meeting the Nazi attacks against the Jews. The Social Democratic Party took a firmer stand, but even here we notice some ambivalence during the last years of the Republic. What about the left-wing intellectuals, most of whom, as stated earlier, were themselves Jews? They were critical spirits who, although socialists, could not be expected to accept unquestioningly the dogmatism of the past.[84] As illustrated earlier, intellectuals were troublesome to the orthodox Marxists, whilst at the same time they rejected the established socialist parties. Such men, for example, deplored the bureaucratic and pragmatic nature of the Communist Party. Their organ, the *Weltbühne*, accused the *Rote Aufbau* of being obsessed with economic considerations, of fulminating against those with true revolutionary spirit.[85]

Yet the *Weltbühne* carried an ecstatic review of Heller's book, stressing that the collapse of bourgeois civilization would also mean the vanishing of the Jew.[86] To be sure, Bruno Frei, author of the review, was one of the few contributors to the *Weltbühne* who consistently favored the Communist Party. He was also the editor-in-chief of the Berlin communist daily *Berlin am Morgen* which, like the *Rote Aufbau*, was controlled by Willi Münzenberg. The review of Heller's book is therefore not really typical of *Weltbühne* attitudes, even though at times the journal linked Jews to anti-Semitic parties which they were said to support out of mistaken self-interest. The *Weltbühne*'s view of eastern European Jewry was not much different from Kautsky's; for example, it accused eastern European Jews of engaging in white slave traffic.[87] On the whole, however, the approach of the left-wing intellectuals differed from that of the communists. They thought of themselves as socialists, as the true heirs of Karl Marx, and yet Marx's analysis of the Jewish question is mentioned only by Bruno Frei.

More typical was Manfred George's *Weltbühne* article on the Jewish revolutionary, a reflection of the left-wing intellectual's personal dilemma. George rejects the bourgeois Jew and the nationalist Jew. There remains only the Jew as revolutionary, but he is doomed to isolation. For the Jew believes in justice and therefore cannot be effective in a time of terror, which is an integral part of revolutionary action. The Jew will be a fertilizer of revolution, but nothing more.[88] This analysis affords deep insight into the make-up of these intellectuals. In 1930, when this article was written, they were indeed isolated and had themselves rejected participation in all political parties. Their view of themselves as Jews, however ambivalent, appeared in stark relief and, in the last resort, made it impossible for them to view the Jewish question in concert with the communists.

It was a subject they would have liked to avoid altogether, but this was impossible in those years of turmoil. George may have spoken the truest words about their situation, but they themselves attempted to face it by dwelling upon the shallow nature of anti-Semitism and by brushing aside the rising power of anti-Semitic National Socialism. Carl von Ossietzky, the editor of the *Weltbühne*, characterized anti-Semitism as a shallow by-product of nationalism. It does not run deep, he said, but has the character of a popular ballad.[89] Walter Mehring, in 1931, agreed with this analysis when he wrote that anti-Semitism was merely the external symptom of the sickness of capitalism. The Nazis did not really believe in their own rhetoric, he said, and Goebbels would just as soon march with the Red Army if it suited his purpose. But his party was dependent on the money contributed by heavy industry and rich Jews as well.[90]

Anti-Semitism could not possibly represent a deeply held conviction; all these men agreed on this point. The rationalism and idealism of the left-wing intellectuals blinded them to the depth and strength of anti-Jewish feeling. Their belief that man is essentially good and that a bad society has only perverted his nature also stood in the way of a realistic assessment of the situation. Ossietzky firmly believed that those writers who advocate anti-Semitism come close to advocating pogroms, for they can claim no case of intellectual substance.[91] Two years earlier, in 1930, the *Weltbühne* had assured its readers that no one takes anti-Semitism seriously; there was no need to get passports and pack one's luggage.[92] This reassurance was needed, for the Nazis had just scored their first spectacular electoral triumph in the Reichstag elections. It is typical that Ossietzky ends his discussion of anti-Semitism with the statement that anti-Semitism had never taken root in the working class.[93] It is this faith that enabled the left-wing intellectuals to brush aside the Nazi successes. After all, the workers were, in their eyes, the least corrupt element in a corrupt society.

In 1931 it was still possible to believe that if Hitler attempted to come to power as Mussolini had done, a general strike would stop him.[94] Those holding this view reassured themselves with the thought of the general strike that had stopped the *Kapp-Putsch* thirteen years earlier. However, it was pandering to illusions to state in February of 1933 that while the Italian working classes were exhausted when Mussolini came to power, the German proletariat was ready and willing to fight.[95] Such an article in the *Weltbühne* demonstrates the extent to which the left-wing intellectuals had lost contact with reality. As we saw earlier, the Austrian Social Democrat, Julius Deutsch, was nearer the mark when he wrote about the German workers' rejection of revolutionary experiments. The only realistic note in the *Weltbühne* was sounded by Ernst Toller, who had some experience in making revolutions. Toller stated that Hitler once he came to power would not give it up. But Toller, in 1930, also thought that the working classes, through the trade unions, could still do something to stop National Socialism.[96]

The intellectuals tried to overcome their feeling of isolation by putting their faith in the working classes. For they saw themselves not as Jews but as the vanguard of an internationalism based upon justice, reason, and the abolition of the capitalist system. In this they were at one with the Jews in the Communist Party, and with liberals who were in opposition to established socialism. Arnold Zweig's review of Simon Dubnow's *History of the Jews* can give us further insight into these attitudes. He treats Dubnow's *History* as the story of a minority that was able to sustain itself against all adversaries, not through an archaic religious faith, but because of its belief in the power of reason. In Zweig's view, the Jews were needed in order that nationalism might be defeated and the barriers between peoples torn down.[97] Carl von Ossietzky shared Zweig's feelings which were, in turn, close to the liberal concept of the supposed "mission of Jews." The solution to the Jewish question lay not in the creation of a separate Birobidjan but in a fusion with a vigorous and unbeaten proletariat. However, this idea of fusion was ambivalent. The original prospectus of the *Weltbühne* called the intellectuals the "council of the wise." They must lead, for only they can have an overall view of society and culture. These intellectuals were not class-bound.[98]

This leadership ideal sprang from their impotence, but it introduced an element of ambivalence into their assimilationist ideal. They loooked back to 1918–19 when Jewish intellectuals had made a revolution in Bavaria; Jews who wanted to be not Jews, but part of the progressive brotherhood of all humanity. Their idealism not only blinded them to the reality of National Socialism; it also made them impassioned enemies of Zionism. Their attitude toward Zionism had some similarities with that of the communists, but it also had its own peculiar twist in tune with their outlook upon the world. The *Weltbühne* stressed that conditions in Palestine were no better than in the Germany of the early thirties. "Where once upon a time love was preached, hatred has remained strongest." In ancient times Jewish sects warred with one another in Palestine, while now Christians, Jews, and Mohammedans lived in a warlike state. These were *Unholy Memories of the Holy Land.*[99]

For these men Palestine was no utopia, no island where rationalism reigned; instead, it was a mirror of all the world's ills. These left-wing intellectuals, unlike the communists, did not make much of the capitalist exploitation of the Jews. Instead, they pictured the Holy Land as unleashing all that is worst in human nature. As committed pacifists they asserted that the word "peace" is as hated in certain Zionist circles as it is in the rest of the world. A lecture in

1932 at the Hebrew University in which Norman Bentwich extolled Jerusalem as a potential center for world peace was interrupted by stink-bombs, whistles, and foot-stamping. The Zionist *Jüdische Rundschau* reported the event with outright condemnation. The misguided revisionist youths, who were responsible for the disturbance, imitated the nationalist current at German universities or in Poland, which took offense at the very word "peace."[100] The *Weltbühne* took up this report, sharpening its tone and making the analogy with Germany more outspoken: Nazi riots on the Kurfürstendamm in Berlin, it said, were reproduced on Mount Scopus. We do not know whether it is true that in the subsequent trial a revisionist lawyer praised Hitler for being the saviour of Germany (he was, after all, still nearly a year from seizing power), as the *Weltbühne* contended. Nor is it certain that he pledged support for the Nazi leader provided Hitler dropped his anti-Semitism. This alleged remark prompted the *Weltbühne*, however, to hazard that next to the call "Germany awake," humanity would finally hear cries of "Zion awake." The headline of the *Weltbühne* article was "Hitler in Jerusalem."[101]

This article is symptomatic of the intellectuals' attitude toward Zionism. The *Weltbühne* took this opportunity to go far beyond the strictures of the *Jüdische Rundschau*: it made an explicit analogy with National Socialism, an analogy not lightly made in 1932. In its view Zionism (and not only the revisionists) had prevented the true universalist and socialist mission of the Jewish people, and of the left-wing intellectuals. Zionist Palestine was indeed an unholy land. But unlike Heller's attack, there was no talk in the *Weltbühne* of the vanishing of the Jewish people, nor was there any reference to Kautsky's or Marx's "Jewish peculiarities" under capitalism.

The absence of the Jewish stereotype did not mean a clear confrontation with National Socialist anti-Semitism. Unlike the communists, they did not toy with the Nazi movement; it was firmly rejected. However, the Jewish question was ultimately dissolved into the general longing for human brotherhood and a more rational world.

In some left-wing intellectuals this produced a painful tension between their "humanity" and their Jewishness. Lion Feuchtwanger, himself a member of the *Weltbühne* circle, provides a good example of this dilemma in his *Josephustrilogie*. The first volume of the novel, *Der jüdische Krieg* (*The Jewish War*) published in 1932, is a song of praise for reason amidst the passion and violence of the age. Reason must triumph if a war in which all truth collapses is to be avoided. Josephus, the hero of the book, opposed both the fanaticism of the Jewish warriors and the barbarism of Rome. Small wonder that another journal close to left-wing intellectuals, the *Tagebuch*, praised the book upon its appearance as an attack upon chauvinism. But it also saw fit to make an analogy with the year 1932. Compared with the excessive nationalism of the Jews of the first century A.D., the Nazis seem like advocates of internationalism. It is surely significant that the review dwells at some length on Jewish chauvinism and ignores Feuchtwanger's description of an even greater Roman ruthlessness.[102] Jews were once more reminded that they must identify themselves with cosmopolitanism, rationalism, and love for all humanity. Nationalism, as we have seen, was opposed to these ideals in the minds of left-wing intellectuals —here no compromise was possible.

The second volume of the trilogy, *Die Söhne* (*The Sons*), which appeared in 1935 after the Nazis had seized power, still exalted reason, but by now despaired of its effects. Reason can fossilize into a rigid and unbending system especially when it is used on behalf of a theocratic nationalism. Moreover, the conflict between Feuchtwanger the left-wing intellectual and Feuchtwanger the Jew comes out in stark relief. He cannot, as yet, resolve this dilemma and both parts of his loyalty exist side by side without joining hands. Feuchtwanger makes Josephus give this description of his famous book on the Jewish war: "It is a Jewish book, but the spirit which informs it is that of a citizen of the world."[103]

The final volume, *Der Tag wird kommen* (*The Day Will Come*), written during World War II and published in 1945, goes one step further. Josephus now "sickens" because of his nationalism. He is said to have betrayed the Jewish state in favor of a cosmopolitan utopia. "He wanted to proclaim the kingdom of reason, of the Messiah . . . he who makes such a prophecy has to pay for it with too many sacrifices. However, it is sweet and honorable to pay allegiance solely to one's people, one's nation."[104] Feuchtwanger the left-wing intellectual had passed from using the Jews as symbols for humanity and rationalism to an attempted confrontation with

Jewish nationalism. To be sure, this was confrontation rather than acceptance, and yet the change from the previous volumes is obvious. One might add that even in the first volume of the trilogy Josephus leaves his people only when the battle is lost. Before this he has fought heroically as a leader of the Jewish cause.[105] Feuchtwanger's Josephus is a very human creature, attracted to worldly power and might. However, the emphasis changes in the three volumes, and together they portray the torn soul of a Jewish left-wing intellectual in his journey from a disillusionment with universalism and rationalism to a confrontation with his Jewishness.

During that journey, typically enough, Feuchtwanger made a foray into communism and paid allegiance to the promise of the Soviet Union. This also ended in disillusionment. He was unwilling to give up altogether what he called "practical socialism as exemplified by the Communists," but was quick to add that his heart and feeling could not affirm it. He never contemplated settling in communist East Germany. Moreover, in his book *Waffen für Amerika* (*Arms for America*, 1947) he returned once more to a belief in the "slow, very slow, yet certain growth of human reason between the last ice age and that which is to come."[106] Feuchtwanger's evolution and hesitations are typical of the generation of intellectuals that had once gathered in the offices of the *Weltbühne*.

V

Confrontation with the Jewish problem was for left-wing intellectuals who traveled this road a consequence of the Nazi triumph and of their own exile. For the majority of such intellectuals, however, exile did not markedly change their political attitudes. The (non-Jewish) novelist Heinrich Mann, for example, whom they admired most, in 1933 criticized the dominance which the persecution of the Jews exercised over all antifascist mass meetings. Hatred of the Jew in National Socialism, he said, took second place to the hatred of human freedom. Humanity was an integral whole, all of which was menaced by fascism. The Jews as Jews had no special claim to attention.[107]

In a critique of their own failure, the Social Democrats attempted to find a new *élan* that would give them a more successful political posture. Some continued to call for a pragmatic approach to politics, but others believed that the masses had to be wedded to the leadership through a renewed emphasis upon the class struggle.

The nationalism that seemed to have led to the party's pragmatic politics came under attack. Youth especially, so it was said, could not live by reason alone.[108] Many Social Democrats came to share with intellectuals like Feuchtwanger a despair in the efficacy of human reason. But the failures with which we have been concerned did not arise from a preponderance of reason, but came rather out of illusions fostered by a Marxist heritage, however much it had been diluted and changed by such men.

The communists continued to take their stand on the same ground that they had occupied under the Republic. Their attitude on the Jewish question remained unchanged. The *Neue Weltbühne*, for example, now published in Prague under communist auspices, asserted that an antifascism based upon the persecution of Jews was mistaken; for Jews themselves were split into social classes and for some the profit motive was more important than antifascist activity. Antifascism must be set in the framework of the international working classes both inside and outside Germany.[109] Soviet attitudes toward Zionism and the Jewish question did not change, and therefore those of the German Communist Party remained constant as well.

The failure of the German Left to present a united and consistent front on the Jewish question was a tragedy for German Jews during this crisis. The Left had let them down in the end, and there seemed little to cling to in the way of allies in the battle that had to be waged. The poignancy of this situation was fully understood by Eva Reichmann in 1932. The general process of radicalization had also gripped Jewish youth, and as they could not join the anti-Semitic radical Right, they joined the radical Left.[110] For such young Jews, the failure of the Left must have been particularly harrowing. The center parties to which many Jews confessed allegiance had shown signs of collapse even before National Socialism arrived on the brink of power. The Right was impregnated with anti-Semitism, though some Jews turned in that direction to find a bulwark against National Socialism. There is hardly any evidence that any Jewish capitalist in desperation turned to the Nazis themselves.[111]

Only the Social Democratic Party seemed to present a barrier of republicanism against the rising tide of the Right. Yet on the whole, a promising avenue of hope had been closed. The noble humanitarian confessions of faith and the Left's utter rejection of racism could not erase the fact that the Jew as a Jew had no place within their ideology. Some Social Democrats like Eduard Bernstein did believe that the affirmation of Jewish identity was a necessary step to world brotherhood. Such men shared the idealism of Gustav Landauer and Martin Buber, but not that of Marx or Kautsky. It was difficult, at best, to combat Nazi racism which attacked the Jew as a Jew, if one could only reply that the Jew as a Jew did not in fact exist. But the inherently noble ideals of the Left seemed sullied when the Jew remained a stereotype, though this was one of their not unexpected consequences. The theories of the Left served to betray the Jew at a moment of crisis while many Jewish intellectuals, after the Nazis had triumphed, were torn between their left-wing allegiance and their Jewishness. Effective resistance to nationalism and fascism was undermined by that world of illusions in which so much of the German Left lived.

Notes

1. Introduction

1. Ernst Toller, "Masse Mensch," *Deutsche Revolutionsdramen*, ed. Reinhold Grimm and Jost Hermand (Frankfurt-am-Main, n.d.), 427.

2. Rosemarie Leuschen-Seppel, *Sozialdemokratie und Antisemitismus im Kaiserreich* (Bonn, 1978), 259, 278.

3. Reinhard Bentmann, Michael Müller, *Die Villa als Herrschaftsarchitektur* (Frankfurt-am-Main, 1970), 125–127.

4. See Peter Uwe Hohendahl, *Das Bild der bürgerlichen Welt im expressionistischen Drama* (Heidelberg, 1967).

5. George L. Mosse, *Germans and Jews, the Right, the Left and the Search for the Third Force in Pre-Nazi Germany* (New York, 1970).

6. George L. Mosse, *The Nationalization of the Masses* (New York, 1975).

7. Berthold Auerbach, *Schrift und Volk* (Leipzig, 1846), 80.

8. J. Wohlfill, "Gesangbuch des neuen Israelitischen Tempels in Hamburg," *Der Jude, Periodische Blätter für Religions und Gewissenfreiheit*, ed. G. Riesser (October 18, 1833), 166–169.

9. George L. Mosse, "The First World War and the Appropriation of Nature," *War, Revolution and Society in Modern Germany, Essays in Honour of Francis Carsten*, ed. W. R. Berghan and Martin Kitchen (London, 1980).

10. Jean Paul Aron, Roger Kempf, *Le pénis et la démoralisation de l'Occident* (Paris, 1978), 31.

11. Michael Foucault, *The History of Sexuality*, Vol. 1 (New York, 1980), 25.

12. David R. Lipton, *Ernst Cassirer* (Toronto, 1978), 92, 111.

13. See Andrew Arato and Paul Breines, *The Young Lukacs and the Origins of Western Marxism* (New York, 1979).

318 / *Notes*

14. Mosse, *Germans and Jews*, 82 ff, 92 ff.
15. See especially *The Crisis of German Ideology* (New York, 1964), *Nazi Culture* (New York, 1966), and *Nazism: A Historical and Comparative Analysis of National Socialism* (New Brunswick, N.J., 1978).

2. Literature and Society in Germany

1. George Lichtheim, *The Concept of Ideology* (New York, 1967), 242.
2. Ralf Dahrendorf, *Society and Democracy in Germany* (New York, 1967).
3. See Jost Hermand, ed., *Das junge Deutschland* (Stuttgart, 1966).
4. See Georg Weerth, *Gedichte, Prosa* (Berlin, 1960), and *Fragmente eines Romans*, ed. Siegfried Unseld (Frankfurt-am-Main, 1965), p. 14.
5. Georg Herwegh, *Werke*, ed. Herman Tardel (Berlin, 1909), Vol. 1, c.
6. *Ibid.*, xciii.
7. Peter Demetz, *Marx, Engels, und die Dichter* (Stuttgart, 1959), 122 ff.
8. See Erich Ruprecht, *Literarische Manifeste des Naturalismus 1880–1892* (Stuttgart, 1962).
9. Susanne Miller, "Critique littéraire de la social-democratie allemande à la fin du siècle dernier," *Le Mouvement Socialiste*, 59 (April–June 1967), 55 and *passim*.
10. *Ibid.*, 58.
11. See Karl Kautsky, *The Class Struggle*, trans. W. E. Bohn (Chicago, 1910), 159.
12. See Ursula Münchow, ed., *Aus den Anfängen der sozialistischen Dramatik* (Berlin, 1964).
13. Alfred Kleinberg, *Die deutsche Dichtung* (Berlin, 1927), 371; Minna Kautsky, *Auswahl aus ihrem Werk* (Berlin, 1965), *passim*.
14. K. Schiffner, *Wilhelm Jordan* (Frankfurt-am-Main, 1889), 138.
15. Josef Victor von Scheffel, *Ekkehard* (Berlin, 1855), 14–15.
16. Felix Dahn, *Erinnerungen* (Leipzig, 1895), Vol. IV, Section II, 649.
17. George L. Mosse, *The Crisis of German Ideology* (New York, 1964), Chaps. 4 and 11.
18. George L. Mosse, "The Image of the Jews in German Popular Culture: Felix Dahn and Gustav Freytag," *Germans and Jews* (New York, 1968), 61–77.
19. Quoted in Jost Hermand, "Zur Literatur der Gründerzeit," *Deutsche Vierteljahrsschrift für Literaturwissenschaft und Geistesgeschichte* (Halle, 1967), Vol. 41, No. 2, 2208.
20. Schiffner, *op. cit.*, 129.
21. See Wilhelm Stoffers, *Juden und Ghetto in der deutschen Literatur bis zum Ausgang des Weltkrieges* (Nymwegen, 1939).
22. Quoted in Eduart Rothfuchs, *Der selbstbiographische Gehalt in Gustav Freytags Werken* (Münster, 1929), p. 69.
23. Julius D. Eckardt, *Lebenserinnerungen* (Leipzig, 1910), Vol. I, 48 and 67.
24. Dahrendorf, *op. cit.*, 36 ff. and 46.
25. Berthold Auerbach, *Schrift und Volk* (Leipzig, 1846), p. 58.
26. Quoted in Joachim Remak, *The Gentle Critic, Theodor Fontane and German Politics, 1848–1898* (Syracuse, N.Y., 1964), 57.

27. Fontane calls him a "Prinzipienreiter," *Effi Briest* (Vienna, 1942), 219 and 244.

28. Theodor Fontane, *Frau Jenny Treibel* (Berlin, 1893), 285 and 320.

29. Fontane, *Effi Briest*, 262.

30. Paul Heyse, *Jugenderinnerungen und Bekenntnisse* (Stuttgart and Berlin, 1912), Vol. 1, 99 and 191.

31. For example, Adolf Bartels, "Die Alten und die Jungen," *Grenzboten*, Vol. 55 (Leipzig, 1869), 277.

32. Paul Heyse, *Kinder der Welt* (Berlin, 1884), Vol. II, 61.

33. *Ibid.*, 262 f.

34. *Ibid.*, 78 and 189.

35. Paul Heyse, "Andrea Delfin," in *Die Reise nach dem Glück* (Stuttgart, 1959), 392.

36. Georg Hermann, *Jettchen Geberts Geschichte* (Berlin, 1912), Vol. 1; Letter from Stefan Zweig to Georg Hermann, October 20, 1935 (Georg Hermann Archive, Leo Baeck Institute, New York).

37. Heyse, *Jugenderinnerungen und Bekenntnisse*, Vol. 1, 239.

38. Dahn, *op. cit.*, Vol. III, 305.

39. E. Marlitt, *Im Hause des Kommerzienrates* (Leipzig, 1877), 218 and 369.

40. *Ibid.*, p. 41.

41. Hermann Zang, *Die Gartenlaube als politisches Organ* (Coburg, 1935), 14 and 17. See also *Die Gartenlaube*, 19 (Leipzig, 1881), 308–314.

42. Ruth Horovitz, *Vom Roman des Jungen Deutschland zum Roman der Gartenlaube* (Breslau, 1937), 71.

43. Eva Becker, "Literarische Zeitkommunikation 1860–1914," mimeographed MS, Proceedings of the Working Party "Deutsche Literaturwissenschaft" of the Fritz Thyssen Foundation (1965), 20; for 1957, see *Der Spiegel*, Vol. 11, No. 30 (Hamburg, July 24, 1957), 37.

44. Ludwig Ganghofer, *Der Dorfapostel* (Stuttgart, 1902), 114.

45. Hans Schwerte, "Ganghofers gesundung," mimeographed MS, Proceedings of the Working Party "Deutsche Literaturwissenschaft" of the Fritz Thyssen Foundation (1965), 95–128.

46. Ludwig Ganghofer, *Lebenslauf eines Optimisten: Buch der Jugend* (Stuttgart, 1930), *passim*.

47. Robert Minder, *Dichter in der Gesellschaft, Erfahrungen mit deutscher und französischer Literatur* (Frankfurt-am-Main, 1966), 277.

48. *Ibid.*, p. 278.

49. Adolf Hitler, *Hitler's Secret Conversations*, trans. N. Cameron and R. H. Stevens (New York, 1953), 257.

50. Viktor Böhm, *Karl May* (Vienna, 1955), 3.

51. Note the stress on Karl May as a genial writer of fairy tales, whose nationalism and Christianity can be discounted, in the novel *Die Aula* by Hermann Kant (Munich, 1966), which was written in the German Democratic Republic. The view of May as a writer of fairy tales is expanded in Ernst Bloch, *Das Prinzip Hoffnung*, Vol. I (Frankfurt-am-Main, 1954), 409 ff.

52. Quoted in Böhm, *op. cit.*, 74.

53. Karl May, *Mein Leben und Streben* (Dresden, 1910), 74–75, 135, and 150.

54. Quoted in Böhm, *op. cit.*, 101.

55. Ludwig Gurlitt, *Gerichtigkeit für Karl May!* (Dresden, 1919), 140.

56. Quoted in Walter Sokel, *The Writer in Extremis* (New York, 1964), 88. The play is *Rektor Kleist* (1905).

57. Friedrich Nietzsche, "Die fröhliche Wissenschaft," *Nietzsches Werke* (Leipzig, 1900), Vol. V, Section I, 41.

58. Sokel, *op. cit.*, 182.

59. Mosse, "Fascism and the Intellectuals," *Germans and Jews*, 144–271.

60. Heinrich Mann, *Der Untertan* (Leipzig, 1918), 454.

61. *Ibid.*, 490.

62. Heinrich Mann, "Zola," *Essays*, Vol. I (Berlin, 1954), 156–236 (especially 166 and 168).

63. *Ibid.*, 189 and 198.

64. Heinrich Mann, *Diktatur der Vernunft* (Berlin, 1923), *passim*.

65. Alfred Kantorowicz, *Heinrich und Thomas Mann* (Berlin, 1956), 24.

66. Lorenz Winter, *Heinrich Mann und sein Publikum* (Cologne, 1965), 32 and 35 f.

67. Thomas Mann, *Betrachtungen eines Unpolitischen* (Berlin, 1918), 71.

68. *Ibid.*, 246.

69. *Ibid.*, 109.

70. Alfred Kantorowicz, *Deutsches Tagebuch*, Vol. II (Munich, 1961), 100.

71. Mann, *op. cit.*, 81, 92 ff.

72. *Ibid.*, 106.

73. *Ibid.*, 47, 84, and 123.

74. Theodor W. Adorno, *Noten zur Literatur*, Vol. III (Frankfurt-am-Main, 1967), 23.

75. See Mosse, *The Crisis of German Ideology*.

3. What Germans Really Read

1. Jost Hermand, *Der Schein des schönen Lebens, Studien zur Jahrhundertwende* (Frankfurt-am-Main, 1972), 14–15.

2. Karl May, *Winnetou* (Bamberg, 1951), II, 446.

3. Ludwig Ganghofer, *Der Dorfapostel* (Stuttgart, n.d.), 114.

4. E. Marlitt, *Im Hause des Kommerzienrates* (Leipzig, 1877), 41.

5. W. Harless in *Marquartsteiner Blätter*, 2 Sondernummer (October 1933), n.p.

6. *Winnetou*, III, 392.

7. *Ibid.*, II, 477.

8. Karl May, *Der Schatz im Silbersee* (Bamberg, 1952), 112.

9. *Schloss Hubertus*, in *Ganghofers Gesammelte Schriften* (Stuttgart, n.d.), I, 86. Von jetzt ab zitiert als *Schriften*.

10. *Im Hause des Kommerzienrates*, 369.

11. E. Marlitt, *Das Geheimnis der alten Mamsell* (Leipzig, n.d.), 98, and Oskar Walzel, *Klassizismus und Romantik als europäische Erscheinung* (Berlin, 1929), 290.

12. *Schloss Hubertus,* in *Schriften* I, xv.

13. Friedrich Theodor Vischer, *Ästhetik oder Wissenschaft des Schönen* (1846–57).

14. Ursula Kirchhoff, *Die Darstellung des Festes im Roman um 1900* (Münster, 1965), 13.

15. *Schloss Hubertus,* in *Schriften,* I, 8.

16. *Der Schatz im Silbersee,* 372.

17. Ernst Moritz Arndt, *Entwurf einer Teutschen Gesellschaft* (Frankfurt-am-Main, 1814), 36.

18. *Das Geheimnis der alten Mamsell,* 88.

19. *Das Zeitalter des Pietismus,* ed. Martin Schmidt and Wilhelm Jannasch (Bremen, 1965), 59.

20. E. Marlitt, *Das Heideprinzesschen* (Leipzig, 1872), I, 109, 61.

21. Ludwig Ganghofer, *Das Gotteslehen. Roman aus dem 13. Jahrhundert,* in *Schriften,* IX, 281 ff.

22. *Winnetou,* III, 523.

23. *Ibid.,* I, 122 f.

24. *Schloss Hubertus,* in *Schriften,* I, 62.

25. *Ibid.,* I, 263.

26. *Ibid.,* II, 288.

27. *Das Heideprinzesschen,* 257.

28. *Das Geheimnis der alten Mamsell,* 201.

29. *Winnetou,* I, 51.

30. *Ibid.,* I, 420.

31. *Ibid.,* III, 266, 269.

32. *Schloss Hubertus,* in *Schriften,* I, 251.

33. Johann Joachim Winckelmann, *Geschichte der Kunst des Altertums,* in *Kunsttheoretische Schriften* (Strasbourg, 1966), V, 153.

34. *Ibid.,* 24.

35. *Im Hause des Kommerzienrates,* 161 ff.

36. *Winnetou,* I, 120; II, 80; III, 36.

37. *Ibid.,* I, 270, 244, 426; II, 88.

38. *Ibid.,* III, 388; *Der Schatz im Silbersee,* 119.

39. *Winnetou,* III, 273.

40. *Der Schatz im Silbersee,* 71.

41. *Winnetou,* I, 384.

42. *Der Schatz im Silbersee,* 59.

43. *Ibid.,* 391. Theodore Ziolkowski, "Der Hunger nach dem Mythos," in *Die sogenannten Zwanziger Jahre,* ed. Reinhold Grimm and Jost Hermand (Bad Homburg, 1970), 169–201.

44. *Der Schatz im Silbersee,* 239.

45. *Ibid.,* 385.

46. *Schloss Hubertus,* in *Schriften,* I, 214.

47. Fritz Fischer, *Krieg der Illusionen* (Düsseldorf, 1969), 65–66.

48. Adolf Hitler, *Hitler's Secret Conversations,* ed. N. Cameron and R. H. Stevens (New York, 1953), 257.

49. Hans Severus Ziegler, *Adolf Hitler aus dem Erleben dargestellt* (Göttingen, 1964), 76.
50. Ludwig Gurlitt, *Gerechtigkeit für Karl May!* (Radebeul, 1919), 140.
51. *Im Hause des Kommerzienrates*, 249.
52. *Ibid.*, 50.
53. *Das Gotteslehen*, in *Schriften*, IX, 207.
54. Dietrich Strothmann, *Nationalsozialistische Literaturpolitik* (Bonn, 1963), 398.
55. *Ibid.*, 345, 338. Uwe-Karsten Ketelsen, *Von heroischem sein und völkischem Tod* (Bonn, 1970).
56. Strothmann, *op. cit.*, 239, 341.
57. H. Schlotz, *Unsere Jungen, Ein Film der nationalpolitischen Erziehungsanstalten* (Göttlingen, 1969), 290.
58. Ziegler, *op. cit.*, 77.
59. Strothmann, *op. cit.*, 398.
60. *Das Gotteslehen*, in *Schriften*, IX, 202.

4. *Death, Time, and History:*
Volkish Utopia and Its Transcendence

1. K. W. Schiebler, ed., *Jakob Böhme, Sämtliche Werke* (Leipzig, 1831), 1, 3.
2. Hermann Stehr, *Der Heiligenhof* (Berlin, 1918), I, 139.
3. Jakob Böhme, *Mysterium magnum*, 40, 8.
4. Martin Buber, "Uber Jacob Boehme," in *Wiener Rundschau* (June 15, 1901), XII, 251–253.
5. Bela Balazs, "Notes from a Diary," in *New Hungarian Quarterly*, XIII, No. 47 (Herbst, 1972), 124–126.
6. Recent scholarship has held that the apocalyptical and millenarian traditions stressed unity rather than a left-wing millenarian enthusiasm—Clark Garrett, "Millenarianism," in *Catholic Historical Review* (n.d.). Donald Weinstein, *Savonarola and Florence* (Princeton, 1970), 178–184.
7. Ernst Heinrich Reclam, *Die Gestalt des Paracelsus in der Dichtung* (Leipzig, 1938), 96, 97.
8. Erwin Guido Kolbenheyer, *Das Dritte Reich des Paracelsus* (Munich, 1926), 310. Alexandre Koyré, *Mystiques, Spirituels, Alchemistes du XVIe siècle allemand* (Paris, 1955), 66 ff.
9. Kolbenkeyer, *op. cit.*, 249.
10. Ernst Bloch, *Thomas Münzer als Theologe der Revolution* (Munich, 1921), 293.
11. Erwin Guido Kolbenheyer, *Sebastian Karst über sein Leben und seine Zeit*, III (Wolfratshausen, 1958), 163.
12. Richard Billinger, "Paracelsus," in *Gesammelte Werke* (Grasse and Vienna, 1960), IV, 11.
13. *Deutscher Ehrenhain für die Helden von 1914–18* (Leipzig, 1931), 8.
14. Julius Petersen, *Die Sehnsucht nach dem Dritten Reich* (Stuttgart, 1934), 27.
15. Kolbenheyer, *op. cit.*, 309.

16. *Die Spielgemeinde* (Gibhard, 1934), 7 Jahrg., No. 10.

17. Heinrich Anacker, "Golgatha," in *Die deutsche Zukunft* (November 1931), 1 Jahrg., Heft 6, 1.

18. Gerhard Schumann, *Heldische Feier* (Munich, n.d.).

19. Rede in *Weltanschauliche Feierstunde der NSDAP* (Munich, 1944), 137–143.

20. Moeller van den Bruck, *Das dritte Reich* (Hamburg, 1931), 235.

21. Ernst Wachler, *Osning* (Leipzig, 1914), 81.

22. Gertrud Prellwitz, *Das Osterfeuer* (Oberhof, 1917).

23. Harry Wilde, *Theodor Plivier. Nullpunkt der Freiheit* (Munich, 1965), Chap. 2.

24. F. Kaufmann connected fairy tales to popular utopian traditions. "Altgermanische Religion," in *Archiv für Religionswissenschaft* (1912), XV, 625; Hans Sints, *Jenseitsmotive im deutschen Volksmärchen* (Leipzig, 1911).

25. *Deutsche Heldensagen*. Neu erzählt von Hans Friedrich Blunck (Berlin, 1938), 427.

26. Ernst Adolf Dreyer, *Hans Friedrich Blunck, Sicht des Werkes* (Stuttgart, 1938), 27; *Die neue Literatur* (July 1931), 308.

27. Peter Aley, *Jungendliteratur im Dritten Reich* (Gütersloh, 1967), 97.

28. Fritz Hugo Hoffmann, *Deutsche Märchen und ihre Deutung* (Frankfurt-am-Main, 1935), 86. This book is normative for the Nazi interpretation of fairy tales. Edmund Mudrak, *Märchen und Sage* (Vienna, 1933).

29. Peter Aley, 95: *Die neue Literatur* (June 1938), 289. I have found no evidence that the production of fairy tales and sagas rose markedly during the Third Reich. They actually declined as dramatic themes—from fifty-four in 1926 to thirty-six in 1934. *Die Neue Literatur* (June 1937), 278.

30. Hans Grimm, *Warum-Woher-Wohin?* (Lippoldsberg, 1954), 549.

31. Arnold Zweig in *Hermann Stehr. Sein Werk und seine Welt*, ed. Wilhelm Meridies (Habelschwerdt, 1924), 61.

32. Dreyer, *op. cit.*, 42.

33. Ernst Wiechert, *Das heilige Jahr* (Munich, 1954; 1. Auflage 1936), "Einführung." ed. Wiechert, *Jahre und Zeiten* (Zürich, 1949), 404.

34. The production figures were given by the Steinkopf-Verlag to Barry Fulkes. I am grateful to him for this suggestion and others that derive from his own research into the book.

35. *Unter dem Schleier der Gisela. Aus Agnes Günthers Leben und Schaffen*, ed. D. Rudolf Günther (Stuttgart, 1929), 224.

36. Albert Ritschl, *Geschichte des Pietismus in der lutherischen Kirche des 17. und 18. Jahrhunderts* (Bonn, 1886), 128, 131, 153, 174.

37. Gerhard Kaiser, *Pietismus und Patriotismus im literarischen Deutschland* (Wiesbaden, 1961), 40.

38. Agnes Günther, *Die Heilige und ihr Narr* (Stuttgart, 1914), I, 15.

39. Hermann Stehr to Martin Buber, December 8, 1914. in Martin Buber, *Briefwechsel aus sieben Jahrzehnten*, ed. Grete Schaeder (Heidelberg, 1927), I, 385.

40. *Die neue Literatur* (October 1933), 553.

41. Hermann Stehr, *Der Heiligenhof* (Berlin, 1919), II, 262.

42. Hermann Stehr, *Sein Werk und seine Welt*, 59, 60; Willibald Köhler, *Hermann Stehr* (Schweidnitz, 1927), 101.

43. *Hermann Stehr–Walther Rathenau. Zwiesprache über den Zeiten*, ed. Ursula Meridies-Stehr (Leipzig and Munich, 1946).

44. Hermann Stehr, *Mein Leben* (Berlin, 1934), 35; ibid., *Gesammelte Werke* (Trier, 1924) III, 94.

45. Köhler, *op. cit.*, 67.

46. Stehr, *Mein Leben*, 37.

47. Certainly about Kolbenheyer. *Sebastian Karst über sein Leben und seine Zeit*, III, 162–163.

48. Heinz Hertl, *Das Dritte Reich in der Geistesgeschichte* (Hamburg, 1934), 14–16, 30.

49. *Die Bücherkunde* (February 1938), 99.

50. Franz Schauwecker in Fritz Büchner, *Was ist das Reich?* (Oldenburg, 1932), 47, 50.

51. *Paul Ernst in St. Georgen. Briefe und Berichte ars den Jahren 1925 bis 1933*, ed. Karl August Kutzbach (Göttingen, 1966), 49. Ernst turned to Hitler's friend and mentor Dietrich Eckart and asked him to publish the *Kaiserbuch* when no other publisher wanted it. But Eckart refused regretfully, saying he was too busy with lawsuits he had started or that were directed against him. *Die Neue Literatur* (August 1935), 457.

52. Georg Lukacs, Paul Ernst. Zu seinem 50. Geburtstag. in *Der Wille zur Form* (1963), No. 9, 385.

53. Georg Lukacs to Paul Ernst, March 12, 1926, in *Paul Ernst in St. Georgen*, 48; ibid., January 29, 1926, 43.

54. *Der wille zur Form*, 390, 392.

55. *Paul Ernst in St. Georgen*, 44.

56. Paul Ernst, "Das tragische Königsideal," in *Die neue Literatur* (February 1935), 65.

57. Paul Ernst, *Das Kaiserbuch* (Munich, 1928), II, 400.

58. Paul Ernst, "Vorwort zum Kaiserbuch," in *Ein Credo* (Munich, 1935), 51.

59. *Paul Ernst in St. Georgen*, 185.

60. Heinrich Anacker, *Die Fanfare. Gedichte der deutschen Erhebung* (Munich, 1936), 116.

61. Gerhard Schumann.

62. Anacker, *Die Fanfare*, 116.

63. Moeller van den Bruck, 243.

64. *Ibid.*, 244.

65. *Ibid.*, 231.

66. Hans-Joachim Schwierskott, *Arthur Moeller van den Bruck* (Göttingen, 1962), 105.

67. See especially Uwe Lars Nobbe, *Rufer des Reiches* (Potsdam, 1935), 71.

68. Zitiert in Ernst Loewy, *Literatur unterm Hakenkreuz* (Frankfurt-am-Main, 1969), 192–193.

69. Will Vesper, *Das harte Geschlecht* (Hamburg, 1931), 5; Herbert A. Frenzel, *Eberhard Wolfgang Möller* (Munich, 1938), 31.
70. Will-Erich Peuckert, *Die grosse Wende* (Hamburg, 1948), 647–649.
71. Hermann Burte, *Wiltfeber, der ewige Deutsche* (Leipzig, 1921), 342.

5. *The Poet and the Exercise of*
Political Power: Gabriele D'Annunzio

1. Sonnet: "Milton! Thou shouldst be living at this hour" in *The Oxford Book of English Verse*, ed. Sir Arthur Quiller-Couch (Oxford, 1939), 617. Two books, above all, extend the analysis of this paper, though they are not specifically concerned with the role of the poet in politics. Michael Ledeen, *The First Duce, D'Annunzio at Fiume* (Baltimore, 1977), excellently puts the political drama in its larger setting, while Renzo De Felice, *D'Annunzio Politico 1918–1938* (Rome, 1978), is the best and most authoritative analysis of his political career and importance.
2. See Essay 6.
3. Ernst Moritz Arndt, *Entwurf einer teutschen Gesellschaft* (Frankfurt-am-Main, 1814), 35–40.
4. Gabriele D'Annunzio, *L'Enfant de volupté* (Paris, 1971), 28 (originally published 1887).
5. J. Huizinga, *The Waning of the Middle Ages* (London, 1924), 186.
6. Quoted in René Gérard, *L'Orient et la pensée romantique allemande* (Nancy, 1963), 170.
7. Allan Mitchell, *Revolution in Bavaria 1918–1919* (Princeton, 1965), 113.
8. Gabriele D'Annunzio, *Die Gloria* (Berlin, 1933), 58, copy from Theodor Herzl's library, Jerusalem, with annotations.
9. Philippe Julian, *D'Annunzio* (Paris, 1971), 56.
10. Gabriele D'Annunzio, *The Flame of Life* (New York, 1900), 12.
11. *Ibid.*, 116 ff, III.
12. *Ibid.*, 126.
13. See Karl Hoffmann, *Des Teutschen Volkes Feuriger Dank und Ehrentempel* (Offenbach, 1915).
14. D'Annunzio, *The Flame of Life*, 74, 75, 90, 296–297.
15. *Ibid.*, 74.
16. See George L. Mosse, *Germans and Jews* (New York, 1970), Chap. VI.
17. Ferdinando Cordova, *Arditi e Legionari Dannunziani* (Padua, 1969), 17.
18. Ferdinando Gerra, *L'Impressa di Fiume* (Milano, 1966), 58.
19. Title page of the *Contemplation of Death* (1917), cited by Julian, *op. cit.*, 134.
20. Christopher Hibbert, *Benito Mussolini* (London, 1969), 60.
21. Renzo De Felice, *Mussolini il fascista*, Vol. I. *L'Organisazione dello stato fascista 1925–1929* (Rome, 1968), 358 n. 2; *Mussolinis Gespräche mit Emil Ludwig* (Berlin, 1932), 70; *Dizionario Mussoliniano* (Milan, 1942), 32. In fact, as early as 1913 Mussolini discounted the importance of religious ritual—Benito Mussolini, *Giovanni Huss il Veridico* (Rome, 1948, first published 1913), 21–22.

22. De Felice, *op. cit.*, 298; there is apparently no trace of Le Bon's influence in D'Annunzio. Le Bon inspired Hitler as well.

23. D'Annunzio, *The Flame of Life*, 124–125. (These words are actually spoken by Stelio Effrena.)

24. *Ibid.*, 206–207. During his journey to Italy, Goethe described the amphitheater at Verona as forming the masses within it into a unity: taking on one form and one spirit—*Italienische Reise* (Munich, 1961), 27–28.

25. D'Annunzio, *L'Enfant de Volupté*, 46.

26. See Friedrich Theodor Vischer, *Aesthetic or the Science of the Beautiful*, a crucial work written in 1846–57.

27. For a discussion of authoritarian rule and literary form, see Mosse, *Germans and Jews*, 158.

28. D'Annunzio, *Enfant de Volupté*, 27.

29. D'Annunzio, *The Flame of Life*, 33; *Die Gloria*, 30.

30. Speech of August 1920, Gabriele D'Annunzio, *Italia e Vita* (Rome, 1920), 64–65.

31. Gabriele D'Annunzio, *Textes Inédits, versions nouvelles souvenirs et essais*, ed. Henri Bedarida (Geneva, 1942), 170–172.

32. *The Complete Diaries of Theodor Herzl*, ed. Raphael Patai, trans. Harry Zohn, Vol. I (New York, 1960), 27. Herzl was also preoccupied with light: a "nation in flames." He connected this somewhat artificially to the Jewish Menorah, "Die Menorah," *Ost und West*, Heft 8–9, IV Jahrg. (August–September 1906), 517–522.

33. D'Annunzio, *Italia e Vita*, 83–94; Gerra, *op. cit.*, 375–377. Leone Kochnitzki, *La Quinta Stagione o I centauri di Fiume* (Bologna, 1922), 24.

34. Ursula Kirchhoff, *Die Darstellung des Festes im Roman um 1900* (Münster, 1968), 7.

35. Renzo De Felice, *Sindicalismo rivoluzionario e fiumanesimo nel carteggio De Ambris–D'Annunzio* (Brescia, 1966), 191–192. Letter of May 30, 1920. Gerra, *op. cit.*, 375–377.

36. Gerra, *op. cit.*, 57, 179, 58.

37. *Ibid.*, 45; D'Annunzio, *The Flame of Life*, 33.

38. Julian, *op. cit.*, 142, 272. The "alala" was also borrowed by Mussolini; Benito Mussolini, *Messagi e Proclami* (Milan, 1929), 29, 34, 62, 73, 77.

39. Gerra, *op. cit.*, 313; Tom Antongini, *D'Annunzio* (London, 1938), 383.

40. Guglielmo Gatti, *Vita di Gabriele D'Annunzio* (Florence, 1958), 350.

41. *Ibid.*, 371.

42. Cordova, *op. cit.*, 103.

43. Gerra, *op. cit.*, 461, 466, 467. De Felice, *Sindicalismo revioluzionario e fiumanesimo nel carteggio De Ambris–D'Annunzio*, 90.

44. Gerra, *op. cit.*, 631.

45. *Ibid.*, 646.

46. Cordova, *op. cit.*, 156.

47. *Ibid.*, 155.

48. *Ibid.*, 146; see especially the remarks on this by Renzo De Felice, *Car-*

teggio D'Annunzio–Mussolini (Milan, 1971), xxviii–xxix; for Mussolini's manipulations against D'Annunzio, see Renzo De Felice, *Mussolini il Fascista*, Vol. I, *La Conquista del Potere 1921–1925*. (Turin, 1966), 65–74.

49. Cordova, *op. cit.*, 132.

50. Camillo Pelizzi, quoted in Mosse, *Germans and Jews*, 160. For other such views, see especially, Michael Ledeen, *Universal Fascism* (New York, 1972).

51. Kurt Pinthus, "Rede fur die Zukunft," *Die Erhebung*, Vol. 1 (1919), 412, 413.

52. Kurt Eisner, *Taggeist* (Berlin, 1901), 44.

53. *Ibid.*, 20, 21; Kurt Eisner, *Feste der Festlosen* (Dresden, 1905?), 255.

54. See *Die Erhebung*, Vol. 1 (1919), 351.

55. Conversation with Albert Speer, March 16, 1972.

56. Robert Brasillach, *Léon Degrelle* (Paris, 1936), 78.

57. William R. Tucker, "Politics and Aesthetics: The Fascism of Robert Brasillach," *The Western Political Quarterly*, XV (1962), 606.

6. Caesarism, Circuses, and Monuments

1. Theodor Mommsen, *Römische Geschichte* (Berlin, 1909), III, 466–471.

2. Cf. Carl von Rotteck (1826), cited in Robert Michels, *Political Parties* (New York, 1962), 47, n. 4.

3. Michels, *op. cit.*, 50.

4. Friedrich Gundolf, *Caesar* (Berlin, 1924); *Caesar in der Deutschen Literatur* (Berlin, 1904); *Caesar in Neunzehnten Jahrhundert* (Berlin, 1926).

5. George Gottfried Gervinus, *Einleitung in die Geschichte des neunzehnten Jahrhunderts* (Frankfurt-am-Main, 1967), 162.

6. Cf. Michael D. Biddiss, *Father of Racist Ideology* (London, 1970), 171.

7. P. J. Proudhon, *Césarisme et christianisme* (Paris, 1883), I, 31, 40.

8. Charles Maurras, *Dictator and King* (1899), quoted in *The French Right from de Maistre to Maurras*, ed. J. S. McClelland (London, 1970), 237.

9. Cf. David Dowd, *Pageant-Master of the Republic, Jacques-Louis David and the French Revolution* (Lincoln, Nebraska, 1948), especially 81–2; Alphonse Aulard, *Christianity and the French Revolution* (New York, 1966).

10. Wilhelm Spohr, *Kultur der Feste* (Munich, 1926), 6.

11. Friedrich Ludwig Jahn, *Deutsches Volkstum* (Leipzig, n.d.), 197, 202; Claude Ruggieri, *Précis Historique sur les Fêtes, les Spectacles et les Réjouissances Publiques* (Paris, 1830), 42, 76.

12. G. Bonet-Maury, *De la Signification Morale et Réligieuse de Fêtes Publiques dans les Républiques Modernes* (Dole, 1896), 3, 26.

13. Martin Paezold, *Sedan Feier* (Gotha, 1908), *passim*; Paul Déroulède, *L'Alsace Lorraine et la Fête Nationale* (Paris, 1910), 26.

14. *Deutsche Nationalfeste, Schriften und Mitteilungen des Ausschusses* (Berlin, 1897–98), 9, 12, 15, 47, 123, 153, 221, 222.

15. A. Soboul, *Paysans, Sansculottes et Jacobins* (Paris, 1966), 197.

16. Spohr, *op. cit.*, 10.

17. Charles Péguy, "Notre Jeunesse," in *Oeuvres Complètes de Charles Péguy* (Paris, 1916), IV, 45.

18. *Der Schulungsbrief*, 1939, 4.

19. Georges Sorel, *Reflections on Violence* (New York, 1950), 78, 209.

20. C. Bessonnet-Faure, *Les Fêtes Républicaines depuis 1789 jusqu'à nos Jours* (Paris, n.d.), 6, 266–270. This book was written some time between 1900 and 1914.

21. *Der Schulungsbrief*, 1934, 16.

22. Quoted in J. L. Talmon, *Political Messianism* (London, 1960), 66.

23. Thomas Nipperdey, "Nationalidee und Nationaldenkmal in Deutschland im 19. Jahrhundert," *Historische Zeitschrift* (June 1968), 559, 576.

24. *Das Nationaldenkmal auf dem Niederwald* (Frankfurt-am-Main, n.d.), *passim*. For earlier attempts to build national monuments, especially the Valhalla of Ludwig I of Bavaria, see Franz Schnabel, *Abhandlungen und Vorträge* (Freiburg, 1970), 134–150.

25. Herman Schmidt, *Ernst von Bandel: ein deutscher Mann und Künstler* (Hanover, 1892), 160, 181, 351; Karl Meier-Lengo, "Das Hermannsdenkmal und sein Schöpfer," *Monatsblätter der Bergstadt* (1924), 5, 353; Nipperdey, *op. cit.*, 570.

26. *Ibid.*, 577–579.

27. Gustave Le Bon, *The Crowd* (New York, 1960), 118.

28. Paul Cornu, *Jules Dalou* (Paris, 1909), 239.

29. *Ibid.*, 230, 242.

30. Maurice Dreyfous, *Dalou, sa Vie et son Oeuvre* (Paris, 1903), 209, 249.

31. Oswald Spengler, *The Decline of the West* (New York, 1926), II, 432.

32. Spengler, *op. cit.*, 464; Meier-Lengo, *op. cit.*, 333.

33. Franz Schonauer, *Stefan George in Selbstzeugnissen und Bilddokumenten* (Hamburg, 1960), 97, 128.

34. *Ibid.*, 66, 102; Friedrich Gundolf, *Caesar im Neunzehnten Jahrhundert* (Berlin, 1926), 56, 64–65; Friedrich Gundolf, *Caesar* (Berlin, 1924), 265.

35. Friedrich Gundolf, *Caesar im Neunzehnten Jahrhundert*, 44, 88.

36. Ernst Kantorowicz, *Kaiser Friedrich der Zweite* (Berlin, 1927).

7. The French Right and the Working Classes: Les Jaunes

1. Arno J. Mayer, *Dynamics of Counterrevolution in Europe* (New York, 1971), 119.

2. See Hans Rogger and Eugen Weber, eds., *The European Right* (London, 1965).

3. Eugen Weber, "Nationalism, Socialism, and National-Socialism in France," *French Historical Studies*, Spring 1962.

4. Israel Schapira, *Der Antisemitismus in der Französischen Literatur: Éduard Drumont und seine Quellen* (Berlin, 1927), 55.

5. *Éduard Drumont ou L'Anticapitalisme National*, ed. E. Beau de Loménie (Paris, 1968), 108.

6. Éduard Drumont, *La Fin d'un Monde* (Paris, 1889), 122, 125; Edmund Sil-

berner, *Sozialisten zur Judenfrage* (Berlin, 1962), 67–70. Drumont's popularity is borne out by Caroline Rémy (Séverine), hardly a friend of his. Hermann Bahr, *Der Antisemitismus* (Berlin, 1894), 151.

7. *Éduard Drumont ou L'Anticapitalisme National*, 357 ff.

8. C. Stewart Doty, "Parliamentary Boulangism after 1889," *The Historian*, February 1970; Jacques Néré, "La Crise industrielle de 1882 et le Mouvement Boulangiste," doctoral dissertation, University of Paris, 1958. For socialists in the Boulangist movement, see especially Patrick H. Hutton, "Popular Boulangism and the Advent of Mass Politics in France," *Journal of Contemporary History*, XI (January 1970), 85–107.

9. Doty, *op. cit.*, 269.

10. Archives de la Préfecture de Police (Quai des Orfèvres), cited hereafter as APP, Report, 27 May 1892, Ba/1108, and General Report on the League, 27 May 1892, Ba/1107. The number of the documents is given when possible; when it is missing the date of the Report by the Sûreté.

11. APP, Report, 23 January 1898, Ba/1107; Archive Nationale, cited hereafter as AN, Report, 24 February 1899, F7/12459.

12. APP, Reports, 22 February 1890, Ba/1107; 22 February 1892, 27 May 1892, Ba/1107; June 1900, Ba/1108.

13. Éduard Drumont, *La France Juive devant l'opinion* (Paris, 1886), 69, 285.

14. For Méry's life see APP, Report, 28 May 1899, Ba/1181.

15. APP, Reports, 25 November 1895, Ba/1181; 27 November 1895, Ba/1515. On the co-operative glass factory, see Harvey Goldberg, *The Life of Jean Jaurès* (Madison, Wis., 1962), 146 ff.

16. APP, Speech of 19 September 1895, Ba/1181; Report, 21 May 1894, Ba/61.

17. APP, Report, 18 November 1892, Ba/1193.

18. APP, Report, 28 November 1891, Cochers grévistes de l'urbaine, Ba/1193.

19. For Morès and anarchists, see APP, Reports, 31 December 1892, Ba/1193; 14 October 1892, Ba/1192; 9 July 1892, Ba/1250. The police found it incredible that anarchist building workers consulted Morès about a demonstration, but their agents confirmed it. The journal he was going to finance was *La Tribune ouvrière*.

20. See Steven S. Schwarzschild, "The Marquis de Morès," *Jewish Social Studies*, January 1960.

21. Cf. Alan B. Spitzer, *The Revolutionary Theories of Louis Auguste Blanqui* (New York, 1967), 22, 81.

22. APP, Ba/885; for Ernest Roche, Ba/869; for these Blanquists, see Charles da Costa, *Les Blanquistes* (Paris, 1912), *passim*. It is typical that while at Rochefort's funeral in 1913 the Ligue des patriotes was represented together with Blanquists, no representative of the Action Française was present. It stood apart from National Socialist circles—APP, Report, 7 July 1913, Ba/252.

23. AN, F7/12793, excerpt from *L'Union ouvrière*, 4 January 1902.

24. Pamphlet, n.d., about a meeting of *Les Jaunes* in Espinal (Paris, Institut Français d'Histoire Sociale).

25. "Origine du Jaune," Report of August 1906, NA, F7/12793.

26. "Conférence par Jules Lemaître," *La Patrie Française*, 19 January 1899, 19, 20.

27. Origine des Jaunes, NA, F7/12793. For agricultural unions, see H. de Gailhard-Blancel, *Quinze années d'action syndicale* (Paris, 1900). Gailhard-Blancel, the moving spirit behind these unions, attended the 1905 congress of Les Jaunes. Xavier Vallat, later commissioner for the Jewish question in Vichy France, was close to Gailhard-Blancel and admired his unions; *La Croix, Les Lys et la Peine des Hommes* (Paris, 1960), 184, 295.

28. Auguste Pawlowski, *Les Syndicats Jaunes* (Paris, 1911), 45; AN, Report, 22 January 1902, F7/12793.

29. Pierre Biétry, *Les Jaunes de France et la question ouvrière* (Paris, n.d. 1907–1908?), *passim;* Pawlowski, *op. cit.*, 116–118.

30. Biétry claimed a membership of 98,000 adherents in February 1902. Report, 10 March 1902, AN, F7/12793.

31. AN, F7/12883, 3/83 (the sum was 200 francs).

32. See AN, F7/12870 1/10; APP, Report, 2 June 1908, Ba/1033. For Déroulède, see Zeev Sternhell, "Déroulède and the Origins of Modern French Nationalism," *Journal of Contemporary History*, October 1971.

33. AN, F7/12793, 242; Eugen Weber, *Action Française* (Stanford, Calif., 1962), 68–70.

34. Drumont, *Concours de la Libre Parole sur la Question Juive* (Paris, 1897), 26.

35. *Le Jaune*, 17 December 1904; *Libre Parole*, 12, 14 April 1905, 17 July 1906; Fédération anti-Juive, NA, F7/12459.

36. NA, F7/12793, from *L'Union ouvrière*, January 1902, edited by Lenoir; F7/12883, 4/135; *Le Jaune*, 8 July 1904.

37. Pictures and text from 1898 in APP, Ba/1341.

38. Drumont, *La fin d'un monde*, 128.

39. The program of *Les Jaunes*, AN, F7/12793; Zeev Sternhell, "Barrès et la gauche: du boulangisme à la cocarde," *Le Mouvement Social*, April–June 1971, 96; now see also his discussion of *Les Jaunes* in his *La Droite Révolutionnaire 1885–1914* (Paris, 1978); *Le Jaune*, August 1909, in NA, F7/12793.

40. Report, L'Union ouvrière, 22–29 February 1902, NA, F7/12793.

41. Biétry, *Les Jaunes de France*, 72–81.

42. For lists of local unions, see NA, F7/12793 264, 368, 375, 438, 464; APP, Collection of newspaper clippings, Ba/1351; *Le Jaune*, 15 October 1904. Among the miners in Carmaux *Les Jaunes* were nearly as strong as the "red" unions. Roland Trempé, *Les Mineurs de Carmaux* (Paris, 1971).

43. R. Michels, *Psychologie der antikapitalistischen Massenbewegungen* (Tübingen, 1926), 299.

44. Pawlowski, *op. cit.*, 42–49.

45. Robert Brécy, *Le Mouvement Syndical en France 1871–1921* (Paris, 1963), 13. He may simply have taken the figure from Pawlowski.

46. Report, August 1906, NA, F7/12793.

47. *Le Jaune*, 20 February, 15 October 1904; 9 June 1905.

48. AN, F7/12739, 472, 473; F7/12717; *Le Jaune*, 22 March 1909; Trempé, *op. cit.*, II, 928.

49. *Le Jaune*, 9, 16 October 1909; Biétry, Foreword to *Les cahiers de l'ouvrier* (n.d.), published by *Le Jaune*.

50. *Le Jaune*, 6 February 1909; they joined with the *Camelots du Roi* of the Action Française.

51. Report on Fédération Nationale anti-Juive, AN, F7/12883, 4/135.

52. Pawlowski, *op. cit.*, 51.

53. *Le Jaune*, 17 December 1904; Reports of 28 September, 6 October, 14 November 1906, AN, F7/12793, 73, 76; AN, F7/12883, 4/135; Drumont, *La fin d'un monde*, 110, 116, 220.

54. AN, F7/12793, 479; Drumont, *La fin d'un monde*, 190. Drumont, *Sur le Chemin de la Vie* (Paris, 1914), 185–209, where he praises the archbishops of Paris and the Jesuits (his delusions of conspiracy were selective: Jews and Freemasons, but not Jesuits).

55. As the police often claimed, AN, F7/12883, 4/135; Report, 14 November 1906, F7/12793.

56. Cf. Trempé, *op. cit.*, II, 764, 812. *Les Jaunes* were succeeded by the *Syndicats Libres* which, founded in 1910, continued into postwar France. They never had much of a following. Brécy, *op. cit.*, 13–14.

57. Rudolf Lebius, *Die Gelbe Arbeiterbewegung* (Berlin, 1908), 6; Anon., *Die Gelben: mit besonderer Berücksichtigung der Gelben in Frankreich* (Cologne, 1907), 16.

58. Rudolf Lebius, *Gelbe Gedanken* (Berlin, 1908), 60, 62; Lebius was a full-time employee of the *Gelben*; Paul Umbreit, *Der Stand der Gelben Organizationen in Deutschland* (Berlin, 1908), 24, 32, 54; *Le Jaune*, 20 February 1909.

59. *Le Jaune*, 20 February 1909; Pawlowski, *op. cit.*, 119, 138, 146.

8. The Heritage of Socialist Humanism

1. Alfred Kantorowicz, *Deutsche Schicksale* (Vienna, 1964), 153. The most helpful discussions of literature in exile for my purposes are Matthias Wegner, *Exil und Literatur* (Frankfurt, 1967) and Hans-Albert Walter, "Literatur im Exil" (mimeographed MS, Suddeutscher Rundfunk, April 3, 1964).

2. Heinrich Mann, *Der Untertan* (Leipzig, 1918), 490.

3. George L. Mosse, "Left-Wing Intellectuals and the Weimar Republic," *Germans and Jews* (New York, 1970) discusses this group up to 1933.

4. Leonhard Frank, *Links ist wo das Herz ist* (Munich, 1952), 66.

5. Quoted in *Lion Feuchtwanger*, ed. Kollektiv fuer Literaturgeschichte (Berlin, 1960), 12.

6. Heinrich Mann, *Diktatur der Vernunft* (Berlin, 1923), *passim*.

7. Lion Feuchtwanger, *The Oppermanns* (London, 1933), 384.

8. Frank, *op. cit.*, 182.

9. *Tagebuch*, II, Jahrg. Heft 27 (July 5, 1930), 1069–1070.

10. *Das Neue Tagebuch*, I, Jahrg. (July 1, 1933), 3.

11. Franz Neumann, *Behemoth* (New York & London, 1942), 464 ff, also for the discussion that follows.

12. *Der Nationalsozialismus* (three articles of the *Tagebuch*) (n.p., 1930), 5, 15.

13. Franz Neumann, *Demokratischer und autoritärer Staat*, ed. Helge Pross (Vienna, 1967), 17, 100 ff. See also H. Stuart Hughes, "Franz Neumann Between Marxism and Democracy," *Perspectives in American History*, vol. II (1968), 446–462. It may have been Neumann's dedication to "unmasking" reality that made him badly underestimate the power of ideology and myth in modern mass movements like Nazism.

14. *Die Neue Weltbühne*, 2 Halbjahr (1933), 1154, 1560.

15. Feuchtwanger, *The Oppermanns*, 382.

16. Alfred Döblin, *Schicksalsreise* (Frankfurt, 1949), 165.

17. I.e., Roland Links, *Alfred Döblin* (Berlin, 1965), 87, 101.

18. Alfred Döblin, *Flucht und sammlung des Judenvolkes* (Amsterdam, 1935), 130, 126, 125.

19. Alfred Döblin, *Jüdische Erneuerung* (Amsterdam, 1933), 45, 86, 87.

20. Döblin, *Schicksalsreise*, 359, 360.

21. *Die Weltbühne*, 28 Jahrg. No. 9 (1932), *passim*.

22. Lion Feuchtwanger, Arnold Zweig, *Die Aufgabe des Judentums* (Paris, 1933), 27 ff.

23. Quoted in Jurgen Rühle, *Literatur und Revolution* (Cologne and Berlin, 1960), 211.

24. Feuchtwanger, *The Oppermanns*, 354, 383.

25. *Ibid.*, 141.

26. Lion Feuchtwanger, *Moskau 1937* (Amsterdam, 1937), 8, 48, 105, 9.

27. Quoted in Wegner, *Exil und Literatur*, 209.

28. Lion Feuchtwanger, "Introductory Remarks" before start of the book, *Proud Destiny* (New York, 1947), The English translation of *Waffen für Amerika*.

29. I.e., Klaus Jarmatz, *Literatur im Exil* (Berlin, 1966), *passim*.

30. Heinrich Mann in *Pariser Tageblatt*, No. 684, 3 Jahrg. (October 27, 1935), 3.

31. Leonhard Frank, *Links ist wo das Herz ist* (Munich, 1952), 228–229.

32. Kantorowicz, *op. cit.*, 169. For a discussion of these "soviets," see Mosse, *op. cit.*

33. Links, *op. cit.*, 103.

34. Mann, *Dikatur der Vernunft*, *passim*.

35. See Emilio Lussu, *Sul Partito d'Azione e gli altri* (Milan, 1968), 40.

9. Toward a General Theory of Fascism

1. The best recent discussion of fascism and totalitarian doctrine is Karl Dietrich Bracher, *Zeitgeschichtliche Kontroversen, um Faschismus, Totalitarismus, Demokratie* (Munich, 1976).

2. Aryeh L. Unger, *The Totalitarian Party, Party and People in Nazi Germany and Soviet Russia* (Cambridge, 1974), 189, 202.

3. *Ibid.*, 1, 264.

4. Cf. George L. Mosse, ed., *Police Forces in History* (London and Beverly Hills, 1975).

5. See J. L. Talmon, *The Rise of Totalitarian Democracy* (Boston, 1952); and the criticism in Peter Gay, *The Party of Humanity* (New York, 1964), 179–181.

6. Mona Ozouf, *La Fête révolutionnaire 1789–1799* (Paris, 1976), 22.

7. For a more thorough discussion of the point, see George L. Mosse, *The Nationalization of the Masses* (New York, 1975), and thē unjustly forgotten Harold J. Laski, *Reflections on the Revolution of Our Time* (New York, 1943), not for his analysis of fascism but for the weakness of parliamentary government.

8. The term "good revolution" is Karl Dietrich Bracher's, *op. cit.*, 68.

9. Renzo De Felice, *Fascism* (New Brunswick, N.J., 1976), 24.

10. Zeev Sternhell, *La Droite révolutionnaire 1885–1914* (Paris, 1978); George L. Mosse, *Towards the Final Solution, a History of European Racism* (London and New York, 1978), Chapter 10.

11. Renzo De Felice, *Mussolini il rivoluzionario* (Turin, 1965), 591; Paolo Nello, *L'Avanguardismo Giovannile alle origini del fascismo* (Rome, 1978), 26–27.

12. George L. Mosse, *Germans and Jews, The Right, the Left, and the Search for a "Third Force" in Pre-Nazi Germany* (New York, 1970), Chapter 1.

13. See Essay 4, Death, Time, and History.

14. Otto-Ernst Schüddekopf, *Linke Leute von Rechts* (Stuttgart, 1960), 84.

15. Joseph Goebbels, *Tagebücher 1945* (Hamburg, 1976), 55, 69–70.

16. Ernst Bloch, *Thomas Münzer als Theologe der Revolution* (Munich, 1921), 295.

17. Victor Klemperer, LTI; *Notizbuch eines Philologen* (Berlin, 1947), 116–118.

18. Clarke Garrett, *Respectable Folly, Millenarians and the French Revolution in France and England* (Baltimore, 1975), 8.

19. Paolo Nello, review of Daniele Marchesini, "La scuola dei gerarchi," *Storia contemporanea* (September 1977), 586.

20. Quoted in George L. Mosse, ed., *Nazi Culture* (New York, 1966), 116.

21. Giuseppe Bottai, *Il Fascismo e l'Italia Nuova* (Rome, 1923), 19.

22. Horia Sima, *Destinée du Nationalisme* (Paris, n.d.), 19.

23. These qualities are taken from *Voor Volk en Vaderland, De Strijd der Nationaalsocialistische Bewegung 14. December 1931–Mei 1941*, ed. C. Van Geelkerken (n.p., 1941), 315.

24. The remarks on World War I are taken from George L. Mosse, "National Cemeteries and National Revival: The Cult of the Fallen Soldiers in Germany," *Journal of Contemporary History* (January 1979).

25. Antoine Prost, *Les Anciens Combattants et la Société Française*, 3 vols. (Paris, 1978).

26. See George L. Mosse, "La sinistra europea e l'esperienza della guerra," *Rivoluzione e Reazione in Europa* (1917–1924), Convegno storico internazionale—Perugia, 1978 (Florence, 1978), Vol. II, 151–167.

27. Mussolini quoted in Umberto Silva, *Kunst und Ideologie des Faschismus* (Frankfurt-am-Main, 1975), 108. For Hitler, see *Die Fahne Hoch!* (1932), 14.

28. Alfred Steinitzer and Wilhelm Michel, *Der Krieg in Bildern* (Munich, 1922), 97; *Der Weltkrieg im Bild* (Berlin-Oldenburg, 1926), Preface.

29. Goebbels, *op. cit.*, 28.

30. Teresa Maria Mazzatosta, "Educazione e scuola nella Repubblica Sociale Italiana," *Storia contemporanea* (February 1978), 67.

31. Peter Hasubeck, *Das Deutsche Lesebuch in der Zeit des Nationalsozialismus* (Hanover, 1972), 77, 79.

32. Ernst Jünger, ed., *Das Antlitz des Weltkrieges* (Berlin, 1930), Preface.

33. Oldo Marinelli, quoted in Emilio Gentile, *Le Origini del' Ideologia Fascista* (Rome, 1974), 92.

34. Ruggero Zangrandi, *Il lungo viaggio* (Milan, 1948); for a recent discussion of this revolt of youth, see Michael Ledeen, *Universal Fascism* (New York, 1972).

35. Drieu La Rochelle, *Socialisme Fasciste* (Paris, 1943), 72.

36. For Hans Naumann's speech, see Hildegard Brenner, *Die Kunstpolitik des Nationalsozialismus* (Hamburg, 1963), 188; Bottai, *op. cit.*, 18 ff; and Jean Denis, *Principes Rexistes* (Brussels, 1936), 17.

37. Hugh Seton-Watson, *Nations and States* (Boulder, Colo., 1977), 420, 421.

38. Charles S. Maier, "Some Recent Studies of Fascism," *Journal of Modern History* (September 1976), 509; and Thomas Childers, "The Social Bases of the National Socialist Vote," in *International Fascism*, ed. George L. Mosse (London, 1979), 161–189.

39. Renzo De Felice, *Fascism* (New Brunswick, N.J., 1976), 46.

40. Gilbert D. Allardyce, "The Political Transition of Jacques Doriot," in *International Fascism*, ed. Mosse, 287.

41. Henry A. Turner, Jr., "Big Business and the Rise of Hitler," in *Nazism and the Third Reich*, ed. Henry A. Turner, Jr. (New York, 1972), 93.

42. Mosse, *Nazi Culture*, 2.

43. See Essays 2 and 3.

44. A list of popular novels under fascism will be found in Carlo Bordoni, *Cultura e propaganda nell'Italia fascista* (Messina-Florence, 1974), 85, but without any analysis of their individual content.

45. *Storia d'Italia*, ed. Ruggiero Romano and Corrado Viyanti (Turin, 1973), 1526; Mosse, *Nationalization of the Masses*, 194.

46. Francesco Sapori, *L'Arte e il Duce* (Milan, 1932), 141.

47. *Ibid.*, 123 ff.

48. Adrian Lyttleton, *The Seizure of Power, Fascism in Italy 1919–1929* (London, 1973), 389.

49. *Storia d'Italia*, 1525; Nello, *op. cit.*, 120.

50. Mosse, *The Nationalization of the Masses*, Chapter 7; unfortunately no detailed analysis of Italian fascist liturgy exists.

51. Anson G. Rabinbach, "The Aesthetics of Production in the Third Reich," *International Fascism*, ed. George L. Mosse (London, 1976), 189–223.

52. Lyttleton, *op. cit.*, 19.

53. Schkem Gremigni, *Duce d'Italia* (Milan, 1927), 116.

54. E.g., *Ausstellung der Faschistischen Revolution, erste Zehnjahrfeier des Mar-*

sches auf Rom (1933). Typically enough, the official poster for the exhibition featured soldiers from World War I.

55. Donino Roncará, *Saggi sull' Educazione Fascista* (Bologna, 1938), 61.

56. Ernst Jünger, *Der Kampf als inneres Erlebnis* (Berlin, 1933), 32 ff.

57. Hitler at the Reichsparteitag, 1935, *Adolf Hitler an seine Jugend* (Munich, 1940), n.p.

58. See Mosse, *Towards the Final Solution.*

59. De Felice, *Fascism*, 56.

60. Roncará, *op. cit.*, 55, 58.

61. *Esposizione Universale di Roma*, MCMXLII, XX E.F. (1942), 83, 88.

62. Giuseppe Bottia wrote that fascism was an intellectual revolution concerned with the problem of its origins—*Pagine di Critica Fascista (1915–1926)* (Florence, n.d.), 322.

63. *Führerblätter der Hitler-Jugend* Nr. (1935), 10.

64. *Lehrplan für Sechsmonatige Schulung* (SS, Hauptamt IV, n.d., n.p.), 25, 79.

65. Typically enough, the newsletter of a Nazi élite school repeated this phrase in Italian, commenting that these ideals werè shared by German and Italian youth—*Reichsschule der NSDAP Feldafing* (1940–41), 73.

66. *Ibid.* (1939–40), 17.

67. La Rochelle, *Socialisme Fasciste*, 72.

68. Charles Beuchat, "Le Quartier Latin aux temps du jeune Brasillach," *Hommages à Robert Brasillach* (Lausanne, 1965), 78.

69. Stanley G. Payne, "Fascism in Western Europe," in *Fascism: A Reader's Guide*, ed. Walter Laqueur (London, 1976), 303.

70. Sapori, *op. cit.*, 15 ff; Mosse, *Towards the Final Solution*, 42, 43.

71. *Rex*, 23 (September 1938); *De Daad*, 2 (September 1933).

72. *Je Suis Partout*, April 18, 1938.

73. Sebastian Haffner, *Anmerkungen zu Hitler* (Munich, 1978).

74. Mosse, *Nationalization of the Masses*, 12, 202.

75. De Felice, *Fascism*, 65.

76. Haffner, *op. cit.*, 154 ff.

77. See, e.g., Percy Ernst Schramm, *Hitler als militärischer Führer* (Frankfurt-am-Main, 1965).

10. The Mystical Origins of National Socialism

1. Cf. Joachim Besser, "Die Vorgeschichte des Nationalsozialismus im neuen Licht," *Die Pforte*, II, 21/22 (November 1950), 763–785. Cf. also Crane Brinton, "The National Socialists' Use of Nietzsche," *Journal of the History of Ideas* (1940), 131–150.

2. It is significant that one common tie among all those men was their frustration in being denied academic recognition. Schuler and List were kept at arm's length by the academic world whose company they sought, while Paul de Lagarde had to teach in a Gymnasium for twelve years before he finally obtained a chair at the University of Göttingen. Julius Langbehn failed to obtain an academic post despite repeated efforts. These experiences un-

doubtedly deepened their aversion to intellectualism and to what they called academic pedantry. Langbehn's *Rembrandt as Educator* is full of diatribes against the professors whose world outlook he opposed. Such men were part of what has been called the "academic proletariat." Langbehn eventually converted to Catholicism (1900). This is not mentioned in C. T. Carr, "Julius Langbehn—A Forerunner of National Socialism," *German Life and Letters*, III (1938–39), 45–54. For Paul de Lagarde, see Robert W. Lougee, *Paul de Lagarde* (Cambridge, Mass., 1962). There is no modern work on List or Schuler.

3. Julius Langbehn, *Rembrandt als Erzieher* (Leipzig, 1900), 8.

4. *Ibid.*, 82.

5. *Eugen Diederichs Leben und Werke*, ed. Lulu von Strauss and Torney-Diederichs (Jena, 1936), 180.

6. *Ibid.*, 82.

7. *Freideutsche Jugend: Zur Jahrhundertfeier auf dem Hohen Meissner* (Jena, 1913), 98 ff.

8. Langbehn, *Rembrandt*, 131.

9. *The Life and Letters of Jacob Burckhardt*, trans. Alexander Dru (London, 1955), 225.

10. Langbehn, *Rembrandt*, 65.

11. R. Burger-Villingen, *Geheimnis der Menschenform* (Leipzig, 1912), 23, 27.

12. Langbehn, *Rembrandt*, 315.

13. *Eugen Diederichs*, 74, 452.

14. Quoted in the National Socialist article, Karl Friedrich Weiss, "Individualismus und Sozialismus," I, *Der Weltkampf*, IV (1927), 66–70.

15. *Paul de Lagarde, Lebensbild und Auswahl*, ed. K. Boesch (Augsburg, 1924), 52.

16. Johannes Baltzli, *Guido von List* (Vienna, 1917), 18, 23.

17. *Ibid.*, 26, 27.

18. Alfred Schuler, *Fragmente und Vorträge aus dem Nachlass*, ed. Ludwig Klages (Leipzig, 1940), 33, 159.

19. *Ibid.*, 51.

20. Claude David, *Stefan George* (Paris, 1952), 200.

21. Baltzli, *Guido von List*, 45; Alvin Boyd Kuhn, *Theosophy* (New York, 1930), 116–117.

22. Baltzli, *Guido von List*, 55n.; Kuhn, *Theosophy*, 144.

23. *Ibid.*, 135, 133.

24. Besser, "Die Vorgeschichte . . . ," 773.

25. Franz Hartmann, *The Life and Doctrines of Jacob Boehme* (Boston, 1891), 166 n. 1.

26. *Erste Gesamtausstellung der Werke von Fidus zu seinem 60. Geburtstage* (Woltersdorf bei Erkner, 1928), 9, 11.

27. *Eugen Diederichs*, 171, 220, 207.

28. *Ibid.*, 267.

29. Langbehn, *Rembrandt*, 93. "With a dose of mysticism one can gild the life of a nation" (203).

30. *Prana, Organ für angewandte Geisteswissenschaften*, VI, 1–2 (1915), 4.

31. *Ibid.*, 348–349. Nourishment and the development of the soul go hand in hand. Anti-alcoholism plays an important role here as well. At the Hohen Meissner gathering, the Temperance League said that it too wanted to serve the race—*Freideutsche Jugend*, 16; see also Langbehn, *Rembrandt*, 296–297.

32. Kuhn, *Theosophy*, 297; *Prana*, 46–47.

33. Arthur Dinter, *Die Sünde wider den Geist* (Leipzig, 1921), 236.

34. Besser, "Die Vorgeschichte . . . ," 773.

35. Baltzli, *Guido von List*, 185. His name was Friedrich Wannieck, and he contributed more to the List Society than all other members put together (79). Wannieck and Franz Hartmann had at least one séance together (185).

36. Langbehn, *Rembrandt*, 94–95. Blavatsky and G. R. S. Meade believed that "of all mystics, Swedenborg has certainly influenced Theosophy most . . . ," though his powers did not go beyond the plane of matter. H. P. Blavatski, *The Theosophical Glossary* (Hollywood, 1918), 293.

37. *Eugen Diederichs*, 15.

38. Baltzli, *Guido von List*, 155, 199.

39. Langbehn, *Rembrandt*, 130–131.

40. *Ibid.*, 158, 159.

41. H. F. K. Günther, *Rîtter, Tod und Teufel* (1920). Quoted in R. Walther Darré, *Das Bauernthum als Lebensquell der Nordischen Rasse* (Munich, 1937), 97. Darré was the National Socialist Minister of Agriculture.

42. Langbehn, *Rembrandt*, 5.

43. *Paul de Lagarde*, 96.

44. *Eugen Diederichs*, 351–352.

45. Langbehn, *Rembrandt*, 158, 160.

46. *Eugen Diederichs*, 72. On *Die Tat*, see Klemens von Klemperer, *Germany's New Conservatism* (Princeton, 1957), 97–100.

47. *Paul de Lagarde*, 64.

48. Langbehn, *Rembrandt*, 218–219.

49. Gerhard Heine, *Ferdinand Avenarius als Dichter* (Leipzig, 1904), 45.

50. Langbehn, *Rembrandt*, 113. Tudel Weller, *Rabauken! Peter Moenkemann haut sich durch* (Munich, 1938), 114; cf. George L. Mosse, "Culture, Civilization and German Anti-Semitism," *Judaism*, VII, 3 (Summer 1958), 256–267.

51. *Weltkampf*, IV (1927), 189.

52. Baltzli, *Guido von List*, 29; Klages in Schuler, *Fragmente*, 43.

53. *Paul de Lagarde*, 104.

54. Schuler, *Fragmente*, 163 ff.; Review of Guido von List, *Die Ursprache der Ario-Germanen und ihre Mysterien-Sprache* in *Prana*, VI, 11–12 (February–March 1916), 560.

55. Langbehn, *Rembrandt*, 353, *Eugen Diederichs*, 84–85.

56. Melanie Lehmann, *Verleger J. F. Lehmann; Ein Leben im Kampf für Deutschland* (Munich, 1935), 23 ff. Lehmann was intimately involved with the growth of the National Socialist Party in Munich.

57. Langbehn, *Rembrandt*, 326–327.

58. *Eugen Diederichs*, 73.

59. Langbehn, *Rembrandt*, 95.

60. Guido von List, *Die Namen der Völkerstaemme Germaniens und deren Deutung* (Leipzig, 1909), 4.

61. *Weltkampf*, IV (1927), 92.

62. Alfred Rosenberg, "Rebellion der Jungend," *Nationalsozialistiche Monatshefte*, Heft 2 (May 1930), 50 ff.

63. Hans Blüher, *Wandervögel, Geschichte einer Jugendbewegung* (Berlin, 1916), II, 83 ff. Blüher blamed Christianity for the degeneration of the romanticism of the *Wandervögel* (172).

64. Alfred Andreesen, *Hermann Lietz* (Munich, 1934), 101.

65. Hermann Lietz, *Deutsche Nationalerziehung* (Weimar, 1938), 123–124.

66. *Ibid.*, 114, 120; H. Lietz, *Lebenserinnerungen* (Weimar, 1935), 41, 47. Christ symbolized struggle (189).

67. For his developing attitude toward Jews, see Lietz, *Lebenserinnerungen*, 115. From 1909 on, only students of Aryan descent were admitted (161). On the Jewish spirit, see Lietz, *Deutsche Nationalerziehung*, 14.

68. *Lebenserinnerungen*, 194; Andreesen, *Hermann Lietz*, iii; for Lietz's own hymn on patriarchal society, see *Lebenserinnerungen*, 194.

69. Hermann Lietz, *Des Vaterlandes Not und Hoffnung* (Haubinda, 1934), 86.

70. *Ibid.*, 76. *Eugen Diederichs*, 64; Lehmann, *Verleger*, 38, 277. The close collaborator was Alfred Andreesen, from 1909 his deputy director at Bieberstein. Lietz, in his social-political confession of faith during the war, tells of his allegiance to the world view of German idealism—*Lebenserinnerungen*, 196. The schools were also represented on the Hohen Meissner in 1913 (*Freideutsche Jugend*, 18).

71. David, *Stefan George*, 208.

72. For the relationship of Strindberg and Lanz von Liebenfels, see Wilfried Daim, *Der Mann der Hitler Die Ideen Gab* (Munich, 1958), 92–99.

11. Nazi Polemical Theater:
The Kampfbühne

1. Gunther Rühle, *Zeit und Theater*, III, *Diktatur und Exil* (Berlin , n.d.), 27, 28.

2. Klau Vondung, *Magie und Manipulation* (Göttingen, 1971).

3. George L. Mosse, *The Nationalization of the Masses* (New York, 1975), 192.

4. Johann von Leers, quoted in Eugen Hadamovsky, *Propaganda and National Power* (New York, 1972), 175, 176; see also "Politisches Streitgesprach ist der Ausdruck Unseres Theaters," *Der Aufmarsch* (März, 1931), 8.

5. Ulrich Mayer, *Das Eindringen des Nationalsozialismus in die Stadt Wetzlar* (Wetzlar, 1970), 46.

6. See, e. g., *Der Junge Nationalsozialist* (September 1932), 12, 13; *Der Junge Sturmtrupp* (März, 1932), n.p.

7. This play is included in the *Eine Materialsammlung Vorgelegt vom Centralverein Deutscher Staatsburger Jüdischen Glaubens* (Berlin, 1932). This collection of documents was to be submitted to President von Hindenburg.

8. Adolf Gentsch, *Die Politische Struktur der Theaterführung* (Dresden, 1942), 303.

9. *Ibid.*, 307; *Illustrierter Beobachter* (1931), 21.
10. Gentsch, *op. cit.*, 305.
11. *Ibid.*, 308.
12. A. E. Frauenfeld, *Der Weg Zur Bühne* (Berlin, 1940), 33.
13. *Illustrierter Beobachter* (1927), 132.
14. *Ibid.*, 312.
15. *Ibid.*, (1930), 14.
16. *Ibid.*, 773.
17. *Ibid.*, 72.
18. *Ibid.*, 14.
19. *Ibid.*, (1931), 119.
20. *Ibid.*, (1930), 13, 14.
21. *Ibid.*, (1931), 321.
22. *Ibid.*, (1930), 211.
23. *Volkischer Beobachter*, 2 Beilage (October 6, 1932), n.p.
24. Richard Biedrzynski, *Schauspieler, Regisseure, Intendanten* (Heidelberg, 1944), 53.
25. Rühle, *op. cit.*, 778.
26. Eberhard Wolfgang Möller, *Rothschild siegt bei Waterloo* (Berlin, 1944), preface to the 4th edn., 11, 41, 124.
27. *Nationalsozialistische Monatshefte* (März, 1934), 109.
28. Erwin Piscator, *Das Proletarische Theater* (Berlin, 1929), 41, 243.
29. *Gott, Freiheit, Vaterland, Sprech-Chöre der Hitler-Jugend* (Stuttgart, n.d.), 7.
30. Mosse, *op. cit.*, 110.
31. Ernst Lenke, "Richard Elsner zu seinem 50. Geburtstage am 10, Juni, 1933," *Das Deutsche Drama* (1933), 9, 13.
32. Hans Brandenburg, *Das Theater und das Neue Deutschland; Ein Aufruf* (Jena, 1919), 36, 20, 11, 33; Mary Wigman, *Die Sprache Des Tanzes* (Stuttgart, 1964), 17.
33. Ernst Brandenburg, *Das Neue Theater* (Leipzig, 1926), 490.
34. *Ibid.*, 449.
35. Hans Brandenburg, "Der Weg zum Nationaltheater. Ein Zweigesprach," *Die Neue Literatur* (July 1936), 402.
36. Christian Jensen, "Hans Brandenburg, Volkhafter Deutscher Dichter," *Die Neue Literatur* (January 1936), 10–15.
37. Rudolf Mirbt, *Laienspiel und Laientheater* (Cassel, 1960), 15, 16.
38. Gerhard Rossbach, *Mein Weg Durch Die Zeit* (Weilburg-Lahn, 1950), 90–93.
39. These are listed and described in *Wille und Werk; Bühnenvolksbund Handbuch* (Berlin, 1928), 96–99.
40. There is unfortunately no investigation of the similarity and differences between plays staged by such organizations.
41. *Das Laienspiel, Erfahrungen, Grundsätze, Aufgaben* (Berlin, Arbeitsfront publication, n.d.), 11.
42. See Eugen Kurt Fischer, *Die Neue Vereinsbühne* (Munich, 1926?), 208.

43. *Das Volksspiel im NS Gemeinschaftsleben* (Munich, 1938), 19.

44. Christian Hermann Vosen, *Kolpings Gesellenverein in Seiner Sozialen Bedeutung* (Frankfurt-am-Main, 1866), 12.

45. *Ibid.*, 17, 18.

46. These and the following plays will be found bound together in the British Museum, London, catalogue number 11747 d. 5. (Familein und Vereinstheater) in Paderborn. They were published as *Kleines Theater.* I owe this reference to Sister Dr. Charlotte Klein.

47. See Adolf Kolping, "Gebet, und es wird euch gegeben," *Ausgewahlte Volkserzahlungen von Adolf Kolping* (Regensburg, 1932), VI, 33–85.

48. Gentsch, *op. cit.*, 53, 203; *Die Volksbühne* (July 1930), 119.

49. Gentsch, *op. cit.*, 206.

50. *Die Volkstümliche Bühne* (1918), 191; *ibid.*, 2 ff, 51.

51. George L. Mosse, *Germans and Jews* (New York, 1970), 50 ff.

52. *Die Volktümliche Buhne* (1918–19), 97 ff.

53. Demetrius Schrutz, *Handlexicon des Theaterspiels* (Munich, 1925), 40.

54. Gentsch, *op. cit.*, 204.

55. *Die Volksbühne* (February 1931), 482.

56. Gentsch, *op. cit.*, 55.

57. Gerschom Scholem, *Walter Benjamin—die Geschichte einer Freundschaft* (Frankfurt-am-Main, 1975), 220.

58. *Dramatiker der HJ, Sonderheft Zur Theaterwoche der Hitler-Jugend verbunden mit einer Reichstheatertagung der Hitler-Jugend*, Vol. II, April 18, 1937 (Bochum, n.d.), 26.

59. Rühle, *op. cit.*, 787.

60. *Wille und Macht* (1937), V, 21.

61. Paul Alverdes, *Das Winterlager* (Munich, 1935), *passim*; Herbert Georg Gopfert, "Paul Alverdes," *Die Neue Literatur* (September 1936), 503–509.

62. Speech by Baldur von Schirach at the Weimarer Tagung of the Hitler Youth, in 1937, *Die Neue Literatur* (May 1938), 223, 224.

63. *Die Spielschaar* (January 1943), 12.

64. *Volktums Arbeit im Betrieb* (Berlin, Kraft Durch Freude publication, 1938?), 23.

65. Hermann Kretzschmann, *Unterricht und Erziehung im Deutschen Arbeitsdienst* (Leipzig, 1933), 8.

66. *Die Neue Literatur* (June 1936), 328. The typical phrase stems from Martin Luserke.

67. Hans Hinkel, *Einer unter Hunderttausend* (Munich, 1937), 261. I am indebted to Barry Fulkes, who supplied the knowledge about Nazi films.

12. Fascism and the Avant Garde

1. Robert O. Paxton, *La France de Vichy* (Paris, 1973), 251.

2. Henry de Montherlant, *Le Songe* (Paris, 1922), 374.

3. Antoine de Saint-Exupéry, "Terre des Hommes," *Oeuvres* (Paris, 1959), 169–170.

4. Quoted in Rolf Italiander, *Italo Balbo* (Munich, 1942), 137. H. G. Wells saw the "Coming of Blériot" (1909) as the end of natural democracy—*The Works of H. G. Wells*, XX (New York, 1926), 422; Guido Mattioli, *Mussolini Aviatore* (Rome, 1936?), 3.

5. Mattioli, *op. cit.*, 3.

6. Bertold Brecht, "Der Ozeanflug," Brecht, *Versuche 1–12* (Berlin, 1959), 14. I owe this reference to Reinhold Grimm.

7. *Ibid.*, 24.

8. Rolf Italiander, *Marschall Balbo*, 11.

9. Giuseppe Fanciulli, *Marschall Balbo* (Essen, 1942), 116.

10. Anson Rabinbach, "The Aesthetics of Production in the Third Reich," *International Fascism*, ed. George L. Mosse (London, 1979), 189–223.

11. Hans Poelzig, quoted in Anna Teut, *Architektur im Dritten Reich* (Frankfurt-am-Main, 1967), 32.

12. See, for example, Jost Hermand and Frank Trommler, *Die Kultur der Weimarer Republik* (Munich, 1978), 382 ff. "Omagio a Terrgani," *L'Architettura: Chronache e Storia*, XIV, No. 3 (July 1968).

13. Hildegard Brenner, *Die Kunstpolitik des Nationalsozialismus* (Hamburg, 1963), 64 ff.

14. *Ibid.*, 73; Barbara Miller Lane, *Architecture and Politics in Germany, 1918–1945* (Cambridge, Mass., 1963), 152, 172 ff. Mies van der Rohe was a member of the Reichskammer für Bildende Kunste, 264, n. 73. He designed an exhibit for the exhibition "German People, German Work" in 1934—Philip C. Johnson, *Mies van der Rohe* (New York, 1947), 53. Mies, so one book claims, did not leave Germany until 1937, while Barbara Miller Lane gives the impression that he left shortly after 1933. Cf. Arthur Drexler, *Mies van der Rohe* (New York, 1960).

15. Albert Speer, *Erinnerungen* (Frankfurt-am-Main, 1969), 94.

16. George L. Mosse, *The Nationalization of the Masses* (New York, 1975), 186. For the relationship of *Neo Klassizismus* and *Neue Sachlichkeit*, see Georg Friedrich Koch, "Speer, Schinkel und der Preussische Stil," in *Albert Speer; Architektur* (Frankfurt-am-Main, 1967), 136 ff.

17. E. Crispolti, B. Hinz, and Z. Birolli, *Arte e Fascismo in Italia e in Germania* (Milan, 1974), 129.

18. "Omaggio a Terragni," 180.

19. Ute Diehl, "Der lange Weg in die Abstraktion. Die italienische Kunst und der Faschismus," *Frankfurter Allgemeine Zeitung*, No. 89 (May 2, 1978).

20. Emilio Gentile, *Le Origini dell' Ideologica Fascista* (Rome, 1975), 6.

21. Alexander J. de Grand, *Bottai e la Cultura Fascista* (Rome, 1978), 251.

22. Calro Bordoni, *Cultura e propaganda nell'Italia fascista* (Messina-Florence, 1974), 167.

23. Cited in *ibid.*, 44, 46.

24. Emilio Gentile, "Bottai e il fascismo. Osservatione per una biografia," *Storia Contemporanea*, X, No. 3 (June 1979), 559.

25. "Novocento," *Enciclopedia Italiana* (1934), XXIV, 995.

26. Mosse, *op. cit.*, 224.
27. "Novocento," *Enciclopedia Italiana*, 994.
28. Adrian Lyttleton, *The Seizure of Power. Fascism in Italy 1919–1929* (London, 1973), 391–393.
29. Francesco Sapori, *L'Arte e il Duce* (Milan, 1932), 37, 49, 66.
30. *Ibid.*, 124, 125, 129; Bordoni, *op. cit.*, 71.
31. Marcello Piacentini, *Architettura d'Oggi* (Rome, 1930), 56–57.
32. George L. Mosse, *Ein Volk, Ein Reich, Ein Führer* (Konigstein-Taunus, 1979).
33. "Omaggio a Terragni," 161.
34. Cited in Nicolas Slonimsky, *Music Since 1900* (New York, 1946), 355.
35. Mussolini ignored Pound, who bombarded him not with poetry but with bizarre political and economic tracts—Niccolo Zapponi, "Ezra Pound e il fascismo," *Storia Contemporanea*, IV, No. 3 (September 1973), 423–474.
36. See George L. Mosse, "Fascism and the Intellectuals," *The Nature of Fascism*, ed. S. J. Woolf (New York, 1968), 205–226.
37. Gottfried Benn, "Rede auf Stefan George" (1934), *Essays, Reden. Vortrage* (Wiesbaden, 1959), 473.
38. *Ibid.*, 627.
39. Crispolti, *et. al.*, *op. cit.*, 59.
40. Renzo De Felice, *Fascism* (New Brunswick, N.J., 1976), 56.
41. "Fascismo," *Enciclopedia Italiana*, XIV (1932), 847.
42. See Robert Soucy, *Fascist Intellectual: Drieu La Rochelle* (Berkeley and Los Angeles, 1979).
43. Drieu La Rochelle, *Gilles* (Paris, 1939), 405–406.
44. See Essay 5, Part I, of this book.
45. Quoted in Soucy, *op. cit.*, 2.
46. David L. Shalk, *The Spectrum of Political Engagement* (Princeton, 1979), 99.
47. J.-L. Loubet del Bayle, *Les non-conformistes des années 30* (Paris, 1969), 101.
48. Walter Z. Laqueur, *Young Germany* (London, 1962), 102.
49. See Ulrich Linse, *Anarchistische Jugendbewegung 1918–1933* (Frankfurt-am-Main, 1976), *passim*.
50. Giovanni Sabbatucci, *I Combattenti nel Primo Dopoquerra* (Rome, 1974), 358.
51. Ferdinando Cordova, *Arditi e Legionari Dannunziani* (Padua, 1969), 22.
52. Donino Roncará, *Saggi sull'Educazione Fascista* (Bologna, 1938), 65.

13. *The Secularization of Jewish Theology*

1. See George L. Mosse, *The Holy Pretence* (2nd ed., New York, 1968). The sources for this paper came almost entirely from the excellent collections of German-Jewish sermons and tracts in the Jewish National and Hebrew University Library, Jerusalem.
2. Ben Joseph Wolf, *Sechs deutsche Reden gehalten in der Synagoge zu Dessau, etc.* (Dessau, 1813), 75, 76.

3. Alexander Altmann, "Zur Frühgeschichte der jüdischen Predigt in Deutschland," *Yearbook of the Leo Baeck Institute*, VI (1961), 16. The continuing attraction of Christian pietism upon Jewish thought may warrant investigation. Gershom Scholem believes that Franz Rosenzweig regarded Judaism as a kind of pietistic Church—*SHDEMOT*, No. 3 (Spring 1975), 21. For Leopold Zunz, see his *Die Gottesdienstlichen Vorträge der Juden* (Frankfurt-am-Main, 1832), 7.

4. Hirsch Traub, *Vier Reden* (Mannheim, 1825), 6.

5. *Ibid.*, 26.

6. *Sulamith*, 2 Jahrg. Vol. I (1808), 224–225.

7. Altmann, *op. cit.*, 11.

8. Friedrich Schleiermacher, *Die neue Liturgie für die Hof-und Garnisons-Gemeinde in Potsdam und für die Garnisonskirche in Berlin* (Berlin, 1816), 13.

9. Moses Mannheimer, *Die Kunst und das deutsche Lied im Israelitischen Kultus* (Darmstadt, 1869), 5, 6, 12.

10. *Gesang-Buch zum Gebrauch bei dem Unterricht in der mosaischen Religion, etc.* (Stuttgart, 1863), v. vi.

11. E. Kley, *Predigten in dem neuen Israelitischen Tempel zu Hamburg*, I (Hamburg, 1819), 33 ff.

12. *Gesang-Buch, op. cit.*, xi.

13. George L. Mosse, *The Nationalization of the Masses* (New York, 1975), 140 ff.

14. Friedrich Schleiermacher, *Die Christliche Sitte*, ed. L. Jonas, *Sämmtliche Werke*, 12 (Berlin, 1884), *passim*. For the new middle-class morality, see George L. Mosse, *The Culture of Western Europe* (Chicago, 1975), 95–102.

15. Ludwig Philipson, ed., *Israelitisches Predigt-und Schul-Magazin*, I (Magdeburg, 1834), 170.

16. Gotthold Salomon, *David, der Mann nach dem Herzen Gottes als Mensch, Israelit und König* (Hamburg, 1837), 96.

17. Abraham Asch, *Der heilige Verein oder die wahre Vaterlandsliebe* (Stern Collection, Archives of the Jewish People, Jerusalem). We know almost nothing about Professor Abraham Asch, who in 1812 adopted the name of Karl Asch—Moritz Stern, *Aus der Zeit der deutschen Befreiungskriege 1813–1818*, Vol. 3 (Berlin, 1935), 15–19.

18. Harold Nicolson, *Good Behaviour* (London, 1955), *passim*.

19. See Christian Boeck, *Schleiermachers Vaterländisches Wirken, 1806–1813* (Berlin, 1920).

20. *Sulamith*, 1 Jahr. Vol. 2 (1807), 12.

21. *Zuruf an die Jünglinge welche den Fahnen des Vaterlandes folgen* (Berlin, 1913), 53. This *Zuruf* was composed by Karl Siegfried Günsburg and Eduard Kley—Stern, *op. cit.*, 9.

22. *Zuruf, op. cit.*, 52.

23. *Gesang und Gebet zum Huldigungstag . . . Friedrich Wilhelm des Zweiten, von der Jüdischen Gemeinde zu Berlin, am Versohnungstage*, 2. October 1786.

24. *Zuruf, op. cit.*, 52; Asch, *op. cit.*, 74.

25. Salomon Plessner, *Der Israelit als Untertan* (Posen, 1861), 17.

26. Asch, *op. cit.*, 72. Asch continued a tradition which in the sixteenth century had ascribed the virtues of David to Arminius—Gerd Unverfehrt, "Ernst von Bandels Hermannsdenkmal," *Ein Jahrhundert Hermannsdenkmal*, Naturwissenschaftlicher und Historischer Verein für das Land Lippe, Vol. 23 (1975), 138.

27. *Jüdische Rundschau*, XIX Jahrg. (August 7, 1914), 343.

28. *Unsere Gefallenen Kameraden, Gedenkbuch Für die im Weltkrieg Gefallenen Munchner Juden* (Munich, 1921), 212. Such a cross was put up in the heat of battle, but there is also some sense that this is the only kind of marker possible for any soldier's grave.

29. Kley, *op. cit.*, 44–46.

30. Zunz, *op. cit.*, 479.

31. J. H. Camper, *Wörterbuch der deutschen Sprache* (Branschweig, 1908).

32. Klaus Hermann, "Weltanschauliche Aspekte der Jüdischen Reformgemeinde zu Berlin," *EMUNA*, Vol. IX (1974), 83–92.

33. *Sulamith*, 2 Jahrg. Vol. II (1811), 32.

34. *Ibid.*, Vol. I (1808), 222.

35. Uriel Tal, *Christians and Jews in Germany* (Ithaca, N.Y., 1975).

36. Caesar Seligmann, *Erinnerungen* (Frankfurt-am-Main, 1975), 143.

37. Walther Rathenau, *Zur Kritik der Zeit* (Berlin, 1912), 219.

38. Seligmann, *op. cit.*, 149.

39. Hans Meyer, *Der Aussenseiter* (Frankfurt-am-Main, 1975), 340 ff.

40. Ismar Freund writing in the 1920s, quoted by Jehuda Reinharz, *Fatherland or Promised Land. The Dilemma of the German Jew, 1893–1914* (Ann Arbor, Mich., 1975), 62.

41. Eugen Fuchs, *Um Deutschtum und Judentum* (Frankfurt-am-Main, 1919), 254, 258.

42. Georg Hermann, *Jettchen Gebert* (Berlin, 1906), 350.

43. Seligmann, *op. cit.*, 162, 163 (from the *Jüdische Rundschau* of 1927).

44. *Ibid.*, 165.

45. Gustav Landauer, "Ein paar Worte der dankbarbeit an Martin Buber" (handwritten note, Mappe 141, Buber Archives, Jerusalem).

46. Georg Lukacs to Martin Buber, December 20, 1911 (Mappe 457, Buber Archives, Jerusalem).

47. Martin Buber and Harry Graf Kessler, January 16, 1928, *Martin Buber Briefwechsel aus sieben Jahrzehnten*, Vol. II, 1918–1938, ed. Grete Schaeder (Heidelberg, 1973), 300.

48. Maximilian Harden in *Die Zukunft* (December 28, 1907) (Mappe 457, Buber Archives, Jerusalem).

14. The Jews and the German War Experience, 1914–1918

1. Karl Hilmar, *Die deutschen Juden im Weltkriege* (Berlin, n.d.) 48.

2. *Am was hat der heimkehrende Kriegsteilnehmer zu denken? Praktische Wegweise*, ed. J. Jehle (Munich, 1918), 3.

3. Paul Fussell, *The Great War and Modern Memory* (London, 1975), 114, 115. I am greatly indebted to this epoch-making book. Hanns Bächtold, *Deutscher Soldatenbrauch und Soldatenglaube* (Strasbourg, 1917) repeats in a German context the superstitions listed for England by Paul Fussell.

4. J. Glenn Gray, *The Warriors* (New York, 1973), xiv.

5. Sir Maurice Bowra, *Poetry and the First World War* (Oxford, 1961), 11.

6. Fussell, *op. cit.*, 115.

7. Walter Flex, *Vom grossen Abendmahl: Verse und Gedanken aus dem Feld* (Munich, n.d.) 43. The citation is from "Machtgedanken," written in 1914.

8. Ludwig Ganghofer, *Reise zur deutschen Front 1915* (Berlin, 1915), 74.

9. Fussell, *op. cit.*, 145.

10. Flex, *op. cit.*, 5.

11. *Ehrendenkmal der Deutschen Armee und Marine* (Berlin and Munich, 1926), 654.

12. See, e.g., *Deutscher Ehrenhain für die Helden 1914–1918* (Leipzig, 1931).

13. Albert Marrin, *The Last Crusade, the Church of England in the First World War* (Durham, N.C., 1974), 135.

14. Immanuel Saul, "An meine Kinder," *Im Deutschen Reich*, Feldbücherei der CVJG (Berlin, n.d.) 55. Other examples of Jews buried under crosses include M. Spanier, *Leutnant Sender* (Hamburg, 1915), 77; *Unsere Gefallenen Kameraden, Gedenkbuch für die im Weltkrieg gefallenen Münchner Juden* (Munich, 1929), 212. Julius Marx writes about a Jew buried under a cross, and that such a cross and the praying soldier in front of it became symbolic for the war—*Kriegs-Tagebuch eines Juden* (Zurich, 1939), 33.

15. *Louis Marshall*, ed. Charles Reznikoff (Philadelphia, 1957), 247, 248. I owe this reference to Professor L. Gartner of the University of Tel Aviv.

16. Ganghofer, *op. cit.*, 150.

17. Unidentified newspaper clipping of February 8, 1816 (Stern Collection, item 212, 17. Archives of the Jewish People, Jerusalem).

18. Cited in Fritz Stern, *Gold and Iron; Bismarck, Bleichröder, and the Building of the German Empire* (New York, 1977), 16.

19. M. Güdemann, "Der jetzige Weltkrieg und die Bibel," *Monatsschrift für Geschichte und Wissenschaft des Judentums*, Vol 23, Neue Folge, (1915), 5; *Zum Gedächtnis an Dr. Moritz Levin*, December 13, 1914, 6.

20. Marx, *op. cit.*, 129.

21. See J. H. Rosny Ainé, *Confidences sur l'amitié des tranchées* (Paris, 1919), *passim*.

22. George L. Mosse, *The Crisis of German Ideology* (New York, 1964), 216.

23. Emil Högg, *Kriegergrab und Kriegerdenkmal* (Wittenberg, 1915), 29; see also George L. Mosse, "National Cemeteries and National Revival: The Cult of the Fallen Soldiers in Germany," *Journal of Contemporary History*, Vol. 14 (1979), 1–20.

24. See *Kriegsgedenkbuch der israelitischen Kultusgemeinde Nürnberg*, ed. Marx Freudenthal (Nuremberg, 1920), *passim*. For the symbolisms referred to, see George L. Mosse, *The Nationalization of the Masses* (New York, 1975).

25. Sammy Gronemann, *Hawdoloh und Zapfenstreich* (Berlin, 1924), 102.

26. *Die Feldgraue, Illustrierte Kriegszeitschrift der 50 I.-D.* (June 1916), 12.
27. Walter Flex, *Der Wanderer zwischen beiden Welten* (Munich, n.d.), 46.
28. Fussell, *op. cit.*, 118–119.
29. Flex, *Der Wanderer zwischen beiden Welten*, 73.
30. *Heldenhaine, Heldenbäume*, ed. Stephan Ankenbrand (Munich, 1918), 28.
31. See *Kriegsgedenkbuch der israelitischen Kultusgemeinde Nürnberg*, 25, 43.
32. Bruno Italiener, *Heimat und Glauben* (Darmstadt, 1917), 9.
33. Johannes Kessler, *Ich schwöre mir ewige Jugend* (Leipzig, 1935), 285.
34. D. E. Dryander, *Weihnachtsgedanken in der Kriegszeit* (Leipzig, 1914), 21; *Die Feldgrauen, Kriegszeitschrift aus dem Schützengraben* (mimeographed, February 1916), 30, 31.
35. Flex, *Vom grossen Abendmahl*, 15.
36. *Gefallene Deutsche Juden, Frontbriefe 1914–1918* (Berlin, 1935), 92.
37. Walther Rathenau, *Eine Streitschrift* (Weilheim/OBB 1917), 20–28.
38. Leo Baecks reports appeared regularly in the *Gemeindeblatt der Jüdischen Gemeinde*, Berlin, from 1914 onwards.
39. See *Jüdische Rundschau* (August 7, 1914), 343; *ibid.* (October 16, 1914), 387; but also Kurt Blumenfeld, "am deutschen Wesen soll die Welt genesen," *ibid.* (February 19, 1915), 65.
40. *Protokoll des II. Ordentlichen Bundestages des Herzl-Bundes Berlin*, (April 17–20, 1918, 7; *Ost und West* (January–May 1915), 14 ff.
41. Quoted in *Jüdische Rundschau* (September 4, 1914), 361.
42. Binjamin Segel, *Der Weltkrieg und das Schicksal der Juden* (Berlin, 1915), 143.
43. *Ost und West*, 14.
44. Ernst Jünger, *Der Kampf als inneres Erlebnis* (Berlin, 1933), 33.
45. Karl Prümm, *Die Literatur des Soldatischen Nationalismus der 20er Jahre* (Kronberg-Taunus, 1974), Vol. 1, 101.
46. Ernst Jünger, *The Storm of Steel* (New York, 1975), 109.
47. *Ibid.*, 126–127.
48. Prümm, *op. cit.*, 101.
49. *Ibid.*, 103 ff.
50. Joseph Goebbels, *Der Angriff; Aufsätze aus der Kampfzeit* (Munich, 1942), 251, 274.
51. Quoted in Lucy S. Dawidowicz, *A Holocaust Reader* (New York, 1976), 133.
52. Otto Binswanger, *Die seelischen Wirkungen des Krieges* (Stuttgart and Berlin, 1914), 27.
53. Prümm, *op. cit.*, 45 ff; Carl Schmitt, *Politische Theologie* (Munich and Leipzig, 1934), preface.
54. Kurt Sontheimer, *Antidemokratisches Denken in der Weimarer Republik* (Munich, 1962), 132.
55. Volker R. Berghan, *Der Stahlhelm, Bund der Frontsoldaten 1918–1935* (Dusseldorf, 1966), 91.

56. Franz Seldte, *Vor und Hinter den Kulissen* (Leipzig, 1931), 56 ff; Mosse, *The Crisis of German Ideology*, 255.

57. Berghan, *op. cit.*, 241.

58. See George L. Mosse, *Germans and Jews* (New York, 1970), 105 ff.

59. Hanns Oberlindober, *Ein Vaterland, das allen gehört!* (Munich, 1939), 10, 11.

60. Oswald Spengler, *Preussentum und Sozialismus* (Munich, 1925), 15, 18.

61. For this see, George L. Mosse, *Toward the Final Solution, The European Experience of Race* (New York, 1978), Chap. XI.

62. Fussell, *op. cit.*, 57.

63. Flex, *Der Wanderer zwischen beiden Welten*, 5, 6.

64. Siegfried Sassoon, *Memoirs of a Fox-Hunting Man* (New York, 1929), 321.

65. Fussell, *op. cit.*, 272.

66. Otto Braun, *Aus Nachgelassenen Schriften eines Frühvollendeten*, ed. Julie Vogelstein (Berlin-Grünewald, 1921), 120.

67. Ernst Jünger, *Der Kampf als inneres Erlebnis*, 33, 56.

68. See *Das Deutsche Grabdenkmal* (February–March 1926), 6; Albert Maennchen, *Das Reichsehrenmal der Eisenbolz am Rhein* (Coblenz, 1927), n.p.

69. Karl von Seeger, *Das Denkmal des Weltkriegs* (Stuttgart, 1930), 22.

70. Willy Lange, *Deutsche Heldenhaine* (Leipzig, 1915), 27; *Das Deutsche Grabdenkmal* (April 1926), 11.

71. See Essay 11, Nazi Polemical Theater—The *Kampfbühne*.

72. Klaus Vondung, "Geschichte als Weltgericht," *Zeitschrift für Literaturwissenschaft und Linguistik*, Beiheft 2 (Göttingen, 1977), 147–168; Dr. Jelski, *Aus grosser Zeit* (Berlin, 1915), 91.

73. Mosse, *Toward the Final Solution*, Chap. XI.

74. Walter Bloem, *Vormarsch* (Leipzig, 1916), 306. Some Englishmen seemed to have agreed with the Germans in viewing the use of imperial black or colored troops in the war as an atrocity—Robert Graves, *Goodbye to All That* (New York, 1957), 185.

75. Eckart Koester, *Literatur und Weltkriegsideologie* (Kronberg-Taunus, 1977), 246.

76. Leo Baeck, *Wege im Judentum* (Berlin, 1933), 390.

15. German Socialists and
the Jewish Question in the
Weimar Republic

1. Hans-Helmuth Knütter, "Die Linksparteien [zur Judenfrage]," in *Entscheidungsjahr 1932. Zur Judenfrage in der Endphase der Weimarer Republik. Ein Sammelband herausgegeben von Werner E. Mosse unter Mitwirkung von Arnold Paucker*, Tübingen, 1965, 1966 (Schriftenreihe wissenschaftlicher Abhandlungen des Leo Baeck Instituts 13).

2. George Lichtheim, "Socialism and the Jews," *Dissent* (July–August 1968), 314–342; Edmund Silberner, *Sozialisten zur Judenfrage* (Berlin, 1962).

3. Karl Kautsky, "Das Massaker von Kischeneff und die Judenfrage," *Die Neue Zeit*, XXI, Vol. 2 (1902–03), 303–309. Although this article had the greatest impact, Kautsky had written another article, "Über das Judentum," in *Die Neue Zeit*, VIII (1890), 23–30, in which he put forward the same theses in a less complete analysis.

4. Karl Kautsky, *Rasse und Judentum* (2nd ed., Stuttgart, 1921), 70.

5. *Ibid.*, 108, 55; Kautsky, "Das Massaker von Kischeneff und die Judenfrage," 306; Eugene Kamenka, *Marxism and Ethics* (London and New York, 1969), 9. While much nonsense has been written about Marx's *Judenfrage*, David McLelland's *The Young Hegelians and Karl Marx* (London, 1969), puts the tract in its proper chronological and ideological setting. As a matter of fact, Marx borrowed heavily from Moses Hess's article "On the Essence of Money." Hess and Marx both agreed in viewing money as the primary symbol of alienation, and on their solution to the Jewish problem. McLelland even holds that Marx copied Hess's ideas at this stage—*ibid.*, 158. Marx's attitude on the Jewish question was not unusual at the time but, unlike Hess, he remained constant in his advocacy of the ideas he had put forward in 1844.

6. Kautsky, "Das Massaker von Kischeneff und die Judenfrage," 304.

7. Kautsky, *Rasse und Judentum*, 107. For the ghetto stereotype, see George L. Mosse, *Germans and Jews. The Right, the Left, and the Search for a "Third Force" in Pre-Nazi Germany* (New York, 1970), 44–46.

8. Kautsky, "Das Massaker von Kischeneff und die Judenfrage," 305, 306.

9. Kautsky, *Rasse und Judentum*, 83 ff.

10. See Werner Blumenberg, *Karl Kautsky's Literarisches Werk* (The Hague, 1960). For Kautsky's influence on Lenin and Stalin, see Marc Jarblum, *Le Problème Juif dans la théorie et practique du Communisme* (Paris, 1935), 18; the influence of Kautsky is obvious in their works, and he is cited with respect. Both, however, devote more space to Otto Bauer's analysis of the nationalities question, partly because he disagreed with them on certain points. Both were, above all, concerned to polemize against the Bund; W. I. Lenin über die Nationale und die Koloniale Nationale Frage (Berlin, 1960), especially 143, 147; Stalin, *Marxismus und Nationale Frage* (Vienna, n.d.), especially 40, 51. In spite of these critiques of Bauer, this leader of Austrian social democracy as well as many others of that party shared Kautsky's basic views on the Jewish question, and carried them over into the postwar world through their discussions of the ever present Austrian nationalities problem. However, we are here concerned with Germany and not with Austria. On Bauer, see Introduction by Robert Weltsch to *LBI Year Book IV* (1959), xviii–xix.

11. Kautsky, *Rasse und Judentum*, 108.

12. *Ibid.*, 73. Hugo Iltis, Kautsky's friend and admirer, expressed his open agreement with the fundamentals of Lamarckianism. Hugo Iltis to Karl Kautsky, April 9, 1930 (Kautsky Familien-Archiv, Portf. 3, Mappe 4, International Archive for Social History, Amsterdam).

13. Hans-Ulrich Wehler, *Sozialdemokratie und Nationalstaat* (Würzburg, 1962), 198.

14. Arjeh Tatakower, "Zur Geschichte des Jüdischen Sozialismus V. Vom Ausbruch des Weltkriegs bis zur Nachwirkung der Russischen Revolution," *Der Jude*, VIII (1924), 642, 643.

15. At least in 1929 the publisher and a party newspaper in Leipzig still possessed a good many copies they wanted to sell. This was the reason why the Dietz publishing house did not want to republish it at that time, as Kautsky was urging. Adolf Schultz to Karl Kautsky, April 18, 1929 (International Archive of Social History, Amsterdam), K.D. IX, 62; Adolf Schultz to Karl Kautsky, May 18, 1929 (International Archive for Social History, Amsterdam), K.D. IX, 64.

16. Karl Kautsky, "Die Aussichten des Zionismus" (International Archive for Social History, Amsterdam), K. A. 154. The article was printed in *Vorwärts* on October 5 & 6, 1929.

17. Hectographed invitation, December 12, 1929 (International Archive for Social History, Amsterdam), K.D. IV 128; Berl Locker to *Chaverim* Louise and Karl Kautsky, September 18, 1937 (International Archive for Social History, Amsterdam), K.D. XVI, 30.

18. Kautsky, "Die Aussichten des Zionismus," 2.

19. Anton Fendrich, *Der Judenhass und der Sozialismus* (Freiburg, 1920), II, 19.

20. Paul Kampfmeyer, *Streifzüge durch die Theorie und Praxis der Arbeiterbewegung* (Stuttgart, 1907), 3; Kampfmeyer, *Die Sozialdemokratie im Lichte der Kulturentwicklung* (Berlin, 1920), 147; Kampfmeyer, *Jüdischer Marxismus* (Berlin, 1923), 4, 5, 7. Similar arguments to those of Kampfmeyer were made from the Jewish side in a leaflet of the CV. See Arnold Paucker, *Der jüdische Abwehrkampf gegen Antisemitismus und Nationalsozialismus in den letzten Jahren der Weimarer Republik* (Hamburger Beiträge zur Zeitgeschichte Band IV) (2nd ed., Hamburg, 1969), 208.

21. *Was muss das schaffende Volk vom politischen, wirtschaftlichen, religiösen Juden- und Rassenhass des reaktionären Faschismus wissen?* Für Redner und Funktionäre, herausgegeben von der Sozialdemokratischen Partei Deutschlands) (Ortsverein-Hanover, 1924). It has been pointed out to me by Arnold Paucker that this social democratic pamphlet is to a very large extent based on defense material of the Centralverein deutscher Staatsbürger jüdischen Glaubens. According to his CV informants, it was probably supplied in toto, as was also most of the propaganda material on the Jewish question (and much of that on Nazism) distributed by the SPD, Reichsbanner, etc., during the last years of the Republic.

22. Éduard Bernstein, "Der Schulstreit in Palästina," *Die Neue Zeit*, XXXII, Vol. I (1914), 752; Bernstein, "Wie ich als Jude in der Diaspora aufwuchs," *Der Jude*, II (1917/18), 191.

23. Kautsky, "Die Aussichten des Zionismus," 2.

24. Éduard Bernstein, in *Sozialistische Monatshefte* (June 1907); "Die demokratische Staatsidee und die Jüdische Nationalbewegung," (MS in the International Archive for Social History, Amsterdam), A. 114.

25. Éduard Bernstein, review of Émile Vandervelde, *Schaffendes Palästina* (handwritten MS in the International Archive for Social History, Amsterdam), A. 126.

26. Salman Rubaschow, *Éduard Bernstein* (MS in the International Archive for Social History, Amsterdam), B. 23, 3.

27. Marc Jarblum to Éduard Bernstein, April 20, 1930 (International Archive for Social History, Amsterdam), D. 305.

28. Rubaschow, *op. cit.*, 7.

29. Éduard Bernstein, "Die Ostjuden in Deutschland" (International Archive for Social History, Amsterdam), A. 790.

30. Paucker, *op. cit.*, 57, 95, 96.

31. "Socialisme et Sionisme," *La Vie Socialiste*, VII, Série Nouvelle No. 168 (December 14, 1929), 7, 9. For Löbe, see *Die blutigen Ereignisse in Palästina (1929) und der Internationale Sozialismus* (Vienna, n.d.), 79.

32. Émile Vandervelde, *Le Pays d'Israël. Un Marxiste en Palestine* (Paris, 1929), 9, 11.

33. H. H. van Kol, *La Démocratie Socialiste Internationale et le Sionisme* (Lausanne, 1919), 5. He also documents the change in socialist attitudes after the war. Jean Longuet supported the Poale Zion, *ibid.*, 4, 11.

34. Kurt Blumenfeld, "Die Zionistische Haltung," *Jüdische Rundschau*, XXXVIII, No. 17 (February 28, 1933), 81; the SPD's reluctance to nominate Jewish candidates is also referred to in the contribution by Werner Jochmann, "Die Ausbreitung des Antisemitismus," in *Deutsches Judentum in Krieg und Revolution 1916–1923. Ein Sammelband herausgegeben von Werner E. Mosse unter Mitwirkung von Arnold Paucker*, Tübingen, 1971 (Schriftenreihe wissenschaftlicher Abhandlungen des Leo Baeck Instituts 25), 498–499; he also gives an excellent bibliography on the anti-Semitic currents in the KPD for the years 1920–1924, 498, n. 331.

35. See *Was muss das schaffende Volk . . .* , 12.

36. Albert Grzesinski to Friedrich Stampfer, September 13, 1932 (International Archive for Social History, Amsterdam), G. 2319.

37. This refers to Kautsky's article of 1890 (see note 3); August Bebel, *Sozialdemokratie und Antisemitismus* (Berlin, 1894), 31.

38. *Protokoll über die Verhandlung des Parteitags der Sozialdemokratischen Partei Deutschlands* (Berlin, 1903), 174, 225.

39. *Sozialdemokratischer Parteitag in Leipzig, 1931, Protokoll* (Berlin, 1931), 265.

40. Hugo Marx *Werdegang eines jüdischen Staatsanwaltes und Richters in Baden* (Villingen, 1965), 195 ff.

41. *Konservative Tendenzen in der Sozialdemokratie? Eine Rundfrage* (Heidelberg, 1930), 8. This was a publication of the *Intellektuellenbund*.

42. *Ibid.*, 12.

43. Hans Jaeger, *Antinaziarbeit bis 1933* (Wiener Library, London, Personal Reports, 3000 Series, No. 3006), 3.

44. *Sozialdemokratischer Parteitag in Leipzig, 1931. Protokoll*, 265.

45. *Ibid.*, 107, 102.

46. Gustav Mayer, *Erinnerungen*, Journalisten zum Historiker der deutschen Arbeiterbewegung (Zurich-Vienna, 1949), 362.

47. Rudolf Hilferding to Karl Kautsky, December 1, 1932 (International Archive for Social History, Amsterdam), K.D. XII, 650; Julius Deutsch to Karl Kautsky, October 19, 1933 (International Archive for Social History, Amsterdam), K.D. VII, 410.

48. W. Dietz to Karl Kautsky, April 27, 1920 (International Archive for Social History, Amsterdam), K.D. VIII.

49. *Zur Judenfrage von Karl Marx*, ed. Stefan Grossmann (Berlin, 1919), 5. Grossmann, the founder of the *Tagebuch*, had become disillusioned with communism and the Soviet Union by 1921. *Das Tagebuch*, II, No. 46 (November 19, 1921), 1399.

50. *Die Rote Fahne*, XV, No. 92 (April 29, 1932).

51. *Ibid.*, XV, No. 175 (August 23, 1932). This was the first reference to Jews in the paper since July 14.

52. *Ibid.*, XV, No. 182 (September 7, 1932).

53. *Der Rote Aufbau*, V, No. 1 (January 1, 1932), 13.

54. *Die Rote Fahne*, XV, No. 76 (April 9, 1932).

55. *Der Rote Aufbau*, IV, No. 3 (March 1931), 158.

56. *Kommunismus und Nationale Bewegung, Schlageter, eine Auseinandersetzung* (Berlin, 1923), 5, 7; Karl Radek, "Kommunismus und deutsche nationalistische Bewegung," *Die Rote Fahne*, VI, No. 188 (August 16, 1923), 50.

57. Ossip K. Flechtheim, *Die Kommunistische Partei Deutschlands in der Weimarer Republik* (Offenbach-am-Main, 1948), 89.

58. *Erwachendes Volk, Briefe an Leutnant a.D. Scheringer* (Berlin, 1931), 13, 21.

59. *Walt am Abend*, IX, No. 179 (August 4, 1931); but it also reprinted a translation of Mike Gold's *Jews Without Money* to show the fate of proletarian Jews under capitalism—*ibid.*, IX, No. 229 (October 1, 1931).

60. Alfred Kantorowicz, "Liquidation der Judenfrage," in *Klärung. 12 Autoren und Politiker über die Judenfrage* (Berlin, 1932), 159–160, 168. Typically enough, Willi Bredel, a leading communist writer, in a novel—*Die Prüfung*, 1935—pictured the Jew as an unpolitical petty bourgeois.

61. Salomon Goldelman, *Löst der Kommunismus die Judenfrage?* (Prague, 1937), 277.

62. *Auf eigener Scholle* (Berlin, 1928), 28, 37. This was a propaganda publication of *Geserd*.

63. Jaeger, *op. cit.*, 1. Stalin dissolved *Geserd* in 1938–39.

64. Babette Gross, *Willi Münzenberg* (Stuttgart, 1967), 175; Tilly Spiegel, *Osterreicher in der belgischen und französischen Résistance* (Monographien zur Zeitgeschichte. Schriftenreihe des Dokumentationsarchivs des österreichischen Widerstandes, Vienna, 1969), 43–44, n. 41. (I am indebted to the late Georges Haupt for this reference.)

65. *Jüdische Rundschau*, XXXVI, No. 99–100 (December 23, 1931), 581.

66. Otto Heller, *Der Untergang des Judentums* (Berlin, 1931), 115, 116, 141, 337. The book was translated into French in 1933.

67. Review by Otto Mänchen-Helfen, *Die Gesellschaft*, II, Vol. 7–12 (1932), 461.

68. Heller, *op. cit.*, 77, 212, 337, 153, 165; M. Alberton, *Birobidschan, die Judenrepublik* (Vienna, 1932), 211.

69. *W. I. Lenin über die Judenfrage* (Berlin, 1932).

70. *Welt am Abend*, IX, No. 285 (December 7, 1931).

71. *C.V.-Zeitung*, IX, No. 9 (February 26, 1932), 77–78; *ibid.*, XI, No. 43 (October 21, 1932), 430; Paucker, *op. cit.*, 116, 274.

72. *Abwehr-Blätter*, XLII, No. 1–2 (February 1932), 103.

73. L. Haddad, *Tag der Fellachen*, Rote Reihe (Berlin, 1932). This was put out by MOPR, the Russian abbreviation for International Class War Prisoners Aid, branch of a Moscow publishing house.

74. *Jüdische Rundschau*, XXXVII, No. 9 (February 2, 1932), 41.

75. Eli Strauss, *Geht das Judentum unter?* (Vienna, 1933).

76. *Jüdische Rundschau*, XXXVII, No. 9 (February 2, 1932), 41.

77. Arthur Holitscher, *Mein Leben in dieser Zeit* (Potsdam, 1925), 188. He also published a book that praised the Zionist experiment: *Reise durch das Jüdische Palästina* (Berlin, 1922). On the effects of the war, see the work by Egmont Zechlin, *Die deutsche Politik und die Juden im Ersten Weltkrieg* (Göttingen, 1969). The intensification of Jewish consciousness as a consequence both of the war and of growing anti-Semitism has now been discussed extensively in the monograph by Eva G. Reichmann, "Der Bewußtseinswandel der deutschen Juden," in *Deutsches Judentum in Krieg und Revolution, 1916–1923*, 511–612.

78. Arthur Holitscher, *Mein Leben in dieser Zeit*, 238; he made similar statements in the *Geserd* publication *Auf Eigener Scholle*.

79. Jaeger, *op. cit.*, 2.

80. *Ibid.*, 10.

81. Quoted in Enzo Collotti, *Die Kommunistische Partei Deutschlands 1918–1933* (Milan, 1961), 35.

82. *Gegen den Strom*, IV, No. 5 (February 28, 1931), 49; *ibid.*, VI, No. 7 (July 1933), 32–33; Otto-Ernst Schüddekopf, *Linke Leute von Rechts* (Stuttgart, 1960), 292, 293.

83. *Der Rote Kämpfer*, I, No. 8 (July 10, 1931), 5, 6; *ibid.*, I, No. 4 (February 15, 1931), 8; see also Olaf Ihlav, *Die Roten Kämpfer* (Meinsenheim-am-Glan, 1969), 40, 41.

84. For a general discussion of such intellectuals, see Mosse, *Germans and Jews*, Chap. VII.

85. *Die Weltbühne*, XXVII, No. 25 (June 23, 1931), 938; for a breakdown of the preponderance of Jews on the journal, see Istvan Deak, *Weimar Germany's Left-Wing Intellectuals. A Political History of the Weltbühne and Its Circle* (Berkeley and Los Angeles, 1968), 24.

86. *Die Weltbühne*, XXVIII, No. 1 (January 5, 1932), 14–17.

87. *Ibid.*, XXIX, No. 8 (February 21, 1933), 298; on Bruno Frei, see Deak, *op. cit.*, 239; *Jüdische Rundschau*, XXXV, No. 101 (December 23, 1930), 683–684.

88. *Die Weltbühne*, XXVI, No. 9 (February 25, 1930), 313–316.

89. *Ibid.*, XXVIII, No. 29 (July 19, 1932), 89.

90. *Ibid.*, XXVII, No. 5 (February 3, 1931), 168–171.

91. *Ibid.*, XXVIII, No. 29 (July 19, 1932), 96–97.

92. *Ibid.*, XXVI, No. 39 (September 23, 1930), 480.

93. *Ibid.*, XXVIII, No. 29 (July 19, 1932), 88.

94. *Ibid.*, XXVII, No. 4 (January 27, 1931), 120.

95. *Ibid.*, XXIX, No. 6 (February 7, 1933), 199.

96. *Ibid.*, XXVI, No. 4 (October 7, 1930), 537, 539.

97. *Ibid.*, XXVII, No. 1 (January 6, 1931), 25, 27.

98. Mosse, *Germans and Jews*, 135–186.

99. This was the title of a book by Horace B. Samuel that had just appeared in England and was reviewed in *Die Weltbühne*, XXVII, No. 7 (February 17, 1931), 247.

100. *Jüdische Rundschau*, XXXVII, No. 13 (February 16, 1932), 62, and leading article in No. 16 (February 26, 1932).

101. *Die Weltbühne*, XXVIII, No. 22 (May 31, 1932), 835, 836.

102. *Das Tagebuch* (December 17, 1932), 1755–1757.

103. Lion Feuchtwanger, *Die Söhne* (Amsterdam, 1935), 81.

104. Lion Feuchtwanger, *Der Tag wird kommen* (Stockholm, 1945), 61 ff.

105. I.e. Gustav Krojanker, "Vom Weltbürgertum," *Jüdische Rundschau*, XXXVIII, No. 18 (March 3, 1933), 87.

106. See Essay 8, The Heritage of Socialist Humanism.

107. See *ibid.*

108. Erich Matthias, *Sozialdemokratie und Nation* (Stuttgart, 1952), 61 ff.

109. *Die Neue Weltbühne*, 2 Halbjahr. (1933), 1154.

110. Eva Reichmann-Jungmann, "Der Untergang des Judentums," *Der Morgen*, VIII (1932), 64.

111. It is, of course, possible that some isolated Jewish capitalist contributed money to the Nazis. Ruth von Mayenburg, *Blaues Blut und Rote Fahnen* (Vienna, 1969), 86, mentions one such case.

Index